Cognition in Human
Motivation and Learning

Cognition in Human Motivation and Learning

Festschrift for J. (R.) Nuttin

Edited by

GERY d'YDEWALLE
WILLY LENS
University of Leuven/Louvain
Belgium

CONTRIBUTORS

J. W. ATKINSON,	*University of Michigan*
J. S. BRUNER,	*Harvard University*
W. K. ESTES,	*Harvard University*
P. FRAISSE,	*Université René Descartes*
H. HECKHAUSEN,	*Ruhr-Universität Bochum*
M. H. MARX,	*University of Missouri*
W. MISCHEL,	*Stanford University*
K. H. PRIBRAM,	*Stanford University*
J. O. RAYNOR,	*State University of New York, Buffalo*
T. A. RYAN,	*Cornell University*
H. THOMAE,	*University of Bonn*

Published jointly by
LEUVEN UNIVERSITY PRESS
LAWRENCE ERLBAUM ASSOCIATES

Leuven University Press v.z.w.
Krakenstraat 3
B-3000 Leuven/Louvain (Belgium)
ISBN 90 6186 099 7
D/1981/1869/8

Lawrence Erlbaum Associates, Inc., Publishers
365 Broadway
Hillsdale, New Jersey 07642

Library of Congress Cataloging in Publication Data
Main entry under title:

Cognition in human motivation and learning.

Festschrift for J. R. Nuttin on the occasion of his
becoming Professor Emeritus at the University of Leuven,
Belgium.
"Selected bibliography of J. (R.) Nuttin": p.
Bibliography: p.
Includes indexes.
CONTENTS: A developmental approach: Bruner, J. S.
The organization of action and the nature of adult-infant
interaction. Heckhausen, H. Developmental precursors of
success and failure. Mischel, W. Objective and subjec-
tive rules for delay of gratification. [etc.]
1. Learning, Psychology of—Addresses, essays lec-
tures. 2. Motivation (Psychology)—Addresses, essays,
lectures. 3. Cognition—Addresses, essays, lectures.
4. Nuttin, Jozef, 1909–   I. Ydewalle, G. d'.
II. Lens, W. III. Atkinson, John William, 1923–
IV. Nuttin, Jozef, 1909–   [DNLM: 1. Cognition.
2. Motivation. 3. Learning. BF311 C6756]
BF318.C64   153   80-23715
ISBN 0-89859-067-1 (L. Erlbaum)

Printed in the United States of America

Contents

Preface

Selected Bibliography of J. (R.) Nuttin

1. **The Organization of Action and the Nature
   of Adult-Infant Transaction   1**
   J. S. Bruner

2. **Developmental Precursors of Success and Failure Experience   15**
   Heinz Heckhausen
   Centering on the Action Outcome: Pleasure in the Outcome   21
   Summary   29

3. **Objective and Subjective Rules for Delay of Gratification   33**
   Walter Mischel
   Introduction   33
   Effects of Attention to the Rewards   35
   Cognitive Distraction   37
   The Role of Symbolically Presented Rewards   43
   Transforming the Stimulus by Cognitive Operations   46
   The Child's Knowledge of the Delay Rules   51
   The Development of Self-Control Competencies   55

4. **Intention and Kinds of Learning   59**
   T. A. Ryan
   Theoretical Implications of the Intention to Learn   60
   Bases for Separating Types of Learning and Memory   65
   A Proposed Classification of Types of Learning and Memory   68
   The Role of Intention in Various Kinds
      of Learning and Memory   72
   Reinterpreting Research on Intentional Learning   78
   Summary   82

5. **Habit Activation in Human Learning   87**
   Melvin H. Marx
   Introduction   87
   From Thorndikean Bond to Memory Store   87
   Reward and Information: Current Issues   89
   Limitations of Cognitive Theory   96
   Habit and Habit Activation: A Reconceptualization   100
   Summary and Conclusions   116

6. **Cognitive Processes in Reinforcement and Choice   123**
   W. K. Estes
   Empirical Domain   124
   Experimental Paradigms   125
   Major Problems Shaping Research   126
   Cognitive Operations in Reinforcement   135

7. **The Brain as the Locus of Cognitive Controls on Action   141**
   Karl H. Pribram
   Introduction   141
   Behavioral Acts   142
   Conclusion   154

8. **Thematic Apperceptive Measurement of Motivation
   in 1950 and 1980   159**
   John W. Atkinson
   The Perspective Around 1950   161
   The Perspective Today (1980)   175
   The Dynamics of Action   176
   Thematic Apperception   177
   The Integrative Principle of a Change in Activity   179
   The Stream of Behavior   180

9. **Future Orientation and Achievement Motivation:**
    Toward a Theory of Personality Functioning and Change   **199**
    Joel O. Raynor
    Overview   199
    Future Orientation   200
    Evaluation of Competence   215
    A Theory of Personality Functioning and Change   219

10. **Cognition of Time in Human Activity**   **233**
    Paul Fraisse
    Two Modes of Knowledge of Time   236
    Perception of Time   238
    Representation of Time   244
    Conclusion: A Model of Duration Estimation   253

11. **Future Time Perspective and the**
    Problem of Cognition/Motivation Interaction   **261**
    Hans Thomae
    Future Time Orientation and
       Phenomenological Theories of Motivation   262
    Future Time Perspective and
       the Structuration of Personality   262
    Future Time Perspective—A Cognitive
       Determinant of Behavior   263
    Expected Definitiveness of Unfavorable
       Life Conditions as an Intervening Variable   266
    Determinants of Future Time Perspective   267
    Concluding Remarks   272

Author Index

Subject Index

Preface

Those who are familiar with the work of Professor J. (R.) Nuttin will understand why "Cognition in Human Motivation and Learning" was selected as the theme of this Festschrift on the occasion of his becoming Professor Emeritus at the University of Leuven in Belgium. Since his pioneering analysis of human selective learning in his doctoral dissertation in 1941, Professor Nuttin has always strongly opposed mechanistic connectionism as the basic explanation of human learning. He distinguishes the rewarding and informational aspects of a behavioral outcome and challenges associationistic learning theories, such as Thorndike's Law of Effect, which consider only the reward aspect. Nuttin holds that learning cannot be identified with stimulus-response connections that are repeated blindly upon the reoccurrence of a stimulus. Instead, learning is to be conceptualized as the selective storing of information about a behavioral act with its outcome as a function of the subject's intentions and interests. That information is retrieved and used in future behavior aimed at the realization of motivational goals and means-end structures. Man seldom repeats learned stimulus-response sequences as a reaction to environmental or internal stimuli; rather, he uses acquired behavioral techniques in subsequent instrumental behavior.

Although Nuttin was one of the first psychologists since Tolman to formulate an integrated cognitive theory of human selective learning, his major work was published in French only (Nuttin, 1953), which inhibited broader circulation and recognition in the Anglo-Saxon world. By the time it was finally published in English (Nuttin & Greenwald, 1968), associationistic psychology had already lost much of its impact and a more cognitive approach was prevailing.

More recently, collaborators in his laboratory (for example, d'Ydewalle and Eelen) have been involved in unravelling the basic processes of human selective learning. Against the older conception of automatic strengthening of response by rewards, the seminal ideas of Estes (1971) and Buchwald (1969) on the cognitive aspects of human learning were tested in various experimental settings. Both Estes and Buchwald acknowledge antecedents of their framework in Nuttin's publications. In d'Ydewalle and Eelen (1975), some elementary mathematical equations were used to predict human performance as a function of the recollection of previously rewarded or punished acts. Although the findings strongly confirmed the basic predictions, a few important problems arose: While predicting a subject's performance by using his recall data was successful, the subject's own report of his performance did not agree very well with assumed cognitive processes (d'Ydewalle, 1978). About at the same time, a paper by Nisbett and Wilson (1977) appeared that treated the issue on a more general level: While a variety of cognitive processes may intervene in many situations, subjects are not well equipped to monitor their own ongoing cognitive activities. Accordingly, some questions and doubts were raised about the entire framework.

But human selective learning, while a hot topic during the debate surrounding the grand-scale learning theories, has moved into the background in recent years. Information processing approaches flourish everywhere now. So it is perhaps an appropriate moment to bring the whole issue of human selective learning back into the mainstream of contemporary experimental psychology. The work of William K. Estes and our own research are attempts to make explicit what kind of information processing does occur in selective learning. It is our opinion that information processing theorists should not lose sight of human action. Already in 1952, Guthrie criticized cognitive psychologists for not linking mental activity to overt behavior.

The gap between cognitive processes and their effects on human action could be bridged by taking the intervening function of human motivation seriously. It is only when the existence of intentional behavior is recognized that cognitive processing of the environment (the situation) makes sense and contributes to a better active adaptation to that situation. This crucial function of human intentions has often been stressed in Professor Nuttin's work on learning and motivation. Contemporary research on information processing would be more fruitful and comprehensive if it approached human action as a function of the interaction between cognitive processes and their underlying motivation.

In this book, outstanding scholars in the field of general psychology (who are also good friends of Professor Nuttin) discuss different ways in which cognition intervenes in behavioral activities on the basis of their empirical research.

Jerome S. Bruner's contribution emphasizes the centrality of man's intentions. For Bruner, intentions are developed by the nature of the "social-technical system" into which man enters. Bruner shows how the intentions of two people (a baby and his mother) are tuned to stimulate the baby's language acquisition. How intentions may influence learning is the topic of Thomas A. Ryan's paper, which shows that the effect of learning intentions has been neglected or minimized by not giving adequate attention to the differences between various types of learning and memory tests.

In the area of human selective learning, William K. Estes reviews a whole range of research including his own and arrives at the conclusion that the effects of reward and punishment can be interpreted in terms of information on the relationship between particular responses producing the desired outcome. Arguing that learning phenomena are not always to be explained by cognitive processes alone, Melvin H. Marx presents a new framework of cognitive and noncognitive factors. Karl H. Pribram's attempt to relate neurological structures to behavioral phenomena leads him to a healthy discussion on what is cognition and what is the relationship between emotion, motivation, decision, reinforcement, attention, cognitive learning, memory, and perception.

All chapters in this volume that discuss the motivational significance of cognition can be related to Professor Nuttin's theory on cognition and human motivation. His work in this field is strongly affected by general ideas on the cognitive and constructive character of human behavior (Nuttin, 1980a). He holds that behavior is a relational function, i.e., the realization of a more or less complex network of relations or interactions between the individual and his environment. Nuttin rejects the conventional conception of personality as being a self-enclosed system. His conceptualization of personality and behavior implies that some types of interactions are necessary for biological and psychological survival or self-realization. By identifying needs or motives with these necessary types of interactions, the Relational Theory of Motivation (Nuttin, 1980a) formulates a truly behavioral definition of what needs are.

Because of his higher cognitive functions, man is not limited to overt interactions with the environment. He also acts on a covert or representational level. Cognitive processes not only guide ongoing overt behavior; they also constitute an autonomous form of behavior. Very often covert behavior is preparatory to overt behavior. On the representational level, needs are cognitively elaborated into specific goals, projects, plans, and means-end structures. These are not merely cognitive structures; they are also dynamically loaded and may instigate and direct subsequent covert or overt behavior. Needs that are cognitively elaborated into goals and means-end structures can be characterized by their motivational content and their future time perspective. Motivational goals are, by definition, situated in the future

(Nuttin, 1980b). Nuttin's insistence on human striving for short-term or long-term goals (related to his conceptual distinction between open and closed tasks in human selective learning; Nuttin, 1953) helped to bring about an important extension of the prevailing expectancy-value models in cognitive motivation research.

Atkinson's expectancy-value model of risk-taking behavior—his theory of achievement motivation—is partly based on the cumulative empirical research into the behavioral effects of individual differences in strength with regard to the need for achievement. The strength of this motive is measured by content analysis of T.A.T. stories, which are samples of verbally expressed covert behavior. In his contribution, John W. Atkinson first explains the basis for this motivational measurement as it was initially developed in the early fifties. Then he cogently demonstrates the construct validity of the need for achievement measure by applying the Dynamics of Action theory—a general theory of motivation that is based on the conceptual analysis of a change in activity instead of isolated actions—to the covert stream of imaginative thought behavior. The translation of this theory into a computer program enables Atkinson to apply computer simulations to the method of measurement that yielded the initial theory. He shows that, contrary to what traditional test theory assumes, reliability (internal consistency) does not set an upper limit for validity. Construct validity does not require internal consistency reliability.

Joel O. Raynor develops a "more general theory" of achievement motivation by elaborating Atkinson's risk-taking model along Nuttinian lines. He incorporates the motivational effects of anticipated future successes and failures contingent upon success or failure in the present achievement task. He also introduces his theory of personality functioning and change in which time perspective becomes a key variable. Heinz Heckhausen presents experimental research with children on the cognitive prerequisites for experiencing an action outcome as success or failure. Great care is given to the problem of detecting at an early age, the signs or expressions of what Nuttin calls "causality pleasure" (Nuttin, 1973).

Walter Mischel's work on the determinants of choosing between an immediate smaller gratification and a more desirable but deferred one shows how mental representations of rewards and other types of ideation affect voluntary delay. Although his research paradigm does not make use of varying time intervals during which instrumental activity must be performed to reach the preferred goal, his findings on the type of cognition that are helpful in coping with a delay period are promising for the development of a cognitive theory of instrumental motivation.

Hans Thomae discusses his research and that of his collaborators showing that future time perspective (future anticipations) as a cognitive variable cannot replace motivational processes as the determinants of directed behavior. He considers the study of the interaction between anticipations of the future and motivational processes as one of the most promising approaches in the study of human behavior. Paul Fraisse describes the different ways in which temporal information is treated by man. He discusses the principal processes occurring in time perception, representation of time, and estimation of time duration. He presents a two-level model to account for the "numerous and sometimes contradictory results" that he reviews.

We want to express our deep gratitude to the scholars who generously accepted our invitation to contribute to this Festschrift. The originality and the high quality of their work is striking and make this book a most valuable source of readings for students of cognition, learning, motivation, and personality psychology. They confirm the appreciation that the international scientific community has for Professor Nuttin's contribution to psychology.

Géry d'Ydewalle
Willy Lens

REFERENCES

Buchwald, A. M. Effects of "Right" and "Wrong" on subsequent behavior: A new interpretation. *Psychological Review*, 1969, *76*, 132–143.

d'Ydewalle, G. The reported number and the repetition of "Right" and "Wrong" responses. *Psychologica Belgica*, 1978, *18*, 160–181.

d'Ydewalle, G., & Eelen, P. Repetition and recall of "Right" and "Wrong" responses in incidental and intentional learning. *Journal of Experimental Psychology: Human Learning and Memory*, 1975, *1*, 429–441.

Estes, W. K. Reward in human learning: Theoretical issues and strategic choice points. In R. Glaser (Ed.), *The nature of reinforcement*. New York: Academic Press, 1971.

Guthrie, E. R. *The psychology of learning* (Rev. ed.). New York: Harper & Row, 1952.

Nisbett, R. E., & Wilson, D. D. Telling more than we can know: Verbal reports on mental processes. *Psychological Review*, 1977, *84*, 231–259.

Nuttin, J. (R.) *Tâche, réussite et échec*. Louvain: Publications Universitaires, 1953.

Nuttin, J. (R.) Pleasure and reward in human motivation and learning. In D. E. Berlyne and K. B. Masden (Eds.), *Pleasure, reward, preference*. New York: Academic Press, 1973.

Nuttin, J. (R.) *Théorie de la motivation humaine*. Paris: P.U.F., 1980. (a)

Nuttin, J. (R.) *Motivation et perspectives d'avenir*. Louvain: Presses Universitaires, 1980. (b)

Nuttin, J. (R.), & Greenwald, A. G. *Reward and punishment in human leaning*. New York: Academic Press, 1968.

Selected Bibliography of J. (R.) Nuttin

Respective effectiveness of success and task-tension in learning. *British Journal of Psychology*, 1947, *38*, 49–55.

Spread in recalling failure and success. *Journal of Experimental Psychology*, 1949, *39*, 690–700.

Psychoanalyse et conception spiritualiste de l'homme: Une théorie dynamique de la personnalité normale. Louvain: Publications Universitaires, 1950 (Also published in English, Dutch, German, Italian, Portugese, and Spanish).

Tâche, réussite et échec: Théorie de la conduite humaine. Louvain: Publications Universitaires, 1953.

Consciousness, behavior and personality. *Psychological Review*, 1955, *42*, 349–355.

Human motivation and Freud's theory of energy discharge. *Canadian Journal of Psychology*, 1956, *10*, 167–178.

La motivation. In P. Fraisse & J. Piaget (Eds.), *Traité de psychologie expérimentale. Vol. V.: Motivation, émotion et personnalité*. Paris: P.U.F., 1963 (Also published in English, Hungarian, Italian, Japanese, Polish, Portuguese, Russian, Slovak, and Spanish).

The future time perspective in human motivation and learning. *Acta Psychologica*, 1964, *23*, 60–82 (Proceedings of the 17th International Congress of Psychology, Washington, 1963).

La structure de la personnalité. Paris: P.U.F., 1965 (Also published in Italian, Polish, Portuguese, and Spanish).

Motivation et fonctions cognitives dans le comportement humain. In *Actes du 18me Congrès International de Psychologie, Moscou, 1966* (XIIIme symposium). Moscow, 1966.

Reward and task-orientation in human learning. *Psychologia* (Tokyo), 1967, *10*, 177–185.

Problèmes de motivation humaine, psychologie des besoins foundamentaux et des projets d'avenir. *Scientia,* 1967, *61,* 464–475.

Adaptation et motivation humaine. In J. Bresson *et al., Les processus d'adaptation.* Paris: P.U.F., 1967.

Reward and punishment in human learning: Elements of a behavior theory. New York: Academic Press, 1968 (in collaboration with A. G. Greenwald).

La perception des réussites et échecs personnels en fonction des résultats d'un partenaire. *Psychologica Belgica,* 1972, *12,* 9–31 (in collaboration with M.-A. D'Amorim).

Pleasure and reward in human motivation and learning. In D. E. Berlyne & K. B. Madsen (Eds.), *Pleasure, reward, preference: Their nature, determinants, and role in behavior.* New York: Academic Press, 1973.

The outcome of behavior and contiguity in motivation and learning. In *Proceedings of the 20th International Congress of Psychology, Tokyo, 1972.* Tokyo: Science Council of Japan-Tokyo University Press, 1974.

Motivation and reward in human learning. In W. K. Estes (Ed.), *Handbook of learning and cognitive processes. Vol. III.: Approaches to human learning and motivation.* Hillsdale, N.J.: Lawrence Erlbaum Associates, 1976.

Frequency perception of individual and group successes as a function of competition, coaction, and isolation. *Journal of Personality and Social Psychology,* 1976, *34,* 830–836 (in collaboration with L. Janssens).

Frequency perception of successes as a function of results previously obtained by others and by oneself. *Journal of Personality and Social Psychology,* 1976, *34,* 734–745 (in collaboration with R. Vreven).

Perception de la fréquence de réussites personnelles et de succès partagés. In G. Oléron (Ed.), *Psychologie expérimentale et comparée: Hommage à Paul Fraisse.* Paris, P.U.F., 1977 (in collaboration with M. Viegas Abreu).

La perspective temporelle dans le comportement humain. In P. Fraisse (Ed.), *Du temps biologique au temps psychologique.* Paris: P.U.F., 1979.

Théorie de la motivation humaine: Du besoin au project d'action. Paris: P.U.F., 1980. (a)

Motivation et perspectives d'avenir. Louvain: Presses Universitaires de Louvain/Leuven University Press, 1980. (b)

1

The Organization of Action and the Nature of Adult–Infant Transaction[1]

J. S. Bruner
Harvard University

I wish to begin by baldly stating a presupposition about the organization of action, one I shall take for granted; I then present evidence from the study of mother–infant interaction that would have forced me to come to a conclusion about the nature of human action very like that I began with as taken for granted. I promise to perform this feat without mirrors. My argument will be simply: How could parent–infant interaction in the human species (and in some higher apes) be as it is unless the nature of human action is as I suppose it to be? This is not such an audacious enterprise as it may seem. It is what we researchers do all the time, though we suppress our presuppositions in communicating our findings and then feign surprise when we state our final conclusions. The evidence I use is material from studies in both the acquisition of language and the assisted acquisition of action routines by infants.

What I take for granted for the moment (until forced later to conclude that I was right) is that most of what we speak of in common-sense terms as human action is steered by intentions of the following kind and in the following way. An intention is present when an individual operates persistently toward achieving an end state, chooses among alternate means and/or routes to achieve that end state, persists in deploying means and corrects the deployment of means to get closer to the end state, and finally ceases the line of activity when specifiable features of the end state are achieved. The elements of the cycle, then, comprise aim, option of means, persistence and

---

[1]A preliminary version of the text was presented at a meeting on the "Organization of action", Maison des Sciences de l'Homme, Paris, 1979.

correction, and a terminal stop order. There are several unspecified features present in this type of cycle. The principal one has to do with the nature of feedback and correction. In the nature of things, feedback in such an action cycle is always context-dependent: It is computed by reference to the feedforward signal inherent in the action aims of the organism. A correction procedure involves a redeployment of means whose objective is to minimize the discrepancy between one's present position and what had been anticipated as the position appropriate to achieving the sought-after end state.

There is another matter hidden in my description that wants to be made explicit. It is not necessary that, in such intended human action, the actor be able to account for or be conscious of the nature of his intentions. Much of intentional action takes place below the threshold of reportable awareness. Driving a motorcar while conversing with a friend provides a familiar case. But I emphasize that a special status inheres in those intentional acts that *are* reportable and conscious. The distinction is important from the point of view of how conscious reportability extends the range of corrections accessible to the actor. Perhaps it is by making conscious intentions more combinable through the case of language. I refer to the support of intentional action in the relation that develops between infant and mother and it matters mightily when and how the child achieves reportable awareness of what he is trying to do.

Another preliminary remark has to do with the graininess of the theory of action I am presenting, its decomposability into elementary units. We know that intentional acts can become constituents of, serve as means subroutines in, other intentional acts. Intentions are obviously nesting and nestable or, in a technical sense, have the property of iterativeness and recursivity. In some systems of intentional behavior, like speaking a natural language, there are discernible, analyzable levels that go to make up a communicative act—say, an utterance. These have the property that they cannot be understood from the bottom up, but are amenable of interpretation only from the top down. When we say that distinctive features are the constituents *en paquet* of a phoneme and that phonemes and their allophonic slippages are constituents of morphemes (whether derivational or inflectional), that morphemes somehow fill the grammatical slots of a sentence, etc., we imply top-down determination. Each level below is constrained by the level above in a fashion that makes it extraordinarily difficult to describe how language is produced or even comprehended. Language is a very special case in the sense that the design features of the system are in many ways quite unlike any other system of intentional action known in the biological world (and I do not mean to exclude the social world by using the term *biological*). Yet, for any system of action—from skilled motor activity to such highly symbolic, rule-governed activities as flirtation or stock brokering—there is a possible description of the manner in which constituents are composed into higher-level action structures. And the crucial point is that it is the task of anybody learning to carry out skilled, intentional action to figure out the rules of composition (and decomposition) of the system.

This brings me to the final preliminary remark. It is quite the most typical thing of the actions of our species that in the course of growth our intentions outstrip our capacities for fulfilling them or, indeed, even for recognizing fully what they are about. The young infant typically will reveal a situation-related restlessness, a general activation before he is fully able to recognize means to an end, and indeed there is a body of data in the field of motivation that suggests that, under such conditons of activation, it may be necessary for the immature organism to learn what the end state is that terminates the diffuse intentionality (if I may use such a bizarre phrase as a synonym for activation). It certainly becomes necessary for him to learn how to deploy the means for achieving the desired end state. It is characteristic of organisms like man, with a conspicuously helpless immaturity, that they cannot operate to achieve their goals (or to learn them, for that matter) by trial-and-error behavior, and they do not have enough of a wired-in repertoire of try out routines to guide them much in such trial and error. In consequence, they are dependent, like no species yet ever evolved, upon a tutoring relationship with adults who can help them learn to carry out their intended actions directed to goals. It is quite obvious that something of this order occurs in language acquisition and in other forms of social skill learning. It is equally obvious that such also occurs when one observes the child learning to cope with the world of objects during the first 2 years of life. Or if it is not immediately obvious, I hope to be able to make it so shortly.

Now, a little reflection upon this problem makes it plain that for such a state of transaction between infant and adult to prevail, adults must have a representation in their heads about the nature of human development. That is to say, to take the case of language, the adult, in order to help the child to his or her goals of linguistic mastery, not only must know what constitutes human mastery but also must have a developmental theory of the performance of the child en route toward that final state. If there is anything to the doctrine of an inbuilt, if not innate, Language Acquisition Device, LAD (Chomsky, 1965), for young children faced with the flow of the language about them, in my view there must be something comparable in the adult that deserves the title Language Assistance Service (LAS). In this view as well, the acquisition of language is a dialogue between the child's acquisition device and the adult's assistance service, between LAD and LAS. Certainly the findings of Shatz and Gelman (1973) on 4-year-olds being able to talk appropriately in "baby talk" register to 2-year-olds suggest that the adult assistance service opens its doors to potential clients at a very tender age indeed. And the past several years of research on mother–infant linguistic interaction points to the fact that there is an enormous amount of fine tuning in the mother's responses to the child's talk (or his very effort to talk) that could not have arrived there simply by virtue of the mother's having been exposed to other babies or having read Lyons (1970) on Noam Chomsky.

With respect to helping the child to handle manipulation of the world of objects, there is a comparable problem. Wood, Bruner, and Ross (1976) have explored what mothers do when helping their child do things like drinking from a cup or putting together an interlocking set of blocks. The mother's performance is an interesting and uncanny set of maneuvers on the theme we have been exploring. She is obviously operating on a very intricate and subtle and updatable theory of the child's performance. Let me specify some of the maneuvers Wood, Ross, and I observed in a study of mothers teaching their 3-to-5-year-olds how to assemble a set of interlocking blocks to make a handsome pyramid.

1. Modeling. The mother typically models not only the final pyramid by constructing it slowly and with conspicuous marking, but also the subassemblies that she recognizes the child needs to create the constituents. She does this only after she has achieved the child's concentrated attention.

2. Cueing. Once the child has achieved a means–end routine of any kind, she cues him or her with respect to the opportunities for using it so that it may reach successful conclusion.

3. Scaffolding. She systematically reduces the number of degrees of freedom that must be controlled by the child in carrying out parts of the task—as in helping him or her guide blocks into place when he or she is attempting to put them into the assembly. She also, by way of diffuse scaffolding, protects him or her from distraction by limiting the site in which the task occurs, and by ritualizing it. I discuss this shortly in the context of language acquisition as "format construction," a means of limiting the complexity of task to situations where the child is able to carry out tasks and to evaluate feedback independently.

4. Raising the Ante. It is characteristic of most mothers we have observed that once the child has mastered one component of the task, they find ways of challenging him or her to incorporate it into a more complex routine for achievement of a more remote end. It often may have the nature of teasing rather than teaching (challenging the child, as one mother put it, to "make the ultimate effort"). But its function is certainly benign and it is a feature of variation in mother–infant interaction that saves the child from being bored out of action by a series of confirming reinforcements when he or she already knows that he or she already knows.

5. Instruction.   And final irony: when the child already knows how to do it and can indeed account for what he or she is doing, at that stage the mother starts using verbal instruction successfully and seriously. There is plenty of talk before that, but it is not "serious." Verbal instruction appears only when the child is able to encode his or her acts in joint reference with the interlocutor, mother.

The conclusion to which I am forced is that the mother is operating as if the child had intentions in mind, as if he or she were trying to deploy means to its realization, were out to correct errors, had a finished task in mind—but is not quite able to put it all together in a fashion to suit him or her or mother. She imposes regularity on the task, takes account of his or her channel capacity for information processing, and keeps him or her activated by managing to keep full effectance just out of reach. I can come to one of two conclusions. Either the mother is a victim of common sense and does not really understand action, else she would put her child into a Skinner box and devise a schedule of reinforcement for his operant responses. Or she is behaving appropriately toward an immature member of the species who does in fact operate along the lines of intentional action I originally proposed. Let me confess at this point that the original view, presented as "taken for granted," may remind you of some things you may have read in the literature, like Von Holst and Mittelstaedt (1950), Bernstein (1967), and Miller, Galanter, and Pribram (1960).

Now language acquisiton. This is not the occasion to go deeply into the question of the functions that language fulfills and the means whereby conventionalized devices or procedures are developed and used for their fulfillment. I do not want to be engaged directly in this issue at this point; enough only to say that something of the order of speech–act theory and the Gricean cycle (Grice, 1957) plus some set of controlling maxims to regulate presuppositions are for me an essential aspect of any linguistic theory and particularly of one that hopes to make contact with work on acquisition. What I would like to do is to take first the case of the child learning to label and then to move on to the child mastering requestive forms, as an illustration of my points.

Consider an infant learning to label objects. Ninio and Bruner (1978) observed Richard in his home every 2 weeks from his eighth month until he was 2 years old, videotaping his actions so that we could study them later. In this instance, he and his mother are "reading" the pictures in a book. Before this kind of learning begins, certain things already have been established. Richard has learned about pointing as a pure indicating act, marking unusual or unexpected objects rather than things wanted immediately. He also has learned to understand that sounds refer in some singular way to objects or events. Richard and his mother, moreover, have long since established well-regulated turn-taking routines, which probably were developing as early as his third or fourth month. And finally, Richard has learned that books are to be looked at, not eaten or torn and objects depicted are to be responded to in a particular way and with sounds in a pattern of dialogue.

For the mother's part, she (like all mothers we have observed) drastically limits her speech and maintains a steady regularity. In her dialogues with Richard in "book reading" she uses four types of speech in a strikingly fixed order. First, to get his attention, she says, "Look." Second, with a distinctly rising inflection, she asks, "What's that?" Third, she gives the picture a label, "It's an X." And finally, in response to his actions, she says, "That's right."

In each case, a single verbal token accounts for from nearly half to more than 90 per cent of the instances. The way Richard's mother uses the four speech constituents is closely linked to what her son says or does. When she varies her response, it is with good reason. If Richard responds, his mother replies, and if he initiates a cycle by pointing and vocalizing, then she responds even more often.

Her fine tuning is fine indeed. For example, if after her query Richard labels the picture, she virtually always will skip the label and jump to the response, "Yes." Like the other mothers we have studied, she is following ordinary polite rules for adult dialogue.

As Roger Brown has described the baby talk of adults, it appears to be an imitative version of how babies talk. Brown (1977) says: "Babies already talk like babies, so what is the earthly use of parents doing the same? Surely it is a parent's job to teach the adult language [p. 10]." He resolves the dilemma by noting: "What I think adults are chiefly trying to do, when they use [baby talk] with children, is to communicate, to understand and to be understood, to keep two minds focussed on the same topic [p. 12]. Although I agree with Brown, I would like to point out that the content and intonation of the talk is baby talk, but the dialogue pattern is adult.

To ensure that two minds are indeed focused on a common topic, the mother develops a technique for showing her baby what feature a label refers to by making 90 per cent of her labels refer to whole objects. Since half of the remainder of her speech is made up of proper names that also stand for the whole, she seems to create few difficulties, supposing that the child also responds to whole objects and not to their features.

The mother's (often quite unconscious) approach is exquisitely tuned. When the child responds to her "Look!" by looking, she follows immediately with a query. When the child responds to the query with a gesture or a smile, she supplies a label. But as soon as the child shows the ability to vocalize in a way that might indicate a label, she raises the ante. She withholds the label and repeats the query until the child vocalizes, then she gives the label.

Later, when the child has learned to respond with shorter vocalizations that correspond to words, she no longer accepts an indifferent vocalization. When the child begins producing a recognizable, constant label for an object, she holds out for it. Finally, the child produces appropriate words at the appropriate place in the dialogue. Even then the mother remains tuned to the developing pattern, helping her child recognize labels and make them increasingly accurate. For example, she develops two ways of asking, "What's that?" One, with a falling intonation, inquires about those words for which she believes her child already knows the label; the other, with a rising intonation, marks words that are new.

Even in the simple labeling game, mother and child are well into making the distinction between the given and the new. It is of more than passing interest that the old or established labels are the ones around which the mother will shortly be elaborating comments and questions for new information:

> Mother: What's that? [with falling intonation]
> Child: Fishy.
> Mother: Yes, and see him swimming?

After the mother assumes her child has acquired a particular label, she generally drops the attention-getting "Look!" when they turn to the routine. In these petty particulars of language, the mother gives useful cues about the structure of their native tongue. She provides cues based not simply on her knowledge of the language but also on her continually changing knowledge of the child's ability to grasp particular distinctions, forms, or rules. The child is sensitized to certain constraints in the structure of their dialogue and does not seem to be directly imitating her. I say this because there is not much difference in the likelihood of a child's repeating a label after hearing it, whether the mother has imitated the child's label, simply said "Yes," or only laughed approvingly. In each case, the child repeats the label about half the time, at about the same rate as with *no* reply from the mother. Moreover, the child is eight times more likely to produce a label in response to "What's that?" than to the mother's uttering the label.

I do not mean to claim that children cannot or do not use imitation in acquiring language. Language must be partly based on imitation, but although the child may be imitating another, language learning involves solving problems by communicating in a dialogue. The child seems to be trying to get through to the mother just as hard as she is trying to reach her child.

Dialogue occurs in a context. When children first learn to communicate, it is always in highly concrete situations, as when mother or child calls attention to an object, asking for the aid or participation of the other. Formally conceived, the format of communication involves an intention, a set of procedures, and a goal. In this sense, the formats of language acquisition are much like the tasks described by Wood, Bruner and Ross (1976).

A second major function of speech is requesting something of another person. Bruner, Roy and Ratner (in press) have been studying its development during the first 2 years of life. Requesting requires an indication that you want *something* and *what* it is you want. In the earliest procedures used by children it is difficult to separate the two. First the child vocalizes with a characteristic intonation pattern while reaching eagerly for the desired nearby object—which is most often held by the mother. As in virtually all early exchanges, it is the mother's task to interpret, and she works at it in a surprisingly subtle way. During our analyses of Richard when he was from 8 to 24 months old and Jonathan when he was 8 to 18 months old, we noticed that their mothers frequently seemed to be teasing them or withholding obviously desired objects. Closer inspection indicated that it was not teasing at all. They were trying to get the infants to reach for what they wanted and to "say something" (as one mother urged her son), pressing them to make their intentions clearer. When the two children requested nearby objects, the mothers were more likely to ask "Do you really want it?" than "Do you want the X?". The mother's first step is pragmatic, to get the child to signal that he wants the object.

Children make three types of requests, reflecting increasing sophistication in matters that have nothing to do with language. The first kind that emerges is directed at obtaining nearby, visible objects; this later expands to include distant or absent objects where the contextual understanding of words like *you/me, this/that* and *here/there* is crucial. The second kind of request is directed at obtaining support for an action that is already in progress, and the third kind is used to persuade the mother to share some activity or experience.

When children first begin to request objects, they typically direct their attention and their reach entirely toward the object, opening and closing their fists, accompanied by a "standard," stereotyped call with characteristic intonation pattern. As this request expands, between 10 and 15 months, an observer immediately notes two changes. In reaching for distant objects, a child no longer looks solely at the desired object, but shifts his glance back and forth between the object and his mother. His call pattern also changes. It becomes more prolonged, or its rise and fall in intonation is repeated, and it is more insistent.

When consistent word forms appeared, they were initially idiosyncratic labels for objects, gradually becoming standard nouns that indicated the desired objects. The children also began initiating and ending their requests with smiles. The development of this pattern is paced by the child's knowledge, which is shared with the mother, of where things are located and of her willingness to fetch them if properly asked. Once the child begins requesting distant and absent objects, the mother has an opportunity to require that the desired object be specified and her emphasis shifts from the pragmatic to the referential. Other conditions begin to be imposed: The request, for example, must be "legitimate" and "appropriate," the object essential, "timetable" conditions must be honored—and when the request is not granted, the child is expected to understand and accept the mother's verbal reasons.

Requests for joint activity contrast with object requests. I think they can be called precursors to invitation. They amount to the child asking the adult to share in an activity or an experience—to look out of the window into the garden together, to play Ride a Cock Horse, to read together. They are the most playlike form of request, and in consequence they generate a considerable amount of language of considerable complexity. It is in this format that the issues of agency and share (or turn) emerge and produce important linguistic changes. Most of these requests are for activities that are quite ritualized and predictable. There tend to be rounds and turns, and no specific outcome is required. The activity itself is rewarding. In this setting the child first deals with share and turn by adopting such forms of linguistic marking as *more* and *again*. These appear during joint role enactment and migrate rapidly into formats involving requests for distant objects.

It is also in joint role enactment that the baby's first consistent words appear and, beginning at 18 months, word combinations begin to explode. *More X* (with a noun) appears, and also combinations like *down slide, Mummy ride, Mummy read, Eileen do.* Indeed, it is in these settings that full-blown ingratiatives appear in appropriate positions, as in prefacing a request with *nice Mummy*. Ingratiatives serve to assure that the other continues to act as a means to the achievement of intention.

After the children were 17 months old, the mothers we studied began to demand that they adhere more strictly to turn taking and role respecting. The demand can be made most easily when they are doing something together, for that is where the conditions for sharing are most clearly defined and least likely, since playful, to overstrain the child's capacity to wait for a turn. But the sharp increase in agency as a topic in their dialogue reflects as well the emergence of a difference in their wishes. The mother may want the child to execute the act requested of her, and the child may have views contrary to his mother's about agency. In addition, the child's requests for support more often lead to negotiation between the pair than is the case when the clarity of the roles in their joint activity makes acceptance and refusal easier. A recurrent trend in development during the child's first year is the shifting of agency in all manner of exchanges from mother to infant. Even at 9 to 12 months, Richard gradually began taking the lead in give-and-take games (Bruner, 1978), and peekaboo games follow a similar pattern (Ratner & Bruner, 1978). In book reading too, Richard's transition was quite rapid. Role shifting is very much part of the child's sense of script, and I believe it is typical of the kind of "real world" experience that makes it so astonishingly easy for children to master soon afterwards the deictic shifts, those contextual changes in the meaning of words that are essential to understanding the language. The prelinguistic communicative framework established in their dialogue by mother and child provides the setting for the child's acquisition of this language function. His or her problem solving in acquiring the deictic function is a *social* task: to find the procedure that will produce results, just as his or her prelinguistic communicative effort produced results, and the results needed can be interpreted in relation to role interactions.

The last type of request, the request for supportive action, has a very special property. It is tightly bound to the nature of the action in which the child is involved. To ask others for help in support of their own actions, children need at least two forms of knowledge. One of them represents the course of action and involves a goal and a set of means for getting to it. The second requirement is some grasp of what has been called the *arguments of action* (Parisi & Antinucci, 1976): Who does it, with what instrument, at what place, to whom, on what object, etc. Once children have mastered these, they have a rudimentary understanding of the concepts that will be encountered later in case grammar (Fillmore, 1968).

The degree to which a child comes to understand the structure of tasks is the degree to which his or her requests for support in carrying them out become more differentiated. These requests do not appear with any marked frequency until he or she is 17 or 18 months old and consist of bringing the "work" or the "action" or the entire task to an adult: a music box to be rewound, or two objects that have to be joined together. In time, a child is able to do better than that. He may bring a tool to an adult or direct the adult's hand or pat the goal (the chair on which he wants "up"). He is selecting and highlighting relevant features of the action, though not in a fashion that depends on what the adult is doing. Finally at about the age of two, with the development of adequate words to refer to particular aspects of the action, the child enters a new phase: He requests action by guiding it successively. The pacemaker of the verbal output is progress in the task itself.

Let me give an instance of this successive guidance system. Richard, it transpires, wishes to persuade his mother to open a cupboard so that he can get something out; she is seated (and very pregnant). Successively, he voices the following requests:

> Mummy, Mummy; Mummy come...Up, up; up...Cupboard...Up cupboard, up cupboard, up cupboard; up...Get up...Cupboard, cupboard... Cupboard up, cupboard up, cupboard up...Telephone...Mummy...Mummy get out telephone.

His mother objects and asks him what it is he wants after each of the first two requests. She is trying to get him to set forth his request in some "readable" order before she starts to respond—to give a reason in terms of the goal of the action. Richard, meanwhile, achieves something approaching a request in sentence form by organizing his successive utterances in a fashion that seems to be guided by his conception of the needed steps in the action. The initial grammar of the long string of task-related requests is, then, a kind of temporal grammar based on an understanding not only of the actions required, but also of the order in which these actions must be executed. This bit of child language is an interpersonal script based on a young child's knowledge of what is needed to reach the goal in the real world; it is the matrix in which language develops.

Requesting, I think, serves as an ideal model for what we have been discussing as our general theme. Its very form in language and in the context of its appropriacy depends on the formulating and the transmitting of intentions and, by its very nature, it forces what at the outset I referred to as explicit, reportable intentions. It is no curiosa that the mother, before the lesson of request is over, insists that the child, almost like a student of the philosophical Anscombe (1957), should make clear (or be prepared, at least, to make clear) what it is that he has in mind in launching on a line of behavior that requires that another enter in to help change his state of the world, to paraphrase Hintikka (1974).

One final point. Intentions involving more than a single person in their execution are the stuff of which social life is composed. Social psychologists refer to their bringing together as a negotiatory process. It is indeed negotiatory, but the negotiation requires a context or format or, as some prefer, a scenario in order for the two or more sets of intentions to be meshed smoothly. Much of earlier developmental psychology stressed that children were egocentric and, by implication, could not enter into scenarios in a way that made it possible for them to see the role of the other. When one observes the conversation of 4-year-olds (as Nelson & Gruendel, 1977, have), it becomes clear that much of what has been taken for egocentrism is simply a failure on the part of the child to grasp the nature of the scenario. They report that 4-year-olds who may show egocentrism in the standard, adulto-centric tasks used in Geneva nonetheless can bring off dialogues over a toy telephone as follows:

Gay: Hi.
Dan: Hi.
Gay: How are you?
Dan: Fine.
Gay: Who am I speaking to?
Dan: Daniel. This is your Daddy. I need to speak to you.
Gay: All right.
Dan: When I come home tonight we're gonna have . . . peanut butter and jelly sandwich . . . uh . . . at dinner time.

Gay: Uhmmm. Where're we going at dinner time?
Dan: Nowhere, but we're just gonna have dinner at 11 o'clock.
Gay: Well, I made a plan of going out tonight.
Dan: Well, that's what we're gonna do.
Gay: We're going out.
Dan: The plan, it's gonna be, that's gonna be, we're going to McDonald's.
Gay: Yeah, we're going to McDonald's. And ah, ah, ah, what they have for dinner tonight is hamburger.
Dan: Hamburger is coming. O.K. Well, goodbye.
Gay: Bye.

To return to my preliminary remarks, there are three alternative views that can be entertained as to why we ever considered that the organization of action was other than I have described it here. One is that at the "natural" or biological level, the "machine language" of the system is in fact as it has been described by exponents of a model of "trial-and-error-cum-reinforcement." I think it can be said that the arguments of Von Holst and Mittelstaedt (1950) and of Miller, Galanter and Pribram (1960) score strongly against this view by demonstrating that at the molecular level as well there must be something "intentional" present that makes possible the generating of a subsequent correction term. The second view is that the socialization process "shapes" human action into its highly intentional form. This is doubtless true, in the sense that ever higher-level intentional systems are called for by adults in their interaction with children. Nonetheless, what is most crucial is that human young have the capacity to respond to such "goading" by adults in the society. The third view holds that intentional activity in man is "required" by the nature of the "social–technical" system into which man enters. The social–technical system of human society can be conceived of as a treasury of "prosthetic devices" in the form of means for achieving ends. The evolution of the species is such as to have shaped man's action patterns into an ever more intention-directed, means-sensitive, corrective form. It is likely that older views of action result from a spirit of reductionism that believed the "true" nature of man could best be explained by using a phylogenetically primitive model that ignored man's evolution into a tool and symbol user.

Let me end where I started. The evidence of child–adult interaction argues strongly, I claim that human behavior is organized under the control of intentions much as I have described the process. The folk wisdom of a species bringing its young into the social and physical envelope of the species' "econiche", human culture, argues much more strongly in that direction than at first seemed to be the case when, unfortunately, we based our inferences about action on models of learning, motivation, and behavior that were remote from the pattern of conduct that one observes man or woman actually indulging in.

REFERENCES

Anscombe, G. E. M. *Intention.* Oxford: Blackwell, 1957.

Bernstein, N. A. *The Coordination and Regulation of Movement.* London: Pergamon, 1967.

Brown, R. Introduction. In C. E. Snow & C. A. Ferguson (Eds.), *Talking to Children: Language Input and Acquisition.* Cambridge, England: Cambridge University Press, 1977.

Bruner, J. S. Learning how to do things with words. In J. Bruner & A. Garton (Eds.), *Human Development* (Wolfson Lectures 1976–1977). Oxford: Oxford University Press, 1978.

Bruner, J., Roy, C., & Ratner, N. The beginnings of request. In K. E. Nelson (Ed.), *Children's Language* (Vol. 3). New York: Gardner Press, in press.

Chomsky, N. *Aspects of the Theory of Syntax.* Cambridge, Mass.: M I T Press, 1965.

Fillmore, C. J. The case for case. In E. Bach & R. Harms (Eds.), *Universals in Linguistic Theory.* New York: Holt, Rinehart & Winston, 1968.

Grice, H. P. Meaning. *Philosophical Review,* 1957, *66,* 377–388.

Hintikka, J. Questions about questions. In M. K. Munitz & P. K. Unger (Eds.), *Semantics and Philosophy.* New York: New York University Press, 1974.

Lyons, J. *Chomsky.* London: Fontana (Modern Masters), 1970.

Miller, G. A., Galanter, E., & Pribram, K. H. *Plans and the Structure of Behavior.* New York: Holt, 1960.

Nelson, K., & Gruendel, J. *At morning, it's lunch time: A scriptal view of children's dialogue.* Paper presented at the Conference on Dialogue, Language Development, and Dialectical Research, University of Michigan, Ann Arbor, December 1977.

Ninio, A., & Bruner, J. S. The achievement and antecedents of labelling. *Journal of Child Language,* 1978, *5,* 1–15.

Parisi, D., & Antinucci, F. *Essentials of grammar.* New York & London: Academic Press, 1976.

Ratner, N.K., & Bruner, J. S. Games, social exchange and the acquisition of language. *Journal of Child Language,* 1978, *5,* 391–401.

Shatz, M., & Gelman, R. The development of communication skills: Modifications in the speech of young children as a function of listener. *Monographs of the Society for Research in Child Development,* 1973, No. 152, *38*(5).

Von Holst, E., & Mittelstaedt, H. Das Reafferenzprinzip. *Naturwissenschaften,* 1950, *37,* 464–476.

Wood, D., Bruner, J. S., & Ross, G. The role of tutoring in problem solving. *Journal of Child Psychology and Psychiatry,* 1976, *17,* 89–100.

2 Developmental Precursors of Success and Failure Experience

Heinz Heckhausen
Ruhr-Universität, Bochum

Inquiring into the nature and antecedents of pleasure, Nuttin (1973) has distinguished between stimulation pleasure and causality pleasure. He offered impressive evidence that event production ("causality pleasure") is more motivating and attractive than mere stimulus change. Five-year olds were confronted with two equal looking automats, each equipped with two colored electrical bulbs and two handles. The bulbs of automat *A* lighted automatically in an alternative rhythm of 0.25 sec. As to automat *B*, the bulbs were either out or on and could be switched on or extinguished, respectively, when the corresponding handle was moved. Each child was free to manipulate each of the two automats for half an hour and again when reintroduced into the experimental room for a second time. Subjects clearly preferred automat *B* over automat *A*, as evidenced by total time spent, spontaneous preference at the beginning of the second session, and verbal communications. Switching off colored light turned out to be more attractive than looking at a continuous change of stimulation.

Similar phenomena have been observed and described by other authors. In a rather general manner, Bühler (1919) labeled the underlying tendency as "function pleasure", and White (1959) as "effectance motivation" (i.e., to deal effectively with the environment). To define White's concept more precisely Harter (1978) proposed and measured four "motivational domains": (1) response variation; (2) curiosity for novel stimulation; (3) mastery for the sake of competence; and (4) preference for challenging tasks. Obviously, the last two of these domains require higher levels of cognitive development than the first two. A very early kind of event production was specified by Piaget (1936) as *secondary circular reactions.* They can be observed 4 months after birth

15

and indicate the beginnings of an intentional production of an effect. Hunt (1965) sees in them the origins of what he calls *intrinsic motivation*. As distinct from other meanings of the term "intrinsic motivation"(Heckhausen, 1980, Chap. 12), Hunt stresses the self-procured gratification derived from information processing, from the activity itself rather than from its intended outcome, let alone from external reinforcement.

Nuttin (1973) puts his observations with 5-year-old subjects into a general explanatory framework. He states:

> The fact that *producing* stimulation is preferred to stimulation as such points to the basic behavioral tendency to *produce* events, or to *do* something in the sense of changing something or *making something happen*. This is what could be called *causality pleasure* ... Generally one of the main sources of pleasure in man is *to do things*. Progressively, he will try to produce them according to his plans and projects. It is in this context that the ego-involved pleasure in the successful outcome of an act is to be situated; succeeding in doing, achieving or producing something (*ego pleasure*) [p. 251–252].

As with White's effectance motivation and its elaboration by Harter, Nuttin's linkage of causality pleasure with an "ego-involved pleasure in the successful outcome of an act" is a bold shortcut, developmentally speaking. It raises several questions like the following: What are the cognitive prerequisites for the experience of a successful outcome of an act? Is causality pleasure a necessary and sufficient condition for experiencing success? What are the earliest indications of causality pleasure? Are there, besides causality pleasure, any other precursors or prerequisites for a fully developed experience of success and failure? I take up these questions in turn.

Cognitive Prerequisites for Experiencing an Action Outcome as Success or Failure

It appears to be safe to say that more than half of all experiments conducted in psychology have attempted, in some way or other, to induce success or failure experiences in their subjects. Therefore, it is striking that the cognitive requirements for such an experience have not been made explicit till now— even in achievement-motivation research. Instead, the terms *success* and *failure* are used more or less intuitively in experimental manipulation. Sometimes the induction techniques have rather questionable results (e.g., when false reference norms are used) (Heckhausen, 1980).

Without going into details (Heckhausen, 1974a), a set of five requirements appears to be necessary for a full experience of success and failure. First, the activity is intended to result in an objectifiable outcome. Second, the action outcome can be evaluated according to some standard of excellence (e.g., some degree of quality or quantity). Third, the actor is not totally sure whether he or she will encounter a successful or an unsuccessful outcome (i.e., the necessary, outcome-producing activity is neither too difficult nor too easy for him or her). Fourth, the actor wants to achieve an action outcome that reaches or surpasses a certain level of excellence. Fifth, the contingency between action and outcome is seen by the actor as, at least to a substantial amount, caused by his or her own ability and effort. If these five requirements are met, an action outcome will, by necessity, be followed by a self-evaluative consequence in the form of an affectively toned experience of success or failure. Such a self-evaluative consequence is a safe sign that the behavior that led to it has been achievement-motivated.

It goes without saying that at least some of the five requirements are not present at birth but need some development and time for their first appearance. In short, and most important, the child must be able to center his awareness not solely on the action–outcome contingency or the ongoing activity itself but also on the outcome as a distinct end term of an action, to evaluate the action outcome according to some standard, however simple, and to attribute the action outcome to the self and, particularly, to some attributes of a personal competence. If we keep in mind these three main requirements for the experience of success and failure, Nuttin's observations of causality pleasure presumably contained a centering on action–outcome contingency of the outcome per se. It is, moreover, questionable that a standard for evaluating the outcome—besides pure contingency between action and outcome—was involved. Finally it is questionable whether Nuttin's subjects attributed the effective handling of automat B to their own personal competence (although children of that age, as will be demonstrated, are able to do so).

Developmental Change as a Guideline for Functional Analysis

In order to unravel the web of complex phenomena that success and failure experiences are, one may make use of developmental change as a guideline for functional analysis. In the following discussion I try to adhere to such a guideline, looking first for behavioral signs of some of the stated prerequisites. However, a word of caution is in order. Searching for "first appearance" of a theoretically circumscribed accomplishment resembles, in a way, the never-ending search of paleontologists for the "missing link." That is to say, in order to make a certain accomplishment observable, one has to construct situations or tasks to which the child can respond. Tasks, however, invariably require in their context other accomplishments beside the accomplishment whose first appearance is looked for. Because the context accomplishments might be more demanding than the one accomplishment looked for, one is never quite sure whether the "first" appearance might not occur even earlier if the requirements of the context accomplishments could be further diminished (i.e., if the researcher discovers and utilizes facilitating conditions).

Meanwhile we know a lot of developmental accomplishments whose well-established first appearances had to be corrected and predated after researchers succeeded in diminishing the task requirements of the context accomplishments, on the one hand by simplifying the cognitive requirements for processing and storage of information and, on the other, by allowing for nonverbal responses. For instance, dramatic shifts of first appearance are obtained when, instead of responding verbally, young children may communicate by way of motoric or expressive equivalences to what they have to "say." A case in point is nonverbal assessment of Piagetian concepts (Miller, 1976). Preschoolers in the preoperational stage, according to Piaget's *méthode clinique,* give evidence of operational thought and nonegocentric behavior (Borke, 1978; Urberg & Docherty, 1976). As shown presently, with respect to causality pleasure, the first appearance of an accomplishment can be blocked even by a development-bound period of "natural deprivation" (Watson, 1966).

The Earliest Signs of Causality Pleasure: Striving for Contingency Awareness

Secondary circular reactions, the third stage of Piaget's (1936) theory of sensory–motor intelligence, already bear all signs of a causality pleasure. The infant repeatedly reacts to a given situation in such a way that the same (or similar) effect is produced in the external environment. There can be no doubt that the infant is aware of a contingency between his or her own reaction and its outcome in the external environment. Moreover, the infant's sustained concentration, his or her centering on the outcome produced, and his or her positive emotional expression leave no doubt that he or she strives for and takes pleasure in contingency awareness.

Whereas secondary circular reactions are the first evidence of learning of reaction–outcome contingencies (operant learning) they do not seem to appear before the fourth month of life. According to Piaget's (1936) stage theory, it takes 3 postnatal months of maturation to become capable of operant learning or, for that matter, of causality pleasure. So many years after Piaget's original observations there should be little doubt that secondary circular reactions do not emerge before the fourth month under natural conditions of physical events. Notwithstanding, attempts have been made to demonstrate operant learning within the first three months of life, but for a long time these attempts have been unsuccessful (Lipsitt, 1963; Rendle-Short, 1961; Wickens & Wickens, 1940). Meanwhile, however, researchers have succeeded even here in finding facilitating conditions of diminished and artificial task requirements under which infants younger than 4 months of life—and even neonates—already demonstrate the capacity for operant learning, for a contingency-aware causality pleasure. The facilitating conditions consisted of a head-turning response after an auditory signal using nutritive sucking (Papoušek, 1961, 1967; Siqueland & Lipsitt, 1966) or colored flashlights (Papoušek & Bernstein, 1969) as reward. Watson (1966) was able to condition the eye movement of a 2-month-old infant. On visual fixation of one of the experimenter's fists, the predetermined hand would open and close.

Under all these conditions there was clear evidence of operant learning, with increasing transfer of learning when the rewarded side was reversed. The infants gained in ability to learn contingencies within a few days or weeks. What is more, in our context, it was not mere learning for obtaining a need-reducing reward. Neither an opening fist nor flashing lights are reinforcements in the sense that they can reduce primary needs. They are reaction-contingent outcomes and not rewarding consequences of reaction outcomes. Even when the outcome consisted of the offering of a small portion of milk, it was not the nutritive reward value per se that kept the infants responding. After maximal satiation (i.e. when the reception of any further milk was refused), the infants still responded to all following signals with rapid and intensive head movements to the correct side and accompanied these reactions with smiling and joyful vocalizations (Papoušek, 1967).

Often the outcome events evoked facial and vocalizing expressions of delight and pleasure. After a certain number of trials these expressions no longer followed but anteceded the occurrence of the outcome. Contingency awareness resulted in a gratifying anticipation of a reaction outcome. This went together with a heightened arousal and a directed attention. At the beginning of a new session, even after an interval of several days, the infant immediately changed into a prepared and responsive subject. One cannot avoid assuming a motivational factor, a striving for contingency awareness. Observing a 2-month-old infant, Watson (1966) states:

> In the initial sessions, my observations provided little evidence that the visual stimulus of hand opening possessed reward or arousal value. In the later sessions, sheer excitement seemed to be obvious, particularly just prior to the start of the game. As the situation was being set up, the infant's arm and leg movement usually increased, his eyes generally widened, and he would begin fixating one then the other of the observer's two fists. The infant's overall visage was one of "positive anticipation". Once the game began, arm and leg movement usualy decreased, and the infant appeared highly focused on "mastering" the contingency available [p. 132].

Observing the newborn's interaction not with the physical, but with the social environment, there can be no doubt of the newborn's capacity for operant learning immediately after birth. The newborn rapidly learns natural contingencies between eye contact with the caretaker and the caretaker's (unconditioned) facial or vocal responses (Papoušek & Papoušek, 1980).

In conclusion, infants within the first 3 months of life—and even neonates—are already capable of operant learning or, in Piagetian terms, of secondary circular reactions. They can be aware of contingencies and show concomitant indications of causality pleasure. One therefore may claim that striving for contingency awareness (reaction–outcome contingencies) is a congenital and pervasive motivation. Within the first 3 months of life, however, contingency awareness (or causality pleasure) occurs only under facilitating conditions (i.e., either in naturally occurring social interaction or when the outcome is artificially mediated by an adult who provides, immediately after the infant's designated reaction, a perceptible and salient outcome in the infant's external environment).

The question that arises is why, under conditions of natural contingencies with physical events, contingency awareness and causality pleasure do not emerge until the fourth month of life, the age at which developmental psychologists observe the first secondary circular reactions. Watson (1966) has proposed an answer to this question. The infant's memory time span has to be sufficiently long for him or her to become aware of a contingency within the temporal limits in which the specified reaction can be reexecuted (i.e., within its recovery speed). Watson assumes that: "during approximately the first three months of life the human infant possesses few, if any, responses which both elicit rewarding stimulation directly from the physical environment and at the same time possess recovery speeds sufficient for the infant's initial level of contingency awareness [p. 127]." On one hand, the young infant may have reactions in his or her repertoire that do elicit interesting outcomes in the external environment but possess too long recovery periods given the temporal limits of contingency awareness. On the other hand, the young infant already may dispose of reactions that have sufficient recovery speed—as is the case with head or eye movement—but such reactions do not directly (i.e., as a natural contingency) elicit outcomes from the physical environment.

The initial retardation of contingency awareness and causality pleasure is caused by a "natural deprivation." The overcoming of such a natural deprivation by the facilitating conditions of an artificial social intervention obviously accelerates the development of increasing temporal limits in the infant's contingency awareness. For Watson reports evidence of an advanced appearance of secondary circular reactions in his 2-month-old infant under natural contingency conditions.

CENTERING ON THE ACTION OUTCOME: PLEASURE IN THE OUTCOME

The first of the three main requirements for experiencing success or failure was stated previously as follows: The child must be able to center his or her awareness not solely on the action–outcome contingency or the ongoing activity itself, but also on the outcome as a distinct end term of an action. To be sure, contingency awareness with the accompanying causality pleasure does not yet fulfill this requirement although it is, obviously, its precursor. In this stage the child still centers on the reaction–outcome contingency and is delighted by its regular reoccurrence. Two things still appear to be lacking. First, the infant's activity still consists of one specific reaction, elicited by a certain stimulus. An action, instead, may be defined as, at least, presupposing the availability of two or more responses by means of which the same outcome can be brought about and the choice of one of the available responses or the modification of an available response in order to alter the outcome. Such a minimal requirement for an action appears to correspond to what Piaget (1936) has observed between 11 and 18 months and described as tertiary circular reactions. Second, the infant still centers on reaction–outcome contingencies and not on the outcome per se. A centering on the outcome implies that the activity is being perceived as leading to a distinct and salient end term, to an outcome that is valued for its own sake and, once established, sought to be maintained for a while, stopping the activity that had led to it. Perhaps the term *outcome* is used appropriately only when the child is able to center on the effect of his or her activity.

In her studies on the child's use of objects, Hetzer (1931) observed children between 1 to 6 years of age who, when building with blocks, stopped and regarded ("respected") their creations. Such an extended attention to the outcome of one's actions first appeared among 1½-year-olds. By the age of 2 all children did this. These first signs of centering on the action outcome fulfill our first requirement for experiencing success or failure, an accomplishment that is necessary but by no means sufficient. Centering on the outcome distinguishes creating a work from pure play; in play, the activity seems to take place for its own sake, and not for an outcome.

Centering on the outcome gives rise, at first, merely to taking note that an intended outcome occurred or failed to occur. In studies of our own, most of the 2- to 3½-year olds simply noted the outcome. Others already showed affective reactions while regarding the established outcome. For example, in a task-choice study (Heckhausen & Wagner, 1965) presenting five levels of difficulty, all of the children recognized the differing degrees of difficulty and occupied themselves happily with each task, moving up and down the various steps of difficulty. No matter how difficult the task was, they registered a positive or negative outcome with or without an affective reaction, but in such a way that their expressive behavior was related to the outcome of their activity and not to perceived personal attributes.

It is important to note that the affective reactions are at first still completely focused on the outcome and related neither to the self of the actor nor to his or her implied competence. If at all, the child at this stage draws the attention of a bystander or observer to the created "work" and not to its producer. It appears to be a later development that the affective reaction involves an attribution of the established action outcome to the self as the originator (self-produced outcome) or to a competence attribute of the actor as a cause. Although systematic observations are incomplete, we found in our studies that 2-year-olds are still fully absorbed by the established outcome.

The crucial point is whether the child's affective responses already contain some indications of self-reference. After a child, for instance, had completed a tower with all available blocks (Heckhausen & Roelofsen, 1962), or lifted a weight on a pulley to a height where it was held in place by a latch (Heckhausen & Wagner, 1965), the child regarded the established outcome with joyful amazement, pleasure, or delight, or the nonestablished outcome—a tower toppled down, a weight not staying up—with surprise, regret, anger, or even rage, although the latter response did not lastingly affect his or her mood. It appeared as if the negative outcome were attributed to the noncomplying task materials. In this age group, the first indication of self-referenced affects appeared only after a positive outcome. Where it did occur, the child no longer simply demonstrated pleasure in the outcome, he or she rejoiced in his or her own power. Interestingly enough, however, these feelings immediately lost their relation to the accomplished outcome.

Although these affective reactions of 2-year-old children generally do not yet represent proper feelings of success and failure, they seem to be precursors of such feelings. What is still lacking are signs in the affectivity involving the self as an agent and—presumably more important—the attribution of the outcome to a personal attribute of competence (third requirement). However, the affective reactions during this stage do meet the first requirement of an outcome-focused awareness. As to the second requirement, evaluation of the outcome according to some standard, there can be no doubt that it is also being met, although in a still rather simple form. The standard is task-inherent and therefore quite obvious: The intended outcome does occur or fails to occur. The child knows what the only desirable effect can be—a nontoppling tower or a weight staying up—and evaluates the outcome accordingly. Of course, such a knowledge has its own cognitive prerequisites.

Attribution to the Self: Pleasure and Pride in a Self-produced Outcome

One may assume an unfolding logic in the progressive relocation of the centering in the child's awareness: from action–outcome contingency to outcome and from outcome to the self and its attributes as a causal agency of the outcome. First signs of referring the outcome to the self mark the origin of the child's ability for making internal attributions. It is persuasive to assume, as already mentioned, a two-step progression of self-reference. The initial step might consist of attributing the outcome entirely to oneself as the actor; in being pleased with, or proud of, the self-produced outcome. The second step then, would be an elaboration of the self-referenced attribution into personal attributes of competence as internal causes of the outcome. However, the assumption of such a distinction and progression is highly tentative. Empirical support would necessitate a close analysis of videotaped reactions to the outcome. But it is not altogether clear how, within the transitional stage, nonverbal reactions can be distinguished as to be indicative either of pure self-reference or of a self-evaluative reference to personal attributes.

A clear indication of a pure self-reference is "wanting to do it oneself" (Fales, cited in Lewin, Dembo, Festinger, & Sears, 1944; Klamma, 1957; Müller, 1958). It is a pervasive phenomenon that arises at the age of 2 and strains the patience of many a mother. The child insists on doing such things himself or herself that have become manageable for him or her. If difficulties arise, however, a child younger than four will accept help. To be sure, "wanting to do it oneself" refers to the activity as such and provides, therefore, only indirect evidence for a centering on a self-produced outcome. But a close correspondence between self-reference in the activity and in the outcome is probable and appears to be captured by White's (1959) "feeling of efficacy."

Attribution of an Action Outcome to One's Own Competence

In any event, an unmistakable criterion for the experience of success and failure seems to be a self-evaluative reaction to the established outcome, as can be observed from expressive behavior. Several of our studies, all cross-sectional and with various age groups, have been designed to tap the earliest signs of self-evaluation. In a first study (Heckhausen & Roelofsen, 1962), the child competed with an adult in placing 12 rings on a rack as quickly as possible. The adult confederate controlled his speed so that the child won half of the time. Before each trial, the confederate asked the child who had finished the previous trial first and, after each trial, who would probably win the next. The dyadic structure of the competition made it particularly important to observe, after task outcome, whether the child's expressive behavior was centered on his or her tower or on the competitor and his tower. Such centerings indicate a narrowed-down or a widened "psychological field," respectively, the importance of which Kurt Lewin (1927) has already pointed out long ago. Besides indices of competitive behavior during tower building (Halisch & Heckhausen, 1977), the following reactions to the task outcome were mainly registered: gazing behavior (e.g., contacting the competitor or turned down), smiling (open or embarrassed), and body posture (stretched or collapsed, relaxed or tight).

Most children of the youngest age group, between 2½ and 3½ years, did not yet compete. They did not understand what it meant to "finish first". When they had finished their towers they raised their hands in an admiring gesture and looked joyously at the completed outcome. As already pointed out, they took pleasure in the outcome. In contrast, as we discuss later, some of the yet noncompeting children also reacted in a self-centered or self-evaluative way. They detached themselves immediately from their work and looked around in an applause-seeking manner at the confederate. Several of the children within this age group who were cognizant of who had finished first looked at the competitor after winning without an observable change in expression. When they had lost, however, they did not remove their eyes from their own tower, which they continued to handle with some embarrassment. After two or three failures, their mood changed, and they stopped the game. These are apparently the earliest signs of a self-evaluative experience of an action outcome, emerging earlier in the case of failure than of success.

By the age of 3½, affective reactions to winning and losing resulting from self-evaluation could be observed in all children. Expressive behavior was remarkably different after success than after failure. It could be elicited reliably and was highly consistent across a series of further studies (Eckhardt, 1968; Halisch, 1979; Heckhausen & Wasna, 1965; Wasna, 1970). The expressive behavior patterns have been documented by pictures (Heckhausen & Roelofsen, 1962) and by a film (Heckhausen, Ertel, & Kiekheben-Roelofsen, 1965). The following quotation from Heckhausen (1973) may serve as a short description:

> If the child has won, he raises his eyes from his own work and looks triumphantly at the loser. His body stretches, the hands are thrown high... His ego is being made larger through his sense of pride and becomes the central point of his experience. If the child, however, has lost, his eyes and hands do not stray from his own work: His psychological field narrows. Facial expression is worth noting. The child tries to cover up his mood with an embarrassed smile of failure. The worst expression of failure is the desire "to disappear from the face of the earth," here to hide from the winner behind the table...
>
> From 4½ on, the expression after either success or failure is much more controlled. If the child has lost, he is often even capable of looking at the winner

with small signs of embarrassment as a slight twitching of the mouth, a quick pulling-in of the lower lip, a sigh, the tone of the voice, all of which show the effect of losing [p. 99; author's translation].

The association of winning or losing with feelings of personal worth became exceptionally clear when the confederate asked "Who finished first?" Almost none of the children younger than four and a half could admit their failure. They remained sullenly silent or simply lied, saying "I was," in a toneless voice and with all the signs of a bad conscience. There was also other evidence of not wanting to admit failure, such as covering up, making excuses, playing down, adverting, and consoling by remembering earlier victories. Other ways of coping with failure outcomes included avoidance (taking a break or stopping), cheating (e.g., impeding the competitor or starting ahead of time), or compensating actions (e.g., "winning" suddenly when removing the rings from the rack).

Because children in our studies showed reactions of self-evaluation by age three, we may conclude that these young children have developed at least a rudimentary concept of their own competence. A direct proof of this claim, however, is methodologically difficult. A possible procedure consists of having children attribute success and failure outcomes to causes. However, task-related requirements in the understanding of concepts and in skill of information integration may set up developmental thresholds below which the accomplishment sought for cannot be uncovered. This appears to be the obvious reason why Ruble, Parsons, and Ross (1976), for instance, did not find any covariation between performance outcome and its attribution to ability and effort in 4- and 5-year-olds, even with the help of a scale in visualized form. Indeed, Ruble et al. (1976) did not find covariation with ability attribution in groups of children younger than 7 to 9 years!

Some of our studies at Bochum have been better adapted to the young child's level of cognitive development. With younger children, it was possible to demonstrate the use of a competence concept by testing their ability to follow the causal schema of simple covariation of cause and effect with picture cards, such as episodes of rope pulling, tower building, carrying a suitcase, etc. The children were told to associate various action outcomes with various actors (children). The pictures showed actors with physical traits either directly suitable for a certain task (e.g., skinny enough to slip through a hole in a wall) or indirectly indicative of attributes pertinent to a specific task (physical stature as an indication of strength or height as an indication of age difference). Gurack (1978; Krug, Gurack & Krüger, in press), using this technique, found a full covariation between a visualized direct index of competence and action outcome in 3½-year olds; at the age of 4, she found similar covariation for indirectly indexed task-relevant attributes. Kuhl (1975) has reported similar results.

To be sure, the initial concept of competence undergoes a long course of development until "ability" can be reliably distinguished from "effort," and conceived of as an individually constant and interpersonally variable construct. I have reviewed this development in detail elsewhere (Heckhausen, in press). Unlike ability, however, varying degrees of effort expenditure can be perceived directly, both in oneself and in others. The covarying degrees of effort in effort-dependent outcome, therefore, might be observed rather early. Krüger (1978; Krug et al., in press) has tested, with picture stories, the matching of effort-related cause and effect. Only 25% of the 3-year-olds produced a full covariation between three degrees of pictorially represented effort (puffed-up cheeks) and their corresponding effects (blown-off seeds of a flower). When the same children blew a cotton ball into a miniature house (with open walls) from three different distances, 64% accurately gauged the amount of effort required; they could not, however, report this in advance as intended effort. When the 3-year-olds were asked to explain what had happened, 60% could not give a cause, or thought the cotton ball had a life of its own (e.g., "It wanted to get into the house"). The others attributed the result to their own competence (e.g., "I'm good at blowing").

Another case in point is choice between tasks of graded difficulty such as pulling weights, building towers, broad jump, or high jump (Heckhausen & Wagner, 1965; Wagner, 1969; Wasna, 1970). The levels of difficulty were obvious; for example, five weights were placed next to each other according to heaviness (increasing size). Because task difficulty and competence are two sides of the same coin, it is interesting to note at what age children attribute action outcome no longer solely to task difficulty (which younger children appear invariably to do) but also to one's own competence. Except for the two youngest children in the Heckhausen and Wagner study (2½ and 2¾), all the children (2 years, 11 months and up) recognized differences in difficulty, as was evidenced by hesitation, long and careful looking, and remarks such as "that won't work." However, none of the children up to the age of three and a half showed a clear self-evaluative reaction to the outcome (e.g., the weight stays up), indicating an attribution to competence. Instead, they simply reacted with joy or, in the case of failure, with surprise, regret, or anger. They performed the tasks following rigidly the order in which the tasks were laid out, from easiest to most difficult and back again. In contrast, the older children revealed behavioral indices of an attribution to competence. They displayed deviations in the order of task choice indicative of self-evaluation, such as jumping to a much heavier weight after success with a light one, or jumping back to a lighter weight after failure with a heavier one.

All of these data from explicit attribution studies and from task-choice studies suggest that 3-year-olds possess rudimentary concepts of competence by the time self-evaluative reactions occur. The most direct evidence consists in the covariation of perceived "ability" and "effort" with action outcomes.

Information-processing Requirements for
Perceiving Standards of Excellence

So far we have clarified, as to their developmental precursors, two of the three prerequisites for self-evaluative consequences upon an action outcome. First, by the age of 1½, children are able to single out an outcome from their transactions as a salient end term and to pay prolonged attention to it. Second, by the age of 3½, children are able to attribute the causes of an action outcome to themselves as actors and to their personal attributes. However, in order to attribute an outcome to causes one has to know how the outcome is to be evaluated, whether it has been achieved, or has fallen short of some given standard of excellence. I have mentioned in passing this last requirement, evaluation according to some standard of excellence, while discussing the pleasure in the outcome when a rather simple form of standard may be entailed (i.e., when an intended task-inherent effect does occur or fails to occur). Inasmuch as, in determining the first appearance of self-evaluative reactions, we have relied on a cognitively more demanding standard of excellence, we should be prepared to observe self-evaluative reactions—and therewith the origin of achievement-motivated behavior—even earlier than by the age of three and a half. We turn now to the issue of whether the cognitive requirements for perceiving a standard of excellence, implied by the experimental task might have set up a developmental threshold for the first appearance of self-evaluative reactions.

Such a developmental threshold obscuring the first appearance of self-evaluative success and failure reaction obviously has been created in a study by Müller (1958). She defined success as the capacity to sort a number of figures within a given amount of time. With such a standard of excellence she did not find self-evaluative reactions before the age of five! In our competition studies the child had to be able to make a simpler judgment about the temporal order of two events (i.e., whether one's own tower, or that of the competitor, had been finished first). Such a comparative temporal judgment is a cognitive accomplishment associated with the mental age of about 3½ (i.e., when all children in our tower-building studies competed and showed self-evaluative reactions). The determination by mental age was confirmed by the administration of the same method with feebleminded (imbecile) children between the ages of 6½ and 14½ whose mental ages lay between 3 and 6 (Heckhausen & Wasna, 1965). Regardless of chronological age, competition and self-evaluative reactions could be observed in those retarded children whose mental ages were 3½ or more.

The findings give rise to the suspicion that self-evaluative reactions might show up still earlier if the cognitive requirements of the standard that determines a successful outcome can be reduced even further. In the initial competition study, all children who competed and reacted in a self-evaluative manner were clearly able to ascertain who, during building, was ahead and who had finished first. There was only one girl, 2 years and 3 months of age, who was capable of time comparison and competed, but gave no evidence of self-evaluation (Heckhausen & Roelofsen, 1962). Instead, she was as happy about the successes of the competitor as about her own. When she did succeed, her expressive behavior was centered joyfully on her own tower; pleasure was found in the outcome, but it was not attributed to her own competence.

To clarify the prerequisite role of the ability to make comparative time judgments ("earlier versus later"), Halisch (1979) has tested in advance this ability in children of the critical transitional period between 2½ and 3½ years of age. According to Piaget (1969), children between 5 and 7 years of age begin to give correct verbal statement as to whether two dolls walking along a track have started at the same time, have arrived at the end point at the same time, or what has been the order in time. In order to answer such questions correctly, the child has to coordinate spatial distance and time, two physical concepts that are connected by the concept of velocity. Longobardi & Wolff (1973) have used a method similar to that of Piaget. Two toy cars had to be rolled on parallel tracks of different length. Even second-grade children were not able to give adequate answers as to how the two cars happened to arrive at the same time (different velocities) or at different times (same velocity). However, and in contrast to nursery children, second graders were able to imitate correctly each of both velocity–time relationships.

Compared to the more complex accomplishment of coordinating spatial distance and time, given same or different moving rates of objects, the requirements of the competition task seem to be easier. The child has only to ascertain the temporal order of two events (i.e., which of the two towers had been finished earlier). Furthermore, a verbal explanation did not need to be given. Halisch (1979) took pains to construct the cognitive test as similar as possible to the competition task, but the construction of an adequate test proved to be much more difficult than expected. In a first attempt, an apparatus was constructed out of which two towers jerkingly grew upward. Only one child of an age group of 2½ to 3¾ years was able to answer correctly across ten trials which tower had attained its full height first. Most of the children became anxious in front of the apparatus, even after some familiarization and some modification of the apparatus with toy symbols. Children who competed and were able to recognize correctly who had finished first in the subsequent tower-building task had, however, not been able to give correct answers in the tower-growing pretest.

Finally, another technique proved to be adequate. Two toy cars (pickups) on parallel tracks of equal length could be moved by preprogrammed electrical devices with different starting times and different velocities. There were three movement patterns which varied in difficulty. One of the two cars was always more rapid than the other one. It started: (1) ahead of the slower car; or (2) at the same time; or (3) after the slower car but took over after a while. In order to elicit nonverbal responses, instead of verbal ones, we loaded the two toy cars with popcorn before the start, and the child was instructed to take the popcorn (and eat it) from the car that had arrived first. In a sample of 62 children between the ages of 2 years, 4 months and 3 years, 8 months, correct solutions of nearly all trials at each difficulty level were observed at age 2 years, 11 months at the earliest and at age 3 years, 7 months at the latest. All children capable of a comparative temporal judgment also competed in the subsequent tower-building task; children not yet capable of the time comparison did not compete, with some correlated gradation of both variables between. In short, the ability to make a comparative temporal judgment was, under the conditions of our competition game, the necessary and sufficient prerequisite for competing and for showing self-evaluative success and failure reactions.

In addition, Halisch (1979) discovered a few children between the ages of 2 years, 8 months and 3 years, 2 months who were not capable of a time comparison and did not compete, but who did show a full-blown self-evaluative success response each time they had completed their tower, regardless of whether they had finished ahead of the competitor or not. Obviously, these children were able to construe another and more simple standard of excellence for themselves: the completion of their own tower. Their affective reactions upon completion of their tower differed clearly from mere pleasure in the outcome. As mentioned earlier, they detached themselves immediately from their work, looked and smiled openly at the competitor, and threw their arms up. In answer to the question of who was first, they invariably declared themselves to be "the first one."

Children at such a developmental level cannot be made to fail in a competition game. In order to elicit corresponding self-evaluative failure reactions in a younger age group also, we presently plan a procedure that allows for perceiving success and failure by means of a rather simple standard of excellence. By using a certain device, the stacking up of the rings can either be completed (success) or becomes impossible because the rings stacked up drop suddenly into a bottom box; perhaps in this way we might succeed in uncovering a still earlier first appearance of contrasting expressions of success and failure experience, and possibly touch upon the first emergence of a causal attribution of an action to oneself as the actor, and to one's personal attributes.

SUMMARY

There are quite a few precursors in the course of development until young children become able to experience success and failure for the first time. Several authors have observed and described early phenomena that appear to be closely related to, if not direct indices of, success feelings or achievement-motivated behavior. Among these phenomena we have discussed Nuttin's causality pleasure, Watson's contingency awareness, Piaget's secondary circular reactions, Bühler's function pleasure, White's effectance motivation and Hunt's intrinsic motivation. However, all these phenomena do not yet reflect achievement-motivated behavior and its affective consequences.

We have defined three cognitive prerequisites for experiencing an action otucome as success or failure: first, ability to focus on an outcome as the end term of one's own action; second, ability to construe some standard according to which an action outcome is evaluated; third, ability to refer an achieved action outcome to one's attributes of competence as causes. The first and the third prerequisite can be ordered into the same line of development. Our review yielded evidence of a developmental progression in the relocation of the child's centering on subparts of the action sequence. The earliest centering of the infant is on the contingency between reaction and outcome (Watson's contingency awareness, Nuttin's causality pleasure, Piaget's secondary circular reactions). Contingency awareness and its affective concomitant of causality pleasure appear to be a congenital endowment of the neonate. The centering on the reaction–outcome contingency progresses to a centering on the action outcome (pleasure in the outcome) and from the action outcome to a centering on the self and its competence attributes as causes of the outcome (origin of internal causal attribution). Self-evaluative reactions of success and failure can be observed in the expressive behavior of all children by the age of 3½. The progressive relocation of the child's centerings looks like an unfolding logic. However, it is not yet clear whether, in self-centering, a general attribution to the self precedes a more specific attribution to competence attributes of the self.

As to the second prerequisite, standards of excellence may entail developmental thresholds obscuring self-evaluative reactions, if the implied standard for success versus failure overcharges the attained developmental level of information processing. It is probable that the emergence of self-evaluative reactions has to be predated below the age of 3½ if the task contains a cognitively less demanding standard than does a comparative temporal judgment (finishing a task ahead of a competitor).

We have pursued the developmental change as a guideline for a functional analysis of the accomplishment in question (i.e., success and failure experience). The results of this pursuit may contribute to a better understanding of what achievement-motivated behavior and its self-evaluative consequences are like. Because of the dearth of longitudinal observations within the first years of life, we had to rely on cross-sectional studies. The contended precursors, and their developmental progression, now suggest longitudinal studies that can provide a detailed picture of intraindividual change from one precursor to the next and, ultimately, will yield a more thorough proof of our functional analysis.

REFERENCES

Borke, H. Piaget's view of social interaction and the theoretical construct of empathy. In L. S. Siegel & C. J. Brainerd (Eds.), *Alternatives to Piaget*. New York: Academic Press, 1978.

Bühler, K. *Abriss der geistigen Entwicklung des Kindes*. Leipzig: Quelle & Meyer, 1919.

Eckhardt, D. *Die entwicklungspsychologische Abhängigheit der Konfliktreaktion vom Grad der Misserfolgswahrscheinlichkeit*. Unpublished Vordiplomarbeit. Psychologisches Institut der Universität Münster, 1968.

Gurack, E. *Die Entwicklung des Fähigkeitskonzepts im Vorschulalter*. Unpublished Diplomarbeit. Psychologisches Institut der Ruhr-Universität Bochum, 1978.

Halisch, C. *Zur kognitiven Grundlage des frühen Wetteiferverhaltens*. Unpublished Diplomarbeit. Psychologisches Institut der Ruhr-Universität Bochum, 1979.

Halisch, C., & Halisch, F. Kognitive Voraussetzungen frühkindlicher Selbstbewertungsreaktionen nach Erfolg und Misserfolg. *Zeitschrift für Entwicklungspsychologie und Pädagogische Psychologie*, in press.

Halisch, F., & Heckhausen, H. Search for feedback information and effort regulation during task performance. *Journal of Personality and Social Psychology*, 1977, *35*, 724-733.

Harter, S. Effectance motivation reconsidered. *Human Development*, 1978, *21*, 34-64.

Heckhausen, H. Die Entwicklung des Erlebens von Erfolg und Misserfolg. In C. F. Graumann & H. Heckhausen (Eds.), *Pädagogische Psychologie* (Vol. 1). *Entwicklung und Sozialisation*. Frankfurt: Fischer-Taschenbuch, 1973.

Heckhausen, H. *Leistung und Chancengleichheit*. Göttingen: Hogrefe, 1974.(a)

Heckhausen, H. *Motivationsanalysen*. Berlin: Springer, 1974.(b)

Heckhausen, H. *Motivation und Handeln*. Berlin: Springer, 1980.

Heckhausen, H. The development of achievement motivation. In W. W. Hartup (Ed.), *Review of Child Development Research*, (Vol. 6). Chicago: University of Chicago Press, in press.

Heckhausen, H., Ertel, S., & Kiekheben-Roelofsen, I. *Die Anfänge der Leistungsmotivation im Wetteifer des Kleinkindes*. Sound Film. Göttingen: Institut für den Wissenschaftlichen Film, 1966.

Heckhausen, H., & Roelofsen, I. Anfänge und Entwicklung der Leistungsmotivation: I. im Wetteifer des Kleinkindes. *Psychologische Forschung*, 1962, *26*, 313-397.

Heckhausen, H., & Wagner, I. Anfänge und Entwicklung der Leistungsmotivation: II. in der Zielsetzung des Kleinkindes. *Psychologische Forschung*, 1965, *28*, 179-245.

Heckhausen, H., & Wasna, M. Erfolg und Misserfolg im Leistungswetteifer des imbezillen Kindes. *Psychologische Forschung*, 1965, *28*, 391-421.

Hetzer, H. *Kind und Schaffen*. Jena: Gustav Fischer, 1931.

Hunt, J. McV. Intrinsic motivation and its role in psychological development. In D. Levine (Ed.), *Nebraska Symposium on Motivation*, 1965. Lincoln: University of Nebraska Press, 1965.

Klamma, M. *Über das Selbermachenwollen und Ablehnen von Hilfen bei Kleinkindern*. Unpublished Vordiplomarbeit. Psychologisches Institut der Universität Münster, 1957.

Krug, S., Gurack. E., & Krüger, H. Die Entwicklung von Anstrengungs- und Fähigkeitskonzepten im Vorschulalter. *Zeitschrift für Entwicklungspsychologie und Pädagogische Psychologie*, in press.

Krüger, H. *Anfänge der Entwicklung des Anstrengungskonzepts im Kindergartenalter*. Unpublished Diplomarbeit. Psychologisches Institut der Ruhr-Universität Bochum, 1978.

Kuhl, U. *Entwicklung der Ursachenerklärung von gelungenen und misslungenen Handlungsergebnissen im Vorschulalter*. Unpublished Diplomarbeit. Psychologisches Institut der Ruhr-Universität Bochum, 1975.

Lewin, K. Kindlicher Ausdruck. *Zeitschrift für Pädagogische Psychologie*, 1927, *28*, 510-526.

Lewin, K., Dembo, T., Festinger, L., & Sears, P. S. Level of aspiration. In J. Mc V. Hunt (Ed.), *Personality and behavior disorders* (Vol. 1). New York: Ronald Press, 1944.

Lipsitt, L. P. Learning in the first year of life. In L. P. Lipsitt & C. C. Spiker (Eds.), *Advances in child development and behavior* (Vol. 1). New York: Academic Press, 1963.

Longobardi, E. T., & Wolff, P. A comparison of motoric and verbal responses on a Piagetian rate-time task. *Child Development,* 1973, *44,* 433–437.

Miller, S. A. Nonverbal assessment of Piagetian concepts. *Psychological Bulletin,* 1976, *83,* 405–430.

Müller, A. Über die Entwicklung des Leistungsanspruchsniveaus. *Zeitschrift für Psychologie,* 1958, *162,* 238–253.

Nuttin, J. Pleasure and reward in human motivation and learning. In D. C. Berlyne & K. B. Madsen (Eds.), *Pleasure, reward, preference.* New York: Academic Press, 1973.

Papoušek, H. Conditioned head rotation reflexes in infants in the first months of life. *Acta Paediatrica* (Uppsala), 1961, *50,* 565–576.

Papoušek, H. Experimental studies of appetitional behavior in human newborns and infants. In H. W. Stevenson, E. H. Hess, & H. L. Rheingold (Eds.), *Early behavior: Comparative and developmental approaches.* New York: Wiley, 1967.

Papoušek, H., & Bernstein, P. The functions of conditioning stimulation in human neonates and infants. In A. Ambrose (Ed.), *Stimulation in early infancy.* London: Academic Press, 1969.

Papoušek, H., & Papoušek, M. Early ontogeny of human social interaction: Its biological roots and social dimensions. In M. V. Cranach, K. Foppa, W. Lepenies, & D. Ploog (Eds.), *Human ethology: Claims and limits of a new discipline.* Cambridge: Cambridge University Press, 1980.

Piaget, J. *La naissance de l'intelligence chez l'enfant.* Neuchâtel: Delachaux & Niestlé, 1936.

Piaget, J. *The child's conception of time.* London: Routledge & Kegan, 1969.

Rendle-Short, J. The puff test: An attempt to assess the intelligence of young children by use of a conditioned reflex. *Archives of the Diseases in Childhood,* 1961, *36,* 50–57.

Ruble, D. N., Parsons, J. E., & Ross, J. Self-evaluative responses of children in an achievement setting. *Child Development,* 1976, *47,* 990–997.

Siqueland, E. R., & Lipsitt, L. P. Conditioned head-turning behavior in newborns. *Journal of Experimental Child Psychology,* 1966, *3,* 356–376.

Urberg, K. A., & Docherty, E. M. Development of role-taking skills in young children. *Developmental Psychology,* 1976, *12,* 198–203.

Wagner, I. *Das Zielsetzungsverhalten von vier ausgewählten Gruppen normaler Kleinkinder in Einzel- und Paarsituationen.* Unpublished Dissertation. Abteilung für Philosophie, Pädagogik, Psychologie der Ruhr-Universität Bochum, 1969.

Wasna, M. *Die Entwicklung der Leistungsmotivation.* München: Reinhardt, 1970.

Watson, J. S. The development and generalization of "contingency awareness" in early infancy: Some hypotheses. *Merrill-Palmer Quarterly,* 1966, *12,* 123–135.

White, R. W. Motivation reconsidered: The concept of competence. *Psychological Review,* 1959, *66,* 297–333.

Wickens, D. D., & Wickens, C. A study of conditioning in the neonate. *Journal of Experimental Psychology,* 1940, *26,* 94–102.

3 Objective and Subjective Rules for Delay of Gratification

Walter Mischel
Stanford University

Given the crucial theoretical role of the concept of reinforcement in psychology, it is surprising how little has been learned until recently about how the mental representation of rewards and outcomes affects the individual's pursuit of them. I have been interested in the problem of reward representation especially when people are attempting to delay immediate smaller gratification for the sake of more desirable but deferred goals. The research I report here focuses on the studies my associates and I have been conducting to understand more deeply how the mental representation of the relevant rewards in a contingency might influence voluntary delay for those outcomes.

INTRODUCTION

Freud's (1911) analysis of the transition from primary to secondary process provides one of the few theoretical discussions of how delay of gratification may be bridged. The psychoanalytic formation suggests that ideation arises intially when there is a block or delay in the process of direct gratification discharge (Rapaport, 1967). During such externally imposed delay, Freud suggested, the child constructs a "hallucinatory wish-fulfilling image" of the need-satisfying object. As a result of frequent association of tension reduction with goal objects, and the development of greater ego organization, the imposed delay of satisfying objects gradually results in the substitution of hallucinatory satisfactions and other thought processes that convert "free cathexes" into "bound cathexes" (Freud, 1911; Singer, 1955). Unfortunately, however, the exact process remains unclear, although there has been much psychoanalytic theorizing about the function of the mental representation of blocked gratifications in the development of delaying capacity.

From a very different theoretical direction it also seemed plausible that "time binding" (the capacity to bridge delay of gratification) might depend on self-instructional processes through which the individual increases the salience of the delayed consequences of his or her behavior. From that viewpoint, any factors (situational or within the individual) that make delayed consequences more vivid should facilitate impulse control. Such a view, while focusing on the self-instructional components of attention to delayed outcomes, also implies covert self-reinforcement processes through which the individual may reinforce his or her own delay behavior by vividly anticipating some of the rewarding consequences that the waiting will produce. Finally, one also could expect that young children would forget easily the deferred outcomes for which they are waiting, and therefore stop waiting unless they are reminded of the relevant contingencies and rewards during the delay period.

In light of these arguments, conditions that help individuals to attend mentally to the delayed reward for which they are waiting should help them to continue to delay. Thus any cues that make the delayed gratification more salient, vivid, or immediate (for example, by letting the children look at them, by picturing them in imagination, or by thinking of the object for which they are waiting) should enhance waiting behavior. These anticipations also seem consistent with findings from previous research on choice of immediate smaller versus delayed but larger rewards (Mahrer, 1956; Mischel, 1966; Mischel & Metzner, 1962; Mischel & Staub, 1965). These earlier investigations indicated that an important determinant of choice preference for delayed rewards is the person's expectation ("trust") that he really will get the delayed (but more valuable) outcome. When the child always can see the relevant rewards, fewer doubts might arise about their ultimate availability than when the rewards are hidden from view. Therefore conditions in which the delayed gratification are visible may increase the individual's willingness to wait by increasing his subjective expectancy that the delayed outcome really will still be there at the conclusion of the delay time.

These considerations led us to predict initially that voluntary delay behavior would be enhanced when the individual converts the delayed object into more concrete form by making it psychologically more immediate, as by providing himself with representations or physical cues about it. To test that notion, the most direct way to increase the salience of the deferred outcomes and to focus attention on them would be to have them physically present in front of the subject so that he can attend to them vividly and easily. To explore how attention to delayed and immediate outcomes influences waiting behavior for them, we varied the availability of those outcomes for attention during the delay period.

EFFECTS OF ATTENTION TO THE REWARDS

For this purpose we needed a paradigm in which very young children would be willing to stay in an experimental room, waiting by themselves for at least a short time without becoming excessively upset (Mischel & Ebbesen, 1970). As a first step (after the usual play periods for building rapport) each child was taught a "game" in which he or she could immediately summon the experimenter by a simple signal. This procedure was practiced until the children obviously understood that they could immediately end their waiting period alone in the room by signaling for the experimenter. The latter always returned immediately from outside the door when the child signaled. The child was then introduced to the relevant contingency. Specifically, the child was shown two objects (e.g., snack-food treats) one of which was clearly preferred (as determined by pretesting), but to obtain the preferred object the child had to wait for it until the experimenter returned "by himself." However, the child was free throughout this delay period to signal anytime for the experimenter to return; if he or she signaled he could have the less preferred object at once but would forego the more desirable one later.

In order to manipulate systematically the degree to which children could attend to the rewards while they were waiting, the reward objects were available to the child's view in all combinations, creating four conditions with respect to the objects available for attention. The children in one condition waited with both the immediate (less preferred) and the delayed (more preferred) rewards facing them in the experimental room so they could attend to both outcomes. In a second group, neither reward was available for the child's attention, both rewards having been removed from sight. In the remaining two groups either the delayed reward only or the immediate reward only was left facing the child and available for attention while he or she waited. The length of time before each child voluntarily terminated the waiting period was the dependent measure.

Our initial theorizing about delay behavior led us to predict results that were the exact opposite of what we found. We had expected that attention to the delayed rewards in the choice situation while waiting would facilitate delay behavior. We found, instead, that attention to the rewards significantly and dramatically decreased delay of gratification. The children waited longest when *no* rewards faced them during the delay period; they waited significantly less long when they faced the delayed reward, or the immediate reward, or both rewards, as Fig. 3.1 indicates, with no significant differences between the reward conditions but a trend for shortest delay when facing both rewards.

To explore what caused these unexpected results, we tried to see just what the children were doing while they were waiting. Therefore we observed them closely by means of a one-way mirror throughout the delay period as they sat waiting for their preferred outcomes in what had proved to be the most difficult situation (i.e., with both the immediate and delayed outcomes facing

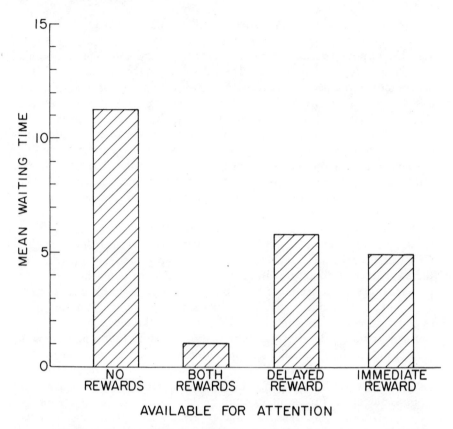

FIG. 3.1.   Mean minutes of voluntary waiting time for the delayed reward in each attention condition (from Mischel & Ebbesen, 1970).

them). These observations were helped by "Mr. Talk Box," a device that consisted of a tape recorder and a microphone that announced its name to the youngster and cheerfully said, "Hi, I have big ears and I love it when children fill them with all the things they think and feel, no matter what." Thereafter, Mr. Talk Box adopted a Rogerian nondirective attitude and acceptingly "uhemed"and "ahad" to whatever the child said to him. In fact, many children quickly seemed to treat Mr. Talk Box as an extension of their psyche and engaged in elaborate, animated discussions with themselves.

Observation of the children during the delay period itself gradually gave us some clues about the mechanisms through which they seemed to mediate and facilitate their own goal-directed waiting. The most effective delay strategies employed by some children were remarkably simple. These youngsters seemed able to wait for the preferred reward for long periods apparently by converting the aversive waiting situation into a more pleasant nonwaiting one. They seemed to manage this by elaborate self-distraction techniques through which they spent their time psychologically doing almost anything other than waiting. Instead of focusing their attention prolongedly on the rewards, they avoided them. Some of these children covered their eyes with their hands, rested their heads on their arms, and discovered other similar techniques for averting their eyes from the rewards. Many children also seemed to try to reduce the frustration of delay of reward by generating their own diversion: They talked quietly to themselves, sang ("This is such a pretty day, hurray"), created games with their hands and feet, and when all other distractions seemed exhausted even tried to go to sleep during the waiting situation—as one child successfully did, falling into a deep slumber in front of the signal bell. These tactics, of course, are familiar to anyone who has ever been trapped in a boring lecture.

Our observations of the children seem consistent with theorizing that emphasizes the aversiveness of frustration and delayed rewards. If the subject is experiencing conflict and frustration about wanting to end the delay but not wanting to lose the preferred, delayed outcome, then cues that enhance attention to the elements in the conflict (i.e., the two sets of rewards) should increase the aversiveness of waiting. More specifically, when the child attends to the immediate reward his motivation for it increases and he becomes tempted to take it but is frustrated because he knows that taking it now prevents his getting the more preferred reward later. When the subject attends to the preferred but delayed outcome he becomes increasingly frustrated because he wants it more now but cannot have it yet. When attention is focused on both objects, both of these sources of frustration occur and further delay becomes most aversive; hence the child terminates quickly (as indeed happened). This reasoning would suggest that conditions that decrease attention to the rewards in the choice contingency and that distract the person (through internal or overt activity) from the conflict and the frustrative delay would make it less aversive to continue goal-directed waiting and thus permit longer delay of gratification. That is, just as cognitive avoidance may help one to cope with anxiety so may it help to deal with such other aversive events as the frustration of waiting for a desired but delayed outcome and the continuous conflict of whether or not to terminate.

COGNITIVE DISTRACTION

The foregoing theorizing suggests that delay of gratification and frustration tolerance should be facilitated by conditions that help the individual to transform the aversive waiting period into a more pleasant nonwaiting situation. Such a transformation could be achieved by converting attention and thoughts away from the frustrative components of delay of gratification.

Thus voluntary delay of reward should be enhanced by any overt or covert activities that serve as distractors from the rewards and thus from the aversiveness of the situation. By means of such distraction the person should convert the frustrative delay-of-reward situation into a less aversive one. Activities and cognitions and fantasy that could distract the individual from the reward objects therefore should increase the length of time he or she would delay gratification for the sake of getting the preferred outcome.

But how can one influence what the child is going to think about? After many poor starts we discovered that even at age three and four our subjects could give us elaborate, dramatic examples of the many events that made them feel happy, like finding frogs, or singing, or swinging on a swing with mommy pushing. In turn, we instructed them to think about those fun things while they sat waiting alone for their preferred outcomes. In some of these studies the immediate and delayed rewards were physically not available for direct attention during the waiting period. We manipulated the children's attention to the absent rewards cognitively by different types of instructions given before the start of the delay period. The results showed that cognitions directed toward the rewards substantially reduced, rather than enhanced, the duration of time the children were able to wait. Thus attentional and cognitive mechanisms that enhanced the salience of the rewards greatly decreased the length of voluntary delay time. In contrast, overt or covert distractions from the rewards (e.g., by prior instructions to think about fun things) facilitated delay of gratification (Mischel, Ebbesen & Zeiss, 1972), as Fig. 3.2 illustrates.

The overall results undermine theories that predict mental attention to the reward objects will enhance voluntary delay by facilitating "time binding" and tension discharge (through cathexes of the image of the object). The data also undermine any "salience" theories that would suggest that making the outcomes salient by imagery, cognitions, and self-instructions about the consequences of delay behavior should increase voluntary delay. The findings unequivocally contradict theoretical expectations that images and cognitions relevant to the gratifications sustain delay behavior. Instead, either looking at the rewards or thinking about them in their absence decreases voluntary delay of gratification. Effective delay thus seems to depend on suppressive and avoidance mehanisms to reduce frustration during the delay period; it does not appear to be mediated by consummatory fantasies about the reward.

The present results suggest that the person can delay most effectively for a chosen deferred gratification if during the delay period he shifts attention from the relevant gratifications and occupies himself internally with cognitive distractions. Situational or self-induced conditions that shift attention from the reward objects appear to facilitate voluntary waiting times appreciably. In order to bridge the delay effectively, it is as if the child must make an internal notation of what he is waiting for, perhaps remind himself of it periodically, but spend the remaining time attending to other less frustrating internal and

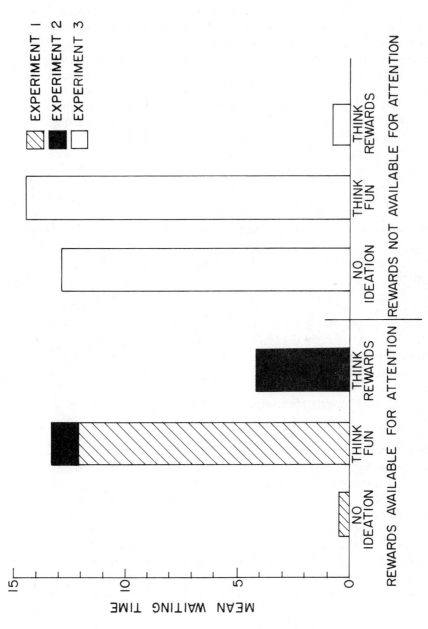

FIG. 3.2. Mean minutes of voluntary waiting time for treatment conditions in Experiments 1, 2, and 3, comparing different ideation instructions with controls (from Mischel, Ebbesen, & Zeiss, 1972).

external stimuli, thereby transforming the noxious into the easy and thus taking the thinking and the worrying out of waiting and "will power."

As early as 1890, William James noted a relationship between attention and self-control and contended that attentional processes are the crux of the self-control phenomena usually subsumed under the label "will" (or, since James' time, under the concept "ego strength"). As James (1890) put it: "Attention with effort is all that any case of volition implies. The essential achievement of will is to attend to a difficult object... [p. 549]." Starting with the work of Hartshorne and May (1928) some correlations have been obtained between indices of moral behavior and measures of attention or resistance to distraction on mental tests (Grim, Kohlberg, & White, 1968). Such correlations have led to the suggestion that a person's ability to resist temptation may be facilitated by how well he attends to a task. "Yielding to temptation"(e.g., cheating) in most experimental paradigms hinges on the subject's becoming distracted from the main task to which he is supposed to be attending. In such paradigms a subject's ability to focus attention *on* the task and to resist distraction automatically may make it easier to resist such temptations as cheating, as Grim, Kohlberg, and White (1968) have noted.

Our findings, however, reveal a quite different relation between attention and self-control: *Not* attending to the goal was what facilitated self-control most dramatically. But it should be recognized that the mental transformations and distractions that occur during delay do not erase or undo the role of the reward contingencies in the waiting situation. This was evident from data which showed that there was little persistence in "thinking fun" or playing with a toy when there was no reward contingency for waiting. The distracting activity itself, although pleasant and distracting enough to maintain the waiting for a contingent reward, did not in itself keep the children in the room for more than a minute when the contingency was removed. Additional evidence that the contingency was available mentally throughout the waiting period is that the children easily reproduced, verbally or by appropriate action, the contingencies at the end of the waiting period. Children who had been busily distracting themselves for the full 15 minutes, playing with a toy or singing songs, immediately and spontaneously ate the appropriate food reward when the experimenter returned. Obviously then, the transformation of the aversive waiting into a pleasant play period does not efface the task-oriented purpose of the behavior and presumably the two processes somehow coexist. Subjects were guided by their goals, even when seemingly absorbed in distractions designed to obscure them. Just how the contingency was operating is an interesting point for speculation. The contingency may have been available but never reproduced mentally until the end of waiting; even more likely, subjects may have reminded themselves of the contingency episodically throughout the waiting period. As mentioned previously, verbalizations of the contingency often occurred when subjects momentarily left their distracting play and seemed about to terminate the waiting period. It is as if subjects periodically remind themselves of the goal for which they are waiting, distract themselves from it to make delay less frustrative, and then repeat the process.

Although the present studies provided reliable findings based on several replications and diverse convergent data, we obviously cannot generalize from them to the role of cognition in forms of self-control other than the delay-of-gratification paradigm. Thus, for example, it might be adaptive to ideate about desired or needed but currently unavailable goal objects, but only in situations in which the subject's actions can be potentially instrumental in producing the desired outcome. When attainment of a positive outcome is contingent on the person's own problem-solving behavior, it might help the person to think about the goal object while seeking means for achieving or reaching it in reality. In the present delay-of-gratification paradigm, in contrast, attainment of the preferred goal required only passive waiting; beyond delaying there was absolutely nothing the subject could do to influence the occurrence of the desired outcome. Moreover, even his or her delay behavior (although a necessary condition for attainment of the preferred outcome) could in no way affect the time at which gratification ultimately would be forthcoming.

Thus the conclusion that aversive stimuli are avoided cognitively may be restricted to paradigms in which the person believes that thinking about the aversive stimulus cannot change the contingencies in the situation. In contrast, when the aversive stimulus (such as an electric shock) can be avoided, subjects may tend to become vigilant, correctly perceiving the stimulus more quickly than do controls (Dulany, 1957; Rosen, 1954). That is, when people potentially can control painful events perhaps they think about them more and become vigilantly alert to them. To the extent that the delay-of-gratification situation produces an aversive frustration effect, people are likely to delay better if they avoid ideating about the rewards, but perhaps only if their own behavior during delay cannot affect the time at which the frustration will be terminated. Whether people react to potentially frustrative or painful stimuli by "blunting" and trying to avoid them cognitively or by "monitoring" and becoming vigilantly alert to them thus may depend in part on what they can do to control them (Miller, 1979; in press).

In sum, the findings up to this point suggested that the capacity to sustain self-imposed delay of reinforcement depends on the degree to which individuals avoid (or transform) cues about the frustrativeness of the delay situation—such as cues that remind them of what they expect and want but are prevented (interrupted, locked, delayed) from getting. This hypothesis would apply equally to the externally imposed delays or interruptions that characterize "frustration" (Mandler, 1964) and to the self-imposed delay behavior that marks "self-control." To increase subjective frustration a person then would have to focus cognitively on the goal objects (e.g., by engaging covertly in anticipatory goal responses); to decrease frustration he would have to suppress the goal objects by avoiding them cognitively. In the delay paradigm, "frustration tolerance" would depend on the subject's ability to suppress his attention to the blocked rewards while remaining in the frustrative situation until the goal is attained. More recent studies by other investigators have confirmed repeatedly that effective self-imposed delay of gratification in preschool children hinges partly on the degree to which the individual can avoid attending to the rewards (outcomes) in the delay contingency (Miller and Karniol, 1976a, 1976b; Schack and Massari, 1973; Toner, Lewis, and Gribble, 1979; Toner and Smith, 1977). These studies consistently indicate that attention and ideation directed at the goal objects in the self-imposed delay-of-gratification paradigm make it extremely difficult for young children to sustain goal-directed waiting.

Although the present interpretation seems reasonable, close observation of the children's behavior while they engaged in voluntary delay indicates that it may be both incomplete and too simple. Sheer suppression or distraction from the frustrativeness of the situation seems to be one important determinant of frustration tolerance but it is unlikely to be the only one. Observation of the children's actions and verbalizations while waiting suggested that those who waited effectively were also engaged in complex self-instructions and internal activities (Mischel et al., 1972).

During earlier studies it was noted, for example, that while the children were waiting for the delayed outcome they often would repeat the contingency aloud (alone in the empty room): "If I wait I get . . ." (naming the more preferred objects), ". . . but if I ring the bell I get . . ." (naming the less preferred). To maintain their delay behavior effectively, it appeared as if they made an internal notation of what they were waiting for (possibly reminding themselves of it by repeating the contingency from time to time), and also reminding themselves of the alternative consequences of continuing to delay or of terminating the delay. Intermittently, when not so occupied, they would spend the time distracting themselves from the frustrativeness of the delay situation (e.g., by singing), thus transforming the noxious delay into a more pleasant activity. Often it seemed as if the subjects also supported their own delay behavior by covert self-reinforcement for waiting. Thus many children performed diverse covert self-congratulatory reactions as they continued to sustain their goal-directed waiting and created special subjective contingencies of their own. For example, "If I just wait a little more I'll get it for sure—yes, he'll come back soon now—I'm sure he will, he must."

THE ROLE OF SYMBOLICALLY
PRESENTED REWARDS

In view of the complex cognitive activity that seems to mediate delay behavior it becomes important to consider and control more precisely the covert activities in the subject during the waiting period. The most relevant condition for further study is the one in which the subject is attending cognitively to the reward objects although the rewards are physically absent. In his formulation of delay of gratification, Freud (1911) suggested that delay capacity begins when the child develops images (mental representations) of the delayed reward in the absence of the object itself. According to that view, the hungry infant may gain some satisfaction by forming a "hallucinatory" image of the mother's breast when she is physically unavailable. Although we tried to manipulate attention to the actual rewards by varying their presence or absence in the child's visual field, how could one manipulate the availability of an *image* of the relevant objects when they were absent physically? A study by Mischel and Moore (1973) tried to approximate this condition at least crudely by *symbolic* presentations of the absent objects during the delay period. For this purpose subjects were exposed to slide-presented images of the absent reward objects while waiting for them. The design compared the effect on delay behavior of exposure to such images of the "relevant" objects (i.e., the rewarding outcomes for which the subject was waiting) with exposure to images of similar objects that were irrelevant to the delay contingency.

In this study preschool children first had to choose between two rewards. They then were allowed to wait for their preferred choice or to signal at any time to obtain the less preferred outcome immediately, just as in the Mischel, Ebbesen, and Zeiss (1972) study. Two different pairs of reward choices were employed; half the subjects chose between two marshmallows and a pretzel and half between two pennies and a token. During the delay period, experimental subjects were exposed to realistic color slide-presented images on a screen that faced them. In one condition the images were slides of the rewards between which the subjects had chosen ("relevant imagery"); in another condition the slides depicted the objects that the subject had not seen before ("irrelevant imagery"). For example, if a subject had been given a choice between two marshmallows and a pretzel, each "relevant imagery" slide would depict those reward objects, whereas each "irrelevant imagery" slide would show the other objects (two pennies and a token) to which he or she had not been exposed previously (i.e., the "irrelevant" rewards with respect to the contingency). Subjects in a third condition were exposed to a blank slide (no picture but illuminated screen). A "no-slide" control group constituted the fourth condition.

In all conditions the slides with *relevant* imagery produced the longest delay times, with the contents of slide-presented images yielding a highly significant main effect ($p < .001$). Thus the effects of relevant slide-presented rewards proved to be the opposite of those found for exposure to the real rewards. Whereas attention to the real rewards makes it much harder for preschool children to delay, slide-presented symbolic presentations of those rewards, for them, were found to facilitate waiting time. Moreover, these opposite effects occurred reliably within the same basic subject population and experimental paradigm at the same preschool. Why?

In a recent experiment we (Mischel & Moore, 1980) tried to resolve this discrepancy and to illuminate why symbolic reward presentations enhance self-imposed delay whereas attention to the actual outcomes impedes it. We reasoned that the highly significant effects found for the mode of presentation of the reward stimuli (real versus slide-presented) occurred because they led children to ideate about the rewards in different ways. Extrapolating from Berlyne's (1960) and Estes' (1972) distinctions, a stimulus may have a motivational (consummatory, arousal) function and an informational (cue) function. The actual reward stimuli (i.e., the real objects) are apt to have a more powerful motivational effect than do their symbolic representations (i.e., slide images). In contrast, symbolic representations of the objects (e.g., through slide pictures) would have a more abstract cue function. Viewing the actual goal objects increases the child's motivation for them, whereas a picture of the rewards serves to remind him or her of them but with less affective arousal. The motivational arousal generated by attention to the rewards themselves is frustrative because it increases the subject's desire to make the blocked consummatory responses appropriate to the outcome (e.g., eat it, play with it). This arousal function of the real stimulus increases the frustration effect (because the children cannot let themselves make the consummatory response), thereby making delay more difficult and shorter (Mischel et al., 1972). In contrast, the cue (informative) function of the symbolic reward stimulus may guide and sustain the children's goal-directed delay behavior. It may do that by reminding the subject of the contingency in the delay situation (a reminder of what the child will get if he delays) without being so real and arousing as to be frustrative.

In sum, exposure to the real reward stimuli may lead the preschool child to become excessively aroused in the self-imposed delay-of-gratification paradigm. Such arousal is frustrative because it makes the child ready to perform the terminal response in a situation in which he or she cannot do so, and hence leads to shorter delay. But exposure to the symbolic representations of the objects in the form of pictures (as on the slides) may retain their cue function without generating excessive arousal; one cannot consume a picture.

To test our conceptualization more systematically, we (Mischel & Moore, 1979) attempted to vary the children's consummatory ideation by manipulating (through instructions) their attention to the arousing qualities of the reward objects. Simultaneously, we varied the slide-presented stimulus content facing the subject during the delay period. In this fashion it should be possible to isolate the role of consummatory ideation and of symbolic presentations of the rewards in delay of gratification.

We hypothesized that the crucial variable would be the nature of the child's ideation about the rewards and not their physical representation during the delay period. Specifically, we attempted to replicate the major Mischel and Moore (1973) finding that exposure to slides of the rewards in the delay contingency leads to significantly longer delay than does exposure to slides of comparable rewards that are irrelevant to the delay contingency. Second, we predicted that this enhancing effect of the slide-presented rewards can be completely wiped out and even reversed when subjects are instructed (before the delay period) to ideate about the consummatory qualities of the relevant rewards while waiting for them (Mischel and Moore, 1980).

In a self-imposed delay-of-gratification paradigm (Mischel et al., 1972) preschool children waited for preferred but delayed rewards (details of the design are in Mischel and Moore [1980]). We systematically varied the contents of slide-presented images of the rewards and instructions about ideation during the delay. The findings unequivocally supported the hypotheses. First, the data replicated the original finding that exposure to slides of the relevant rewards leads to significantly longer self-imposed delay than does exposure to slides of the comparable rewards that are irrelevant to the delay contingency (Mischel & Moore, 1973). But more important, the study also showed that the delay-enhancing effects of the relevant slides can be completely wiped out when subjects are instructed (before the delay interval) to ideate about the consummatory qualities of the relevant rewards (e.g., the taste and texture of food objects) while waiting for them. Presumably the delay-enhancing effects of exposure to the symbolic presentation of the rewards in the waiting contingency hinge on their helping the child to ideate about them but in a nonconsummatory fashion. In contrast, consummatory ideation about the relevant rewards, whether induced by instructions, as in this study, or by exposure to the actual rewards (Mischel & Ebbesen, 1970; Mischel et al., 1972), prevents effective delay of gratification.

Specifically, the child's consummatory ideation (induced by instructions before the delay period) about the rewards, and not the content of the slide-presented image facing him during the waiting period, was found to be the crucial determinant of voluntary delay of gratification. Instructions to focus on the consummatory qualities of the rewards in the delay contingency consistently produced the shortest delay times. When instructed to ideate about the consummatory qualities of the objects in the waiting contingency ("relevant rewards"), the children delayed gratification significantly less long than when they were given the same instructions focused on comparable rewards irrelevant to the delay contingency. Moreover, the debilitating effect of consummatory ideation regarding the rewards in the contingency occurred regardless of the physical stimulus facing the subject during the delay period (Fig. 3.3).

TRANSFORMING THE STIMULUS BY COGNITIVE OPERATIONS

The effects of attention to the rewards upon delay behavior probably depend on *how* the subject attends to them rather than simply on whether or not he or she does attend to them. In that case, if attention is focused at the nonconsummatory (more abstract, informative) cue properties of the reward stimuli, delay behavior should be facilitated. In contrast, attention to the motivational or arousing qualities of the rewards should increase the frustrativeness of delay and interfere with effective self-control. If Freud's (1911) conceptualization of the positive role of the "hallucinatory image" of the blocked gratification in the development of delay of gratification refers to the motivational properties of the image, he was probably incorrect. But if his formulation referred to the nonconsummatory, more abstract cue properties of the image it may still prove to be of value.

To test these theoretical possibilities, some of our studies have explored how the impact of attention to the rewards in the delay paradigm can be modified by the specific *cognitive transformations* that the subject performs with regard to them. In these studies, just before the start of the delay period, children are given brief instructions designed to encourage them to ideate in different ways during the actual delay time. For example, one study compared the effects of instructions to ideate the motivational (consummatory) qualities of the "relevant" rewards with comparable instructions to ideate about their nonmotivational (nonconsummatory) qualities and associations (Mischel & Baker, 1975). The same two types of instructions also were used for the "irrelevant" rewards. "Relevant" and "irrelevant" were operationalized as in the Mischel and Moore studies. All children had to wait while facing the relevant rewards in the contingency.

We found that through instructions the child can cognitively transform the reward objects that face him or her during the delay period in ways that either permit or prevent effective delay of gratification. If the child has been instructed to focus cognitively on the consummatory qualities of the relevant reward objects (such as the pretzel's crunchy, salty taste or the chewy, sweet, soft taste of the marshmallows) it becomes difficult for him to wait. Conversely, if he cognitively transforms the stimulus to focus on nonconsummatory qualities (by thinking about the pretzel sticks, for example, as long, thin brown logs or by thinking about the marshmallows as white, puffy

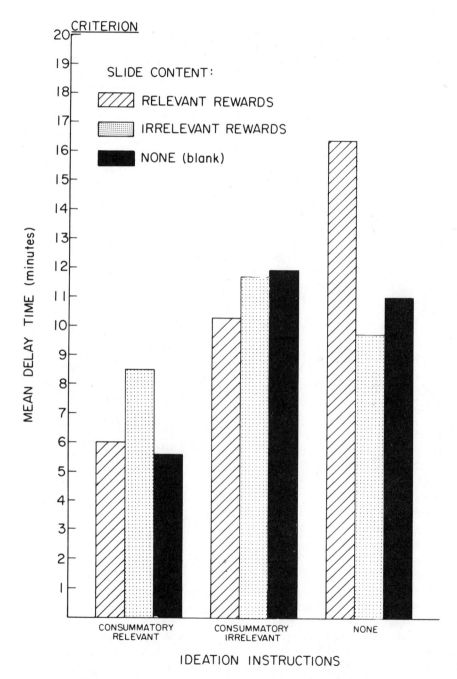

FIG. 3.3.   Effects of ideation and slide content on delay time (from Mischel &
Moore, 1980).

TABLE 3.1
Mean Delay Time in Each Ideation Instruction Condition
(from Mischel and Baker, 1975)[a]

Rewards in Ideation	Content of Ideation	
	Consummatory	Nonconsummatory
Relevant[b]	5.60	13.51
Irrelevant[b]	16.82	4.46

[a]Maximum possible delay time is 20 minutes. All subjects facing the rewards. Data are in minutes.
[b]To contingency in the waiting situation.

clouds or as round, white moons) he can wait for long time periods (Mischel & Baker, 1975). The main results are shown in Table 3.1.

Most interesting, transformations of the reward objects that focus on their nonconsummatory qualities provide more than mere cognitive distraction. The Mischel and Baker (1975) study compared, in this regard, the effects of instructions that focus on nonconsummatory qualities of the relevant reward objects (i.e., those for which the subject is actually waiting) with the same instructions for irrelevant rewards. When the children had been instructed to ideate about nonconsummatory qualities of the relevant rewards their mean delay time was more than 13 minutes (20 minutes was the maximum possible). In contrast, when subjects had been given the same instructions with regard to the irrelevant rewards (i.e., comparable but not in the delay contingency) their average delay time was less than 5 minutes. Thus attention to the non-consummatory qualities and associations of the actual reward objects in the delay contingency substantially enhances the ability to wait for them, and does so more effectively than when the same ideation instructions focus on comparable objects irrelevant to the delay contingency.

One might argue that the relatively low delay time obtained when instructions dealt with ideation for the "irrelevant" rewards reflects that young children simply have trouble thinking about reward objects that are not present. Note, however, that the longest mean delay time (almost 17 minutes) occurred when subjects were instructed to ideate about those same objects but with regard to their consummatory qualities (Table 3.1). This finding also is provocative theoretically. It suggests that whereas consummatory ideation about a potentially available object makes it difficult to delay gratification, similar consummatory ideation about an outcome that is simply unattainable in the situation (i.e., the "irrelevant" rewards), rather than being aversive, is highly pleasurable and may serve to sustain prolonged delay behavior. That is, consummatory ideation about reward objects that are not expected and not available in the delay contingency (the irrelevant rewards) may serve as an interesting effective distractor, hence facilitating waiting. In contrast, similar ideation about the relevant but blocked rewards heightens the frustration of wanting what one expects but cannot yet have and, by making the delay more aversive, reduces the length of time that one continues to wait.

Further support for the powerful role of cognitive transformations in delay behavior comes from studies showing that through instructions the children can easily transform the real objects (present in front of them) into an abstract version (a "color picture in your head"), or they can transform the picture of the objects (presented on a slide projected on a screen in front of them) into the "real" objects by pretending in imagination that they are actually there on a plate in front of them, with predictable opposite effects on their delay time. Specifically, Moore, Mischel, and Zeiss (1976) exposed preschool subjects either to a slide-presented image of the rewards or to the actual rewards. In each of these conditions half the children were instructed before the start of the delay period to imagine a "picture" of the reward objects during the delay period. For example:

> ... Close your eyes. In your head try to see the picture of the _____ (immediate and delayed rewards). Make a color picture of (them); put a frame around them. You can see the picture of them. Now open your eyes and do the same thing. (more practice)... From now on you can see a picture that shows _____ (immediate and delayed rewards) here in front of you. The _____ aren't real; they're just a picture... When I'm gone remember to see the picture in front of you.

Conversely, half the children in each of the conditions were instructed before the delay period (with similar techniques) to imagine the *real* rewards actually present in front of them while waiting. Details of the instructions were adapted to make them plausible in each condition and a maximum delay of 20 minutes was possible. The results indicated that the crucial determinant of delay behavior was the subject's cognitive representation, regardless of what was actually in front of the child. When imagining the rewards as a picture, the mean delay time was almost 18 minutes, regardless of whether the real rewards or a picture of them actually faced the child. But when representing the rewards cognitively as if they were real, subjects' delay time was significantly and very substantially lower, regardless of whether the slide or the actual set of rewards was objectively in front of them (Table 3.2).

In sum, our overall findings on cognitive stimulus transformations clearly reveal that how children represent the rewards cognitively (not what is physically in front of them) determines how long they delay gratification. Regardless of the stimulus in their visual field, if they imagine the real objects as present they cannot wait very long for them. But if they imagine pictures (abstract representations) of the objects they can wait for long time periods

TABLE 3.2
Mean Delay Time as a Function of Cognitive Transformations (from
Moore, Mischel, & Zeiss, 1976)[a]

Objectively Facing Subject	Cognitive Representation of Rewards as:	
	Pictures	Real
Picture of Rewards	17.75	5.95
Real Rewards	17.70	7.91

[a]Maximum possible delay time is 20 minutes. Data are in minutes.

(and even longer than when they are distracting themselves with abstract representations of objects that are comparable but not relevant to the rewards for which they are waiting). By means of instructions (given before the child begins to wait) about what to imagine during the delay period, it is possible to alter completely (in fact, to reverse) the effects of the physically present reward stimuli in the situation and to control delay behavior cognitively with substantial precision. Whereas arousal-generating cognitions about the real objects in the contingency significantly impede delay, cognitions about their nonconsummatory (nonmotivational) qualities or about their abstract representations enhance delay.

Thus *how* the subject ideates about the outcomes (rather than whether or not he does) appears to be crucial. In the delay paradigm, cognitive representations of the rewards (goals, outcomes) that emphasize their motivational (consummatory, arousal) qualities, we suggest, prevent effective delay by generating excessive frustration, at least in young children. The more the subject focuses on the arousing qualities of the blocked goals, the more intense and aversive the choice conflict and the delay become, and the sooner they terminate the situation. Conversely, cognitive representation of the same objects that focuses on their nonconsummatory (more abstract, less arousing) qualities appears to facilitate the maintenance of goal-directed behavior. In future research it will be important to explore the exact mechanisms that underlie this facilitation. It seems likely that abstract cognitive representations of the rewards permit the subjects to remind themselves of the contingency, and to engage in self-reinforcement for further delay, without becoming debilitatingly aroused and frustrated, but the specific processes require further study. Hopefully such work will continue to clarify not only the mechanisms in delay of gratification but also how the mental representation of goal objects ("rewards") motivates and guides complex waiting and working. The present studies have demonstrated that the specific ways in which rewards are represented cognitively, rather than their physical presence or absence, determine the impact of those rewards on the subject's ability to control his or her behavior in pursuit of them. Future efforts hopefully will provide an increasingly comprehensive analysis of the cognitive mechanisms that permit human beings to achieve such self-control.

THE CHILD'S KNOWLEDGE OF THE DELAY RULES

The results summarized in earlier sections provided evidence about conditions that may facilitate waiting for deferred outcomes. But remarkably little is known about the subject's own understanding and strategies for coping with various types of delay. For example, does the preschool child know that consummatory ideation about the rewards will make self-imposed delay more difficult? Thus, we now know a considerable amount about delay-enhancing stimulus conditions but almost nothing about children's awareness of effective attentional strategies during delay of gratification. To begin to fill this gap, in one recent set of studies we began to explore young children's verbal preferences and actual use of different attentional strategies for sustaining delay of gratification (Mischel, Mischel, & Hood, 1978; Mischel, Mischel, & Hood, 1978; Mischel & Mischel, 1979; Yates & Mischel, 1979). Our results ultimately should help clarify the degree to which young children know and utilize delay-facilitating attentional strategies when faced with situations requiring them to wait for deferred outcomes and should illuminate the development and implications of such strategies.

To begin to investigate children's preferred attentional strategies for delaying gratification, we (Yates & Mischel, 1979) modified the delay paradigm developed by Mischel et al. (1972). Instead of placing fixed stimuli in front of the child for the entire delay, we designed equipment that allowed the subject to self-regulate the presentation of stimuli throughout the delay period. Each child had available for self-presentation one of the two types of stimuli that facilitate self-imposed delay (SID)[1] and one of the two types of stimuli that hinder it. Different groups of children had available for viewing one of the four possible pairings of the two SID-facilitating and two SID-hindering stimuli. We recorded the amount of time that the children actually

---

[1] In an important series of related subsequent studies, Miller and Karniol (1976a, 1976b, 1979), have distinguished between self-imposed delay (SID), of the sort studied in the paradigm of Mischel and his associates, and externally-imposed delay (EID), in which the subject cannot voluntarily terminate the delay in favor of an alternative immediate but less preferred reward. Miller and Karniol believe that the findings of Mischel and associates apply to SID but not to EID. They argue that when individuals have no choice but to endure the delay it is adaptive to focus on the rewards and they have provided some empirical support for their view. Miller and Karniol's conclusions should still be seen as tentative, but their work does underline the need to distinguish between the two types of delay and therefore we have been examining both the SID and EID paradigms separately to determine whether different rules apply.

viewed the different types of stimuli during either a self-imposed delay of gratification (SID) or during an externally imposed delay (EID) of equal duration and also assessed their preferences verbally after completion of the delay.

Taken as a whole, the results of our series of four experiments lead to several conclusions concerning the nature and consequences of young children's preferred attentional strategies during delay of gratification. To summarize briefly, Experiment 1 showed that during both self-imposed delay (SID) and externally imposed delay (EID), preschool children prefer to view real stimuli rather than symbolic (pictorial) representations of them, regardless of their relevance to the rewards in the delay contingency. No differences in preference patterns were found in SID versus EID. The same pattern of preferences was replicated in Experiment 2, which also found no significant effects of age within the three age categories sampled (ages 3 to 4.3 years, 4.6 to 5.9 years, and 6 to 7 years).

Experiment 3 allowed us to distinguish clearly between children's attentional preferences during delay when they are oriented to attend to the stimuli that they want to view (wish strategy) as opposed to those stimuli that they believe would help them wait most (efficacy strategy). The results revealed that when following a wish strategy children attended significantly more to the real rewards rather than to their more abstract (pictorial) representations, further replicating the finding of Experiments 1 and 2. But when following an efficacy strategy the children did not show any systematic preference for viewing relevant real as opposed to relevant symbolic stimuli: Presumably they simply did not know which of these two types of stimuli would help more and chose quite randomly.

The data from the older children (grades 1, 2, 3) obtained in Experiment 4 were dramatically different and suggest a change in delay strategies in the course of development, beginning around age seven. Specifically, when waiting for food, these older children systematically preferred viewing reward irrelevant stimuli and were aware that this strategy would help them delay gratification best. This was true in externally imposed as well as in self imposed delay situations. The fact that the older children preferred to view the irrelevant stimuli during externally imposed food delay as well as during self-imposed delay raises serious questions about whether the attentional strategies that facilitate EID as opposed to SID are really different and suggest that Miller and Karniol's (1976) conclusions about the facilitating effects of attention to the rewards during EID (but not SID) may be premature. Given the potential theoretical importance of the EID–SID distinction, further work to assess closely its empirical status seems crucial.

The Yates and Mischel (1979) finding that the younger children spontaneously prefer to view the real stimuli during delay of gratification seems to be congruent with Freud's (1911) classical theory of wish-fulfilling ideation during delay: When the desired object is blocked, the frustrated child tries to self-present it, to "have it." But our previous research suggests that in so doing, young children are making self-imposed delay not less but more difficult for themselves! That happens because reward-relevant ideation increases their desire and hence enhances the frustrativeness of the delay (Mischel, 1974)—especially if this ideation is consummatory rather than more abstract (Mischel & Baker, 1975; Moore, Mischel, & Zeiss, 1976). The youngsters are then trapped in a delay-defeating cycle, attending to the consummatory qualities of what they really want and becoming increasingly frustratively aroused, thereby making it even harder to wait successfully. Thus young children's preference for attending to the real rewards rather than to more symbolic representations of them helps to explain why it is so difficult for them to tolerate voluntary delay of gratification. By attending to the real rewards young children may make such delay especially frustrative and arousing, thereby defeating their own ability to wait for what they want. These interpretations are supported by the fact that it has been demonstrated repeatedly that attention to the real stimuli increases the frustrativeness of self-imposed delay and reduces the length of voluntary waiting (Mischel, 1974; Schack & Massari, 1973; Toner & Smith, 1977).

The young children's preferences for real stimuli over abstract or symbolic ones in the delay situation and their inability to discriminate effective and ineffective delay strategies probably reflect their cognitive developmental immaturity. With greater cognitive development, the child comes to recognize and prefer attentional strategies (e.g., focusing on irrelevant rather than relevant rewards) that avoid frustrative arousal (Experiment 4). As children increase their ability to deal with stimuli more abstractly, they also can transform them in delay-facilitating ways (Mischel, 1974; Moore et al., 1976). Specifically, we suggest that the older child can focus more on the abstract rather than consummatory qualities of incentives, thereby avoiding excessive frustration while remaining oriented to and guided by preferred but delayed goals. Support for that hypothesis, however, still requires empirical work.

Although Yates and Mischel (1979) found that their younger subjects did not systematically prefer effective delay strategies, it would be premature to conclude that such young children are totally unaware of the conditions that facilitate delay. Yates and Mischel confined their investigation to preferences that would require a fairly complex level of knowledge about delay. For example, one group of children was asked to choose between viewing the real object for which they were waiting and a picture of this reward and another group to choose between a picture of the reward for which they were waiting and a picture of another (irrelevant) object. Although young children do not correctly select the best delay strategies from such complex choices, they might be aware of more basic rules for successful delay. Indeed, as Gelman (1978) noted perceptively, the traditional account of the younger child has been couched in terms of the capacities he or she *lacked*; we share, instead, Gelman's focus on exploring what the young child *can* do and are impressed by how much at least some preschool children seem to know about effective ways to delay gratification as revealed in our preliminary work. It will be a challenge to assess whether different measurement conditions might reveal systematic knowledge of effective delay at earlier ages, and studies exploring such early knowledge are now in progress.

To illustrate, in one study (Mischel, Mischel, & Hood, 1978), in a delay-of-gratification paradigm, children of different ages (preschool and grades 3 and 6) were asked whether it would help them to wait if the delayed rewards were exposed or covered during the delay period. They were then instructed to suppose that the rewards would be exposed and were asked what they could *think* about to help them to wait. After the children's spontaneous ideas were elicited, pairs of alternative ways of ideating about the rewards were presented with the instruction to choose the one from each pair that would most help the child to wait for the rewards (Table 3.3). One choice was between the consummatory ("hot") properties of the delayed rewards and their abstract, nonconsummatory ("cool") properties. A second choice was between hot ideation about the rewards and task-contingency ideation. The sequence in which the choice pairs, and the items in each pair, were presented was randomized. Following each choice the child was asked the reason for choosing as he or she had. To test for possible preferences for hot or cool ideation apart from the delay-of-gratification context, one-half of the subjects in each group served as their own controls, first making the choice between hot and cool ideation about the reward objects in a nondelay situation and later choosing in the delay context. This control allowed us to assess whether any age-related changes in hot–cool ideation preferences reflected the child's changing knowledge of delay rules or merely developmental changes in preferences for hot–cool ideation regardless of its value for effective delay.

TABLE 3.3
Ideation Alternatives[a] (from W. Mischel, H. N. Mischel, &
S. Q. Hood, 1978

Hot:	"The marshmallows taste yummy and chewy."
Cool:	"The marshmallows are puffy like clouds."
Task-Contingency:	"I am waiting for the two marshmallows."

[a]Subjects chose between hot versus cool and hot versus task-oriented ideation. (The table shows the alternative when the delayed rewards were two marshallows.)

THE DEVELOPMENT OF SELF-CONTROL
COMPETENCIES

We (Mischel & Mischel, 1979) have been finding that children's spontaneous delay strategies show a clear developmental progression in knowledge of effective delay rules. A few preschoolers suggest a self-distraction strategy or even rehearsal of the task-contingency. Most children below the age of 5 years however, do not seem to generate clear or viable strategies for effective delay; instead they tend to make waiting more difficult for themselves by focusing on what they want but cannot have. By the age of 6 years they know that covering the rewards will help them wait for them while looking at them or thinking about them will make it difficult. By third grade, children spontaneously generate and reasonably justify a number of potentially viable strategies and unequivocally understand the basic principles of resistance to temptation. For example, they avoid looking at the rewards because: "If I'm looking at them all the time, it will make me hungry... and I'd want to ring the bell." Often they focus on the task and contingency, reminding themselves of the task requirement and outcomes associated with each choice ("If you wait, you get _____; if you don't, you only get_____"). They also often indicate the value of distraction from the rewards or of negative ideation designed to make them less tempting ("Think about gum stuck all over them"). A small minority still suggest that positive ideation about the rewards ("The marshmallow looks good and fluffy") will help, and one wonders if these are the very youngsters for whom delay is likely to be most difficult. Most third graders clearly know that task-contingency ideation helps delay more than hot reward ideation but they still do not know that cool reward ideation is better than hot reward ideation. By the time they reach sixth grade, the children's spontaneous strategies (just like their formal preferences), show considerable sophistication. Now most of these youngsters seem to recognize clearly the advantage for delay of cool rather than hot ideation about the rewards. The basic delay rules have been firmly mastered.

Perhaps, most important, we are finding the same meaningful developmental sequence in children's growing knowledge of effective self-control rules when we explore the everyday self-control situations they deal with in their lives (waiting for birthdays, cookies, Christmas, the family ski trip) as we find when we examine their delay knowledge in our experimental situations.

In sum, a comprehensive, coherent account of the genesis of knowledge about delay of gratification seems to be emerging. In the course of development children show increasing awareness of effective delay rules and come to generate the strategies necessary for effectively reducing frustration and temptation. They progress from a systematic preference for seeing and thinking about the real blocked rewards and hence the worst delay strategy (Yates & Mischel, 1979) to randomness, to a clear avoidance of attention to the rewards and particularly of consummatory hot reward ideation. Systematically they come to prefer distraction from the temptation, self-instructions about the task-contingency, and cool ideation about the rewards themselves. These developmental shifts seem to reflect a growing recognition by the child of the principle that the more cognitively available and "hot" a temptation the more one will want it and the more difficult it will be to resist. Armed with this insight the child can generate a diverse array of strategies for effectively managing otherwise formidable tasks, and for overcoming "stimulus control" with self-control. It will be important to trace further not only the development of this cognitive application to relevant self-control tasks as well as the conditions that might impede or enhance the developmental progression. Whereas knowledge of self-control rules is only one component of the growth of effective self-control, it appears to follow a predictable developmental sequence of potential theoretical and practical importance. We will want to know not only when do children know what rules but also what determines the cognitive availability, the accessibility of those rules when they are needed, and their activation to guide behavior, so that we can understand more fully the links between cognitive competence and self-regulatory behavior.

ACKNOWLEDGMENTS

Preparation of this chapter and the research by the author was supported in part by Research Grant MH-6830 from the National Institute of Mental Health and by Grant HD MH 09814 from the National Institute of Child Health and Human Development.

REFERENCES

Berlyne, D. E. *Conflict, arousal, and curiosity.* New York: McGraw-Hill, 1960.
Dulany, D. E., Jr. Avoidance learning of perceptual defense and vigilance. *Journal of Abnormal and Social Psychology,* 1957, *55,* 333–338.
Estes, W. K. Reinforcement in human behavior. *American Scientist,* 1972, *60,* 723–729.
Freud, S. Formulations regarding the two principles in mental functioning. In *Collected papers* (Vol. 4). New York: Basic Books, 1959. (Originally published in 1911.)
Gelman, R. Cognitive development. In M. R. Rosenzweig & L. R. Porter (Eds.), *Annual review of psychology* (Vol. 29). Palo Alto, Calif.: Annual Reviews, 1978.
Grim, P. F., Kohlberg, L., & White, S. H. Some relationships between conscience and attentional processes. *Journal of Personality and Social Psychology,* 1968, *8,* 239–252.
Hartshorne, H., & May, M. A. *Studies in deceit.* New York: MacMillan, 1928.
James, W. *The principles of psychology* (Vol. 1). New York: Holt, 1890.
Mahrer, A. R. The role of expectancy in delayed reinforcement. *Journal of Experimental Psychology,* 1956, *52,* 101–105.
Mandler, G. The interruption of behavior. In D. Levine (Ed.), *Nebraska symposium on motivation.* Lincoln: University of Nebraska Press, 1964.

Miller, D. T., & Karniol, R. Coping strategies and attentional mechanisms in self-imposed and externally imposed delay situations. *Journal of Personality and Social Psychology, 1976,34,* 310–316.(a)
Miller, D. T., & Karniol, R. The role of rewards in externally and self-imposed delay of gratification. *Journal of Personality and Social Psychology, 1976, 33,* 594–600.(b)
Miller, D. T., & Karniol, R. *The process of reward re-evaluation in delay of gratification situations.* Paper presented at the meeting of the Society for Research in Child Development. San Francisco, March 18, 1979.
Miller, S. M. Controllability and human stress: Method, evidence and theory. *Behaviour Research and Therapy, 1979, 17,* 287–304.
Miller, S. M. When is a little information a dangerous thing? Coping with stressful events by monitoring versus blunting. In S. Levine & H. Ursin (Eds.), *Coping and health: Proceedings of a NATO conference.* New York: Plenum Press, in press.
Mischel, H. N., Mischel, W., & Hood, S. Q. *The development of knowledge about self-control.* Unpublished manuscript, Stanford University, 1978.
Mischel, W. Theory and research on the antecedents of self-imposed delay of reward. In B. A. Maher (Ed.), *Progress in experimental personality research* (Vol. 3). New York: Academic Press, 1966.
Mischel, W. Processes in delay of gratification. In L. Berkowitz (Ed.), *Advances in experimental social psychology* (Vol. 7). New York: Academic Press, 1974.
Mischel, W., & Baker, N. Cognitive appraisals and transformations in delay behavior. *Journal of Personality and Social Psychology, 1975, 31,* 254–261.
Mischel, W., & Ebbesen, E. B. Attention in delay of gratification. *Journal of Personality and Social Psychology, 1970, 16,* 329–337.
Mischel, W., Ebbesen, E. B., & Zeiss, A. R. Cognitive and attentional mechanisms in delay of gratification. *Journal of Personality and Social Psychology, 1972, 21,* 204–218.
Mischel, W., Ebbesen, E. B., & Zeiss, A. Determinants of selective memory about the self. *Journal of Consulting and Clinical Psychology, 1976, 44,* 92–103.
Mischel, W., & Metzner, R. Preference for delayed reward as a function of age, intelligence, and length of delay interval. *Journal of Abnormal and Social Psychology, 1962, 64,* 425–431.
Mischel, W., & Mischel, H. N. *The development of children's knowledge of self-control.* Paper presented at the meeting of the Society for Research in Child Development. San Francisco, March 18, 1979.
Mischel, W., Mischel, H. N., & Hood, S. Q. *The development of knowledge of effective ideation to delay gratification.* Unpublished manuscript, Stanford University, 1978.
Mischel, W., & Moore, B. Effects of attention of symbolically-presented rewards on self-control. *Journal of Personality and Social Psychology, 1973, 28,* 172–179.
Mischel, W., & Moore, B. The role of ideation in voluntary delay for symbolically presented rewards. *Cognitive Therapy and Research, 1980, 4,* 211–221.
Mischel, W., & Staub, E. Effects of expectancy on working and waiting for larger rewards. *Journal of Personality and Social Psychology, 1965, 2,* 625–633.
Moore, B., Mischel, W., & Zeiss, A. R. Comparative effects of the reward stimulus and its cognitive representation in voluntary delay. *Journal of Personality and Social Psychology, 1976, 34,* 419–424.
Rapaport, D. On the psychoanalytic theory of thinking. In M. M. Gill (Ed.), *The collected papers of David Rapaport.* New York: Basic Books, 1967.
Rosen, A. C. Change in perceptual threshold as a protective function of the organism. *Journal of Personality, 1954, 23,* 182–195.
Schack, M. L., & Massari, D. J. Effects of temporal aids on delay of gratification. *Developmental Psychology, 1973, 8,* 168–171.
Singer, J. L. Delayed gratification and ego development. Implications for clinical and experimental research. *Journal of Consulting Psychology, 1955, 23,* 428–431.

Toner, I. J., Lewis, B. C., & Gribble, C. M. Evaluative verbalization and delay maintenance behavior in children. *Journal of Experimental Child Psychology,* 1979, *28,* 205–210.

Toner, I. J., & Smith, R. A. Age and overt verbalization in delay-maintenance behavior in children. *Journal of Experimental Child Psychology,* 1977, *24,* 123–128.

Yates, B. T., & Mischel, W. Young children's preferred attentional strategies for delaying gratification. *Journal of Personality and Social Psychology,* 1979, *37,* 286–300.

4
Intention and Kinds of Learning

T. A. Ryan
Cornell University

Other contributors to this volume undoubtedly are inspired by Nuttin's recent works in the field of motivation. Important as these works are, however, I wish to refer back to earlier work, *Tâche, Réussite, et Échec* (1953), a book whose importance has not been adequately appreciated in the United States and which is highly relevant to the theme of the volume. The failure of many American specialists in learning to take account of the book was partly due to their general tendency to overlook contributions from abroad, but it was also due to its being ahead of its time. It emphasized the role of cognitive factors in reinforcement before cognitive psychology had come into fashion. Even today, the kind of cognitive psychology that is prevalent in the United States, particularly in the field of learning and memory, is still basically behavioristic in its underlying assumptions. Greenwald's translation of parts of the book (Nuttin & Greenwald, 1968) helped to bring the work to the attention of American psychologists, but its implications often met resistance rather than understanding. A major theme of *Tâche, Réussite, et Échec* was of course the important, indeed essential, role of the "open task" (*tâche ouverte*) in learning based on reward and punishment or reinforcement. The purpose of this chapter is to explore further implications of the role of tasks in learning, particularly the open task to learn a given set of materials, information, or responses.

My principal thesis is that a more complete understanding of the role of the task or intention to learn depends on the recognition that there are several distinct kinds of learning and memory and that the role of intention is likely to be quite different in these different processes. Most discussions of the problem have assumed explicitly or implicitly that there is a single set of principles governing all kinds of learning and memory. Thus it is assumed that results found in experiments using the free-recall technique can be used to explain what happens in serial memorization or recognition. Yet the evidence to support the assumption of a single set of principles for all learning is scanty or nonexistent. The assumption seems to be based upon habits of thought carrying over from the early days of associationism or from those of reinforcement theory—habits of thought that have received little critical examination.

I propose further that an adequate classification of types of memory needs to be based on phenomenal experience as well as on response criteria. Even recent theories of memory that are called *cognitive* have been reluctant to deal with experience and are apparently under the inhibitions generated by years of dominance of behavioristic theories. Now is the time for cognitive theory to become truly cognitive—to become a psychology of what we know and experience as well as of what we do. Certainly a book in honor of Nuttin is a most appropriate place to support a move in this direction.

THEORETICAL IMPLICATIONS OF THE INTENTION TO LEARN

Before dealing with the problem of types of learning, it is helpful to consider the implications of experiments on intention to learn for various theories of learning. The initial impetus for studying the role of intention in learning arose from association theory. The theoretical importance of the task to learn can be best seen in Lewin's thesis on the Ach problem (Lewin, 1921–1922; Ryan, 1970). In essence, Lewin concluded that the "associative tendency" postulated by Ach and taken for granted by most psychologists of the time did not exist; that is, contiguity alone was not responsible for learning—it was effective only in conjunction with a task to learn or some other relevant task.

Although the importance of contiguity theory waned over the succeeding years, there were, and still are, some theories in which contiguity plays an important role. Theories of this kind find the phenomena of intentional learning an embarrassment, and their exponents must try to explain away the effects—they must show that the effect of intention is somehow to increase the number of repetitions. Rehearsal theories are the simplest proposals of this kind. The explanation is inadequate because the rehearsals themselves are intentional. Unintentional rehearsal (i.e., rehearsal without the intent to learn) is known to produce little or no learning, at least in rote memorizing, the method used in the early experiments on intention to learn.

Contiguity theory, like almost all learning theories down to the present, was a monolithic theory in that contiguity was considered an essential principle of *all* learning. The possibility that some kinds of learning would be dependent on contiguity whereas other kinds of learning would not depend on contiguity simply was not considered. As a result of this assumption, intentional learning experiments became *crucial* experiments; that is, unless intentional learning could be accounted for in terms of contiguity, the principle would fail. The possibility that memorizing lists would require intention to learn, whereas recollection of personal history could depend on contiguity alone, simply was not considered.

In the era of the dominance of Thorndike and Hull, contiguity theory was replaced by reinforcement theory. Although reinforcement has a number of definitions and therefore is involved in a number of distinct theories, they all share one important characteristic. Reinforcement, however defined, has an automatic effect that does not depend on the subject's intentions nor even on his being aware of the relation of the reinforcer to the response. *Tâche, Réussite, et Échec* gives a detailed analysis of this feature of Thorndike's theory, and a similar analysis could be made of Hull and his successors. Hull himself emphasizes this point in *Principles of Behavior* (1943).

The series of cleverly designed experiments on open and closed tasks developed by Nuttin added a mass of evidence to the earlier studies of Wallach and Henle (1941, 1942), giving strong support to the conclusion that reinforcement does not act automatically but depends on the task of the subject. Although the results involved only certain forms of human learning, they were closely similar to kinds of learning that had been interpreted by Thorndike and others as illustrations of the "blind" operation of the law of effect.

In spite of this strong evidence, reinforcement theory remained quite influential in American psychology for a number of years longer and is still supported in some quarters. The justification seems to be: (1) that reinforcement theory is eventually able to explain the effects of intention in terms of reinforcement theory itself (although no strongly convincing theory has yet been offered); and (2) that experiments on "learning without awareness" supposedly show cases in which learning occurs without any intention or even any awareness of what is being learned. The work on learning without awareness generated a considerable body of work but the results were highly controversial. I summarized the results earlier and the results are not any more definite now than they were at that time. My abbreviated conclusion at the time was (Ryan, 1970): ". . . reinforcement normally operates by giving the individual information about what he is expected to do in the situation, information which he uses intentionally to behave in accordance with the perceived demands of the situation. If he is somehow prevented from perceiving this information, perhaps the law of effect or other mechanical principles may take over. Evidence for this latter possibility is, however, still extremely shaky [p. 231]." Such a conclusion is, of course, unacceptable to the confirmed reinforcement theorist because he assumes that *all* learning is based on the principle. Opponents of reinforcement theory may also find the conclusion unacceptable, because they often seem to be supporting the position that reinforcement *never* operates.

Coming down to the past 5 to 10 years, there has been a gradual shift of point of view resulting from the influence of cognitive theory and concepts of information processing. Current theories are still in a process of flux and are harder to pin down on specific issues. The writers seem more cautious about making broad assumptions and profess to be aiming only at minitheories of specific phenomena. Implicitly, however, there still seems to be an assumption that all learning and memory can be accounted for on the basis of a few basic principles, and that they all involve essentially the same component processes. Sometimes there are proposals for dual mechanisms, for example, distinct processes for recognition and for recall, or two kinds of memory, one for verbal material and one for perceptual patterns. Such proposals are considered radical, however, and there is a tendency to resist such subdivisions. Rarely is there a consideration of multiple processes. Tolman's (1949) proposal of six kinds of learning would still be considered very reckless.

The fashionable language has changed in current theories and there has been some change of emphasis as a result. What used to be called learning is now more likely to be called "encoding." This change has also been coupled with an emphasis on what used to be called "single-trial learning" or memory for a single event. In terms of experimental procedures the single presentation of material followed by "free recall" tests is more widely used than Ebbinghaus' memorizing of serial lists. Theoretically, encoding implies that something is done to the material received—it is worked on or changed in some way and not just received. The use of the term *memory* for the topic, and the use of the term *retrieval* instead of retention or recall also involves some shift of emphasis. The theories are about the retrieval or recall of information about past events. Little attention is paid to the learning of motor patterns or habits and their retention. In spite of these changes in emphasis, however, many of the theories retain a familiar associationistic flavor. As Wickelgren (1979) has put it:

> With a time period of development spanning over two thousand years of human history, the doctrine of the association of ideas is to this day the dominant theory of the mind. I imagine there were always protesters who claimed that the mind was too complex to be encompassed by such associationism. However, until recently, there was no comparably elegant and general alternative theory. Now there is such a theory, though as is so often the case, the new theory is more of an extension than a repudiation of classical associationism [p. 44]

At present we pass over the specific nature of this "elegant" alternative theory, because we are concerned now with overall impressions of the current state of affairs in theories of learning and memory. I note only in passing that Wickelgren also has a twofold separation of kinds of learning, apparently intended to apply to all learning and memory.

Although it is risky to generalize about current theories, there does seem to be considerable uniformity in the treatment of intentional learning. Postman (1964) is still cited as evidence that differences between intentional and incidental learning can be eliminated by controlling the "processing strategies" of the subject and that there is no essential difference between intentional and incidental learning. It should be noted that the conclusion is stated in general terms—for all learning, not just for one particular kind.

It is true that Montague (1972) has asserted that the newer view of learning is radically different from that of behaviorism. He says: "Gradually, it has become apparent that the learner controls much, and in some cases all of what he learns in experiments relatively independently of the *E*. What has happened is that the *S*, with his mind and knowledge, his imagination and his reminiscences, has crept back into the research spotlight from which he was banished by the behaviorists [p. 225]." I fear, however, that Montague's assessment is overly optimistic. There is still a strong tendency to avoid dealing with the problem of intentional learning as an integral part of a learning theory. Instead the tendency is to deal with it as a side issue and to assume that it has a simple solution. Before the cognitive revolution, we were offered solutions in terms of "representational responses" or "differential responses." Now, the approach is to substitute the language of information processing for the behavioristic language but still to think in terms of a single simple solution to the problem applicable to all learning. For example, Hyde and Jenkins (1973) interpret their experiments as showing that "semantic processing" of words automatically leads to retention so that the effect of intention can be "explained" by the kind of processing that it produces. The fact that we do not know any more about the nature of semantic processing than we did about differential responses and that neither can be given any independent definitions or indicators does not seem to bother those who favor this approach. A similar view is expressed by Craik and Lockhart (1972), who suggest that there are "levels of processing" and that the degree of retention is greater the "deeper" the processing. Presumably, semantic processing is deeper than processing for visual pattern alone, so a task that requires understanding of the words *automatically* leads to retention.

Such "explanations" of the role of intention in memory are almost completely circular. The experimenters find that a task that requires understanding of the words leads to greater recall in the special tasks used in these experiments. This result is explained by the principle that understanding the words leads to recall. At best this is an empirical generalization from the facts of the experiment. It could become a low-level explanatory principle if it were validated on a number of other experimental methods and situations. Certainly nothing is added to the explanation by renaming understanding of the words as semantic processing (see Nelson, Walling, & McEvoy (1979) for a further analysis of this problem).

If it can be established as a general empirical principle that understanding of words leads to automatic retention without intention to learn and it is shown that this principle can account for all the effects of intention on learning, then we would have reduced the effects of intention to a simpler, or at least a more manageable process. A review of the literature shows, however, that the largest known effects of intention are found in the memorization of serial lists. The current experiments, however, deal only with free recall after a single presentation of a list—quite likely an entirely distinct kind of learning and recall.

At this point we need to look closely at the logic of the current conclusions on the role of intention in learning, making explicit the assumption that is implicit in the current discussions. The argument runs as follows: (1) The early work on intentional learning found substantial differences between retention following repetitions under the task to learn and retention following repetitions induced by some "cover" task not calling for learning. (Note that the task was serial memorization and that it required repetition for mastery.) (2) In experiments like those of Hyde and Jenkins (1973) or Craik and Lockhart (1972) a list of words is presented once (occasionally two or three times) and recall is tested immediately by a free-recall test, counting number of words correctly recalled without regard to order. Here semantic processing (a task emphasizing understanding of the meaning of the words) can lead to recall scores almost as good as those resulting from a task to learn—the differences are often insignificant, but usually the small differences still favor the task to learn, although occasionally incidential learning is even better then intentional learning. For the sake of the argument here, however, we can accept the authors' interpretation that semantic processing leads to about the same amount of recall as intent to learn. (3) There is an implicit assumption that the kind of learning involved in the one-presentation-free-recall experiments is the same as the kind of learning involved in Ebbinghaus's serial list memorization method, and both are representative of all learning. (4) Another implicit assumption is that the two conditions that produce similar quantitative results—equal success in recall—involve similar processes. (5) Therefore one explanation of the effect of intention is that it produces a more meaningful kind of processing of the materials to be learned.

Without assumption 3, of course, the final conclusion must be much more limited, applying only to the particular kind of free-recall method used by these investigators. My major purpose here is to question the validity of assumption 3. Assumption 4 is also questionable, of course. It must be taken as a preliminary working hypothesis to use until such time as we have other criteria for evaluating the nature of the underlying processes. Equal performance could, of course, be produced by entirely different processes and this possibility must be kept in mind—assumption 4 must be kept explicit rather than implicit, and it must not be forgotten. We can consider equal performance as a necessary *but not sufficient* basis for judging that two conditions produce similar learning and memory processes. Further refinements must await the development of independent criteria of types of learning process.

Most of the research on intentional learning or forgetting has aimed at reducing the effects of intention to some simpler, known process. There can be no objection to this aim—it is, after all, the goal of all science. What I do object to is the hasty oversimplification due to the attitude that this is not a very important problem and that the sooner we dispose of it the sooner we can get on to more important matters. The erroneous belief that the problem has been solved reflects a weakness in current theories of learning and memory that are attempting to substitute a new monolithic theory for an older one. Without the assumption that all learning depends on a single set of basic principles, the results of current research on incidental and intentional learning take on an entirely different meaning.

BASES FOR SEPARATING TYPES OF LEARNING AND MEMORY

Despite the common assumption of a single set of principles for learning and memory, there has been, over the years, a number of proposals for a classification of types of learning. A few examples are those of Gagné (1965), Tolman (1949), and Wickens (1964), schemes that aim to categorize the whole range of learning processes. Oxendine (1968) presents a chart comparing a number of these categorizations. There are some common elements—for example, a number take development of motor skill as a separate category. There are also considerable differences among the schemes. For example, Kingsley (1946) takes "memorizing ideas or verbal responses in fixed sequences" as a separate category, whereas Tolman and others fail to mention it at all—Tolman probably because he is not considering human learning, but others because they use quite different dimensions as criteria. Some include perceptual learning as a category; others do not mention it at all. Clearly there is yet no well-established subdivision of the types of learning, and various proposals have had little effect on learning and memory theories. In fact, the schemes are often considered only as a convenient way of setting up chapter headings or areas of application, which are then treated as different areas to be dealt with by the same set of underlying principles. None of the schemes I know of place any important weight on phenomenal experience as an essential criterion.

More recent information-processing approaches have not attempted general schemes like those mentioned previously. They have produced a number of proposals for categorization within a part of the total domain. Sometimes they also seem to be proposals for dividing the whole of learning and memory into two divisions. It is often difficult to tell which is involved because there is no specification of what the total domain is considered to be. Some examples that we examine in greater detail later are Tulving's (1972) separation of episodic and semantic memory, and proposals that recognition and recall involve distinct underlying processes (Broadbent & Broadbent, 1975, 1977).

A definitive scheme for subdividing learning and memory is not developed overnight, or indeed over a period of a few years. The validity of proposed distinctions must be tested in a number of ways, just as there is now a whole series of articles dealing with comparisons of recognition and recall. The various proposed complete systems of classification and the proposals for dual categorizations must all be treated as preliminary proposals or suggestions until the evidence is assembled and evaluated. Any proposals that I make here are similarly incomplete and tentative, although I give as much evidence as I can for their usefulness.

Perhaps more important than any particular classification is a recognition of the need for developing a valid classification. The more cautious and more rigorous approach is to assume that different kinds of learning follow distinct principles and involve different processes until there is evidence to the contrary. Psychologists have been so impressed with the value of parsimony in their theories that they have allowed the criterion of parsimony to take precedence over the criterion of validity. Only after two theories have been shown to have equal explanatory or predictive power should the criterion of parsimony be appealed to.

Where classifications of types of learning have been attempted, a number of factors have been considered. Some of the most common are: (1) experimental paradigms, such as trial and error learning, conditioning, discrimination learning, and serial learning; (2) theoretical constructs such as drive learning and expectancy learning; (3) the nature of the outcome or practical result, such as concept learning, motor pattern learning, attitude learning, verbatim recall; (4) differences in experimental effects. For example, the greater accuracy of recognition over recall has been taken by some as evidence of differences in process, although more recently others have questioned whether there really is an essential difference in accuracy. Differences in experimental effects would seem to be an important final criterion of the accuracy of a classification. It cannot be used alone, however, because there must be other identifying characteristics that allow us to separate the types before their functional characteristics are compared. The first three criteria are not independent and they are often mixed together in the same classification. They are not independent because experimental methods are usually based either on theoretical constructs or on the desire to study a certain kind of practical outcome.

The previous considerations are certainly useful and need to be taken into account. They pay relatively little attention to what I consider a very important aspect of learning and memory—how it is experienced by the learner. The classifications, and indeed theories of learning themselves, have concentrated on the objective accomplishments or responses. Why should not theories of memory account for how things appear in recall, as well as the correctness of responses? It should be part of the task of the theories to account for the characteristics of experience, not only to satisfy general curiosity but also because these experiences are practically important to our behavior. How well I trust my memory is not determined directly by its factual correctness because usually there is no way to check it, but by the clarity, detail, and form of the recall experience. In fact, it is questionable whether a theory that attempts to account only for responses can ever be very successful. That is why $S-R$ theories have failed, but current theories seem to be making the same mistakes over again.

Whereas the phenomenal experience of the learner should be an important consideration in separating types of learning, I am not claiming that the type of learning can be ascertained solely by questioning the experimental subject. He is frequently too busy to give us accurate descriptions, and he is likely to lack the terminology for accurate characterization of the processes involved. Moreover it is possible that similar phenomenal experiences could result from dissimilar underlying processes. Therefore phenomenal report must be coupled with other kinds of information and must be validated on the same basis as other factors in classification.

Separation of types of memory therefore needs to be based on multiple criteria. Emphasis should be given to phenomenal experience, coupled with information about the experimental situation, methods of testing memory, the instructions given by the experimenter and with the pattern of results coming from the variation of experimental conditions. We can also obtain useful information from nonexperimental data, such as clinical results on amnesia.

It must also be recognized that different kinds of learning may be mixed together in a single experimental or practical situation. In fact, mixture might be the rule rather than the exception. Even though mixture is possible and even frequent, the kinds of learning that I propose are of a "molar" rather than a "microscopic" nature. They are kinds of learning that *can* stand alone and be exhibited in relatively pure form, not atomic components that must always be combined to form the total performance.

TABLE 4.1

Subdivision of Learning and Memory—A Tentative Classification

1. Recollection—recall of past events as experienced.
2. Memorization (rote or meaningful)—the task requires retention of an amount of information or details that is more than can normally be recollected. Usually involves repetition of the details with a task to memorize.
3. Recognition:
   a. Identified as previously perceived in a particular context.
   b. Identified as familiar only—no context specified.
4. Learning to understand—perceiving or understanding a pattern of relationships. Once the pattern is clarified, it can be recollected later as in subdivision 1. Problem is not a simple quantitative overload as in memorization.
5. Developing the general cognitive background:
   (Long-term accumulation of knowledge rather than processes localized in time as in subdivision 1–4).
   a. Perceptual framework such as geographical organization of the world, commonsense physics, and mechanics.
   b. Social groups, organizations, and institutions as understood.
   c. Conceptual systems such as political theories, geometry, physical theory.
   d. Conceptions of the self.
   e. Norms, moral standards.
6. Language learning—involves all of the previous processes, but may be more than just a combination of them.
7. Learning perceptual skills (e.g., increasing accuracy of perceiving simple dimensions such as pitch; discrimination and identification of standard forms such as letters, words, triangles; perceived cause and effect, other mechanical relationships; social and physiognomic properties of persons).
8. Localized or short-term habits and responses.
   a. S—expectation or anticipation—variable responses to expectation.
   b. S–R "connections."
   It is possible that S–R connections develop out of learned expectations as in entry a or from other variable patterns, but some may be learned directly by a process like reinforcement.
9. Developing motor skill.
   a. Relatively invariant routines, components already learned (e.g., maze learning).
   b. Learning repertory of component skills (e.g., walking, handling tools).
   c. Adaptive patterns (e.g., driving).
10. Learning specific interests, likes and dislikes, fears, etc.
11. Learning generalized attitudes, motives, topical interests, etc.

A PROPOSED CLASSIFICATION OF TYPES OF LEARNING AND MEMORY

The proposals that I make here are based on multiple criteria as described previously. Table 4.1 gives the complete list in an arbitrary order based on ease of exposition rather than order of importance or any particular logical scheme. The separation is based primarily on the nature of the outcome or result, but it is the outcome or result for the individual rather than the outcome as observed by an experimenter. In addition, the nature of the experience at the time of learning is also considered.

My hypothesis is that these 11 headings represent *at least* 11 distinct kinds of learning-and-memory process. I say at least because I believe that it is more likely that some of these headings have to be subdivided further as research progresses and that these further separations more than offset any cases where two headings are found similar enough to be treated as a single process. For example, under the heading of perceptual skill, it would seem that increasing accuracy of pitch perception would be a quite different process from that of learning to identify letters or words. Certainly the two outcomes are sufficiently different to lead to a presumption of difference in process in the absence of evidence to the contrary. The same argument holds for many of the other subdivisions within the 11 categories, as well as for comparisons across categories.

Space does not permit me to treat each of the categories in detail—a complete treatment of the meaning of the separations and the evidence for them would require a book. I consider in some detail the distinctions between the first two types—*recollection* and *memorization*— because these are very relevant to the current literature on intention to learn and because the distinction is frequently ignored.

Recollection Versus Memorization

The distinction between recollection and memorization has been lost sight of in recent times. The distinction is between memory of past events *as past* and more or less as they were previously experienced and recall of information from the past without phenomenal reference to the past. Thus, I can *recollect* a spelling bee held in my second-grade classroom. In contrast I know how to spell *Mississippi* with no experience of when or where I learned to spell it. It is simply part of my memorized repertory of information. I can recollect hearing Wertheimer lecture on thinking at Cornell and even recall the lecture hall where he spoke and some of the people who were present. My knowledge of the principles of gestalt psychology is, in contrast, not associated with any particular events in my past—I just know it.

Various terms have been used for what I call recollection. Meumann (1913), stressing the learning or "encoding" phase, called this process "observational noting." Bartlett (1932) called it "remembering" and wrote an excellent book about it. Stern (1935) called it "Erinnerung" and translated it as "remembrance." He carried out much research on the subject of the accuracy of testimony and even founded a journal devoted to the topic—a topic in which the accuracy of recollection is of great practical importance. The chapter on "Remembrance" in Stern's book (1935) is an excellent description of the phenomenon. Because neither "remembering" nor "remembrance" seemed to be used solely for this kind of memory, I later proposed (Ryan, 1948) to use the term *recollection* as more usually implying an autobiographical kind of memory. Common usage does not always restrict the term to this kind of recall, but I am making this restriction for the purposes of this discussion.

Another term that is partially related is *memory for form* and the literature on this topic provides one source of information about recollection. Recollection is, however, not necessarily visual, and it is probably possible to recall a form (e.g., the Mona Lisa) without reference to any autobiographical event. By and large, however, memory for form can be considered as one aspect of recollection. Literature on this topic was well summarized by Woodworth (1938) and there has been a revival of interest in this topic in recent years.

Another related separation of types of memory is Tulving's (1972) separation of "episodic" and "semantic" memory. He apparently considers that all memory can be divided into these two categories, although one wonders where he puts motor skill, the retention of musical themes, etc. Without concerning ourselves with other possible kinds of memory that Tulving does not mention, the role of experience in the dichotomy of episodic and semantic memory is not at all clear. Tulving first defines semantic memory as whatever is involved in understanding language and episodic memory as everything else. Tulving (1972) has written: "I refer to this other kind of memory, the one that semantic memory is not, as 'episodic memory' [p. 384]." He also says: ". . . semantic memory, among other things, is not the kind of memory that psychologists have been studying in their laboratories since the time of Ebbinghaus [p. 384]." Thus Ebbinghaus's studies of serial learning are considered in the domain of "episodic memory." In the initial definition of episodic memory then, experience plays little part, but at this stage it is also not very clear what episodic memory *is*.

Tulving (1972) then goes on to characterize episodic memory more fully, and says: "Episodic memory receives and stores information about temporally dated episodes or events and temporal spatial relations among these events. A perceptible event can be stored in the episodic system solely in terms of its perceptible properties or attributes, and it is always stored in terms of its autobiographical reference to the already existing contents of the episodic memory store [p. 385–386]." Semantic memory, on the other hand, is "the memory necessary for the use of language."

Here it appears that Tulving's characterization of episodic memory is based on experiential criteria, and that he is talking about what I call recollection. If we take his statements about "temporal dating" as a description of experience, there is a conflict between this description and his earlier definition. Verbal-learning studies since Ebbinghaus would fit Tulving's first definition of episodic memory because it covers everything except understanding language. It is doubtful if they would fit the criterion of temporal dating. We are able to produce much information—reciting poetry, giving the product of 8 and 7, the capital of California, and the definition of specific gravity—without referring to, knowing, or being able to report the time when we learned or stored the information. It is true that in many verbal-learning studies the subjects have to identify which list among several is being tested, and to this extent the "autobiographical" side enters into the recall. But the emphasis has been mainly on the retention of undated information—on the retention of the information rather than the event of learning it. Thus, we can think of the verbal-learning studies as involving a mixture of two kinds of memory—episodic memory characterized by temporal dating (*recollection*) and another kind that has no standard name that might be called *memorized information.*

In earlier studies of verbal learning the emphasis was on the memorization of information—acquiring the dateless material such as the correct order of the list. In more recent times where the interest has shifted to free-recall tests of retention, there is a greater admixture of recollection. In fact, where the studies deal with only a single presentation of a list followed soon after by a free-recall test, we may be dealing with an almost pure form of recollection. It is a very sweeping assumption however, to consider all verbal-learning experiments of the past 90 years as involving solely episodic memory, thus lumping together serial anticipation, serial recall, paired associate, recognition, free recall, and prompted recall, as all involving the same kind of memory. They are probably all different from what is called semantic memory, but why must we have a dichotomy of only two kinds of memory?

Tulving did say that a number of different dichotomous classifications of memory have been proposed and that his proposal is surely not the only correct one. If we think of the problem as a sort of "feature analysis" of kinds of learning, then Tulving is really proposing two independent features: (1) the episodic character—dated in the past versus not dated in the past; and (2) something involved in the understanding of language versus not involved in the understanding of language. Perhaps these are empirically not completely independent—usually the understanding of language is not dated in the past. It is possible, however, that some understanding does require a reference to specific past events that are recalled in a quasi-perceptual manner. In other words, the two characteristics are conceptually independent. Looking at it from the point of view of episodic memory as referring to the recollection of specific past events as events of the individual's past life, nonepisodic memory can certainly involve more than language understanding.

Recall of events *as* events rather than as motor habits or verbal automatisms is certainly one important distinguishing feature of kinds of memory. Language is clearly a special kind of activity uniquely human, or nearly so, so that whatever is involved in understanding speech is probably different from other forms of memory or knowledge. There probably are other kinds of memory involved in the abilities to read, to play tennis, and to appreciate painting.

The distinction between recollection or episodic memory and other kinds seems an especially important distinction to maintain, not only for theoretical reasons but for practical reasons as well. The practical importance lies in the fact that recollection is so pervasive in our lives that disturbances of recollection become profoundly upsetting to the individual, and because his whole orientation toward reality depends on it.

Even though the distinction between memorization and recollection has been recognized by a substantial number of writers on memory, like those cited earlier, there have been even more who consider that there is no essential difference between the two. Ebbinghaus (1885) seemed to believe that his studies of memorized lists were representative of all memory—certainly his title, "Ueber das Gedächtnis," implies as much. Later this tendency was strengthened by the prejudice against phenomenal experience as a legitimate datum for scientific psychology. Looked at only from the response side, there is little difference between reciting a series of words previously memorized and verbal report of a past autobiographical event—both are verbal responses. Even recent cognitive psychologists, who might be expected to consider the possibility that the two cases involve different "encoding" processes or at least different kinds of stored information, fail to recognize the distinction. Wickelgren (1979), for example, having stated his modern form of associationistic theory (quoted earlier) proceeds to apply it primarily to human amnesia. Even though the most striking features of amnesia are clearly failures of recollection rather than of memorized information, Wickelgren does not even consider this distinction as possibly relevant to the problem.

THE ROLE OF INTENTION IN VARIOUS KINDS OF LEARNING AND MEMORY

1. Recollection, and 2. Memorization.   We come now to our original reason for developing a separation of types of memory. The earlier literature on the effect of intention or the task to learn, going back to Jenkins (1933), to Lewin (1921), and even earlier, demonstrated very marked effects on memorizing serial lists. In fact, for the incidental tasks that they employed there was very little or no incidental learning. It appeared that repetition in the absence of a task to learn was almost without effect, and we have discussed earlier the theoretical implication of these facts.

Although serial memorization depends on repeated trials with an intention to learn, recollection seems to depend usually only on a single trial without any specific intention to recall. I say "seems to" because there is almost no experimental research on the role of intention in recollection, even by those who make a distinction between the two kinds of learning. Meumann (1913) cites a considerable number of qualitative and quantitative studies of recollection or "observational noting." With reference to the effect of intention, however, he makes a statement of its importance [p. 74] but provides no specific references to support the statement. Many of the testimony experiments involved incidental observation without a task to learn but there was no control *with* a task to learn. Incidental recollection under these circumstances was often highly inaccurate, a result that is of great practical importance, but we have no proof that the accuracy would improve with intent to learn. Stern (1935), like Meumann, assumes that accuracy is increased if the subject is prepared for later recall, and he may be right, but he also cites no specific evidence.

On the other hand, whereas recollection may contain many errors, there is still a large amount of information that is retained without an intention to retain being present at the time of the original perception of the event. It would seem from common observation that the sheer amount of incidental retention in the form of recollection is much greater than the amount of memorization that takes place incidentally. Of course, it is difficult to make such estimates because the conditions for incidental memorization—repetition of a complex sequence—are perhaps not very frequent in ordinary life. It can be argued that the typical task of memorization involves the kind of information that cannot be recollected on the basis of either intentional or incidental observation. When we need or want information of this kind such as the verbatim recall of a poem or a lengthy string of numbers like a social security code, even intentional observation for purposes of recall is not enough. At this point we are forced to bring in other resources and repetition in order to accomplish the task. The evidence indicates that these processes must involve more than simply repeated perception; instead some kind of new process is required. So far, no one has found an "orienting task" or "cover task" that is successful in promoting serial memorization without an intention to learn. Only repetition *with* intent to learn is successful in providing mastery of complex sequences. Thus it seems justified to conclude that recollection and memorization differ not only in terms of the phenomenal outcome but in terms of their dependence on an intention to learn or recall. In fact, their differences with respect to the role of intention could be considered as another strong reason for considering them as qualitatively different processes. A very important task for students of memory is to explore further the differences between the two processes.

3. Recognition.   Although the test of recognition has traditionally been classed as just another test for the recall of memorized material, phenomenally recognition is more similar to other kinds of memory. In some ways it is closely related to recollection. For example, the detailed recognition that this is a person that I talked to at a certain meeting may be accompanied by a recollection of the original event. On the other hand, there may be the "bare recognition" that the person is familiar with no recollection of an earlier event. In this case, recognition might be considered as a form of perceptual learning—the familiarity is a property of the perceived object with no specific reference to the past, just as the property "triangle" may become a property of a perceived form. Bare recognition and detailed recollection prompted by perception may represent extremes of a continuum with various gradations between. That is why I have tentatively listed recognition as a separate category of memory. If we had only the two extremes, one could be considered as an aspect of recollection, bare familiarity could be considered as a form of perceptual learning, and no separate heading would be needed. In any event, recognition seems to be qualitatively different from the recall of memorized material. Recently there have also been discussions of other differences, quantitative as well as qualitative (Broadbent & Broadbent, 1975, 1977) although some still contend that recognition is based on the same processes as recall (usually not recognizing the distinction between rote recall and recollection; Rabinowitz, Mandler & Patterson, 1977; Watkins & Tulving, 1975).

In the light of my argument that different phenomenal forms of memory should be considered distinct until there is good evidence that they depend on similar underlying processes and in view of the conflicting evidence from studies based on response criteria, we should assume that recognition is distinct from recall of memorized material. Moreover there is extensive evidence that intention has relatively little effect on recognition tests in verbal learning experiments. With the material and other conditions constant, recall tests show the effect of a task to learn as compared to an incidental task, whereas the recognition tests show little or no effect of intention to learn (de Montpellier, 1972; Estes & DaPolito, 1967; Mulhall, 1915; Postman, Adams, & Phillips, 1955).

Thus we can conclude that recognition is distinct from the recall of memorized information, not only on phenomenal grounds and on evidence based on response criteria but also because of the sharp differences in the effect of intention to learn. Much confusion has been generated in studies of intentional and incidental learning by those who ignore the above results and assume that recognition tests are interchangeable with other recall tests.

4. Learning to Understand.   This is normally an intentional activity—the individual is *trying* to solve a problem, to understand a particular concept or method. He may be trying to understand only for an immediate purpose or satisfaction (out of curiosity) or he may also be trying to retain the solution or understanding for future use. The calculus student studying a particular proof, for example, is trying not only to understand the proof now but to be able to apply it in future. A problem here is to find whether the task to retain is more effective in later recall than the task to understand without reference to the future. In other words, is the open task effective or necessary for this kind of learning?

5. Developing the General Cognitive Background.   I would expect that the bulk of this background is put together incidentally in the process of carrying out other tasks. For example it is doubtful that we deliberately set out to formulate a conception of ourselves, although some part of this conception probably is subject to deliberate study and modification in the course of psychotherapy. Our knowledge of geography is partly the result of systematic study in the case of the global structure, but our picture of local geography is picked up without special study. We develop a commonsense understanding of the mechanics of everyday objects without deliberate study. Then that understanding may be modified by the formal study of physics. An important problem in this area is, then, the degree to which the cognitive background that is picked up incidentally can be modified by formal study.

6. Language Learning.   Young children seem to be trying to learn to speak, sometimes striving or struggling very hard. The task is probably not to learn a language as an abstract entity but to learn to communicate. What aspects of language are picked up incidentally and which are the result of a specific task is an important problem in this area.

7. Learning Perceptual Skills.   As pointed out before, this is probably a group of several distinct kinds of learning process that needs to be sorted out. Probably the role of intention varies from one kind to another just as it does in the other major categories of learning. Learning to identify forms or letters is likely to be an intentional activity, like learning the language, whereas our learning of physiognomic properties of persons is more likely to be learned incidentally.

8. Localized or Short-Term Habits and Responses.   Reinforcement theory is probably invalid as a general theory of all learning. On the other hand, it is still possible that the principle of reinforcement as defined by Thorndike or Hull could apply to certain limited kinds of learning—the learning of specific nonvarying responses to stimuli. Other habits may begin as more flexible forms of cognitive learning involving expectations and then change to automatized responses without any conscious expectation and with less flexibility of the response. Whatever their origin, specific *S-R* connections or habits do develop and may represent a process of learning that is different from that involved in our other categories.

If the principle of reinforcement does account for some kinds of habits, it implies that the habits are learned without awareness and without any intention to learn. They are difficult to unlearn intentionally also and may have to be broken by a process of reinforcement.

There is, of course, a very large literature on "learning without awareness," which I do not try to summarize here. (See Ryan, 1970, for a more extended account.) I merely point out that it is very difficult to find clear-cut cases of learning without awareness in which there is no suspicion of cognitive factors involved. Nevertheless, it is still possible that such cases exist, and they are most likely to be found in the case of simple motor habits. Experiments on learning without awareness have often involved complex kinds of learning (e.g., learning to say more plural words) where cognitive factors are very difficult to eliminate. The formation of simpler motor habits has more possibility of following reinforcement or classical conditioning principles. Pavlovian or operant conditioning paradigms are simple to set up, but the control of cognitive factors for human subjects in these experiments is very difficult. There is an extensive body of research to show that cognitive factors *can* play a considerable role in these paradigms. Conclusive evidence that cognitive factors can be eliminated to produce a purely automatic kind of learning is more difficult to achieve. The possibility has not, however, been eliminated. The whole problem takes on a new appearance if we accept the possibility that there are different kinds of learning. Then the demonstration that certain kinds of complex learning of language behavior depend on cognitive factors has no bearing on the problem of cognitive factors in simple conditioning or habit formation.

9. Developing Motor Skill.   Some of the activities usually lumped in this category may turn out to be essentially similar to memorizing—learning a fixed sequence of components that are themselves already available. Other kinds of motor skill may turn out to be essentially like language learning. Such a reshuffling awaits the development of our knowledge about all categories of learning. Meanwhile I again argue that the cautious approach is to assume that motor skills have their own special characteristics until all the evidence is in.

Early hope that motor skills could be understood as combinations or chains of simple habits has been largely discredited. Lashley's (1951) article is still highly influential on this topic, and Halwes and Jenkins (1971) provide a later critique of an associationistic model of skill. Even if an elementaristic account of motor skill could be shown to be correct, it still would not necessarily be very useful in dealing with practical problems of learning skills.

A skill is made up of so many component movements that the description of the skill in these terms would be extremely complex and cumbersome. Unless the theory could also tell us which details are practically important in improving the skill and how to manipulate them, the theory would be of little practical value. Elementaristic theories so far proposed have not been helpful in this regard even if they were correct.

Much of the development of motor skill is intentional—the individual is trying to improve his performance at some task whether it be playing tennis, playing the violin, or driving nails with a hammer. Although he intends to improve, he does not necessarily know how to improve—he does not necessarily know what he should attend to or how he should practice for more effective learning. Even so, it appears that practice with the intent to improve is effective—the individual does improve even though he does not know how the improvement is produced. On the other hand improvement can probably be enhanced with the aid of a skilled teacher or coach. Much of our information on this problem is anecdotal rather than data from controlled experiments, but it does seem that some teachers are successful in finding ways of directing the attention of the learner to critical factors in the skill. Such things are "keeping the eye on the ball," changes in posture, or relaxing certain muscles do seem to be more effective than simply "trying hard." The success of the teacher depends on his hitting on relevant factors in the skill that can be attended to. He could not be effective, however, unless the learner is trying to learn and is looking for aid in this endeavor. The teacher's suggestions must be made part of the learner's detailed intentions—he must deliberately try to attend to certain details of posture or muscle tension or to attend visually to certain aspects of the situation. The study of the detailed characteristics of the intention to learn is therefore a very important topic for research on motor skill—the more stylish term for this topic is the *strategy* of the learner.

10 and 11. Learning of Specific or General Interests and Attitudes. These headings have been included here only to make the classification as complete as possible. Involving all motivational theory as they do, even a sketchy treatment would require another chapter. I content myself here with a brief note about the nature of the problems without getting into substance at all.

Many accounts of motivation have applied standard learning theories, especially reinforcement theory to the development of interests and attitudes. Such an account is obligatory if one starts with the belief in a single set of principles of all learning. If, on the other hand, there is a number of independent kinds of learning, the learning of motivational characteristics such as interests and attitudes may involve one or more new kinds of learning. This means that the data on development and change of interests and attitudes must be examined with a neutral eye, looking for both resemblances and differences between these kinds of learning and others. Only after a set of empirical generalizations has been worked out for these kinds of learning and for each of the other classes can we begin to look for communalities and the possibilities of combining different categories.

It would appear that the learning of motivational characteristics is largely unintentional, but even this assumption is open to question until the empirical study of these kinds of learning is more fully developed.

It should be emphasized again that the classification of types of learning is only tentative, even though I have made it as accurate as I could on the basis of present evidence. I am firmly convinced that some such classification is necessary and that serious efforts should be devoted to collecting further evidence and developing a more definitive categorization.

The purpose of the brief discussions of each heading was not to justify the categorizations but to show what consequences could follow from such a classification. These consequences emphasized the role of intention in the various kinds of learning, but they could be extended to many other aspects of learning.

REINTERPRETING RESEARCH ON INTENTIONAL LEARNING

The Free-Recall Method and Types of Memory

As mentioned earlier, much of the recent research on intention to learn has made use of the method of free recall, usually following a single presentation of a list of words. Under the assumption that learning is learning (or encoding is encoding), this quick and convenient method has been considered as giving results comparable to those obtained by serial memorization. Unless you believe in a monolithic theory of learning and memory, this assumption is of extremely doubtful validity. From my point of view, the important question is: What kind of memory is involved in the free-recall method?

I do not know of any systematic studies of the phenomenal experiences involved in free-recall experiments (or for most other kinds of memory experiments for that matter). In the absence of systematic studies I would conjecture from my own experience that the free-recall test involves primarily a form of recollection, particularly when the material has been presented only once or a few times; that is, the subject probably remembers the whole event of the presentation, aurally and/or visually, and some of the details of the actual words heard or read. It is recollection of a relatively short term, because most of the experiments involve recall after a few minutes. We might call it *RSTM* because *STM,* in current theoretical discussions, refers to a span of only a few seconds. Whether there are any essential differences between recollections over a few-minute period and those over spans of days, months, or years we do not know, but I would expect the differences to be quantitative rather then qualitative.

If my hypothesis is correct, then much of the recent literature on intentional and incidental learning bears on the role of intention in *recollection,* mostly for *RSTM,* but occasionally for somewhat longer periods. Under the instruction to learn, the subject may attempt to use some of the strategies that he would use to memorize, but with the single trial there is little chance of these strategies becoming effective, and the subject cannot reach the stage of true memorization. The first few trials in a serial memorization experiment probably also involve primarily recollection rather than a distinct process of memorization. Even though the free-recall experiment involves recollection, the material is of limited scope, almost always involving word lists and therefore a quite narrow range of material. I do not review the relevant literature in detail here. The earlier material is reviewed in McLaughlin (1965) and Ryan (1970, Chapters 6 and 7). I am preparing a literature review of the research since then. To summarize briefly, the task to learn produces significantly higher accuracy of recall than "nonsemantic" orienting tasks like counting the number of letters in each word or looking for all the *e*'s. Tasks that involve understanding the meaning of the words, however, produce recall as accurate, or almost as accurate, as the task to learn.

Thus, for one rather narrow sample of recollection, there is evidence that the task to learn or retain is effective (at least more effective than some incidental orienting tasks). One possible way in which the task to learn may operate is by making the subject pay more attention to the meaning of the words. The effect of intention *could* be produced in this way, but the experiments do not prove that this is the way in which intention actually works for any of the subjects. There is still the possibility that the task to learn produces other changes in "processing" that have not yet been described and that are just as effective as "semantic processing."

There is a further complication in the interpretation of the results of the free-recall experiments. The incidental tasks that produce poorer recall than the task to learn usually seem to *interfere* with intentional learning when the two tasks are combined. Unfortunately the whole situation is so artificial that there is no "normal," "standard" or even "usual" condition for comparison. The neutral instruction to "just listen to the list of words" has to be avoided because the subjects are likely to suspect that this is a learning experiment and engage in intentional learning anyway. It is possible, then, that the task to learn is no more effective than simple perception and understanding of the words with no particular task. What may happen in the experiments is that some incidental nonsemantic tasks *reduce* recall compared to a "neutral" perception, whereas intention to learn has little or no effect. In this interpretation, the "semantic task" also has no effect beyond what would happen in a more passive or neutral task such as "just listen" or "just watch" that the subject carries out without adding any tasks of his own.

Under this interpretation, then, the results may not reflect any effect of either intent to learn or semantic processing, on recollection. The results could reflect only an interfering effect of some artificial tasks that reduce the normal attention to the meaning of the words. The outcome of this argument is that an understanding of the role of intention in free-recall experiments alone requires the investigation of more different kinds of "orienting tasks" and particularly an attempt to produce conditions in which the subject listens or reads attentively, but with no task to do anything further—trying to come as close as possible to a neutral condition in which the only task is to perceive.

To summarize my conclusions on the research dealing with intention to learn in free-recall experiments:

1. These experiments probably deal primarily with recollection and are not relevant to the earlier research dealing with intent to memorize.

2. Incidental tasks calling attention to the meaning of the words (*semantic processing*) produce about as much recall as the task to learn. Both produce better recall than some other incidental tasks that call attention to aspects of the words other than their meaning.

3. Relative to some hypothetical "neutral" condition, the results could be interpreted as either an increase in learning due to intention or a task emphasizing the meaning of the words, or as due to an interfering effect of tasks that deflect attention from the meaning (or both could be true).

4. *If* the task to learn has an effect on performance in free-recall experiments, then one possible mechanism of the effect is that the task to learn produces more attention to the meaning of the words. The equivalence of performance for incidental tasks involving semantic processing and intentional learning shows the *possibility* of this explanation of the effect of intention. There is no conclusive evidence, however, that this is the way the task to learn actually works or that it is the only way that it works.

Paired-Associates Experiments

A few of the experiments on intention to learn have employed paired words with a test for recall of the second member of the pair and have obtained results similar to those summarized earlier for free recall. These cases all involve, however, only one or two presentations of the list before testing. Paired-associates tests clearly involve memorization when carried to mastery. As noted previously for serial memorization, the first few trials probably make more use of recollection than they do the processes of memorization.

Our conclusions for paired-associates experiments are therefore the same as for the free-recall experiments.

Nuttin's Experiments on Open and Closed Tasks

Although these experiments were directed specifically at reinforcement theory, we should also consider where they fit into the separate types of learning and memory. Several of the experiments can be described by the following general outline:

1. The experimenter presents some series of items.
2. The subject is to make some response to each item (e.g., estimate the number of objects in a picture).
3. Each response is called "right" or "wrong."
4. In the second trial, the subject is asked to recall his response on the first trial.

In the "open" task, the subject expects to be given further trials like the first one, so that there is some advantage in recalling which responses were correct. In the "closed" task, the subject does not expect to repeat the responses. It is the closed-task condition that is new, because the earlier Thorndikean experiments had all been carried out under the open-task condition with the subject expecting to continue until he has learned the "correct" responses.

In the closed-task situation, the materials in several experiments were presented once. Then the series was presented once more with the new instructions to recall what the previous response had been. Here the "law of effect" failed to operate and the successful and unsuccessful responses were recalled about equally well.

In these cases of a single learning trial, we can assume that we are dealing with recollection rather than the process of memorization. Because the individual recollects his previous responses better if he has the open task (corresponding to a task to learn) than he does under the incidental or closed task, we have clear-cut evidence of the role of the task in recollection.

These results are less equivocal than the results from the later free-recall experiments summarized in the previous section. The only difference between the open and closed tasks is the expectation of repeated trials, and there is no basis for supposing that the closed task would have an interfering effect. There is nothing in the closed task to distract attention from the essential features of the situation, in particular the success or failure, in favor of some other aspects.

Consequently, these experiments provide important evidence that intention does affect recollection and help to clarify the results of the free-recall experiments.

It should be emphasized that these conclusions are completely independent of the issue raised by Postman (1966) as to whether the Nuttin experiments are irrelevant to the law of effect. Postman argued that the law concerned only the repetition of *responses* as a function of previous reward and that recall (recollection) of previous responses is not predicted by the law of effect. I agree with Nuttin's argument (1953, Chapter VI, especially pp. 309 ff.) that the law of effect is supposed to apply to all learning and consequently should apply to recollection of previous responses as well as to the learning of responses themselves. In fact, he argues that recollection of previous responses is a better test of strength of connection than repetition of the response itself. This is, however, a separate issue. The effect of the task to learn upon the recollection of previous responses is an interesting and important problem in its own right, regardless of the bearing of these results upon the law of effect. Buchwald (1969), d'Ydewalle and Eelen (1975), and d'Ydewalle and Buchwald (1976) have concerned themselves with the factual question of the relationship between recollection of earlier responses and rewards on the one hand and actual responses on succeeding trials on the other. This is an important problem in understanding performance in reinforcement experiments. Again, however, my concern here is with the recollection itself and not with its effects on subsequent response or performance.

Unfortunately, later results from the laboratory at Leuven and elsewhere complicate the picture, even for the separate problem of recollection of previous responses. For example, d'Ydewalle and Eelen (1975) found cases where the "right" responses were not recollected any better than the "wrong" responses, even under the open task to learn. d'Ydewalle (1976) found that the effect of the task to learn depends on the specific nature of the instructions and the expectations of the subjects. Results varied with whether the subject expected multiple learning trials or only two trials and with the introduction of familiarization trials. We are left with the impression that the task or expectation of the subject does affect his recollection of previous right and wrong responses. It is not, however, a simple matter of whether the task involves learning or not. More specific expectations about the number of trials and other aspects of the expected procedure also play an important role.

SUMMARY

Starting from the inspiration of Nuttin's important book, *Tâche, Réussite, et Échec* (1953), this chapter has pursued further the theoretical problems involved in the open task or the task to learn. The early work on the differences between intentional and incidental learning in memorizing created serious theoretical difficulties for the prevalent associationistic theories of the time, and it still creates difficulties for more recent forms of associationism. Nuttin's experiments on open and closed tasks created the same kinds of theoretical difficulty for the law of effect and reinforcement theory.

Attempts to understand *how* the intention to learn produces its effect and to reconcile the effect with current theories of learning have produced a considerable body of research in the past 20 years. Most of this research has utilized free-recall tests of memory after one or only a few learning trials. Yet these results are considered as representative of all learning and memory and are supposed to explain how intention worked in the original research that used memorization of serial lists as the experimental method.

The main thesis of this chapter is that we must assume the existence of a number of distinct types of learning and memory that follow different principles and are subject to different controlling conditions. The role of the task to learn or the open task is expected to differ for the different kinds of learning. As a consequence it cannot be assumed that the recent work with free-recall tests is relevant to the role of intention in other kinds of learning.

It is also argued that an adequate separation of types of learning and memory must take the phenomenal experiences of the learner as well as his responses into account. Based on this assumption a tentative classification of types of learning and memory is presented, together with a discussion of the possible role of intention in the various classes of learning.[1]

REFERENCES

Bartlett, F. C. *Remembering.* Cambridge, England: Cambridge University Press, 1932.

Broadbent, D. E., & Broadbent, M. H. P. The recognition of words which cannot be recalled. In P. M. A. Rabbitt & S. Dornic (Eds.), *Attention and Performance* (Vol. V). New York: Academic Press, 1975.

Broadbent, D. E., & Broadbent, M. H. P. Effects of recognition on subsequent recall: Comments on "determinants of recognition and recall: accessibility and generation" by Rabinowitz, Mandley, & Patterson. *Journal of Experimental Psychology: General,* 1977, *106,* 330–335.

Buchwald, A. M. Effects of "right" and "wrong" on subsequent behavior: A new interpretation. *Psychological Review,* 1969, *76,* 132–143.

Craik, F. I. M., & Lockhart, R. S. Levels of processing: A framework for memory research. *Journal of Verbal Learning and Verbal Behavior,* 1972, *11,* 671–684.

---

[1]Since this chapter went to press we have received a relevant and interesting paper by Hasher and Zacks. (L. Hasher & R. T. Zacks, Automatic and effortful processes in memory. *Journal of Experimental Psychology: General,* 1979, *108,* 356–388). They have categorized all kinds of learning along a single dimension from automatic to effortful, the latter being equivalent to intentional learning as discussed in this chapter. They state: "Operations that drain minimal energy from our limited-capacity attentional mechanism are called automatic: their ocurrence does not interfere with other ongoing cognitive activity. . . . They occur without intention and do not benefit from practice [p. 256]." This article raises a number of important questions that, unfortunately, it is too late to address here. I shall mention here only that a number of the instances of "automatic" memory are probably instances of recollection—they involve recall of spatial location, frequency, and other temporal information. They are considered automatic because memory is not improved by intent to learn or the expectation of a test.

de Montpellier, G. Nature et méchanisme de l'apprentissage intentionnel. *Psychologica Beligica*, 1972, *12*, 33–44.

d'Ydewalle, G. Recall of "right" and "wrong" responses as a function of instructions for intentional learning and task familiarization. *Psychological Reports*, 1976, *38*, 619–624.

d'Ydewalle G., & Buchwald, A. Effects of "right" and "wrong" as a function of recalling either the response or the outcome. *Journal of Experimental Psychology: Human Learning and Memory*, 1976, *2*, 728–738.

d'Ydewalle, G., & Eelen, P. Repetition and recall of "right" and "wrong" responses in incidental and intentional learning. *Journal of Experimental Psychology: Human Learning and Memory*, 1975, *1*, 429–441.

Ebbinghaus, H. *Ueber das Gedächtnis.* Leipzig: Dunker & Humboldt, 1885.

Estes, W. K., & DaPolito, F. Independent variation of information storage and retrieval processes in paired-associate learning. *Journal of Experimental Psychology*, 1967, *75*, 18–26.

Gagné, R. M. *The conditions of learning.* New York: Holt, Rinehart & Winston, 1965.

Halwes, T., & Jenkins, J. J. Problem of serial order in behavior is not resolved by context-sensitive associative memory models. *Psychological Review*, 1971, *78*, 122–129.

Hull, C. L. *Principles of behavior.* New York: Appleton-Century, 1943.

Hyde, T. S. & Jenkins, J. J. Recall for words as a function of semantic, graphic, and syntactic orienting tasks. *Journal of Verbal Learning and Verbal Behavior*, 1973, *12*, 471–478.

Jenkins, J. G. Instruction as a factor in "incidental" learning. *American Journal of Psychology*, 1933, *45*, 471–477.

Kingsley, H. L. *The nature and conditions of learning.* Englewood Cliffs, N.J.: Prentice-Hall, 1946.

Lashley, K. S. The problem of serial order in behavior. In L. A. Jeffress (Ed.), *Cerebral mechanisms in behavior.* New York: Wiley, 1951.

Lewin, K. Das Problem der Willensmessung und das Grundgesetz der Association, I. *Psychologische Forschung*, 1921, *1*, 191–302; II. *ibid.*, 1922, *2*, 65–140.

McLaughlin, B. "Intentional" and "incidental" learning in human subjects: the role of instructions to learn and motivation. *Psychological Bulletin*, 1965, *63*, 359–376.

Meumann, E. *The psychology of learning.* New York: Appleton, 1913.

Montague, W. E. Elaborative strategies in verbal learning and memory. In G. H. Bower (Ed.), *The psychology of learning and motivation* (Vol. 6). New York: Academic Press, 1972.

Mulhall, E. F. Experimental studies in recall and recognition. *American Journal of Psychology*, 1915, *26*, 217–228.

Nelson, D. L., Walling, J. R., & McEvoy, C. L. Doubts about depth. *Journal of Experimental Psychology: Human Learning and Memory*, 1979, *5*, 24–44.

Nuttin, J. *Tâche, Réussite, et Échec.* Louvain: Publications Universitaires de Louvain, 1953.

Nuttin, J., & Greenwald, A. G. *Reward and punishment in human learning.* New York: Academic Press, 1968.

Oxendine, J. B. *Psychology of motor learning.* New York: Appleton-Century-Crofts, 1968.

Postman, L. Short-term memory and incidental learning. In A. W. Melton (Ed.), *Categories of human learning.* New York: Academic Press, 1964.

Postman, L. Reply to Greenwald. *Psychological Bulletin*, 1966, *65*, 383–388.

Postman, L., Adams, P. A., & Phillips, L. W. Studies in incidental learning: II The effects of association value and of method of testing. *Journal of Experimental Psychology*, 1955, *49*, 1–10.

Rabinowitz, J. C., Mandler, G., & Patterson, K. E. Determinants of recognition and recall: Accessibility and generation. *Journal of Experimental Psychology: General*, 1977, *106*, 302–329.

Ryan, T. A. Recollecting, imagining, and thinking. In E. G. Boring, H. S. Langfeld, & H. P. Weld (Eds.), *Foundations of Psychology.* New York: John Wiley & Sons, 1948.

Ryan, T. A. *Intentional behavior: an approach to human motivation.* New York: Ronald Press, 1970.

Stern, W. *Allgemeine Psychologie auf personalistischer Grundlage.* The Hague: Martinus Nijhof, 1935.

Tolman, E. C. There is more than one kind of learning. *Psychological Review,* 1949, *56,* 144–155.

Tulving, E. Episodic and semantic memory. In E. Tulving (Ed.), *Organization of memory.* New York: Academic Press, 1972.

Wallach, H., & Henle, M. An experimental analysis of the law of effect. *Journal of Experimental Psychology,* 1941, *28,* 340–349.

Wallach, H., & Henle, M. A further study of the function of reward. *Journal of Experimental Psychology,* 1942, *30,* 147–160.

Watkins, M. J., & Tulving, E. Recall and recognition: A reply to Light, Kimble, and Pellegrino. *Journal of Experimental Psychology: General,* 1975, *104,* 37–38.

Wickelgren, W. A. Chunking and consolidation: A theoretical synthesis of semantic networks, configuring in conditioning, $S-R$ versus cognitive learning, normal forgetting, the amnesic syndrome, and hippocampal arousal system. *Psychological Review,* 1979, *86,* 44–60.

Wickens, D. D. The centrality of verbal learning: Comments on Professor Underwood's paper. In A. W. Melton (Ed.), *Categories of human learning.* New York: Academic Press, 1964.

Woodworth, R. S. *Experimental Psychology.* New York: Holt, 1938.

5 Habit Activation In Human Learning

Melvin H. Marx
University of Missouri—Columbia

INTRODUCTION

In this chapter I attempt to deal with the general issue of cognitive–behavioral interaction by focusing on the theoretical explanation of human selective learning. The role of cognition has of course been accorded recognition at a rapidly increasing pace over the past few years, as is demonstrated by the following pages and the other chapters in this volume. Nevertheless, purely cognitive explanations of learning, even human learning, do not seem to be sufficient. It is the present contention that they generally need a fuller account of the role of motivation. Most of the recent cognitive interpretations of human learning either gloss over the problem by giving what amounts to a kind of lip service to motivation or ignore the problem entirely by simply assuming that the human learner is adequately and appropriately motivated. The present treatment attempts to fill that gap by reconceptualizing the role of motivational factors in instrumental learning and memory.

FROM THORNDIKEAN BOND TO MEMORY STORE

Although readers of this volume are no doubt reasonably familiar with the history of the human learning problem, at least as it has been approached by American theorists, some review is desirable to set the stage for the following discussion.

The Bond

Throughout the first half of the century, there was one outstanding theoretical position, that of Edward Lee Thorndike. Thorndike (1898, 1911) early formulated his *law of effect,* according to which responses are strengthened (and thereby selected and ultimately fixated) or weakened (and eventually eliminated) on the basis of the satisfyingness or nonsatisfyingness of the consequences of those responses. Thorndike developed an association-istic, stimulus–response (S–R) conceptual framework in which the concept of the S–R bond was focal. It was the bond, the hypothetical connection between stimulus and response, which was strengthened by satisfying aftereffects and not simply the response itself.

As Thorndike's research interest shifted from animals to people, he shifted his law of effect as well. The law of effect was initially based on Thorndike's own (and others') prior work with animal subjects. But as a result of massive empirical investigations with human subjects over many years, Thorndike (1931) became convinced that the law of effect, or at least the part of it involving positive aftereffects and response fixation in selective learning, was equally applicable to humans. For many years during the first half of the century, this theoretical position was largely uncontested as the primary American interpretation of human learning, in educational psychology as well as the psychology of learning.

Few seriously doubt the *empirical* validity of either the Thorndikean law of effect or its contemporary counterpart, Skinner's highly influential *principle of reinforcement.* For some time, however, the theoretical underpinnings of these two statements of substantially the same generalization have been in disarray. There has been a widespread abandonment of the law of effect by human-learning theorists (Buchwald, 1969; Estes, 1971, 1972; Nuttin, 1976). This situation has been of little apparent concern to Skinnerian (operant conditioning) researchers because following Skinner's lead they rarely concern themselves directly with theoretical problems of this kind, remaining largely content to demonstrate empirical relationships and refine exper-imental procedures. The result of this wholesale dismissal, on the one hand, and general neglect, on the other hand, by former and present proponents of the reinforcement principle, is that the field of human learning has been left to the currently popular, strictly cognitive interpretations.

The Memory Store

The contemporary cognitive theory of human selective learning is remarkably simple in its core structure. The basic theory simply holds that humans store in memory both their responses and the outcomes of those responses, which in the typical Thorndikean multiple-choice learning situation consist of the verbal signals, "right" and "wrong", or some other cues indicative of correctness or incorrectness. Rehearsal, designed to transfer correct responses from short-term memory (STM) to long-term memory (LTM), is assumed to occur whenever time and other task constraints permit. A variety of encoding strategies, by which correct answers are made more meaningful and thus easier to store in memory, have been demonstrated (Montague, 1972). Then, on subsequent tests in the same stimulus situation, the human subject retrieves from LTM both the previous responses and their outcomes and deliberately repeats the previously correct responses and varies the incorrect responses, so as to maximize the opportunity for correct responses.

This nut-shell description of what seems to be little more than a commonsensical portrayal of human learning does not do justice to the ingenuity of the experimentation that has been designed to test it (Estes, 1969, 1976), the elegance of its mathematical formulation (Buchwald, 1969; d'Ydewalle & Buchwald, 1976; d'Ydewalle & Eelen, 1975), or the breadth of innovative conceptualization that has been developed to relate it to ongoing motivations (Nuttin, 1973, 1976). By and large, the cognitive view would seem to have met Thorndikean theory on its own ground (i.e., the multiple-choice learning task) and to have overwhelmed it. There is really no question but that human subjects can do all the things attributed to them by cognitive theory. Nevertheless, some doubts remain as to the completeness of the strictly cognitive account. Before we lay the issue to rest and concur with the more enthusiastic of the cognitivists that the core problem of human selective learning has been solved, let us therefore look more closely and analytically at some broader questions concerning the relationship between cognition and learning.

REWARD AND INFORMATION: CURRENT ISSUES

The Automaticity Issue

The theoretical heart of the Thorndikean law of effect is the automaticity with which rewards are presumed to operate. Thorndike was well aware of cognitive learning processes and, as a matter of fact, designed his human experiments so as to eliminate cognitive factors as far as possible (as by requiring too many S-R connections to permit ready memorizing of them all, presenting stimuli at a rapid rate so as to prevent rehearsal, etc.). He felt that it was, fundamentally, the automatic strengthening of the S-R bond that accounted for selective learning, and that when the cognitive overlay was removed this automatic effect would be more clearly revealed.

A substantial part of my research program over the past decade has been concerned with one version of this issue. It is quite clear that providing human subjects (and probably all higher organisms as well) with information is a sufficient operation to insure learning, defined as the acquiring of new S–R connections that can then be demonstrated in behavior. But the issue with which I have been concerned is whether there are any *additional* properties that are mediated by reward, defined simply as *the satisfaction of motivation.* In other words, are responses that have been accompanied by reward, as compared with those acquired through information alone, not only acquired more readily but also do they show greater durability or transfer more readily? Note that these questions do not necessarily deal directly with the automaticity issue, as such, but are more broadly phrased and can be tested without making any assumptions about automaticity.

Reward Versus Information–Research Paradigm

The paradigmatic experimental operation that was developed to test these questions (Hillix & Marx, 1960) involves the comparison of the behavior of experimental subjects, whose acquisition of S–R connections is accompanied by verbal feedback (or some similar rewarding signals), with control subjects who are shown the responses and given equivalent information as to their outcomes. Typically this comparison is provided by a within-subjects design in which pairs of subjects work together in acquisition. Subjects in each pair alternate between roles in which they *perform* (respond and receive feedback) and *observe* (watch the responses and their outcomes). Because observer acquisition needs to be compared with performer acquisition, special test trials, on which both performers and observers respond individually to all stimuli, are interpolated among acquisition trials. The presumption is that such test trials reveal any differences between learning with reward and learning by information alone. Information is assumed to be equivalent for the two task conditions so that differences may be attributed to the reward function. This design also permits both within-subjects and between-subjects comparisons; the latter, although not controlling for individual differences, does offer the opportunity of controlling for other factors, such as learning materials; and in some studies only the between-subjects comparison has been used. It should also be noted that there is a fundamental difference between this use of performer and observer to control the role of information, and the superficially similar use of performer and observer where the performer serves as a behavioral model, as in social-learning research (Bandura, 1969).

Acquisition. The prototypic study (Hillix & Marx, 1960) showed unexpectedly superior acquisition by the control—observing—subjects. The same result was found consistently in a large number of studies by Rosenbaum (Rosenbaum & Arenson, 1968). In all of this research the tasks used were some form of serial multiple-choice learning (e.g., tracing of a circuit through a matrix of switches, only one of which in any given row is correct). In more recent discrete-item multiple-choice tasks, we have typically found no acquisition difference between performance and observation, as far as number of correct responses is concerned (Marx, Witter, & Mueller, 1972). Only in two experiments with grade-school children were reliable differences of this kind found, in each case favoring the performers. Marx and Marx (1970) reported an interaction between performance/observation (P/O) and school grade, with younger children (grades 4 and 5) learning more under performance. Reanalysis of those data by grades taken separately indicates that there were reliably more children in grades 4 and 5 who learned more P than O items than there were children who learned more O than P items [29 against 15 in grade 4, 22 against 9 in grade 5; $\chi^2(1) = 4.54$ and 5.45, assuming a 50–50 baseline]. The slight superiority of $O > P$ learners in grade 6 (24 against 19) was not reliable, $\chi^2(1) = .58$. Marx and Marx (1976) found that fourth to sixth grade children learned to spell very difficult words more effectively under P than O conditions, but this study was run under somewhat unusual conditions, with correct spellings provided only after performers had attempted to spell six words; observers may have been handicapped by the massing of correct responses, and the contribution to the general problem may therefore be questioned.

In most of the later studies a more analytic measure than number of correct responses has been used. This measure is proportion of correct and incorrect responses repeated from study to test trial as a function of performance or observation in study. Justification for its use was indicated by the results of one experiment (Marx & Witter, 1972) in which no difference in number of correct responses was found, but performers clearly repeated both correct responses and incorrect responses more often than observers. In this case, the failure to find any overall difference in number of correct responses was presumably due to the performers' increased repetition of errors (and therefore reduced opportunity for changing to correct responses), offsetting their increased repetition of the correct responses themselves. This same kind of result was replicated in a later study (Witter, Marx, & Farbry, 1976) in which the reliably greater performer tendency to repeat both correct and incorrect responses persisted over a 1-month interval between the two experimental sessions.

One potentially interesting trend was observed in these studies. This was the tendency for performer superiority in repetition of correct responses to develop over trials. In Witter, Mueller, and Marx (1971), for example, there was no P/O difference in number of correct responses in early trials but a performer advantage in later trials. Marx, Witter, and Farbry (1973) also found that performers repeated less correct responses on early trials but repeated more correct responses on later trials, and, in the Witter, Marx, and Farbry (1976) study mentioned earlier, there was also an interaction between trials and correct response repetition in the first session, with no first-trial differences but performers repeating more thereafter.

We may refer now to some unpublished results as well as two other lines of published research that bear on the reward/information issue. One unpublished study is especially worthy of mention here and is examined more closely later. Again there were no simple main effect P/O differences but some intriguing interactions. Marx and Conover (In preparation) found that in binary tasks, performers repeated correct responses reliably more than they varied incorrect responses, and increasingly over trials, whereas observers did not do so. It may be mentioned, in passing, that like certain of the earlier studies, this one revealed a large number of interactions between sex of subject and P/O,—most notably indicative of female superiority as observers—but these are not described here because of their apparently tangential relationship to the primary issue.

Transfer.   It should be emphasized that the purpose in initiating this research was not to compare acquisition under P/O conditions but rather to test transfer after P versus O acquisition. This was indeed the objective of the first study (Hillix & Marx, 1960). The acquisition tests used in that experiment were designed to insure the comparability of P and O learning. The fact that unexpectedly greater O acquisition occurred, led not only to an immediate replication, with the same results, but also to the further studies described previously. Moreover, this observer superiority in acquisition has tended to obscure the transfer results that were obtained. Mainly these results showed that when the acquisition differences were statistically controlled, by analysis of covariance, subjects who had served as performers and presumably been "rewarded" by positive feedback, did, in fact, tend to select previously learned responses more than control observers in the transfer test.

Similar results, with greater transfer following P rather than O acquisition, have been found in subsequent experiments. Two experiments involved identification of faces and facial features. Marx and Witter (1972) found that college-student performers, more often than observers, identified correctly the full faces from which the particular features on which they had been trained were taken. Marx (1980), using line-drawn facial materials in high-school classes, found some rather complex interactions that were interpreted as suggesting greater transfer of learning under performance on relatively easier materials and greater transfer following observation on more difficult materials.

Two other transfer studies, utilizing personality evaluations as a kind of "cover" for the true purpose of the research, have provided some measure of positive support for the proposition that reward produces more transferable learning than information. Marx (1978) reported that male performers were more influenced by prior reinforcement than either male observers or female performers or observers, and Marx and Marx (1978) reported a similar result for all subjects using three different transfer tests.

Retention.   I turn now to one final, and quite different, experimental approach to the problem at hand. This is the more direct manipulation of reward, defined as *motivation satisfaction,* within the Zeigarnik-effect situation; in that situation, the incompletion of a task, which may be considered to produce motivation persistence, has been shown to result in superior recall of the task name (Prentice, 1944; Zeigarnik, 1927). The experimental design called for the introduction of a clue, following a short period of effort on each of a sequence of tasks that were too difficult to permit easy or quick solution. Half the clues were constructed to facilitate task solution, and half to inhibit it; the experimental prediction was that successful clues would be better recalled than unsuccessful, in contrast to the anticipated superior recall of the names of the uncompleted tasks themselves, in accordance with the usual Zeigarnik effect. "Problem" tasks, requiring the development of patterns of behavior not already in the subject's response repertoire, were used rather than the more typical "performance" tasks, in which already established responses are simply run off (e.g., naming cities or book authors, connecting scattered dots by pencil line, crossing out letters), so that learning would be more clearly involved in the task behaviors.

In the first study (Bottenberg, Marx, & Pavur, 1976), reliably more clues than problem names were recalled, and in both cases, there was greater recall following solution than nonsolution of the tasks. More important, there was a reliable interaction between the two variables, so that although only a slightly greater proportion of completed problem names was recalled, a very marked increase in recall of selected clues occurred.

The second study (Marx, Pavur, & Seymour, 1977) used the same experimental design but new problem tasks, 28 five-letter anagram words—problems—that were to be transformed into new anagrams—solutions—with the aid of associated-word clues; the clue was to be combined with the solution so as to produce a colloquial expression (e.g., "cheap skate," "lost cause"). These more homogeneous materials permitted better control of time of task presentation and timing of the interruption. One new variable (set) was added; half the college-student subjects were told to expect a recall test and half were not so informed.

In general the results replicated those of the earlier study. Both kinds of words from solved problems were recalled more often, and more clue than problem words were recalled. Problem words were recalled equally well for solved and unsolved tasks, but again, clue words from solved tasks were recalled much more frequently. Although the main effect of set was not reliable, the word-by-set interaction was reliable, with subjects in the incidental-learning group recalling reliably more clues than subjects in the intentional-learning group and the latter recalling slightly more problem words.

It seems clear enough from these two experiments that under the conditions used, the names of successful secondary instructions (clues) are better recalled, whereas there is no tendency for task (problem) names themselves to be better recalled after task interruption (incompletion).

Whether these results can be interpreted in terms of depth of processing (Craik & Lockhart, 1972) or the more recently emphasized elaboration or spread of processing (Craik & Tulving, 1975) needs to be determined on the basis of more specifically designed research. This is also true for the failure of the Zeigarnik effect to occur even for problem names. In any case, the results can be viewed as supporting the proposition that the names of successful instrumental activities (clues) are more likely to be recalled than the names of either unsuccessful instrumental activities or the names of the problems, whether solved or not.

Theoretical Implications.   In this section we described a number of published and unpublished studies relating to the role of reward in human selective learning. Here some of the more immediate aspects of their theoretical implications are treated before our attention returns to certain of the broader issues involving verbal report, motivation, reward, and learning.

With respect to the acquisition data, it is apparent that the cited experiments have provided little in the way of support for the proposition that learning with reward is different from learning by information alone. Certainly some of the differences that have appeared can be attributed to differential learning strategies. The initial superiority of observational learning emphasized in cognitive interpretation (Hillix & Marx, 1960), for example, was very likely due, in large part if not entirely, to the much greater opportunity for rehearsal of correct responses afforded the observer (because the performer was distracted by the extra requirements of his task, especially when more extended behavior was involved in the making of the response).

In all the later work, however, wherever differences occurred, they have favored the performer. But even in these cases, the role of reward is questionable because of the fact that, typically, the increased tendency to repeat rewarded responses was accompanied by a similarly increased tendency to repeat nonrewarded responses in performance. The implication here is that the making of the response itself is somehow reinforcing, without the need to invoke any role for reward, suggesting, rather, a combination of a kind of self-determination factor and perhaps frequency of occurrence. Marlatt (1972) has reviewed evidence from the clinical literature that also suggests greater stability for responses that are actually performed.

The theoretical significance, if any, of the gradual development of greater correct-response repetition by performers is not entirely clear, but it is possible that whatever behavioral processes occur with rewarding feedback of the kind used in these studies are cumulatively more effective in establishing S–R connections than is information.

The theoretical implications of the result described from the Marx and Conover (In preparation) study is potentially more important. This is the reliably greater repetition of correct responses, relative to the changing of errors (where correct and incorrect signals were equally informative, in the binary situation), that occurred for performers but not for observers. The theoretical suggestion is that directly rewarded responses were more strengthened, and increasingly so over trials, than were "observed" correct responses, relative to the degree to which incorrect responses were varied on test trials. These data are important because they are not subject to the criticism that Nuttin and Greenwald (1968, Chapter 5 and Appendix, p. 173) have made of the typical experiment demonstrating superior learning after symbolic "reward" compared to symbolic "punishment." This criticism points to the fact that in such experiments, subjects are more motivated to retain rewarded responses, so that there is a built-in bias in favor of rewarded-response repetition when it is compared with error repetition. Performers and observers are equivalent in this respect.

All in all, the acquisition data are seen as comfortably congruent with the negative results of various of the other experiments recently reported to test the same general proposition (Estes, 1969; Nuttin & Greenwald, 1968, p. 160ff), at least until more definitive data of the type reported by Marx and Conover (In preparation) are available.

However, the negative tone of this conclusion needs to be tempered by the fact that, as already mentioned, our initial purpose in setting up this line of research was to test for transfer rather than acquisition effects. And when the transfer results are considered, a somewhat more favorable picture emerges. Both the Hillix and Marx (1960) and the Marx and Witter (1972) studies found reliably greater transfer after performance. Some evidence is thereby available that rewarded responses operate more strongly, when called upon to provide new patterns of behavior in transfer-type situations. The more recent experiments, run under the personality-evaluation cover (Marx, 1978; Marx & Marx, 1978), also yielded partially positive results, interesting and suggestive in their own right in spite of the preliminary character of the research. The affective transfer that they seem to demonstrate is similar to certain earlier reported results. Association of neutral objects with rewards has been reported to increase children's positive verbal evaluation as well as their selected attention and their expectation of reward in a new game (Nunnally, Duchnowski, & Parker, 1965; Nunnally, Stevens, & Hall, 1965).

When these various positive transfer results are placed alongside the even more clearly positive retention results of the clue-reinforcement experiments in the Zeigarnik-effect setting, a definitely more suggestive theoretical picture begins to emerge. Implication of some kind of effective role for reward appears to be a theoretical problem once more worthy of serious consideration. Particularly noteworthy is the fact that reliably more successful clues were recalled in the absence of instructions that there would be a recall test (Marx, Pavur, & Seymour, 1977). Greenwald (Nuttin & Greenwald, 1968, p. 159) has pointed out the "decisive" role of any demonstration of greater learning after reward in cued incidental learning, which is functionally equivalent to a "closed" task. Nuttin (Nuttin & Greenwald, 1968, p. 66ff) has allowed for the role of reward in helping to establish chains of goal-directed behavior, but only in a subsidiary, if important, role (i.e., in conjunction with on-going motivations and not as an independent reinforcer in anything like the Thorndikean sense). The data that he has reported are quite consistent with this provocative formulation; rewarded responses are better recalled only when subjects have reason to anticipate their future utility (i.e., in the "open" set) and not otherwise (closed set). But the instrumental meaningfulness of the clues in our experiments, as crucial aids in problem-solving tasks, would seem to be appreciably greater than that provided in the more traditional memorization tasks; the resulting difference in effectiveness of the reward process may account for the different results in the two sets of studies.

LIMITATIONS OF COGNITIVE THEORY

Human selective learning is quite clearly a prime example of cognitive functioning. The information-processing model that has recently been so effectively applied to this problem, obviously describes the way in which the human organism can function, and typically does function in the kind of multiple-choice task that Thorndike developed, as well as a large number of other tasks and situations.

Granted that human learners are superb information processors, however, must one then conclude that this is all there is to the story? If cognitive processes are as all powerful as suggested, not only by some cognitive theorists themselves but also by certain of the experimental results cited earlier, why is it necessary to continue to examine the role of other factors in human learning and memory? Should we not simply accept their influence as sufficiently documented and proceed to investigate the ways in which cognitions operate to fixate responses in human learning?

Well, hardly, in my view, at least not quite yet. Although there can be no doubt as to the power of cognitive processes, in "higher" organisms especially, of course, but also even in lower ones, in varying degrees, there are nevertheless some very good reasons for doubting that cognition is such an all-powerful process. Here we consider certain of the features of cognitive theories applied to human learning that are most open to criticism (notably, their overly rational orientation, with the apparent assumption of dichotomous rather than continuous underlying functions and their dependence on some form of verbal report of conscious processes), as well as certain commonplace observations that indicate very clearly the limitations of cognitively focused factors in determining some behaviors.

Commonplace Observations of Cognitive Insufficiency

Starting with the last of the conditions listed previously, one can readily point to a number of familiar illustrations of the failure of cognitive factors to effect desired behavioral changes. The sometimes ineffectual role of cognitively mediated motivational factors in learning is dramatically indicated by some strongly entrenched habits that have proved to be totally resistant, in many instances, to modification by cognitive means: Witness, most notably, cigarette smoking, drug and alcohol intake, and simpler, less directly "physiological" habits like nail-biting, thumb-sucking, head-scratching, or any of a host of less obvious but nonetheless persistent, idiosyncratic personal habits that each of us develops—and often finds very difficult indeed to change, in spite of strong intentions to do so. Although some of these habits (e.g., cigarette smoking) are apparently learned under cognitive controls, many of them are not. As a matter of fact, we are very often unaware of their existence, until they are pointed out to us by others (Duncan & Fiske, 1979).

Because the more dramatic of these habits (e.g., drug or alcohol addiction) are obviously related to powerful physiological mechanisms, the relevance of ordinary, more strictly behavioral processes in them, as alternatives or complements to cognitions, may be questioned. Recent research on drug addiction, however, has given very clear evidence of the central role played by learning. For example, Siegel (Siegel, 1975, 1976, 1977; Siegel, Hinson, & Frank, 1978) has shown that morphine tolerance (and hence addiction) in laboratory rats is highly specific to the particular environment in which the drug has been administered and is readily interpretable in terms of classical conditioning principles. Strongly suggestive evidence in support of this kind of learning component in human drug addiction, in which cognitive processes may be more confidently assumed to operate, is also available in the clinical literature (Cochin, 1972; Levine, 1974; Wikler, 1973). Thus it seems safe to conclude that it is not simply pharmacological processes that compete with cognition in these illustrations but also noncognitive types of learning processes whose complementary operation needs to be related to the cognitive processes themselves, as well as the physiological mechanisms.

Relationship Between Cognitive and Noncognitive Processes

The human-learner model employed in recent cognitive theories is clearly an extremely rational one. As long as this model is restricted to informational learning tasks of the sort we have been considering, the fit is more than adequate; in intellectual games of this sort, the human learner, and especially the college student who is the typical subject used, is a sharply honed information-processing machine ideally suited to this kind of task. By the same token, human selective learning offers an especially rigorous test of other, noncognitive factors, as we have already seen.

However, even if wholly rational cognitive processes are sufficient to account for much of human verbal and symbolic learning, requiring no special input from reward or other form of reinforcement factors, then how is one to explain their failure to account for other behavioral phenomena? Are entirely different principles needed, as Nuttin (1973) has seemed to suggest in his drawing a clear distinction between cognitive and noncognitive functions? Nuttin's position is explicit. He has stated:

> The cognitive type of learning just described is not the only way in which man learns: It is the way in which *information* is acquired.... Important other things to be learned are directly related to the response side of behavior....[And he continues] It should be emphasized that cognitive or noncognitive learning processes are not to be considered as two separate ways in which man acquires new behavioral forms of dealing with objects. Both processes contribute in variable doses—according to the cognitive development of the living being involved, and his actual state of cognitive alertness or vigilance—to the man's progressive building of his behavioral and cognitive repertoire [p. 267–268].

The implication in this last quotation is, again, clearly that the human organism is, first and foremost, a highly rational cognitive learner and performer—note the qualification concerning "alertness or vigilance"—and that the extent of the contribution of noncognitive factors is determined by the level of cognitive activity. This may well be, certainly under some conditions, but even this position appears to give insufficient recognition to the role of motivation. As one British reviewer (Claxton, 1978) has recently noted: "The goal of forming a meaningful representation of the world is subordinate to the goal of doing something about it. And as long as cognitive modellers ignore their behaviourist colleagues' concern with action and its consequences, their products will remain fundamentally incomplete [p. 514]."

Other relationships between cognitive and noncognitive factors may be conceived. For example, in the habit-activation conceptualization, to be described, it is not necessary to make a priori theoretical decisions ordering the various determinants of habit activation; rather, because they all funnel into a single activating mechanism, questions of relative importance and the interactions among the determinants are best left to further empirical research. This more flexible theoretical framework has the advantage of providing what seems to me a better balance between cognitive and noncognitive processes than the typical cognitive position.

Veridicality of Verbal Reports

Among the advantages afforded by the use of human organisms is the fact
that such subjects have the ability to provide the researcher with copious
amounts of verbal reports that presumably more or less directly reflect the
crucial cognitive functions that are assumed to be responsible for so much of
his learning and overt behavior. Indeed, it is the readily elicited verbal report
that offers promise of being an essential measure in the cognitive theories that
have become the predominant force in contemporary interpretations of
human learning. Granted this special status of the verbal report, some serious
questions may be raised concerning the extent to which cognitive theory may
reasonably be expected to incorporate learning phenomena in the light of the
current controversy over the veridicality of verbal reports.

The recent sweeping attack by Nisbett and Wilson (1977; Wilson & Nisbett,
1978) on verbal reports as accurate reflections of underlying cognitive
functions has been answered by Smith and Miller (1978) and Ericsson and
Simon (1980). There is no room in this chapter for anything like an adequate
consideration of this fundamental methodological issue, but certain observations most pertinent to the present problem may be made.

The arguments and data advanced by Nisbett and Wilson do not appear to
be directly relevant to the cognitive theories of human selective learning, at
least in the way in which these theories have thus far been empirically tested;
that is to say, the kind of inaccuracies and omissions noted in verbal reports
do not apply to the relatively simple and straightforward recall of responses
and their outcomes in the typical multiple-choice research situation. Nevertheless, if Nisbett and Wilson are correct in their contention that higher
mental processes are often not directly accessible to introspection and thus
are not available for verbal report, judgment must be reserved as to whether
human learners can be depended on to identify sources of response
strengthening in any but the simplest situations.

The reasons subjects give for their judgments and choices in more complex
situations are especially prone to omission of demonstrably potent conditions
and dependence on culturally prescribed rules and practices. It is in such
situations that the usefulness of introspective reports, and perhaps also the
sufficiency of cognitive theory, can be most seriously questioned. Moreover,
these questions pose equal risks for the kind of explicitly rational account of
motivation that Nuttin (1973, 1976), for example, has proposed. Although
Nuttin has qualified his cognitive theory (Nuttin & Greenwald, 1968) by
conceding that: "cognitive elaboration of needs does not necessarily imply
clear awareness [p. 12, footnote]," it is nonetheless very difficult to see how
strict cognitive accountability for motivational systems can be long maintained once such exceptions are admitted.

The problem of defining cognition is particularly relevant to any discussion
of the issues under consideration. One may define cognition narrowly, in

terms of consciousness and related verbal report; this is more or less the way in which the term seems to be implicitly implemented in the typical cognitive theories of human learning that have been considered (Buchwald, 1969; Estes, 1969; Nuttin & Greenwald, 1968). But it is also possible to define cognition more broadly, so as not to restrict the term to mental processes accompanied by verbal reports. Because of the continuity between conscious and unconscious processes, if for no other reason, the broader definition would certainly seem to be a more reasonable procedure. This kind of continuity has been emphasized, in the formalization of the commonsensical notion that consciousness is active in the early phases of learning but decreases and eventually disappears as tasks become highly routinized (Schank & Abelson, 1977; Schneider & Shiffrin, 1977). The role of unconscious functions in cognitive processing is nicely indicated by Marcel's (1978) demonstration of "unconscious reading"; semantic processing is evidenced even when the subject is unable to identify masked words tachistoscopically presented.

On the basis of these various kinds of evidence, there is little reason for restricting cognitive processes to conscious events. But then it is important that conclusions based on such a broad definition of cognition, one that includes unconscious processes, not be carelessly transferred to propositions incorporating, implicitly, a definition relating the term strictly to conscious processes and verbal reports on such. Moreover, once conscious or verbal reports are removed as necessary indicators of cognition, the door is clearly opened to the acceptance of other, more general types of learning and performance (motivational) factors, such as the habit-activation construct next to be considered, that can hardly be considered cognitive in the narrow sense.

HABIT AND HABIT ACTIVATION:
A RECONCEPTUALIZATION

Habit-Activation Construct

The core of the present proposal is that we need to conceive of: (1) *habit,* or the S–R connection; and (2) *habit activation,* or the contemporary strength of the S–R relationship, as independently generated and separately manipulable functions. In accordance with the orthodox cognitive and certain of the S–R viewpoints (Guthrie, 1959), habit is simply assumed to be established by contiguity alone. This contiguity is between some form of stimulus and response components but can be cognitively—imaginatively—as well as physically—behaviorally—mediated. Habit activation is also multiply determined. Once established, however weakly, a habit, as here conceived, can be activated or energized by cognitive ("voluntary") processes alone—so strongly, as a matter of fact, that there is really no need to look for any immediate noncognitive determinants. And, more or less in accordance with traditional S-R reinforcement theory, a habit can be energized by behavioral events, such as reward—also so strongly, as a matter of fact, that the response is highly probable in the appropriate stimulus situation with or without conscious accompaniment.

From an orthodox theoretical point of view, this proposal of a single basic mechanism (habit activation) for response strengthening may be related to the long-accepted distinction between learning and performance. First emphasized by Tolman, who in turn credited Blodgett, and, earlier, Lashley (Tolman, 1959, p. 149), that distinction focused on the *consummatory* motivation of the organism and showed it to be a crucial determinant in the expression of learning; in other words, how much learning is evidenced in behavior (performance) depends not only on the degree of learning itself but also on how strongly the learner is motivated to perform. In a somewhat similar way, the present proposal focuses on *instrumental* learning and motivation. It holds that no matter how strongly a given habit or S-R connection has been expressed in the past, its present expression depends on the contemporary level of activation. It differs from the traditional learning–performance dichotomy, however, in that it refers not to the motivation of the organism but rather to the degree of activation of particular habits.

By accepting both cognitive and behavioral (reinforcement) determinants, the habit-activation model invites not only the separate investigation of each of these types of factors, as has been traditional in learning research, but also and more meaningfully, the experimental analysis of their interaction. Historically, most if not all of the variation underlying performance differences has been assigned to the habit construct itself. This general practice has had the effect of sharpening the distinction between S-R and cognitive theoretical orientations and by the same token of course has rendered their integration more difficult.

The important theoretical question is how a given instrumental habit is activated so as to be behaviorally expressed. It is not hard to understand why subjects with good memory retrieval of previously made responses with clear-cut outcomes repeat rewarded ones and vary incorrect ones. But when there are substantial gaps or rips in the cognitive fabric or when emotional factors are deliberately or otherwise introduced, the task of the experimenter and the theorist is much more difficult, albeit perhaps more interesting and challenging. Understanding why particular instrumental habits are now less likely to be demonstrated, in spite of high levels of prior acquisition, depends on how well we are able to pinpoint specific activation agents and their interaction.

Theoretical Advantages of Habit Activation

A major theoretical advantage of the proposed model is the common conceptual framework afforded both cognitive and noncognitive behavioral processes. With this kind of framework assumed, there is no longer any need to continue to lay down special conditions and qualifications of the sort that has so long plagued us. There is, for example, no need to argue for or against the "automaticity" of reward; rather, experimental investigations of the various types of determinants of activation of habits are needed. Apparent automaticity, when it occurs, is seen as resulting from minimal involvement of conscious factors and maximal influence of reward, or some other mechanism that is nonconscious (but not necessarily noncognitive, depending of course on one's definitional preferences). Freed from doctrinaire shackles (the need to push for data against an opposing doctrine), protagonists can turn their attention and their conceptual, theoretical, and experimental ingenuity more directly to a host of challenging problems, some of which are subsequently described in this chapter.

At first glance, this compromise proposal may seem to be an attempt to have one's cake and eat it at the same time. In some respects it *is* just that. It is a release from decades of doctrinaire argumentation, from one side or the other of the dispute between cognitivists and reinforcement theorists based in each instance on the selective viewing, often with obvious theoretical blinders, of the wealth of contrary empirical evidence that has been accumulated over the decades.

On the positive side, however, the proposal is more than a mere compromise. It is, in my view, an attempt to represent, as fairly as possible, the legitimate claims of these two traditionally opposed points of view. Moreover, the apparent simplicity of its single basic motivational mechanism (the elevation or reduction in activation level for particular habits) is deceptive; it not only offers a realistic picture of learning and performance through a very wide range of organisms but also provides a conceptual framework that can be just as stimulating of experimental research as the more traditional theoretical viewpoints. The remaining sections of this chapter are devoted to a detailed exposition of the more salient features of the habit-activation model and its major theoretical implications, with reference to its implications for past and future research problems.

Determinants of Habit Activation

Let us start with what is probably the most immediate question, that of the determinants of habit activation. A guiding principle in answering this question is that there is really no need for any radically new sources of evidence.

Primacy and Recency.   The familar phenomena of primacy and recency offer as good a starting point as any. Superior recall of the first and last items in a list or set is so commonplace an event that experimenters routinely place buffer items, not to be scored, in these positions. A fairly obvious interpretation of recency effects is in terms of differential dissipation of hypothesized memory traces, at least for relatively short time intervals between study and test. But primacy effects are not quite so readily interpreted. For a first approximation, primacy is probably best understood in terms of the special attention and correspondingly greater amounts of processing received by introductory items. In this respect, primacy is similar to other especially potent learning and memory determinants, such as the von Restorff effect (Wallace, 1965), in which items that are somehow "isolated" are more readily recalled.

Frequency.   The frequency with which a given S–R relationship has occurred seems to be a prime determinant of its contemporary strength, or in present terms, degree of habit activation. In everday life, we are all familiar with many highly stereotyped response patterns, in ourselves and (sometimes more clearly noted) in others. These are most obvious when they occur as idiosyncratic behaviors, which are too commonplace to require illustration.

In laboratory studies, nevertheless, frequency as a determinant of response strength has proved to be a surprisingly elusive factor to test. The difficulty is produced by the need to dissociate the frequency variable per se from its normal links with information processing and other sources of reinforcement. In recent verbal-learning research, this objective has been achieved by the use of incidental-learning designs. Retention of items presented with no instructions that they should be learned is measured as a function of the number of such occurrences of the items.

A recent experiment of this kind has been reported by Cowan (in press). Following semantic processing of items (judgment of "good" or "bad"), recall increased reliably with number of word presentations for delayed as well as immediate tests, and incidental learning was not reliably different from intentional learning.

In a recent comprehensive critique of the influential depth-of-processing view (Craik & Lockhart, 1972), Nelson (1977) has focused on the presumption that repetition without further processing does not facilitate memory. Results contrary to this presumption were reported in three experiments involving structural processing, and earlier reported failures to show such positive results were questioned on methodological grounds.

Other recent experiments have utilized a different technique within the incidental-learning paradigm. Subjects are instructed to learn a set of digits. They are also instructed to repeat some given word at a regular rate after the digits are presented, ostensibly to prevent digit rehearsal during the time interval. The time interval is varied systematically so as to manipulate the item frequency variable. Then, after the anticipated retention test for the digits, the subjects are given unexpected retention tests of the words that they had repeated. The general results of this kind of "distractor recall test" (Glenberg & Adams, 1978; Glenberg, Smith, & Green, 1977; Rundus, 1977) are that retention is a function of frequency of repetition of the distractor words when the measure is recognition but not when it is recall.

Extension of the repetition-memory effect to recall is suggested by the results of Cowan's most recent experiment (Cowan, personal communication, 1979). In that study, repetition (two occurrences versus one) reliably improved both recall and recognition under severely "impoverished" learning conditions (incidental learning of briefly exposed nonsense syllables, a strictly structural task, and interpolated arithmetic problems to eliminate recency effects).

In sum, these results suggest that the frequency with which a given response occurs is a determinant of its strength or probability of subsequent identification, at least as far as typical memory tests are concerned. If these results can be extrapolated to the habit-activation construct on the grounds that the retention test constitutes a measure of response strength, then frequency of occurrence can be regarded as an effective determinant of habit activation.

An important by-product of frequency, *familiarity,* is one of the more neglected sources of habit activation. Familiar objects, events, and surroundings are potent reinforcers. Although this is probably as true for humans as for lower organisms, an illustration from rodent behavior is instructive. Given the opportunity, laboratory rats, like some of their nonlaboratory counterparts, show an enormous amount of hoarding behavior—repeatedly carrying back to the home–cage food pellets (or other objects) in quantities far greater than can be very soon consumed. But this behavior develops only if the home cage is really and truly "home" to the rat. And "hominess" to the rat is, apparently, primarily a matter of smell. Thus, if the old shavings are replaced by new, aseptic shavings, the typical rat will not hoard. (see Marx, 1950, for a review and some interpretation.)

How far the familiarity determinant can be pushed as an explanatory factor in human learning has not been intensively pursued, but common observation suggests that it is by no means an unimportant determinant.

Reward. For present purposes, reward as a process may be briefly defined as the satisfaction of some motive. A distinction must be drawn between extrinsic reward, such as food or a passing mark in a college course or a college degree, all of which are consummatory-type satisfactions (that is, ultimate behavioral objectives in their own right) and the kind of reward that is more appropriately related to instrumental responses. Instrumental satisfaction may be generally identified as either: (1) the continuation of the goal-directed chain of behavior, permitting subsequent instrumental responses to be made; or (2) the consummatory behaviors themselves, at the end of the instrumental chain.

The line between instrumental and consummatory satisfactions, as defined previously, is not always easy to make or maintain. The major reason for this difficulty is that clearly instrumental behaviors can also have—or develop—consummatory properties. Consider the passing mark in a course; is this more of an instrumental satisfaction because it permits the continued progress toward the college degree and a subsequent career, or is it more of a consummatory satisfaction because it is obviously an objective? Or, more at hand, consider the symbolic reward mediated by the "right" signal in a human learning task of the Thorndikean multiple-choice variety; is this more appropriately regarded as instrumental because it contributes to the overall performance level, or an objective in its own right? Obviously many such objectives have both instrumental and consummatory properties, and no hard and fast distinction can be readily made. (For an especially perceptive discussion of this general problem see Nuttin, 1976). In any event, whether there is any important difference between these two types of reward with respect to the elevation of the instrumental habit-activation factor, and more generally whether there are any effects of reward that cannot be reasonably attributed to information processing, remains to be determined by appropriately designed experimentation.

Cognition.   Within the currently popular information-processing framework, and particularly within the depth-of-processing version of this framework, the cognitive elaboration of perceptual processing is the primary, if not the exclusive determinant of memory and, consequently, response strength. The various recent demonstrations of the powerful role that cognitive processes can play in human selective learning (Buchwald, 1969; Estes, 1969; Nuttin & Greenwald, 1968) leave no doubt of the effectiveness of this kind of determinant.

Although the role of cognition has been most often related to the information-processing procedure, as exemplified in the typical learning experiment where the informational role of reward is demonstrated, it should be noted that implicit verbal processes may also play a much broader role in directing explicit verbalization and other overt behaviors. In other words, any of the determinants of habit activation described earlier can be overriden by deliberate conscious intentions. Moreover, there are various other experimental reports that indicate the effective way in which cognitive processes interact with reward, as in "insight" learning by infrahuman organisms (Tolman & Honzik, 1930). But these facts should not be construed as indicative of absolute supremacy of cognitive processes over all others, even in selective learning and other symbolically mediated behavior. There is much other evidence, such as that discussed earlier, that suggests just as clearly that there are serious limitations to the role of conscious factors. We may conclude that cognition, powerful as it can be in human behavior, is by no means the exclusive determinant of habit activation.

Key Theoretical Issues

At this point, it might be well to make explicit certain questions concerning the relationship between the habit and habit-activation constructs that may have been raised for some readers. For example, if the various determinants described previously directly affect habit activation, do they also somehow affect habit? In other words, how do habits gain increased strength? Or, more specifically, does habit itself change over trials and events as a function of habit activation, or habit performance?

A tentative start at answering these questions may be made. It seems clear that the habit-activation factor is especially important during the early phases of learning, whereas the habit itself is not well developed. Later, after a strongly entrenched habit has developed, the habit-activation factor may play a much less significant role. In other words, the strongest habits appear to be activated on a kind of all-or-none basis, given appropriate stimulating conditions. Our individual habits of speech and thought, for example, once well established, tend not to be differentially activated by the same conditions that during their earlier development were effective.

More definitive answers to such questions raised by the present formulation must await the accumulation of a great deal of specifically designed research. The purpose of the present chapter is to suggest a new framework for thinking on these fundamental theoretical issues and thereby encourage the kind of experimentation that makes possible more satisfactory answers.

It is not my intention to try to provide anything more than the most tentative suggestions of lines along which such answers might profitably be sought. The theoretical tone of this chapter has therefore been kept relatively loose, with the tightening of theoretical formulations deliberately left to the future.

Research Problems

In line with the immediately preceding paragraph, this section considers some contemporary research areas that have special significance for the habit-activation model. Although space restrictions limit the number of topics that can be treated, there is some sampling of relevant contemporary research within the information-processing framework.

Because of the overwhelmingly powerful role played by conscious cognitive functions in ordinary information processing and retrieval, it may not be possible to detect the more subtle reinforcement effects, such as those possibly initiated by reward, unless special experimental conditions are imposed. These conditions might well include very brief (tachistoscopic), masked, distorted, or incomplete presentation of cues, requiring either very rapid responses so as to minimize, if not eliminate, normal cognitive activities or encourage the substitution of nonconsciously directed responses for such normal cognitive processes. In responding quickly to cues, subjects may well be expected to reveal differential response strengths that are normally overshadowed, much as free association tests can reveal relationships that ordinary cognitive processes apparently obscure. Such further experimental tests, within the framework of reaction time and vigilance tasks, are now being conducted in my laboratory. Direct instigation of habit activation, by means of differential go–no go instructions in the reaction time situation, is also under investigation. The results of these preliminary experiments directly attacking the core habit-activation construct should indicate its theoretical life expectancy as well as its more immediate heuristic value in stimulating experimental research.

Coding of Habit Activation. If not much in the way of new principles seems necessary, at least at this time, for the detection of the major determinants of the habit-activation construct, the same thing can certainly not be said for the problem of coding. Indeed, the central problem posed by the introduction of the habit-activation construct is how it is encoded, particularly with respect to the encoding of the habit factor itself, and how the two components are decoded so as to produce the responses that identify learning. If the model is accepted, as at least a provisional basis for research, it suggests a number of what seem to me interesting and testable experimental issues.

With respect to the primary question of how the activation and habit components of an S–R relationship are related in coding, it is necessary that habit-activation strength be independent of habit, or association potential. Indeed, the need for flexibility in S–R strength, as in the interpretation of extinction data, was the initial impetus for the development of the construct (Marx, 1966). Experiments in which the S–R relationships are first establish-ed, and then their value or applicability in test situations is differentially manipulated, as by rewards or instructions, are indicated.

Another central coding problem for the habit-activation hypothesis is how the different levels of activation are marked or indicated in a particular S–R association. Lowering of a high habit-activation level by extinction and rapid renewal of extinction-reduced levels by new reinforcement (Bunch, 1963) are among the common phenomena that require explanation. One way to handle these questions is to posit a high degree of stimulus specificity in the encoding operation, as by the development of elaborated stimuli by various discrimina-tive, occasion-setting cues as markers for different levels and types of habit activation.

Fisher and Craik (1977) have asked how a "strength" type of memory-trace notion, such as Wickelgren's (1970), can handle the retrieval results they found as a function of different retrieval environments. One answer is by adopting the specificity of the stimulus element in the S–R relationship. Although the Fisher and Craik results may be difficult for any fixed-strength view of the memory trace to handle, they can be readily accommodated within the present conceptual framework by relating different levels of habit activation to the various stimulus refinements in the experimental environments.

Nilsson (1976) has reported an interesting demonstration that responses are learned equally well when followed by monetary gains or losses and symbolic ("right" or "wrong") outcomes. Nilsson also found, however, that retrieval was more affected by symbolic outcomes, suggesting a greater amount of information processing. That more processing activity occurred with symbolic outcomes was also indicated by the poorer retention found for the responses immediately following the better remembered positive outcomes. This result, which was interpreted as reflecting the reduced time available for processing items that followed highly processed items, confirmed an earlier report (Cohen & Nilsson, 1974).

It should be noted that monetary rewards and penalties in Nilsson's (1976) study were not response contingent (i.e., they were given independently of the particular responses made). This fact places the experiment in a different conceptual context from the typical design in which response-contingent consequences are used.

Because of the difficulty Nilsson's (1976) subjects had in remembering response outcomes, he interpreted his results as contradicting Buchwald's (1969) hypothesis that outcomes are encoded along with responses. Similar difficulties in recalling outcomes compared to responses had earlier been reported by Nuttin and Greenwald (1968) and Longstreth (1971).

These difficulties in recalling outcomes relative to responses suggest that, for whatever reason (e.g., insufficient attention and processing, especially to be expected when outcomes are not response contingent), outcomes typically operate by directly elevating or depressing the activation level associated with habits and are not independently encoded to the same extent as responses. In any event, further analysis of behavioral differences resulting from symbolic and nonsymbolic outcomes, with special attention to determination of retrieval as well as encoding variations, seems to be one of the more fruitful directions that future research should follow.

Directed Forgetting.   In all the burgeoning research on human memory, there is probably no phenomenon that, on its face at least, seems to be more immediately relevant to the habit-activation proposal than directed forgetting. Subjects instructed to remember or to forget individual items, *after* they are presented for processing, are generally able to discriminate on subsequent tests between the to-be-remembered (TBR) and to-be-forgotten

(TBF) items. For example, Woodward and Bjork (1971) found that even when the TBR and TBF items were presented very haphazardly and rapidly, so as to prevent rehearsal and organization into categories, subjects were still able to remember about one-half of the TBR items with only 2 or 3% of the TBF items intruding. This ability suggests that positive ("remember") and negative ("forget") tags are directly applied to individual memory traces, more or less as hypothesized by the habit-activation proposal.

On the basis of several other studies showing even more impressive differentiation between TBR and TBF items achieved in spite of especially complex and difficult processing conditions, Bjork and Geiselman (1978) concluded that Bjork's (1972) interpretation of directed forgetting in terms of selective rehearsal and selective grouping was incomplete. The results of their three experiments led them somewhat reluctantly to state that at least part of the "missing mechanism" consists of differential tagging of TBR and TBF items. Bjork and Geiselman (1978) have stated: "For the moment, it appears that we are stuck with the tagging hypothesis [p. 356]." The "compelling evidence" that forced this conclusion was the continued finding of end-of-list discrimination between TBR and TBF items in two carefully controlled experiments even when there were no differences in subsequent recall or recognition tests between the same TBR and TBF items. Bjork and Geiselman were apparently a little more comfortable with the tagging hypothesis because of earlier results reported by MacLeod (1975): Subjects were able to discriminate TBR and TBF items on a recognition test administered a full 2 weeks after acquisition.

From the present point of view, the remember tag produces an elevation in the habit-activation level of TBR items, and conversely the forget tag a lowering of that level for the TBF items. Because the remember and forget instructions are provided after presentation and presumed initial processing of TBR and TBF items, and in the Bjork and Geiselman experiments also came after one or more arithmetic problems administered to prevent further rehearsal or other processing, differential processing of items during the study trial cannot readily be used to explain the end-of-list discriminability in recall. Moreover, the fact that equivalent final levels of retention were subsequently found for TBR and TBF items, in both recall and recognition tests, strengthens the argument by showing the essential equivalence of the "habit" components. Perhaps this generalized explanation renders the tagging hyothesis less objectionable because of its apparent "magical" character to researchers such as Bjork and Geiselman. In any event, the directed-forgetting phenomenon appears to provide a fruitful problem for future investigation of the habit-activation hypothesis, which in one form or another should certainly be considered as a potential explanatory factor in this kind of research.

Processing of Positive Versus Negative Responses.   A number of recent experiments, conducted within the framework of information processing, have shown very clearly that positive responses (i.e., "Yes") are better remembered than negative responses (Brimer & Mueller, 1979; Coltheart, 1977; Fisher & Craik, 1977; Glanzer & Ehrenreich, 1979; Goldman & Pellegrino, 1977; Morris, Bransford, & Franks, 1977; Moscovitch & Craik, 1976; Schulman, 1971, 1974).

Because a positive response would normally be expected to induce an elevation in any associated action tendency, this surprisingly robust result appears to offer, on its face at least, support for the habit-activation hypothesis. It is therefore examined in some detail.

The Craik and Tulving (1975) study, consisting of a series of 10 separate experiments, is the most elaborate of the cited reports. The typical procedure they used was first to pose a question requiring some degree of processing and then show a word cue that elicited either a positive or a negative answer. Three general levels of processing were used: (1) structural: "Is the word printed in capital letters?"; (2) phonemic: "Does the word rhyme with_____?"; and (3) semantic: "Is the word an animal name?". In general, these experiments showed a consistent superiority in retention of cue words that elicited positive answers, especially for semantically processed cues.

Craik and Tulving interpret these results in terms of the congruency principle earlier advanced by Schulman (1974) to explain similar results. In brief, the congruency view is that positive answers provide a more integrated or compatible whole that is more readily retrieved. However, the only experimental results presented by Craik and Tulving directly in support of this notion is an experiment (Experiment 6) in which greater or lesser than comparisons were involved; a slight nonreliable difference (39% compared to 36% recall probabilities) in favor of the negative responses occurred. It should be noted that this procedure confounded the yes/no answer dimension with the greater/lesser than comparison, which can also be considered as a positive (greater) versus negative (lesser) dimension. The experimenters did not report any analysis of the recall data in terms of the greater/lesser variable, and these results are therefore somewhat suspect. Moreover, their conclusion that the results demonstrate the preeminent role of spread or elaboration of processing rather than the positive/negative variable, is seriously weakened by the data of their own Experiment 7: Positive and negative responses were varied over 3 degrees of sentence complexity, but the greater degree of elaboration benefitted only the positive responses.

A second type of cognitive interpretation of the greater recallability of positive responses is suggested by Glanzer and Ehrenreich (1979). They found that true sentences were recalled more often than false sentences and interpret this result as due to the double encoding of true sentences. Both truths and falsehoods have episodic representation, but only truths provide new markers for semantic memory (e.g., for the true proposition that a camel is an animal, in contrast to the false proposition, not in semantic memory, that a camel is a machine). This reasonable suggestion clearly merits independent experimental test. In an earlier study, Glanzer and Koppenaal (1977) found that their living–nonliving classification yielded a memory advantage for living instances, a fact that they interpreted as additional evidence for the superiority of positive over negative types of cues.

It is interesting but hardly surprising that no strength-type interpretation of the general advantage of positive over negative responses has yet appeared. From the present point of view, as suggested previously, this persistent advantage of positive responses may be readily interpreted in terms of differential habit activation tendencies. Positive responses are typically accompanied by the "go"-type cues, negative responses by no-go type (if not outright inhibition). Thus we may expect this persistent general tendency to provide a similarly persistent higher baseline of habit activation for positive responses.

The fact that Craik and Tulving report the yes/no difference only for the more highly processed (phonemic and semantic) yes responses is inconsistent with this interpretation, or at least with the most straightforward application of it to the present case. But Craik and Tulving's (1975) unqualified statement that: "positive and negative decisions are equally well retained after typescript judgments [p. 282]" may be questioned on the basis of their own data. It is true that no yes/no differences occurred in several of their experiments for the typescript judgment, but clear suggestions of advantages for the yes items did appear in several other experiments [Nos. 3, 4, 5, and 8; Fig. 3, p. 277; Fig. 4, p. 278; and Table 5, p. 286]. Moreover, in these experiments there was no interaction of the reliable yes/no variable and the task (type of processing) variable; this absence of a reliable interaction was explicitly stated for Experiment 5 [p. 281] and may be inferred in the other three cases because of the absence of any positive statement to the contrary.

An additional difference between the typescript items and the phonemic and semantic items has been noted by Postman (1976, p. 29). The same question was asked about all the typescript items ("Is the word printed in capital letters?"), whereas rhymes and categories tended to be more uniquely queried (e.g., "Does the word rhyme with TRAIN?"; "Is the word a type of FISH?"). The increased individuality of the phonemic and semantic items might, therefore, be expected to raise the general level of recallability and hence permit increased differentiation by the yes/no variable. The yes/no differences noted for the more poorly recalled typescript items in roughly half the experiments become even more meaningful in the light of this kind of floor effect.

The very substantial study by Goldman and Pellegrino (1977) provided some results indicating that, for recognition measures, positive decisions on orthographic (structural) and acoustic (phonemic) cues are better retained than negative. In fact, with single encodings, the advantage of positive over negative acoustic recognition scores exceeded the comparable semantic difference, and multiple encodings resulted in greater positive–negative differences for both orthographic and acoustic compared with semantic (Fig. 2, p. 35). Matlin and Stang (1978) have recently assembled a great variety of evidence in support of a "Pollyanna" (positive over negative) principle.

The generality of the habit-activation type of construct for positive–negative comparisons is suggested by some interesting results on latencies of responses to verbal stimuli. Although Craik and Tulving (1975) did not find any consistent differences in latencies of decisions for yes or no judgments, Osgood and Hoosain (Osgood, 1980) found that affectively positive words elicited faster vocal reactions (the statement "positive") than affectively negative words (the statement "negative"). This persistent difference was demonstrated for various lexical types (nouns, adjectives, verbs) and for 27 of 28 subjects in one of their "Pollyanna" experiments and for 16 of 18 subjects in a second experiment. The wide scope of the effect is also indicated by the fact that 53 of the items showed the predicted positive advantage compared with 12 exceptions (and 2 ties) in the first experiment, and 55 items conformed against seven exceptions (and 5 ties) in the second experiment.

One of the more interesting subeffects reported by Osgood concerns the fact that in the lexical breakdown, by far the greatest mean difference was observed for verbs (a whopping 170 milliseconds, with no item exceptions, as compared with mean differences of 29 milliseconds for nouns, with three exceptions, and 27 milliseconds for adjectives, with two exceptions). The great advantage shown for positively affective verbs is entirely consistent with the habit-activation proposition because of the obviously greater congruence between the action orientation in verb form and the habit-activation function. Whether or not this particular ad hoc application of the habit-activation hypothesis holds up in specific experimental tests remains to be seen, but it certainly seems to merit such a closer examination.

In sum, although this kind of linguistic research design is obviously tangential to the present problem, a clear-cut latency difference in favor of affectively positive cues is, at least, suggestive of a very broad occurrence in cognitive function of differential activation conditions of a sort postulated by the habit-activation proposal.

Interaction of Response Systems. The scope of the S and R components in habits is another important variable that needs to be experimentally manipulated. Interactions among response systems resulting from reward were theoretically suggested (Marx & Bunch, 1951) and empirically demonstrated (Marx & Bernstein, 1955a, 1955b) in my own laboratory. In the older experimental literature, there have been other hints that reinforcement produces more effective verbal-behavior transfer than verbal instructions. Masters and Branch (1969), for example, found that syntagmatic responding (using sequential words) transferred to a new free-association test after social reinforcement (e.g., "good") with both delayed and immediate tests, and even with a change in stimulus conditions (room, experimenter). Such transfer occurred after verbal instructions (to respond syntagmatically) only in the immediate test and only if there was no change in stimulus conditions. The transfer difference was especially impressive, because the subjects given verbal instructions showed the greatest amount of syntagmatic responding in the original list under all conditions. For another example, Phillips (1968) reported that with control of some previously uncontrolled conditions, direct reinforcement was clearly more effective than vicarious reinforcement (hearing some one else's taped verbal output reinforced) in the production of specified types of verbal responses.

Interpretation of affective transfer (Marx, 1978; Marx & Marx, 1978), described earlier, is fairly straightforward in terms of interacting S-R systems. Elevation of the habit-activation level of a particular S-R relationship (as by reinforcement of some personality evaluation of a facial photograph) simply operates to increase the habit-activation level of subsequent S-R relationships with the same stimulus (such as judging the same face on some new personality attribute). Increased excitation of the new response in the transfer test because of a common stimulus would thus be a kind of stimulus generalization involving the habit-activation component rather than the habit itself, as assumed in orthodox S-R theory.

A recently reported experiment by Wilson and Nisbett (1978) offers further support for the general proposition that differential activation of response systems can be indirectly manipulated. In that experiment, subjects who had been exposed to paired-associate learning and esthetic judgments of colored slides were subsequently found to emit more target responses in association tests (e.g., responding "grapes" after having learned "jelly–purple" and/or having judged a picture of a fruit stand). Approximately twice as many of eight target words were given, following such suggestive cuing than following neutral cuing. However, when subjects were later asked why they had made target responses, only 2 of 94 proffered explanations referred to the word cues, which proved nonetheless to be far more potent than the pictures. This failure to report presumably crucial stimuli, which was interpreted by Wilson and Nisbett as support for their general methodological position (Nisbett & Wilson, 1977, discussed earlier), could not be explained on the basis of retrieval failure; at the end of the experiment the subjects were able to recall a mean 11.4 words of the 16 words they had learned as paired associates.

Marcel's (1978) demonstration of semantic instigation of "guesses" about stimulus words that are masked and therefore not correctly perceived, is a more recent and particularly convincing indication of similarly induced behavior that can be interpreted as due to differential activation of response systems in the absence of conscious correlates; in that experiment, responses such as *yellow* and *king* were made to the masked cues *red* and *queen*. In a more traditional investigation, Light and Carter-Sobell (1970) demonstrated the interaction of response systems by showing strong context effects in the recognition of homographic words.

Straws in the Wind

In this final section we examine a number of recent indications of how the research winds may be shifting so as to blow more in accordance with the kind of motivational interpretation presented in this chapter. This highly selective sampling provides illustrations of some clear and potentially significant changes in the overly rationalistic tilt so long characteristic of much cognitive theory. Space restrictions prevent anything but the briefest mention of two of these trends, but I think their cumulative impact is suggestive.

Depth of Processing.   Morris, Bransford, and Franks (1977) have very clearly demonstrated the conceptual and empirical inadequacy of the original formulation of Craik and Lockhart (1972) as well as most if not all of the subsequent "elaborations." They argue that: "particular acquisition activities are never inherently 'superficial' or 'nonmeaningful'" and that "task meaningfulness must be defined relative to particular learning goals [p. 519]." Their data amply support this argument (for example, subjects given a rhyming acquisition mode consistently surpassed subjects given a semantic acquisition mode when the recognition test was based on rhyming-type distractors).

In somewhat similar veins, Davies and Cubbage (1976) have shown an interaction between initial orienting task (rhyming, categorizing, or imaging) and the types of errors made on recognition tests (i.e., types of distractors selected); Anderson and Pichert (1978) have very convincingly demonstrated that a shift in set enables subjects to recall substantial amounts of previously unrecalled information from narratives (this study also provides an especially good example of the effective use of subjects' verbal protocols), and Anderson, Reynolds, Schallert, & Goetz (1977) have shown the dependence of understanding and recall of discourse on the type of superordinate schemata—orienting frameworks—used; and Klein and Saltz (1976), in their dimensional analysis *within* processing levels, have invoked the concept of: "activation of levels of meaning which is so new that the extent of applicability of this process has been relatively unexplored [p. 679]."

Other indications of the more active role of the subject in determining encoding and/or retrievability of cues are provided by Spyroupolos and Ceraso (1977), who stress the limitations on access to recall associated with categorizing of attributes, pointing to what the subject regards as the "defining property" of a memory unit as a crucial factor; by Bellezza, Cheesman, and Reddy (1977), who found that use of a story and an alphabetic mnemonic improved recall, relative to extended semantic elaboration; their conclusion was that some such organization is necessary for further improvement in memory once a certain minimal amount of semantic processing has occurred; by Keenan, MacWhinney, and Mayhew (1977), who, heeding Neisser's (1976) call for greater ecological validity in memory research, showed that such "pragmatic information" as the "speaker's intentions, beliefs, and attitude toward the listener"—collectively labeled "interactional context"—are important determinants of long-term memory for statements; and by Rogers, Kuiper, and Kirker (1977), who demonstrated the overriding potency of self-references in processing; self-reference is apparently a maximally significant habit-activation determinant!

Schematic Versus Categorical Organization. The most recent general trend to hit memory research may be the growing emphasis on schematic, as opposed to categorical, organization. That contrast is very nicely described by Mandler (1979) in her excellent review. Memory experiments have traditionally been concerned with categorical organization, mainly studied with word lists. But memories are also and perhaps more importantly ordered by schemas, which are not based on class memberships or relationships. Rather, a schema, according to Mandler (1979): "is a spatially and/or temporally organized cognitive structure in which the parts are connected on the basis of contiguities that have been experienced in space or time.... A schema is formed on the basis of past experience with objects, scenes, or events and consists of a set of (usually unconscious) expectations about what things look like and/or the order in which they occur" [p. 263].

Schemas are believed to be responsible for maintaining most of our encoded information (of the type classified by Tulving, 1972, as "episodic") in long-term memory. Mandler (1979) says they also provide: "a more powerful set of retrieval cues than does a taxonomic organization ... and a much more active and constructive type of retrieval mechanism." Further, they are "automatically activated by familiar situations regardless of age, culture, or schooling" [p. 286]. Finally, with respect to the comparison of schematic and categorical organization in memory, "Taxonomic structures seem to be added onto a knowledge base that is basically schematically organized and which probably remains so in adulthood. It also seems clear that we use schema-based organizations for most of our daily negotiations with the world and for much of our daily remembering" [p. 292]. Especially impressive results have been obtained in schematically oriented research on developmental problems (Mandler, 1978; Mandler & Day, 1975; Mandler & Robinson, 1978; Nelson, 1978; Schank & Abelson, 1977).

At this point, the reader may be thinking: "This stress on schematic organization and related factors is all well and good, but what does it have to do with habit activation?" The answer to this quite reasonable query is that the schema construct provides a ready-made (and readily made) framework in which perceptual and cognitive habits may exhibit high activation levels for a great variety of related responses without special effort (note that schemas are "automatically activated by familiar situations," according to Mandler, as quoted earlier). Although there has been less attention paid to the response side of the behavioral chain, in contrast especially to cognitive organization, greater amounts of such emphasis may be expected in the future. That development should be facilitated if the potentially important role of concepts such as habit activation is recognized.

SUMMARY AND CONCLUSIONS

This chapter has reviewed a number of research efforts in my laboratory to isolate any special influence of rewarding aftereffects in human selective learning, apart from the strictly informative function of reward; has suggested some of the limitations in a purely cognitive interpretation of human learning; and has proposed a reconceptualization of the role of motivation in which habit (associative) and habit-activation (instrumentally motivational) components of S–R relationships are separated.

Overall, the research program outlined has produced, in my opinion, a sufficient amount of "suggestive" evidence of a relatively "hard" variety to justify paying continued experimental and theoretical attention to the proposition that habits that are learned with rewarding feedback are in some ways more influential in subsequent tests, especially in transfer situations, than comparable responses learned by information processing alone.

In the habit-activation conceptualization, reward is only one of a number of factors determining performance. Conscious, deliberate intention is a common, obvious determinant, which can easily override the various other more subtle determinants, although it too has some limitations. Relevant parts of the rapidly growing experimental literature on encoding were examined, particularly the work on directed forgetting, and the consistent finding that positive responses are faster and better remembered than negative responses. Also cited as generally supportive of the habit-activation proposition were a number of experimental demonstrations of interaction among S–R systems and selected instances of memory research stimulated by the depth-of-processing framework and the more recent emphasis on schematic as contrasted with categorical organization.

The habit-activation construct has been conceived within an S–R framework and is designed to retain the major advantages of that framework (e.g., the "strength" concept applied to responses, the theoretical flexibility permitted by stimulus refinements). At the same time, however, by separating habit activation from habit, and thus avoiding postulation of any "absolute" response strength, the concept is also enabled to enjoy the major advantages of the cognitive (information-processing) conceptual framework.

Some final comments may be directed at this somewhat unusual combination of S–R and cognitive frameworks. Are they really so readily combined? It has been, in my view, a mistake to assume, as protagonists on both sides of the issue so often have seemed to do, that either the S–R or the cognitive view must be the only valid account of human learning. It is, of course, possible that one or the other of these two apparently contradictory positions, or some variation of one or the other of them, will ultimately prevail. But it is also quite possible that a compromise position of the sort suggested here can be more satisfactorily developed. Extreme positions may have some methodological merit, in that they encourage pushing theoretical views to their limits and may therefore facilitate more vigorous and more rigorous empirical tests. But I think in the present case at least, this historically important contribution has served its purpose. The time has come for the more widespread removal of the conceptual blinders that have afflicted so many of the more dogmatically inclined protagonists of one view or the other. More open-minded attitudes are quite consistent with effective experimental and theoretical efforts. Apart from the merits of the particular case that I have tried in this chapter to make for a combination of reward and information factors in human learning theory, it is in the best interests of our science, and in my opinion ultimately necessary, for learning researchers more generally and more seriously to consider various forms of such a combination.

ACKNOWLEDGMENTS

Supported in part by a Research Career Award from the National Institute of Mental Health and a grant from the Army Research Institute for Behavioral and Social Science. The opinions herein are those of the author and are not to be construed as endorsed by the U.S. Army. I thank the following for their critical reading of an early draft of this paper: Marion Bunch, Robert Cowan, Andrew Homer, Donald Kausler, John Mueller, Edward Pavur, and Richard Petty.

REFERENCES

Anderson, R. C., & Pichert, J. W. Recall of previously unrecallable information following a shift in perspective. *Journal of Verbal Learning and Verbal Behavior,* 1978, *17,* 1–12.
Anderson, R. C., Reynolds, R. E., Schallert, D. L., & Goetz, E. T. Frameworks for comprehending discourse. *American Educational Research Journal,* 1977, *14,* 367–381.
Bandura, A. *Principles of Behavior modification.* New York: Holt, 1969.

Bellezza, F. S., Cheeseman, F. L. II, & Reddy, B. G. Organization and semantic elaboration in free recall. *Journal of Experimental Psychology: Human Learning and Memory*, 1977, *3*, 539-550.

Bjork, R. A. Theoretical implications of directed forgetting. In A. W. Melton & E. Martin (Eds.), *Coding processes in human memory*. Washington, D.C.: Winston, 1972.

Bjork, R. A., & Geiselman, R. E. Constituent processes in the differentiation of items in memory. *Journal of Experimental Psychology: Human Learning and Memory*, 1978, *4*, 347-361.

Bottenberg, R. A., Marx, M. H., & Pavur, E. J., Jr. Differential recall of problem names and clues as a function of problem solution or nonsolution. *Bulletin of the Psychonomic Society*, 1976, *7*, 445-448.

Brimer, R. W., & Mueller, J. H. Immediate and final recall of pictures and words with written or oral tests. *American Journal of Psychology*, 1979, *92*, 437-447.

Buchwald, A. M. Effects of "right" and "wrong" on subsequent behavior: A new interpretation. *Psychological Review*, 1969, *76*, 132-143.

Bunch, M. E. Experimental extinction in learning and memory. *Journal of General Psychology*, 1963, *69*, 275-291.

Claxton, G. Special review feature: Memory research. *British Journal of Psychology*, 1978, *69*, 513-520.

Cochin, J. Some aspects of tolerance to the narcotic analgesics. In J. M. Singh, L. Miller, & H. Lal (Eds.), *Drug addiction 1. Experimental pharmacology*. New York: Futura, 1972.

Cohen, R. L., & Nilsson, L. G. The effect of monetary reward and punishment on the repetition of responses under open and closed task conditions. *Quarterly Journal of Experimental Psychology*, 1974, *26*, 177-188.

Coltheart, V. Recognition errors after incidental learning as a function of different levels of processing. *Journal of Experimental Psychology: Human Learning and Memory*, 1977, *3*, 437-444.

Cowan, R. E. Effect of instructions to learn and repeated semantic processing on long-term free recall. *American Journal of Psychology*, in press.

Craik, F. I. M., & Lockhart, R. S. Levels of processing: A framework for memory research. *Journal of Verbal Learning and Verbal Behavior*, 1972, *11*, 671-684.

Craik, F. I. M., & Tulving, E. Depth of processing and the retention of words in episodic memory. *Journal of Experimental Psychology: General*, 1975, *104*, 268-294.

Davies, G., & Cubbage, A. Attribute coding at different levels of processing. *Quarterly Journal of Experimental Psychology*, 1976, *28*, 653-660.

Duncan, S., Jr., & Fiske, D. W. Dynamic patterning in conversation. *American Scientist*, 1979, *67*, 90-98.

d'Ydewalle, G., & Buchwald, A. M. Effects of "right" and "wrong" as a function of recalling either the response or the outcome. *Journal of Experimental Psychology: Human Learning and Memory*, 1976, *2*, 728-738.

d'Ydewalle, G., & Eelen, P. Repetition and recall of "right" and "wrong" responses in incidental and intentional learning. *Journal of Experimental Psychology: Human Learning and Memory*, 1975, *1*, 429-441.

Ericsson, K. A., & Simon, H. A. Verbal reports as data. *Psychological Review*, 1980, *87*, 215-251.

Estes, W. K. Reinforcement in human learning. In J. Tapp (Ed.), *Reinforcement and behavior*. New York: Academic Press, 1969.

Estes, W. K. Reward in human learning: Theoretical issues and strategic-choice points. In R. Glaser (Ed.), *The nature of reinforcement*. New York: Academic Press, 1971.

Estes, W. K. Reinforcement in human behavior: Reward and punishment influence human actions via informational and cybernetic processes. *American Scientist*, 1972, *60*, 723-729.

Estes, W. K. Some functions of memory in probability learning and choice behavior. In G. H. Bower (Ed.), *The psychology of learning and motivation* (Vol. 10). New York: Academic Press, 1976.

Fisher, R. P., & Craik, F. I. M. Interaction between encoding and retrieval operations in cued recall. *Journal of Experimental Psychology: Human Learning and Memory*, 1977, *3*, 701–711.

Glanzer, M. & Ehrenreich, S. L. Memory for truths and falsehoods. *Memory and Cognition*, 1979, *7*, 13–18.

Glanzer, M., & Koppenaal, L. The effect of encoding tasks on free recall: Stages and levels. *Journal of Verbal Learning and Verbal Behavior*, 1977, *16*, 21–28.

Glenberg, A., & Adams, F. Type I rehearsal and recognition. *Journal of Verbal Learning and Verbal Behavior*, 1978, *17*, 455–463.

Glenberg, A., Smith, S. S., & Green, C. Type I rehearsal: Maintenance and more. *Journal of Verbal Learning and Verbal Behavior*, 1977, *16*, 339–352.

Goldman, S. R., & Pellegrino, J. W. Processing domain, encoding elaboration, and memory-trace strength. *Journal of Verbal Learning and Verbal Behavior*, 1977, *16*, 29–43.

Guthrie, E. R. Association by contiguity. In S. Koch (Ed.), *Psychology: A study of a science* (Vol. 2). *General systematic formulations, learning and special processes*. New York: McGraw-Hill, 1959.

Hillix, W. A., & Marx, M. H. Response strengthening by information and effect in human learning. *Journal of Experimental Psychology*, 1960, *60*, 97–102.

Keenan, J., MacWhinney, B., & Mayhew, D. Pragmatics in memory: A study of natural conversation. *Journal of Verbal Learning and Verbal Behavior*, 1977, *16*, 549–560.

Klein, K., & Saltz, E. Specifying the mechanisms in a levels-of-processing approach to memory. *Journal of Experimental Psychology: Human Learning and Memory*, 1976, *2*, 671–679.

Levine, D. G. "Needle freaks": Compulsive self-injection by drug users. *American Journal of Psychiatry*, 1974, *131*, 297–300.

Light, L. L., & Carter-Sobell, L. Effects of changed semantic context on recognition memory. *Journal of Verbal Learning and Verbal Behavior*, 1970, *9*, 1–11.

Longstreth, L. E. Relationship between response learning and recall of feedback in tests of the law of effect. *Journal of Experimental Psychology*, 1971, *90*, 149–151.

MacLeod, C. M. Long-term recognition and recall following directed forgetting. *Journal of Experimental Psychology: Human Learning and Memory*, 1975, *1*, 271–279.

Mandler, J. M. A code in the node: The use of a story schema in retrieval. *Discourse Processes*, 1978, *1*, 14–35.

Mandler, J. M. Categorical and schematic organization in memory. In C. R. Puff (Ed.), *Memory, organization, and structure*. New York: Academic Press, 1979.

Mandler, J. M., & Day, J. Memory for orientation of forms as a function of their meaningfulness and complexity. *Journal of Experimental Child Psychology*, 1975, *20*, 430–444.

Mandler, J. M., & Robinson, C. A. Developmental changes in picture recognition. *Journal of Experimental Child Psychology*, 1978, *26*, 122–136.

Marcel, A. J. Unconscious reading: Experiments on people who do not know that they are reading. *Visible Language*, in press.

Marlatt, G. A. Task structure and the experimental modification of verbal behavior. *Psychological Bulletin*, 1972, *78*, 335–350.

Marx, M. H. A stimulus–response interpretation of the hoarding habit in the rat. *Psychological Review*, 1950, *57*, 80–93.

Marx, M. H. The activation of habits. *Psychological Reports*, 1966, *19*, 527–550.

Marx, M. H. Transfer of rewarded responses in personality judgments. *Bulletin of the Psychonomic Society*, 1978, *11*, 112–114.

Marx, M. H. Multiple-choice learning of line-drawn facial features: III. Transfer as a function of performance or observation. *Bulletin of the Psychonomic Society,* 1980, *15,* 57–59.

Marx, M. H. & Bernstein, B. Generalization of reinforcement among responses to synonyms. *Journal of General Psychology,* 1955, *52,* 49–64. (a)

Marx, M. H., & Bernstein, B. Generalization of reinforcement among similar responses made in altered stimulus situations. *Journal of Experimental Psychology,* 1955, *50,* 355–360. (b)

Marx, M. H., & Bunch, M. E. New gradients of error reinforcement in multiple-choice human learning. *Journal of Experimental Psychology,* 1951, *41,* 93–104.

Marx, M. H., & Conover, J. N. Sex differences in multiple-choice learning under performance and observation conditions. In preparation.

Marx, M. H., & Marx, K. Observation versus performance in learning over the fourth to sixth grades. *Psychonomic Science,* 1970, *21,* 199–200.

Marx, M. H., & Marx, K. Learning to spell as a function of trial-and-error performance or observation. *Bulletin of the Psychonomic Society,* 1976, *8,* 153–155.

Marx, M. H., & Marx, K. Affective transfer as a function of reward and sex of subject. *Bulletin of the Psychonomic Society,* 1978, *12,* 159–161.

Marx, M. H., Pavur, E. J., Jr., & Seymour, G. E. Differential recall of problems, clues, and solutions from completed and uncompleted tasks. *Bulletin of the Psychonomic Society,* 1977, *9,* 322–324.

Marx, M. H., & Witter, D. W. Repetition of correct responses and errors as a function of performance with reward of information. *Journal of Experimental Psychology,* 1972, *92,* 53–58.

Marx, M. H., Witter, D. W., & Farbry, J. Greater repetition of errors under performance compared to observation in multiple-choice human learning. *Perceptual and Motor Skills,* 1973, *37,* 949–950.

Marx, M. H., Witter, D. W., & Mueller, J. H. Interaction of sex and training method in human multiple-choice learning. *The Journal of Social Psychology,* 1972, *88,* 37–42.

Masters, J. C., & Branch, M. H. Comparison of the relative effectiveness of instructions, modeling, and reinforcement procedures for inducing behavior change. *Journal of Experimental Psychology,* 1969, *80,* 364–368.

Matlin, M., & Stang, D. *The Pollyanna principle: Selectivity in language, memory, and thought.* Cambridge, Mass.: Schenkman, 1978.

Montague, W. E. Elaborative strategies in verbal learning and memory. In G. H. Bower (Ed.) *The psychology of learning and motivation* (Vol. 6). New York: Academic Press, 1972.

Morris, C. D., Bransford, J. D., & Franks, J. J. Levels of processing versus transfer appropriate processing. *Journal of Verbal Learning and Verbal Behavior,* 1977, *16,* 519–533.

Moscovitch, M., & Craik, F. I. M. Depth of processing, retrieval cues, and uniqueness of encoding as factors in recall. *Journal of Verbal Learning and Verbal Behavior,* 1976, *15,* 447–458.

Neisser, U. *Cognition and reality.* San Francisco: Freeman, 1976.

Nelson, K. How young children represent knowledge of their world in and out of language: A preliminary report. In R. Siegler (Ed.), *Children's thinking—What develops?* Hillsdale, N.J.: Lawrence Erlbaum Associates, 1978.

Nelson, T. O. Repetition and depth of processing. *Journal of Verbal Learning and Verbal Behavior,* 1977, *16,* 151–171.

Nilsson, L. G. The role of two types of outcome on storage and retrieval processes in memory. *Quarterly Journal of Experimental Psychology,* 1976, *28,* 93–104.

Nisbett, R. E., & Wilson, T. D. Telling more than we can know: Verbal reports on mental processes. *Psychological Review,* 1977, *84,* 231–259.

Nunnally, J. C., Duchnowski, A. J., & Parker, R. K. Association of neutral objects with rewards: Effect on verbal evaluation, reward expectancy, and selective attention. *Journal of Personality and Social Psychology,* 1965, *1,* 270–274.

Nunnally, J. C., Stevens, D. A., & Hall, G. F. Association of neutral objects with rewards: Effect on verbal evaluation and eye movements. *Journal of Experimental Child Psychology*, 1965, *2*, 44–57.

Nuttin, J. R. Pleasure and reward in human motivation and learning. In D. E. Berlyne & K. B. Madson (Eds.), *Pleasure, reward, preference: Their nature, determinants, and role in behavior*. New York: Academic Press, 1973.

Nuttin, J. Motivation and reward in human learning: A cognitive approach. In W. K. Estes (Ed.), *Handbook of learning and cognitive processes* (Vol. 3). Hillsdale, N.J.: Lawrence Erlbaum Associates, 1976.

Nuttin, J., & Greenwald, A. G. *Reward and punishment in human learning*. New York: Academic Press, 1968.

Osgood, C. E. In P. Levelt (Ed.), *Lectures on language performance*. New York: Springer-Verlag, 1980.

Phillips, R. E. Comparison of direct and vicarious reinforcement and an investigation of methodological variables. *Journal of Experimental Psychology*, 1968, *78*, 666–669.

Postman, L. Methodology of human learning. In W. K. Estes (Ed.), *Handbook of learning and cognitive processes* (Vol. 3). Hillsdale, N.J.: Lawrence Erlbaum Associates, 1976.

Prentice, W. C. H. The interruption of tasks. *Psychological Review*, 1944, *51*, 329–340.

Rogers, T. B., Kuiper, N. A., & Kirker, W. S. Self-reference and the encoding of personal information. *Journal of Personality and Social Psychology*, 1977, *35*, 677–688.

Rosenbaum, M. E., & Arenson, S. J. Observational learning: Some theory, some variables, some data. In E. C. Simmel, R. A. Hoppe, & G. A. Milton (Eds.), *Social facilitation and imitative behavior*. Boston: Allyn & Bacon, 1968.

Rundus, D. Maintenance rehearsal and single-level processing. *Journal of Verbal Learning and Verbal Behavior*, 1977, *16*, 665–681.

Schank, R. C., & Abelson, R. P. Scripts, plans, and knowledge. Proceedings of the fourth international joint conference on artificial intelligence. Tbilisi, 1975. (Reprinted in P. N. Johnson-Laird & P. C. Wason (Eds.), *Thinking: Readings in cognitive science*. Cambridge, Eng.: Cambridge University Press, 1977.)

Schank, R. C., & Abelson, R. P. *Scripts, plans, goals and understanding: An inquiry into human knowledge structures*. Hillsdale, N.J.: Lawrence Erlbaum Associates, 1977.

Schneider, W., & Shiffrin, R. M. Controlled and automatic human information processing: I. Detection, search, and attention. *Psychological Review*, 1977, *84*, 1–66.

Schulman, A. I. Recognition memory for targets from a scanned word list. *British Journal of Psychology*, 1971, *62*, 335–346.

Schulman, A. I. Memory for words recently classified. *Memory and Cognition*, 1974, *2*, 47–52.

Siegel, S. Evidence from rats that morphine tolerance is a learned response. *Journal of Comparative Physiological Psychology*, 1975, *89*, 498–506.

Siegel, S. Morphine analgesic tolerance: Its situation specificity supports a Pavlovian conditioning model. *Science*, 1976, *193*, 323–325.

Siegel, S. Morphine tolerance acquisition as an associative process. *Journal of Experimental Psychology: Animal Behavior Processes*, 1977, *3*, 1–13.

Siegel, S., Hinson, R. E., & Frank, M. D. The role of predrug signals in morphine analgesic tolerance: Support for a Pavlovian conditioning model of tolerance. *Journal of experimental Psychology: Animal Behavior Processes*, 1978, *4*, 188–196.

Smith, E. R., & Miller, F. D. Limits on perception of cognitive processes: A reply to Nisbett and Wilson. *Psychological Review*, 1978, *85*, 355–362.

Spyropoulos, T., & Ceraso, J. Categorized and uncategorized attributes as recall cues: The phenomenon of limited access. *Cognitive Psychology*, 1977, *9*, 384–402.

Thorndike, E. L. Animal intelligence: An experimental study of the associative processes in animals. *Psychological Review Monograph Supplement*, 1898, *2*, (8).

Thorndike, E. L. *Animal intelligence*. New York: Hafner, 1911.

Thorndike, E. L. *Human learning*. New York: Century, 1931.

Tolman, E. C. Principles of purposive behavior. In S. Koch (Ed.), *Psychology: A study of a science,* (Vol. 2). New York: McGraw-Hill, 1959.

Tolman, E. C., & Honzik, C. H. "Insight" in rats. *University of California Publications in Psychology,* 1930, *4,* 215–323.

Tulving, E. Episodic and semantic memory. In E. Tulving & W. Donaldson (Eds.), *Organization of memory.* New York: Academic Press, 1972.

Wallace, W. P. Review of the historical, empirical, and theoretical status of the von Restorff phenomenon. *Psychological Bulletin,* 1965, *63,* 410–424.

Wickelgren, W. A. Multitrace strength theory. In D. A. Norman (Ed.), *Models of human memory.* New York: Academic Press, 1970.

Wikler, A. Dynamics of drug dependence. *Archives of General Psychiatry,* 1973, *28,* 611–616.

Wilson, T. D. & Nisbett, R. E. The accuracy of verbal reports about the effects of stimuli on evaluations and behavior. *Social Psychology,* 1978, *41,* 118–131.

Witter, D. W., Marx, M. H., & Farbry, J. Long-term persistence of response-repetition tendencies based on performance or observation. *Bulletin of the Psychonomic Society,* 1976, *8,* 65–67.

Witter, D. W., Mueller, J. H., & Marx, M. H. Correction procedures in observational learning. *Psychonomic Science,* 1971, *22,* 94–95.

Woodward, A. E., & Bjork, R. A. Forgetting and remembering in free recall: Intentional and unintentional. *Journal of Experimental Psychology,* 1971, *89,* 109–116.

Zeigarnik, B. Das Behalten erledigter und unerledigter Handlungen. *Psychologische Forschungen,* 1927, *9,* 1–85.

6 Cognitive Processes in Reinforcement and Choice

W. K. Estes
Harvard University

In the present state of research on reinforcement in human behavior, it is hard to remember that only a couple of decades ago the major issue was the adequacy of the interpretations of reward and punishment as direct actions of aftereffects on response strengths or probabilities (Estes, 1959; Postman, 1962). Up to the early 1960s the dominant view of reinforcement (the term being used here descriptively to encompass operations of reward and punishment) comprised the stimulus–response theories of Hull (1943, 1952) and Skinner (1938) at the level of animal learning and neo-Thorndikean interpretations of the law of effect at the level of human learning, the latter being epitomized in a review of the literature by Postman (1962). Though at a theoretical level, interpretations of both animal and human behavior were extensions and elaborations of the law of effect, major differences appeared at the level of application. The reinforcement theories led directly to the vast technology of operant conditioning and behavior modification (Buchwald, 1976; Kanfer & Phillips, 1970; Verhave, 1966). In contrast, research on human learning conducted under the influence of the law of effect led to some gradual resolution of problems having to do with the role of awareness but contributed very little in the way of applications to problems of human behavior.

The beginnings of a shift in the dominant viewpoint on reinforcement were associated with increasing evidences of dissatisfaction over the lack of continuing theoretical progress within the reinforcement framework (Estes, 1959; Miller, 1963) and gathered momentum gradually in the climate provided by the emergence of the information-processing movement, in which such influential adherents as Hunt (1962) and Miller, Galanter, and

Pribram (1960) coupled proposals for new approaches with slashing criticisms of the traditional conceptual framework. However, no amount of criticism suffices to weaken greatly the sway of an entrenched theoretical position. Nothing achieves that end but the building of a new theory. Here a great deal has happened during the past dozen years, the outcome being not a new monolithic theory of reinforcement comparable to those of Thorndike and Hull but rather a broadly based body of theory that seeks to interpret reinforcement within the framework of information-processing models and, more broadly, cognitive psychology.

In this chapter I wish to review some of these developments with a view to pointing up some of the new sources for the interpretation of reinforcement and choice that have been contributed by empirical and theoretical advances in the study of human information processing. Without wishing in any way to claim credit for all the developments of the past two decades, I make it my first order of business to draw together and reorganize the threads of my own researches over this period, because I am obviously in a good position to do so and because other approaches are covered by other chapters in this volume.

By way of preview I identify three principal stages in the development of what I take to be the currently most acceptable view of the role of memory in reinforcement and choice behavior. The first stage was the clear identification and experimental isolation of the process of acquiring information concerning relationships between situations, actions, and outcomes, as distinguished from response-contingent motivational effects of outcomes on action tendencies. The second stage was the evolution of our conception of the role of memory in this informational process from a simple paired-associate conception to one more in keeping with present theories of organization in memory. The third stage has to do with recognition of the role of perception in the encoding of relationships between tasks and situations; I hasten to add that this stage should not be considered chronologically later than the others, because seminal ideas were contributed by Nuttin (1953) much earlier, though kept by sluggishness in international scientific communication from reaching their full influence until perhaps midway in the period I am reviewing.

EMPIRICAL DOMAIN

Broadly speaking, the extent of applicability of theories of reinforcement and choice to behavior outside the laboratory is an open question, the answer depending on the generality of mechanisms or processes embodied in the theories and the technical knowledge or intuition of those who attempt applications to relatively complex situations. In fact, however, throughout the history of research in this area, experiments have been fairly closely modeled on common and relatively simple types of learning situations encountered in everyday life, and these have constituted the domains to which the results of research should be applicable with some confidence.

For historical reasons one major class of these situations has to do with gambling. A number of forms of gambling, as those employing dice and roulette wheels or the equivalent, have taken remarkably constant forms over a very long period of time, thus providing an almost uniquely well-structured problem for psychological analysis. The problem piqued the interest of mathematicians in the early eighteenth century and motivated the early development of probability theory. One of those mathematicians, Daniel Bernoulli, went further than most in the psychological direction and formulated the distinction between utility and subject probability that has pervaded much theorizing in economics and the psychology of gambling down to the present (Luce & Suppes, 1965).

Much later but still early on the time scale of most of the research to be discussed in this chapter, simulated gambling situations provided the context for the initial efforts of experimental psychologists to provide tests under laboratory conditions of models that had grown up in this rationalistic tradition (Preston & Baratta, 1948). Following the appearance of the game theory of Von Neumann and Morgenstern (1944), interest in gambling as a problem for psychological theories of choice broadened to include games of strategy (Estes, 1957; Suppes & Atkinson, 1960) and such economic activities as bargaining (Siegel & Fouraker, 1960).

The second broad class of situations to which early theories of reinforcement and choice were thought to be applicable constitutes simple forms of trial-and-error learning, as the process of learning to choose the most efficient of alternative routes to a goal, the highest quality brand among those marketed by alternative makers of a product, or the most efficacious of alternative medications available for a particular ailment.

EXPERIMENTAL PARADIGMS

A great part of the research carried out during the past half century with a view to analyzing the empirical domain just outlined can be characterized in terms of a single basic paradigm. On any one trial of an experiment, the experimental subject is presented with a problem defined by an initiating signal, a set of admissable responses, a set of possible rewarding or punishing outcomes, and a probability distribution over the outcomes. In general, the subject is given full information in advance concerning the relationship between the signal and the set of alternatives together with varying degrees of information concerning the possible reward values and probabilities of outcomes and, over repeated trials, has the task of learning by experience which response yields the most satisfying outcome (in uncertain situations, which response yields the outcome of greatest average value). In order to increase the difficulty of the task so that for normal adult subjects learning is not too rapid to yield informative data, it is usual to combine a number of such problems into a list and to cycle repeatedly through the list in random order until the subject reaches some criterion of correct or optimal performance on the list as a whole.

In a typical variant of this paradigm first studied intensively by Thorndike, the signal stimuli take the form of single letters of the alphabet, nonsense syllables, or common words; the response alternatives constitute a set of digits; and the outcomes are the speaking of the words "right" or "wrong" by the experimenter. Unknown to the subject, the experimenter assigns some one digit as the correct response to each signal stimulus and the task of the subject is simply to discover by trial and error what this correct response is for each stimulus. The Thorndikean experiment in its simplest form was analyzed and interpreted by Thorndike himself (Thorndike, 1931) and later, with important variations, in the research programs of Buchwald (Buchwald, 1967, 1969; d'Ydewalle & Buchwald, 1976) and Nuttin (Nuttin, 1953; Nuttin & Greenwald, 1968).

In variations of this paradigm closer to the gambling motif, the outcomes are qualitatively graded; usually amounts of money or the equivalent and a number of different outcome values may have finite probabilities following the occurrence of any one of the admissable responses; hence there is no one correct answer but there is still the possibility of improving average payoffs by profiting from experience (Myers & Atkinson, 1964; Siegel, 1961).

MAJOR PROBLEMS SHAPING RESEARCH

Direct Versus Indirect Action of Aftereffects.   From the appearance of the earliest studies of Thorndike (1898) to about 1960, the story of research on reinforcement in human learning appears in hindsight to be one of successive generations of investigators trying to fight their way free of the highly restrictive framework provided by Thorndike's law of effect. On the face of it, the law of effect seems simply to codify the everyday life observation that in a trial-and-error situation a response followed by reward increases in its likelihood of recurrence. What did not become obvious until much systematic research had been accomplished was the fallibility of everyday-life observation, in particular, the habitual failure of people to notice the great frequency with which responses followed by reward do not increase in likelihood of occurrence. A very large number of studies was carried out over an extended period of years with various limited variations on Thorndike's original trial-and-error paradigm (thoroughly reviewed by Postman, 1962).

However, in the evolution of scientific ideas, sheer numerousness of studies or results counts for very little so long as all are interpreted within the same basic philosophical and theoretical framework, in this instance in the tradition of philosophical and psychological hedonism. A substantial shift in the dominant viewpoint on reinforcement only began to appear about 1960 with the gathering momentum of an alternative theoretical framework, that of the information-processing movement, which drew its concepts and methods not from the tradition of research on conditioning and learning but rather from the analogy between human mental activities and those of digital computers.

Actually Thorndike himself was not wholly committed to the law of effect. In some of his theoretical writings (Thorndike, 1931) he outlined as an alternative what he termed a *representational hypothesis* according to which the learner in the trial-and-error experiments forms a representation in memory of the reward value associated with an action and then utilizes this memory as a guide to action on subsequent occasions. However, this alternative hypothesis virtually dropped from view for a long period of time, perhaps because it did not fit in well with the studies of reward in animal learning that were largely responsible for the reinforcement theories associated with Hull (1937, 1943), Skinner (1938), and Spence (1960). In any event, the two alternative views that Thorndike had initially considered to be the principal competitors were again put forward on that basis by Hillix and Marx (1960) but formulated in terms more congenial to the new information-processing movement. Stating the issues in terms of *information versus effect,* Hillix and Marx cast the issue in a form amenable to lines of research opened up by investigations of memory in human learning.

Experimental research bearing on the issue of information versus effect took a number of forms. Perhaps the largest group of studies constituted investigations of observational learning under various designs. All of these studies had in common the feature that the experimental subject has an opportunity to observe relationships between actions and rewarding or nonrewarding outcomes without himself actually performing the actions. The results were uniformly that the observer learned to select the correct or higher-paying member of a set of alternatives in much the same way under these conditions as under the usual conditions in which he or she made the choices on which the rewards or nonrewards were contingent (Bandura, 1965; Farley & Hokanson, 1966; Nunnally, Duchnowski, & Parker, 1965; Nunnally, Stevens, & Hall, 1965). In a number of variations on the original Thorndikean trial-and-error experiment conducted by Buchwald (1967, 1969; d'Ydewalle & Buchwald, 1976), the outcomes were contingent on the subjects' responses but the informational aspects of the outcomes were delivered at various delays and with varying amounts of information concerning the action–outcome relationship. The results led to Buchwald's model for the Thorndikean situation in terms of which the individual's changes in performance are interpreted solely in terms of *independent memories* for stimuli, responses, and outcomes.

In some rather intricately designed experiments reported by this writer (Estes, 1969), evidence was sought as to whether a relationship of contingency between action and outcome adds anything to the effectiveness of reinforcing events when informational factors are fully equated. The answer appeared to be uniformly negative. Keller et al. (1965) took the alternative tack of holding the relationship of contingency between response and outcome constant but varying the amount of information conveyed by the outcomes. In their situation each problem comprised a stimulus together with two response alternatives to each of which a quantitative reward value was assigned. Under a full information condition, following the subject's choice on each trial, information was given as to the reward value of the alternative chosen and also the reward value of the alternative not chosen. In a partial information condition, information was given only as to the value associated with the chosen alternative. The salient results were that, under the partial information condition, speed of learning was systematically and strongly related to the difference in reward values between the two members of a pair of alternatives, whereas under the full information condition speed of learning was entirely independent of this reward differential.

A conclusion from this entire wave of research seemed to be that, whatever the direct motivating effects of rewards or punishments on performance, the effects on learning could be interpreted wholly in terms of the information conveyed by the reinforcement procedures concerning relationships among stimuli, actions, and outcome values.

Representation of Reinforcement Values in Memory.   Given that for normal adults trial-and-error learning is primarily a matter of acquiring information about values of aftereffects of responses and using this information to guide choices, interest naturally turns to the form in which this information is represented in memory. The question can be pointed up in terms of an illustrative example of a segment of a multiple-choice experiment in which, say, the subject is presented on some trials with a choice between alternatives A_1 and A_2 with associated reward values 4 and 2, respectively, and on other trials with a choice between A_3 and A_4 having associated reward values 6 and 9, respectively; that is,

$$4 \qquad\qquad 2$$
$$A_1 \quad \text{versus} \quad A_2$$

$$6 \qquad\qquad 9$$
$$A_3 \quad \text{versus} \quad A_4.$$

After a little experience with these problems, adult subjects would of course always choose A_1 from the first pair and A_4 from the second pair. A conceptualization of what had been learned in terms of the earlier law-of-effect framework might simply be that tendencies to approach A_1 and A_4 had been strengthened by the effects of reward and that tendencies to avoid A_2 and A_3 had been strengthened by nonreward. In fact, when experiments of this design were conducted with sufficiently young children, the data supported just that interpretation (K. W. Estes, 1971). With adults, however, that conceptualization does not suffice, as can be demonstrated by means of transfer tests. If, for example, the subjects were tested with A_4 versus A_2, they would be expected to choose A_4 on any interpretation (that is, the strengthened response prevailing over the weakened one). If, however, A_4 were tested against A_1, the prediction would not be as clear; and if A_3 were tested against A_1, the prediction based on the law of effect (that the formerly approached alternative A_1 should be chosen over the formerly avoided alternative A_3) turns out to be incorrect both for older children (K. W. Estes, 1971) and for adults (Estes, 1966). The observed transfer results for older children and adults could be quite well interpreted on the supposition that during the training phase the individuals learn to associate each stimulus alternative with its assigned numerical reward value and then on transfer tests recall the values associated with each of the transfer stimuli and choose the stimulus with the higher associated value.

Although the interpretation of selective learning in such situations in terms of memory for stimulus–reward combinations seems parsimonious and intuitively plausible, further analysis has shown it to be inadequate. Influenced by the instructive results of the use of memory probes in other current work in cognitive psychology (Murdock, 1974; Neisser, 1967), Allen and I conducted selective learning experiments with problems of the kind just illustrated but with the added procedure of interrupting the sequence of trials at certain points and asking subjects to attempt to recall the reward values when presented with only the stimulus members of the various problems individually. Memory for values of outcomes associated with the choice alternatives proved surprisingly poor and the results showed clearly that, in general, subjects in these experiments reached criteria of 100% choice of the higher-paying alternative of each problem in a list long before they were able to recall the reward values (Allen, 1972; Allen & Estes, 1972).

The results that Allen and I obtained should perhaps not be surprising if one takes into account the general assumption that performance in these experimental problems reflects processes that govern trial-and-error learning outside of the laboratory, and the obvious fact that much trial-and-error learning outside of the laboratory concerns events whose values to the individuals doing the learning are not calibrated in numerical units. It appears, rather, that during experience with a set of outcomes of differing values the individual builds up a representation in memory having the properties of a"utility" scale on which the different events are represented in positions reflecting their relative value. Then on any type of test, whether during a learning series or during transfer tests, the individual would be conceived to deal with a test problem by retrieving from memory information about the relative positions of the alternatives on the value scale and choosing the alternative expected to lead to the outcome of higher value. In essentials, this conception is a model put forward by the writer (Estes, 1966, 1972, 1976).

So stated, however, the model seems incomplete in that we are given no idea as to how an individual might proceed to convert his/her different reactions to outcomes of differing values into relative positions on an internalized memory scale. The answer I have recently proposed entails the recognition of additional cognitive operations in the chain leading from the observation of choice stimuli to the actual making of choice responses. The suggestion depends on the assumption that an individual has relatively complete short-term memory for his reaction to an event, including the affective reaction that would lead him to characterize it verbally as being of higher or lower value. Further, it is assumed that these short-term memories persist sufficiently long that over a sequence of occasions, such as the successive trials in a selective learning experiment, an individual is able to compare his/her reaction on a given trial with his/her memory of his/her reaction to the outcome of a previous trial and judge whether the current one should be described as being of higher or lower value. The remaining principal component of the model is the assumption that in fact this process of comparison of the subjective values of pairs of successive trial outcomes does occur and leads to a recoding of the value of a given trial outcome as "higher" or "lower" than that of the one preceding. These "higher" and "lower" judgments are then presumed to enter into memory for frequency just as any other events, and the relative frequency with which a particular trial outcome is associated with the judgment "higher" determines its placement on the memory scale of relative value. These assumptions set down in quantitative form prove to lead to a promising account of detailed data of learning and transfer series in a number of experiments (Estes, 1976).

With these results we have come quite a way from the law-of-effect theory that influenced much work on reward and punishment in human learning over a number of decades. For one thing, we now recognize that the cognitive operations and the demands on memory capacity entailed by the problem of adapting to relative reward values of actions are just as complex, and indeed of the same kind, as those involved in tasks that would more customarily be denoted *cognitive*. In payment for adding some conceptual elaboration to the austerely simple law-of-effect model, we are not only able to interpret a wider range of phenomena but also find that research on reinforcement and choice in human beings is brought much closer to other lines of research and theory dealing with human cognition and intellectual function.

Memory for Alternatives. Almost all research on multiple-choice behavior, and indeed preferential choice in general, has been quite unrepresentative of choice situations in normal environments in a major respect. Almost without exception, on an experimental trial in studies of choice behavior or differential reward learning, the subject is presented with a specific subset of alternatives from which to choose, the subset always including the correct alternative if there is one and otherwise the one that is optimal on some criterion. Thus the most that can be learned from such experiments is how feedback from the consequences of past choices influences the individual's tendency to select one or another member of such a subset of alternatives and how a decision is generated given the subset and the individual's state of information concerning outcome probabilities.

But outside the laboratory it is often, perhaps most often, the case that an individual who must choose an action is not confronted with some fixed set of alternatives before making a choice. If an individual is ill and must choose treatment or is bored and wishes to find some recreation, he or she generally must first recall or discover by some search process a set of relevant actions and then generate expectations about possible outcomes and arrive at a choice. The failure of traditional lines of experimentation to capture the process of recalling or otherwise generating the set of relevant alternatives has been well appreciated by some investigators of choice behavior, in particular R. D. Luce (this reference is based on informal conversations—I don't recall whether Luce has recognized this limitation in publications), but nonetheless the problem remains almost untouched in the research literature.

In some exploratory research on the problem, I have started with the presumption that the availability in working memory of a set of alternatives including the best available choice is a major factor in many choice situations and that availability in memory is determined in part by the outcomes of past choices and in part by information concerning values, delays, and probabilities of possible outcomes that may be obtained or transmitted by other means. Further, I have assumed that the whole body of concepts and theory of long-term memory storage and retrieval is relevant and should be brought to bear on the problem.

In one situation that appears promising on the basis of preliminary investigation, subjects are given opportunity to learn to maximize payoffs with respect to a set of problems of the same character as those used in the earlier studies of Allen (1972), Estes (1966), and Keller et al. (1965). Each problem consists of an identifying stimulus symbol together with a set of two or more response alternatives, each of which is assigned a reward value. In the earlier experiments the standard procedure was to cycle the subject through a sequence of such problems in random order repeatedly with the task of learning to choose the highest valued alternative from the subset associated with each problem. The essential modification of the paradigm to enable study of memory for alternatives was to present on each trial only the symbol identifying the problem and require the subject to recall relevant alternatives before making a choice.

The subject was instructed that the symbol identifying each problem signified an illness, the response alternatives represented possible treatments, and the numerical reward values displayed following choices indicated the percentages of instances in which a treatment would be effective. When the symbol was presented on a trial, the subject first attempted to recall the relevant treatments and, if successful, was then permitted to choose one of the alternatives and observe the outcome.

In one of these experiments that I will describe in some detail for illustrative purposes, the subjects were 22 young adults. During the experiment a subject was seated in front of a Teletype on which stimuli were presented under control of a PDP-8/I computer situated in an adjoining control room. The Teletype keyboard was also used to record the subject's responses, made by typing single letters that denoted the admissable response alternatives. The stimuli were six arbitrary symbols representing problems, and to each symbol two alternative responses were assigned, represented by letters that could be typed in the keyboard. A symbol together with the alternative responses was presented to the subject as a simulation of an illness (the symbol) together with possible treatments (the responses). Each pair of alternative treatments was assigned a combination of numerical reward values: 8-0, 7-6, 6-4, 5-3, 4-2, 2-1. Each subject received a different random assignment of symbols to response letters and reward values, but the reward combinations within each problem remained constant throughout the experiment for all subjects.

The task was explained to the subject as a simulation of an outpatient service or first-aid station in which the subject's task was to learn to select the most appropriate treatment for each of a number of illnesses. On a cycle of information trials, the subject was shown on each trial one of the symbols followed by one of the admissable response alternatives, each symbol appearing once with each of its alternative responses during the cycle. The subject's task on these trials was simply to learn the alternative treatments for each problem. On a cycle of test trials the symbols were presented alone, and when each appeared the subject was first to recall and type the letters denoting the two admissable alternative treatments. Whenever a subject recalled both alternative treatments for a problem correctly, the computer would ask him to make a choice and, as soon as the subject had made the choice, the numerical value associated with that treatment was printed out next to the response. The numerical value indicated to the subject how many times out of 10, the treatment selected would prove successful on the average. From the beginning of the experiment information and test cycles were alternated but, as soon as a subject had remembered both alternative treatments for all problems correctly at least once, the information trials were discontinued.

The overall results are summarized in Table 6.1, both for the more conventional measure of percentages of correct choices on the different pairs

TABLE 6.1
Percentages of Correct Choices and Recalls in Study of Memory for Alternatives

Response Category	8–0	7–6	6–4	5–3	4–2	2–1	avg.
	Reward Values of Pair						
Choices							
Correct	83	70	63	73	64	76	72
Correct if higher alternatives recalled first	89	76	68	71	68	76	75
Correct if lower alternatives recalled first	73	60	54	76	62	76	67
Recalls							
Correct	67	69	70	71	69	71	70
Recall higher alternatives first if incorrect choice on previous trial	59	48	52	74	29	66	52

of alternatives and for the more novel measure, percentages of recalls of alternatives.

The most striking trend with regard to recalls is the extreme constancy over the pairs of alternatives having different reward values. These percentages, presented in the first row under Recalls in Table 6.1, show very little variation around the mean value of 70. However, the tendency to recall the higher alternative (i.e., the alternative that has the higher assigned reward value) first on a given trial does depend on the choice of the preceding trial. Comparing the second and third rows under Recalls, it is seen that there is an overall mean difference of 64 versus 52% recalls of the higher alternative depending on whether it or the other member of the pair was chosen on the previous trial ("previous trial" referring here to the most recent trial involving the same pair of alternatives). This differential tends to be largest for pairs in which the higher alternative has a large absolute value (6, 7, or 8).

The more conventional dependent variable (percentage of correct choices) does show some dependence on reward differential in that the highest value is observed for the 8–0 pair, but there is no systematic relationship. A more systematic relationship does emerge, however, if we consider choices conditional on whether the higher- or lower-valued alternative was recalled first. Comparison of the second with the third row of Table 6.1 shows a substantial dependence of choice on recall. The degree of dependence, as measured by the difference between the values in the second and third rows within any column, is strongly related to the absolute value of the recalled alternative but not uniformly related to the reward differential of the pair.

The pattern of results takes on significance especially in relation to the model for choice in this type of situation put forward earlier by the writer (Estes, 1960, 1972). The sequence of events on a trial, conceptualized in the model, begins with the presentation to the subject of a pair of alternatives, say A_1 and A_2. Then the individual is presumed to orient mentally toward one of the alternatives (to recall it, in terms of the present experiment) and accept or reject it, the decision depending on the remembered reward value. If the alternative is accepted, the trial ends. If not, reorientation occurs and the process continues until one alternative or the other is accepted. It is assumed that the tendency to accept a given alternative when it is under consideration increases by a linear increment on any trial when that alternative is chosen, the extent of the increase in general depending on the reward value. The probability of recalling an alternative is assumed to increase similarly whenever that alternative is chosen and to decrease when the other alternative of the pair is chosen.

Among specific predictions of the model are the following. First of all, for any pair the proportion of choices of the higher-values alternative should change from the initial value toward an asymptote that depends on the reward values of the pair (in a quantitative fashion detailed in Estes, 1960). The probability that the higher-valued alternative of a pair is recalled first is predicted to approach the same asymptote. We are not in a position to check on the prediction about asymptotic relationships, because learning was obviously incomplete within the number of trials given in this experiment. However, it is observed that the proportion of first recalls of the higher alternative does run below the proportion of correct choices and that the two measures are fairly well correlated over pairs. A stronger prediction is that the tendency to recall the higher alternative first on any trial should depend on the choice made on the previous trial. Reference to the last two rows of Table 6.1 shows that this expectation is confirmed overall and more strongly so for the pairs involving outcomes of higher absolute values. Also, other things equal, the alternative first recalled on a trial should be the one most likely to be chosen—a prediction similarly supported by the data in Table 6.1.

The process conceptualized in the model and receiving some support from these results is a positive feedback system in which the alternative first recalled has an advantage with respect to choice, and in turn the alternative chosen on a given trial is more likely to be recalled first on the next, with this tendency being related to the value of the outcome.

A long-standing question in this area has been that of whether memory for items of information (words, symbols, or whatever) is a function of the value attaching to these items of information in whatever task is engaging the individual. Our analysis shows that the question as posed is too general to admit a satisfactory answer. Thus, in the specific case in which the items of information were simply the symbols representing the admissable alternatives for a problem in the present experiment, the sheer acquisition of information, as measured by the ability to recall the alternatives when the problem was presented, proved entirely unrelated to associated reward values. However, given that the individual has stored information concerning both alternatives of a pair to the point of being able to recall them, the tendency to recall one rather than another member of the pair first on a given occasion does prove to be systematically related to the reward values. I would not want to press the point too far until the analysis is carried further, but the flavor of the result would seem to be quite well captured by saying that the storage of information about the alternatives is unrelated but that retrieval is systematically related to reward value.

COGNITIVE OPERATIONS IN REINFORCEMENT

Hypothesis Testing.   Much of the research on reinforcement and its control of human performance from Thorndike through the behaviorists of the 1930s and 1940s and down through much of that discussed in the present chapter has been carried out within a basic stimulus–response framework. For most investigators of human behavior in this tradition, *stimulus* and *response* are generally not as narrowly defined as in reflexology or even in the behavioral theories of Skinner or Hull; but nonetheless relatively simple and discrete actions are taken as the behavioral units whose probabilities, rates, or latencies in relation to their aftereffects constitute the dependent variables of theories. In a somewhat different approach to human performance, it is conceived that, at least for adult human beings, choices do not ordinarily involve selection among specific alternative actions but rather selection between alternative strategies, a strategy once adopted controlling a sequence of actions that may extend over a considerable period of time. In this approach the individual's cognitive activity in a problem situation is assumed to be primarily that of sampling from a set of possibly relevant hypotheses or strategies, then selecting from these on the basis of the consequences until the optimal hypothesis or strategy for the given situation is discovered and adopted as a guide to action (Levine, 1971; Restle, 1961; Trabasso & Bower, 1968). Theoretical issues involved in the choice between the stimulus–response and the hypothesis-testing approaches have been critically reviewed by Falmagne (1974).

In my own previous discussions of this issue (Estes, 1970), I have suggested that although hypotheses and strategies are undoubtedly important constitutents of human performance, theories such as that of Levine (1971), formulated solely in terms of strategies, are not sufficiently analytical. The hypothesis-testing models have proven valuable in elucidating how people select from among previously specified sets of hypotheses but do not address problems of explaining why and how effective hypothesis selection is constrained by capacity limitations of the human cognitive system or how hypotheses and strategies take form as behavioral units that come under the control of particular kinds of aftereffects. I think it is fair to say that for the most part investigators of human reinforcement and choice within the framework of present-day cognitive psychology tend to take no firm position on the side of the unit of action and proceed on the working assumption that the determinants of choice can usefully be studied somewhat independently of questions having to do with the organization and detailed control of sequences of actions (Atkinson & Wickens, 1971; Buchwald, 1969; Estes, 1969, 1972).

Comparison and Classification. Just as the research on information versus effect showed that the effects of reinforcement on adult human behavior involve more than a simple strengthening or weakening of response tendencies, continuing investigation in the framework of cognitive psychology has shown further that, generally, choices represent the outcome of a more complex ensemble of processes than simple consultation of memory for the events experienced on an earlier occasion. Among the most important additional cognitive operations commonly implicated, we must surely count that of perceiving relationships of category membership between a situation existing on a particular occasion when choices are followed by rewarding or nonrewarding aftereffects and broader classes of situations that may obtain in the future. Consider, for example, investigations of discrimination learning on the part of young children by K. W. Estes (1976). She noted that when a young child has chosen one from a pair of alternative stimulus boxes, turned it over, and obtained the reward (as a bit of candy or a raisin), the child on the next trial might well remember that the reward had been removed from under the "correct" block and thus choose the other, therefore apparently failing to profit from the previous experience of reward for a correct choice. An important aspect of learning for the child, in contrast to the adult, thus might be to learn that there was a rather abstract uniformity among all types of trials in the experimental situation such that the stimulus choice was followed by reward on one trial would be followed by rewards on others. Appropriate experimental manipulations showed that indeed the discrimination learning of young children was facilitated when conditions were arranged to make it less taxing to detect such uniformities and was hindered when it was made more taxing.

A similar idea had been developed much earlier by Nuttin (1947) in relation to adult learning in Thorndikean trial-and-error experiments. He noted that experiments in which satisfying aftereffects of choices apparently exerted no strengthening effect on the rewarded action often were characterized by an absence of any information that would signify to the learner that the situation was of a class in which the reward contingencies observed on a particular occasion could be expected to obtain on future occasions. Following up this idea systematically, Nuttin developed the conception of a classification of experimental tasks, those of the kind just mentioned being termed *closed* tasks and, in contrast, those in which information is available to indicate generality of observed contingencies across variations in the experimental situation *open* tasks (both the theory and the supporting research having been fully reviewed in Nuttin & Greenwald, 1968). Follow-up of my own hypothesis as to the basis for the differences between open and closed tasks has showed, with some additional controls, that the effectiveness of rewards and punishments for adult human learners can be varied substantially even within a single task, depending on the individual's state of information concerning the probable generality of an observed relationship between an action and a rewarding or nonrewarding consequence (Estes, 1972).

The operation of comparing current perceptions with memories of previous experiences, or with memory structures based on previous experiences, must be conceived to extend throughout the process of generating a decision in any instance of human learning. In choice situations of the kind treated in this chapter, we have just noted the importance of the learner's initial classification of a given situation relative to broader classes he has had experience with. But also, within a single trial, it appears that the learner compares the value of the observed outcome with those of previous trials still represent in short-term memory and converts the currently experienced absolute value to a representation of relative value in long-term memory (Estes, 1976). It is an interesting question whether this process of comparison and classification proves to be related in a theoretically significant way to phenomena of "behavioral contrast," familiar in the literature of animal learning (Hilgard & Bower, 1966).

Retrieval from Memory. An important constituent of any cognitive interpretation of reinforcement is the process of searching memory and retrieving information concerning the previously experienced relationships between the possible available actions and their outcomes in one's previous experience before making a decision at a point of choice. The search and retrieval processes involved are part of general theories of memory and presumably apply to situations involving reinforcement and choice as well as to any other activities with cognitive aspects. However, the specific question often arises whether actions or experiences associated with rewarding events are better remembered than those not associated with rewarding events. Everyday observation suggests that the answer may well be "yes" at a purely empirical level but provides little insight into the factors responsible. The earlier experimental research on the problem, reviewed by Weiner (1966), suffered from a failure to include controls sufficient to show whether any effects of rewards are exerted by modifying the process of encoding and storing information about events in memory or by way of modifying the retrieval process. Weiner's analysis indicated that once information is stored the rewards exert little or no effect on the efficency of retrieval. Later work by Loftus and Wickens (1970) suggested that at least in situations involving only short-term memory, the larger effect of rewards is on the efficiency of encoding but that there may also be some effect on the efficiency of retrieval. The interpretation proposed by Atkinson and Wickens (1971) is that in either case the effects are indirect, being mediated by the tendency of rewards to instigate rehearsal activity that in turn modifies both the likelihood of storage of information in memory and its availability for ready retrieval.

From the standpoint of the present chapter, much of the research conducted hitherto on the relation between retrieval and reinforcement may be rather peripheral to theoretically significant issues. Nearly always, the question posed for research has had to do with the existence or magnitude of a simple and direct relationship between reward value associated with an alternative and retrievability in memory for that alternative. However, some of the analyses discussed in previous sections of this chapter make it clear that no such relationship may exist even in a situation where other evidence reveals a significant role of retrieval. The moral would seem to be that the focus of research in this area should be shifting from the search for differences or "effects" to the assembling of evidence regarding interacting processes.

ACKNOWLEDGMENT

Research reported in this chapter was supported in part by USPHS Grant MH33917 (formerly 16100).

REFERENCES

Allen, G. A. Memory probes during two-choice, differential reward problems. *Journal of Experimental Psychology,* 1972, *95,* 78–89.

Allen, G. A., & Estes, W. K. Acquisition of correct choices and value judgments in binary choice learning with differential rewards. *Psychonomic Science,* 1972, *27,* 68–72.

Atkinson, R. A., & Wickens, T. D. Human memory and the concept of reinforcement. In R. Glaser (Ed.), *The nature of reinforcement.* New York: Academic Press, 1971.

Bandura, A. Influence of models' reinforcement contingencies on the acquisition of imitative responses. *Journal of Personality and Social Psychology,* 1965, *1,* 589–595.

Buchwald, A. M. Effects of immediate versus delayed outcomes in associative learning. *Journal of Verbal Learning and Verbal Behavior,* 1967, *6,* 317–320.

Buchwald, A. M. Effects of "right" and "wrong" on subsequent behavior: A new interpretation. *Psychological Review,* 1969, *76,* 132–143.

Buchwald, A. M. Learning theory and behavior therapy. In W. K. Estes (Ed.), *Handbook of learning and cognitive processes* (Vol. 3). Hillsdale, N.J.: Lawrence Erlbaum Associates, 1976.

d'Ydewalle, G., & Buchwald, A. M. Effects of "right" and "wrong" as a function of recalling either the response or the outcome. *Journal of Experimental Psychology: Human Learning and Memory,* 1976, *2,* 728–738.

Estes, K. W. Transfer following two-choice differential reward learning in children. *Psychonomic Science,* 1971, *25,* 317–321.

Estes, K. W. An information-processing analysis of reinforcement in children's discrimination learning. *Child Development,* 1976, *47,* 639–647.

Estes, W. K. Of models and men. *American Psychologist,* 1957, *12,* 609–617.

Estes, W. K. The statistical approach to learning theory. In S. Koch (Ed.), *Psychology: A study of a science* (Vol. 2). New York: McGraw-Hill, 1959.

Estes, W. K. A random-walk model for choice behavior. In K. J. Arrow, S. Karlin, & P. Suppes (Eds.), *Mathematical methods in the social sciences.* Stanford, Calif.: Stanford University Press, 1960.

Estes, W. K. Transfer of verbal discrimination based on differential reward magnitudes. *Journal of Experimental Psychology,* 1966, *72,* 276–283.

Estes, W. K. Reinforcement in human learning. In J. Tapp (Ed.), *Reinforcement and behavior.* New York: Academic Press, 1969.

Estes, W. K. *Learning theory and mental development.* New York: Academic Press, 1970.

Estes, W. K. Reinforcement in human behavior. *American Scientist,* 1972, *60,* 723–729.

Estes, W. K. Some functions of memory in probability learning and choice behavior. In G. H. Bower (Ed.), *The psychology of learning and motivation* (Vol. 10). New York: Academic Press, 1976.

Falmagne, R. J. Mathematical psychology and cognitive phenonema: Comments on preceding chapters. In R. C. Atkinson, D. H. Krantz, R. D. Luce, & P. Suppes (Eds.), *Learning, memory, and thinking* (Vol. 1). San Francisco: W. H. Freeman and Company, 1974.

Farley, J. A., & Hokanson, J. E. The effect of information set on acquisition of verbal conditioning. *Journal of Verbal Learning and Verbal Behavior,* 1966, *5,* 14–17.

Hilgard, E. R., & Bower, G. H. *Theories of Learning.* New York: Appleton-Century-Crofts, 1966.

Hillix, W. A., & Marx, M. H. Response strengthening by information and effect in human learning. *Journal of Experimental Psychology,* 1960, *60,* 97–102.

Hull, C. L. Mind, mechanism, and adaptive behavior. *Psychological Review,* 1937, *44,* 1–32.

Hull, C. L. *Principles of behavior.* New York: Appleton-Century-Crofts, 1943.

Hull, C. L. *A behavior system.* New Haven, Conn.: Yale University Press, 1952.

Hunt, E. B. *Concept learning.* New York: Wiley, 1962.

Kanfer, F. H., & Phillips, J. S. *Learning foundations of behavior therapy.* New York: Wiley, 1970.

Keller, L., Cole, M., Burke, C. J., & Estes, W. K. Reward and information values of trial outcomes in paired-associate learning. *Psychological Monographs,* 1965, *79*(Whole No. 605).

Levine, M. Hypothesis theory and nonlearning despite ideal S-R-reinforcement contingencies. *Psychological Review,* 1971, *78,* 130–140.

Loftus, G. R., & Wickens, T. D. Effect of incentive on storage and retrieval processes. *Journal of Experimental Psychology,* 1970, *85,* 141–147.

Luce, R. D., & Suppes, P. Preference, utility, and subjective probability. In R. D. Luce, R. R. Bush, & E. Galanter (Eds.), *Handbook of mathematical psychology* (Vol. 3). New York: Wiley, 1965.

Miller, G. A., Galanter, E., & Pribram, K. H. *Plans and the structure of behavior.* New York: Holt, Rinehart & Winston, 1960.

Miller, N. E. Some reflections on the law of effect produce a new alternative to drive reduction. In M. R. Jones (Ed.), *Nebraska Symposium on Motivation.* Lincoln, NE: Nebraska University Press, 1963.

Murdock, B. B., Jr. *Human memory: Theory and data.* Hillsdale, N.J.: Lawrence Erlbaum Associates, 1974.

Myers, J. L., & Atkinson, R. C. Choice behavior and reward structure. *Journal of Mathematical Psychology,* 1964, *1,* 170–203.

Neisser, U. *Cognitive psychology.* New York: Appleton-Century-Crofts, 1967.

Nunnally, J. C., Duchnowski, A. J., & Parker, R. K. Associations of neutral objects with rewards: Effects on verbal evaluation, reward expectancy, and selective attention. *Journal of Personality and Social Psychology,* 1965, *1,* 274–278.

Nunnally, J. C., Stevens, D. A., & Hall, G. F. Associations of neutral objects with reward: Effect on verbal evaluation and eye movements. *Journal of Experimental Child Psychology,* 1965, *2,* 44–57.

Nuttin, J. R. Respective effectiveness of success and task tension in learning. *British Journal of Psychology,* 1947, *38,* 49–55.

Nuttin, J. R. *Tâche, réussite, et échec.* Louvain, Belgium: Publications Universitaires, 1953.

Nuttin, J., & Greenwald, A. G. *Reward and punishment in human learning.* New York: Academic Press, 1968.

Postman, L. Reward and punishment in human learning. In L. Postman (Ed.), *Psychology in the making.* New York: Knopf, 1962.

Preston, M. G., & Baratta, P. An experimental study of the auction-value of an uncertain outcome. *American Journal of Psychology,* 1948, *61,* 183–193.

Restle, F. *Psychology of judgment and choice: A theoretical essay.* New York: Wiley, 1961.

Siegel, S. Decision making and learning under varying conditions of reinforcement. *Annals of the New York Academy of Science,* 1961, *89,* 766–783.

Siegel, S., & Fouraker, L. E. *Bargaining and group decision making.* New York: McGraw-Hill, 1960.

Skinner, B. F. *Behavior of organisms.* New York: Appleton-Century-Crofts, 1938.

Spence, K. W. *Behavior theory and learning: Selected papers.* Englewood Cliffs, N.J.: Prentice Hall, 1960.

Suppes, P., & Atkinson, R. C. *Markov learning models for multiperson interactions.* Stanford, Calif.: Stanford University Press, 1960.

Thorndike, E. L. Animal intelligence: An experimental study of the associative processes in animals. *Psychological Review Monograph Supplement,* 1898, *2,* (8).

Thorndike, E. L. *Human learning.* New York: Appleton-Century-Crofts, 1931.

Trabasso, T., & Bower, G. H. *Attention in learning theory and research.* New York: Wiley, 1968.

Verhave, T. *The experimental analysis of behavior.* New York: Appleton-Century-Crofts, 1966.

Von Neumann, J., & Morgenstern, O. *Theory of games and economic behavior.* Princeton, N.J.: Princeton University Press, 1947.

Weiner, B. Motivation and memory. *Psychological Monographs,* 1966, *80* (Whole No. 626).

7

The Brain as the Locus of Cognitive Controls on Action

Karl H. Pribram
Stanford University

INTRODUCTION

Psychology has made great strides over the past century and a half in providing experimental observations in an area of inquiry that hitherto had been the exclusive domain of philosophical analysis. However, the science of psychology is now beset with the difficulty of organizing its data into a coherent body of knowledge. This lack of organization becomes a critical factor when the results of neurobehavioral experiments are reported: The relationship of brain organization to mind as adduced from the effects of brain recordings, lesions, and excitations must be framed coherently to be communicated. Yet, in my own work for example, I have completed some 30 experiments on the functions of the frontal cortex in as many years in order to obtain some idea of what might have been the effects of the human lobotomy procedures—only to find that these effects can be couched in the language of motivation and emotion, decision theory, operant reinforcement theory, or the paradigms used by experimentalists interested in attention, cognitive learning, memory, or even perception. Now it is certainly possible that perhaps all psychological processes are influenced by the frontal lobe of the brain, but if this is so, there should still be a way of systematically reporting how. For an understanding of mechanism one must at least have some rudimentary idea of what one is searching a mechanism for—in short, what is the relationship among emotion, motivation, decision, reinforcement, attention, cognitive learning, memory, and perception?

The fact that the various approaches to psychology have produced a variety of conceptual and experimental frames of psychological inquiry is obvious.

Each "school" of psychology is concerned mainly with its own body of evidence and only dimly aware that alternate schools exist. Such dim awareness can take the form of complete dissociation and denial, of a more or less mild "put down," or of active conflict. Only rarely (Estes, 1970; Pribram, 1970a) is any effort made to examine the relationship of the alternate conceptual–evidential frames to one another. What appears to be lacking is some set of operational definitions that lead from one conceptual domain to another. Only when such definitions become available will there be a nontrivial modus operandi for coming to grips with the Tower of Babel that now constitutes scientific psychology.

BEHAVIORAL ACTS

Central to this confusion in which psychology finds itself is the topic of this chapter: the relationship of cognition to behavior. At the root of the difficulty is a failure to define what is meant by *behavior* and an often overgenerous interpretation of what is encompassed by *cognition*. For example, experimentalists dealing with human behavior would readily acknowledge cognitive factors in motivation. Experimentalists concerned with animal behavior would have difficulty in understanding the issue: For them, motivation deals largely with the physiological mechanisms comprising hypothalamic and perhaps limbic brain function. And, even more devastating, the animal behaviorist understands by motivated behavior a particular sequence of muscle contractions such as those that produce a sexual display or birdsong, whereas the observer of the human scene is interested in describing the factors responsible for the success or failure of sexual encounters, the production of a musical symphony, or linguistic communication.

As noted, the root of the difficulty lies with the definition of behavior. Ethologists and physiological psychologists ordinarily use the terms *movement* and *behavior* synonymously. Movement is a sequence of muscular contractions. Behavior is therefore identified with series of muscular contractions. By contrast, most experimental and social psychologists use the term *behavior* to denote an action (i.e., an environmental consequence of a series of muscular contractions). Thus the particulars of the muscular sequence or even of which muscles are used become irrelevant. It matters little as to whether writing is accomplished with the left or right hand or even with toes: It is the writing as behavior that is the object of investigation. Skinner, when asked for a definition of behavior, once remarked that the behavior of his pigeons and people was the cumulative record that he took home with him each night to study.

The problem for the physiologically oriented psychologist has been to discern a brain mechanism that can organize actions and not just movement. Such a mechanism, by definition, must account for the potential equivalence among series of muscular contractions, the potential equivalence of movements in the production of an act. In a series of experiments (reviewed in Pribram, 1971) this problem was investigated and evidence was obtained to show that the cerebral motor cortex was involved in action rather than just in the control of muscles or movement. The mechanism appears to be that individual cells in the motor cortex respond to the forces exerted on muscles and sensed by the muscle receptors rather than to the lengthening, shortening, or tonicity of the muscles per se.

The question remained as to how these forces on muscles could become complimented by neural mechanisms in such a way that actions become organized. Experiments by Bernstein (1967) and his successors, Gel'fand, Gurfinkel, Tsetlin, and Shik (1971), and by Turvey and his group (1973) have shown that there is a hierarchy of systems of "coordinate structures" that control muscular sensitivity, movement, and action. Our own work and that of many other neurophysiologists (Granit, 1975; Miller, Galanter, & Pribram, 1960; Pribram, 1971) has suggested that these coordinate structures are composed of feedback servo-loops (Test–Operate–Test–Exit [i.e., TOTE] sequences) that, when arranged in parallel, become feedforward predictive mechanisms.

Neural Holograms

In addition, Bernstein's (1967) work and our own leads to the formulation that the cortical representation of the forces exerted on muscles depends on the fluctuations of such forces. Fluctuations, whether of the vocal apparatus, of gravitational influences in walking, or of the repetitious swinging of a hammer, can be analyzed into their regular sine-wave components according to Fourier's theorem. In fact, Bernstein performed a Fourier analysis of acts and showed that such an analysis provided him with remarkable predictive power.

I have reviewed elsewhere (Pribram, 1971, 1974, 1977, 1978a) the evidence that the cerebral cortex operates as an analyzer of the frequencies of fluctuation, of vibration, and of the sensory input. Over a century ago Ohm (of Ohm's law of electricity) suggested that the auditory nervous system operates as a frequency analyzer, and Helmholtz provided much experimentally obtained support for Ohm's thesis. Bekesy then refined Helmholtz's work and showed that the same principles operated for tactile sensation. Finally, over the past 10 years, largely through the work of Fergus Campbell and John Robson at Cambridge University but supported by experiments performed in Piza, Leningrad, and at Harvard, MIT, Berkeley, and Stanford (Pribram, 1978a; Pribram, Nuwer, & Baron, 1974), it has been shown that the visual system performs an analysis of the frequency of alternations of light and dark in spatial patterns. It has become clear that sensory and motor mechanisms of the brain depend on such frequency analyses for operation.

This formulation of the brain mechanisms involved in sensory and motor processes has had important consequences for understanding perception and action. These consequences derive from utilizing holograms as analogues to these mechanisms. Holograms are technical instantiations of mechanisms that utilize frequency analysis: image processors (also called optical information processors). Initially, holography was a mathematical invention (Gabor, 1969). Its realization in hardware has been accomplished by storing (on film) the interference patterns of waveforms produced by reflection and diffraction from and through objects. Illumination of the stored interference patterns recreates an image of the objects in a plane removed from the stored patterns. The mathematical descriptions of this holographic process and the brain process delineated previously are identical. A model of holographic brain processes has been developed (Pribram, 1971; Pribram, Nuwer, & Baron, 1974). This model accounts for many hitherto difficult to explain brain-behavior relationships such as the failure of even very large brain lesions to eradicate specific memory traces (engrams) and the facts of equivalence in both sensory and motor function that were noted earlier.

Equivalence and memory sparing come about in holography by the same mechanism. Both are due to the fact that Fourier and similar procedures, called "spread functions," distribute information over wide areas. In short, they blur a point source of light. Many such blurs, which can be likened to ripples emanating from point sources of pebbles thrown into a quiet pool, form interfering wave fronts. When frozen onto a film, a hologram results. An inverse transform (simply performing the Fourier operation a second time) reconstructs the point sources (i.e., the image, much as would showing a film of the ripples on the pond in reverse).

The spread of information over the surface of the encoding medium assures that damage to any one portion of the medium does not delete the information. At the same time, reconstruction of image (and act) can proceed from any location within the hologram (this is called *translation invariance*). Thus equivalence can be accounted for.

To summarize the preceding sections: Our understanding of the relationship between cognition and behavior depends on our definitions and understanding of the concepts involved. We have reviewed the confusions attendant to the term *behavior*, which sometimes refers to movements and at other times to actions. We have developed in some considerable length the concept of behavioral "act" because it is the root concept in experimental and social psychology. Not only can act be defined as the environmental consequence of movement but the neural mechanism that is responsible for the organization of action can be detailed.

This root definition in hand, let us turn to the problem of specifying what we mean and don't mean by *cognition.* Here, no hard and fast boundaries can be established without consensual consent. For instance, even the limits of what is a language must be agreed upon socially. Purists identify language and speech because the term *language* is derived from *lingua,* Latin for tongue. But in everyday usage we talk about sign language, pictorial language, etc. The problem is not a trivial one but one that must await consensus for solution (Pribram, 1978b).

With this caveat in mind I first attempt some definitions of subject-matters that are often included in cognitive psychology but are not perhaps "cognition" in any strict sense. These definitions form the context for what might then become a more restricted pursuit of what cognitive processes are all about.

Consciousness as Attentional Control

The separateness of various conceptual frames in the study of psychology depends to a large extent on overall organization, not on elements of content (Pribram, 1970a). This is reminiscent of actual psychological experience that is characterized as taking place in a variety of states of consciousness. The same elements can be identified in a dream as in an ensuing hypnogogic period and in ordinary awareness. A bilingual person (Kolers, 1966, 1968) refers to the same content in both languages, just not at the same time nor according to the same rules of reference (or perhaps even grammar). What is composed during a creative period of authorship is recognized later in ordinary perception—it only seems strange that authorship should have occurred at all. Even extraordinary states share considerable content with ordinary ones (Barron, 1965). Thus psychological processes appear to operate within one or another frame or state that excludes for the time being other states. There is evidence, some of which is presently reviewed here, to the effect that a good deal of behavior, behavior modification (learning), verbal communication, verbal report of awareness, and feeling is state dependent. We therefore proceed to explore the assumption that psychological inquiry mirrors the fact that psychological processes are organized into states.

The determination of these brain states can be defined in terms of *attention.* Attention is also central to our understanding of the variety of conceptual frames that characterize current experimental psychology. Attention (from the Latin *hold to*) can be defined as *holding* to one rather than another program. Holding implies span, competency, and effort, all topics of considerable interest and the focus of much experimental activity in contemporary attention theory (Kahneman, 1973; Pribram & McGuinness, 1975). Holding also implies that certain consistency over time that characterizes a state. Different conscious states are therefore due to the maintenance in operation (i.e., the holding or attending) of different neural programs that structure mnemic events, sensory, and physiological invariants in different ways. William James (1890), in fact, suggested that all problems of consciousness are reducible to problems of attention.

At least three sources can be identified as giving rise to the events operated upon by attention: sensory input, physiological stimuli arising within the body to which the central nervous system is directly sensitive, and mnemic stimuli stored within the brain tissue. The fact that a diversity of states shares, to some considerable extent, the content given by these sources suggests that the separateness of these states cannot be attributed per se to sensory processes, to mechanisms arising in body physiology, nor to the way in which memory storage occurs. This does not mean that such stimuli cannot serve as triggers that initiate one or another of the states—in fact there is good evidence (Ornstein, 1972, 1973; Tart, 1971) that triggering stimuli of all three sorts occur in abundance. However, the organization of a particular state cannot be coordinate with stimulus content but must reflect some particular attentional control process.

What, then, characterizes a particular attentional organization in one or another psychological state? We have already ruled out the structure of the sensory input, of physiological stimuli, or of the memory store as critical. There must therefore be involved some organizing process akin to that responsible for retrieval. Such processes are usually referred to as *programs* or as *control functions* (Miller, Galanter, & Pribram, 1960). These map the array of anatomical receptor-brain connectivities into physiological ambiences, ambiences that process invariances in the stimulus configuration into more or less coherent and identifiable structures. In short, the conclusion to be drawn is that differences in psychological states (i.e., states of consciousness) are due to differences between control processes exercised by the brain on sensory and physiological stimulus invariants and on the memory store, not on differences in stimuli or the memory store per se. Let us now take up in detail the varieties of controls as they operate on sensory input, physiological stimuli, and the memory store.

Perception as Feedback Control of Sensory Input

Even before the heydey of classical behaviorism, it was considered a truism that the brain controlled motor function as expressed in behavior. This control was conceived to take place by way of abstractive and associative mechanisms that progressively recoded the input into adaptive motor organizations, the hierarchy of coordinate structures described in the section on behavioral acts. Today there is a considerable body of evidence that supports the conception that neural systems provide "feature analyses" and that an "association by contiguity" takes place in the brain. However, additional insights have been achieved into feature organization and what is meant by "contiguity" (Pribram, 1971, Chapter 14).

The best known of these insights is the fact that everywhere in the central nervous system closed loops are formed by neural connections. These closed-loop circuits feed part of the output signal back to their input source. Thus subsequent input comes under the influence of previous input. A good deal of neurophysiology of the 1950s and early 1960s, some in my own laboratory, was addressed to discerning the feedback characteristics of such circuits (Pribram, 1974; Pribram & McGuinness, 1975).

Neural control circuits were well-known before the last 25 years, of course. Walter Cannon's laboratory (Cannon, 1929) established the concept of homeostasis to describe the finding that physiological stimulation from an organism's body was under feedback control. What was new was the discovery that feedback control existed everywhere in the central nervous system and regulated sensory as well as physiological input to the brain (Dowling, 1967).

The ubiquity of feedback control made it necessary to alter our conception of what constitutes "association" (Pribram, 1971, Chapter 14). Contiguity no longer refers to just an accidental coincidence in time and place but to a controlled influence of temporally and spatially connected feedback units. Homeostats were found (Ashby, 1960; Pribram, 1969) to be multilinked to produce stable systems that could be perturbed only by gradually establishing new and independent input circuits (habituation). Such systems have the characteristic of matching input to the stable current organization— perturbations indicated novelty; their absence, familiarity. The stable system provides the context in which the input or content is processed. "Association by contiguity" therefore turns out to refer to a context–content matching procedure, not just a simple, haphazard conjoint happening.

In addition, it was possible to establish which parts of the brain accounted for the maintenance of a stable context and which were directly involved in habituation to novelty. A feedback control model of the perceptual functions of the brain thus emerged from a variety of neurophysiological and neurobehavioral studies (Pribram, 1971, Chapter 11).

Emotion and Motivation as Feedback Controls of Physiological (Internal) Stimuli

The actualization of the operation of one or another of these feedback controls constitutes a motivational or emotional process. Emotions and motivations occur where the operation of a feedback is stopped or initiated. The neural substrates of "stop" and "go" mechanisms have been thoroughly investigated (Pribram, 1971; Pribram & McGuinness, 1975). The stop signals appear to be the more primitive and homeostatic whereas go involves the entire intentional system of neural programs that is discussed more fully in the next section.

The identification of stop and go mechanisms has eased difficulties of definition that have beset the concepts *emotion* and *motivation* (Pribram, 1971, Chapters 9, 10). The difficulties disappear in part by initially correlating emotion with stop mechanisms and motivations with go mechanisms. More complete resolution comes when the more subtle distinction is made between feeling and expression (Pribram, 1970a, 1970b). Feelings, both emotional and motivational, are found to be homeostatically controlled. Thus the stop mechanisms (that process input from both physiological drive and from sensory stimuli and are located in the diencephalic and limbic basal ganglia regions of the brain) sense that equilibrium has been achieved. This corresponds to the emotional feelings of satiety that stop behavior. These same mechanisms sense the perturbation and mismatch that correspond to affect produced by interruption of ongoing behavior.

Expression or intended expression (i.e., motivation), on the other hand, involves still an additional mechanism that entails the cerebellar circuit and cerebral cortex. The problem is that of distinguishing between motivational feelings and motivational intent. Thus, a person is declared guilty of a crime on the basis of his intentions, not his (emotional or) motivational feelings, though these may be taken into account in assigning the penalty. A crime may be undertaken for love or for need—both eminently respectable motivational feelings in our society. It is the intended or actual expression of these motives in behavior that is judged (Miller, Galanter, & Pribram, 1960).

Intention and Decision as Feedforward Controls

Beginning in the mid-1960s concerted effort was directed to the study of these intentional go mechanisms per se. A new theoretical distinction was achieved when it was realized that open-loop, helical organizations characterized certain brain organizations, making intentional, voluntary, and other forms of preprogrammed behavior possible (MacKay, 1969; McFarland, 1971; Mittelstaedt, 1968; Pribram, 1971; Teuber, 1972). Such behavior runs its course insensitive to the effects it is producing. Of course, most behavioral processes combine feedback and feedforward operations, but there are a sufficient number of relatively pure cases of each to make the analysis possible.

The classical example of feedforward behavior is eye movement. Once initiated, an eye movement is insensitive to feedback from that movement. Corrective influence must await its completion (McFarland, 1971; Pribram,

1971). The problem of control is limited to initiation and cessation, although of course a program must have been constituted either genetically or through previous learning for the behavior to be carried through. Feedforward control is therefore programmed control and shows considerable similarity to the operations performed in today's serial computers.

The distinction between closed-loop feedback associative control and open-loop helical feedforward control is not a new one in science. Feedback control is error-sensitive control. It is therefore sensitive to the situation, the context in which the operation takes place. By contrast, feedforward control operates by virtue of preconstituted programs that process signals automatically and essentially free from interference from the situation in which the program is running. Interference can only stop the program. As already noted, homeostatic mechanisms are error processing—every action begets an equal and opposite reaction when the feedback is inhibitory, leaving the system essentially unchanged. Feedforward control, on the other hand, proceeds to change the basic operating characteristics of the system. This change can be quantitatively represented as a change in efficiency of operation.

These concepts were initially embodied in the first and second laws of thermodynamics. The first law deals with the inertia or stability of systems—their resistance to change. The second law provides a measure (entropy) of the efficiency of operation of the system—the amount of work (i.e., organization)—the system can accomplish per unit time. More recently the second law was shown to apply not only to engines but to communications systems where the term *information* is used to indicate the reciprocal of entropy. Feedforward systems that exercise control through programs are therefore properly called *information-processing systems* (Brillouin, 1962).

The distinction between error-processing feedback organizations and programmed information-processing feedforward control is a useful one. Elsewhere (Pribram & Gill, 1976) I have detailed the suggestion that this distinction brings into sharp focus an earlier one made by Sigmund Freud. Psychoanalytic metapsychology, which concerns the mechanisms that underlie psychological processes, distinguishes between primary and secondary processes. Primary processes are composed of homeostatic feedback associative mechanisms; secondary processes are cognitive, volitional, and programmed, under the control of an executive (the ego) much as in today's time-sharing information-processing computer systems. The terminology *primary* and *secondary processes,* however, is not unique to psychoanalysis. Other biologically oriented disciplines have expressed similar insights. Thus, at a recent meeting of experimentalists working on hypothalamic function, it was proposed and agreed to that primary, diencephalic, homeostatic regulations were influenced by secondary, higher-order programs originating in the forebrain.

The primary–secondary process distinction, which was originally based on clinical observation, has thus been given a more substantive theoretical foundation based on a variety of experimental and analytic techniques. Clinically based concepts by necessity are often plagued by considerable vagueness that gives rise to unresolvable conflict of opinion. The sharpening that occurs when data from other disciplines become available to support and clarify a distinction is therefore a necessary preliminary if the conceptions are to be more generally useful in scientific explanation.

Cognition as Mnemonic Control

This distinction between primary processes that are organized according to feedback and associative principles and secondary processes that are organized in a feedforward manner leads us to a precise definition of cognitive processes: We subsume under cognition those intentional and decisional processes that operate on experience and behavior by virtue of feedforward mechanisms (i.e., stored programs acquired or of genetic origin).

Thus the memory store must be composed in part of items representing events and in part of programs that organize the items into usable information. In the section on the Neural Hologram, I detail the evidence that items of information become distributed in the brain and stored in holographic fashion. Of course, item storage also occurs in the environment—in our homes and other familiar places, in libraries, etc.

The problem for the brain sciences has been to discover the rules of interaction among neurons that constitute program storage. A good deal of this work is proceeding in invertebrates (Teyler, 1978) but a few impressive advances are being accomplished in mammals as well (Mountcastle, Lynch, Georgopoulos, Sakata, & Acuna, 1975).

Cognition and The Linguistic Act

Perhaps the most profound insights into the relationship between cognition and behavior have come from studies of language. Language has been, in fact, identified by some (Pattee, 1971) as *the* behavioral manifestation of cognition although others (Chomsky, 1979) see language as only one form of cognitive expression. My own view (Pribram, 1979b) is that audio–vocal communication and writing are two forms of cognitive ability that share with others such as mathematics, logics, and music certain complex structures that are akin to each other and to still other forms of cultural activity. These structures are often labeled *linguistic* or *linguistic-like* because of their commonality, and it is a matter of a convention as yet to be developed as to whether we call mathematics, music, etc., "languages" or whether we restrict the term to its root meaning (derived from *lingua,* the tongue). The facts are that speech (audio–vocal communication) can be relatively highly developed in persons who are otherwise cognitively deficient (with intelligences rated in the IQ 40 range). Similarly, there are "idiot savants" who can accomplish remarkable arithmetic calculations whereas other cognitive competencies are normal or below normal. In addition, brain lesions in different locations produce cognitive deficits (agnosias) related to different sensory modalities although the aphasias (brain lesion-produced disturbances of speech) follow damage restricted to a still different part of the cerebral hemisphere (around the sylvian fissure). These "experiments of nature" clearly indicate that cognitive competencies are several of which the speech competency is but one.

The relationship between cognitive competencies and their linguistic-like structures is reasonably clear (Pribram, 1971a). Each sensory mode is embedded in neural systems that are concerned with *iconicity*—the initial step in image processing (Paivio, 1971). Simultaneously, most likely by way of preprocessing initiated in other neural systems (Pribram, 1971, 1974), categorical perceptions arise that distinguish features of that icon. Using Charles Peirce's (1934) terminology, such categorizing of features *"index"* an icon. Indicators have deictic functions.

Iconic and indical processing is further embedded in neural systems that allow arbitrary representations to be made. Thus *signs* develop when iconicity is being communicated and *information,* considered as alternatives (Miller, 1953), results when the communication concerns indicators. In most right-handed persons, the right hemisphere of the brain has become specialized for image processing and significant communication whereas the left hemisphere is especially efficient in information processing.

Note the dependence of the development of arbitrary representations (tokens) on communication. I mean by communication some organism—environmental interaction that allows the consequences of that interaction (i.e., the inter*act*) to become "presented" (i.e., present) in the brain of the organism or in an artifact in the environment. For example, in music such communication may lead to the development of a symphonic form or to the construction of a musical instrument. Of course, once such presentations have been developed, brain re-presentations of the instrument and environmental re-presentations of the symphony (in score, performance, tape, or disc) are readily achieved (Pribram, 1979c).

This development of a hierarchy of presentation → representation and by repetition of the process, re-representation, can be illustrated by drawing a plausible scenario of the beginnings of audio–vocal linguistic communication by man. There is considerable evidence that, initially, primate communication proceeded by establishing a reciprocal relationship between icon and index using visual–gestural mechanisms. Thus, apes have been taught to indicate their communications by American sign language (Gardner & Gardner, 1969) and the cave paintings of early man suggest considerable skill at iconic representation. Perhaps due to darkness in caves, distance, or other awkward circumstances, initial iconic gestural representations became expressed in vocalizations that then became differentiated and used as tokens even when the gestures were no longer visible. After awhile, the more universally usable audio-vocal expressions supplanted the now redundant gestures as the primary medium for communication.

Syntax, Semantics, and Pragmatics

The rules by which communicative action, the hierarchy of presentations–representations and rerepresentations, etc., take form are known as the *syntax* or *grammar* of the interactions. Grammatical rules apply not only to audio–vocal interactions but also to play, as shown in our laboratory (Reynolds, 1968), and to music (Bernstein, 1976), and may in fact be the rules by which the coordinate structures of all action are organized (Pribram, 1971; Turvey, 1973).

The content of communication—what the communication is about—is ordinarily subsumed in linguistics under the heading *semantics*. Semantics purports to deal with the meanings of communicative acts. However, philosophers have sharply distinguished between meaning and reference. Reference refers to the environmental events that form the content of the communication: the in-formation about those events. Meaning is more elusive: Meanings are defined as intending, as conveying, as the instrumental vehicles of the communication. The term *mean* is derived from the middle English "mene" and "menen," tend where the tending is toward a common (i.e., average) understanding. Thus the various meanings of mean: to be common, penurious; the statistical average; the intension (with an *s*) of an expression (Searle, 1969).

Ordinarily, semantics is especially concerned with the referential (i.e., the extensive) aspects of linguistic communications. The examples of the development of hierarchically ordered re-presentations described previously give a fair view of how the referential process becomes organized. In philosophy such referential processes are defined as "extensional" and in neurology they are said to exhibit "local sign" (i.e., they refer to "locations" in space and time). Such referential organizations are disrupted by lesions of brain systems that involve the posterior cortical convexity.

What about the "intensive" aspects of communication? In part they are of course derived from the intensity with which the communication takes place. But this is only a part of the meaning of intension. As noted earlier, intension also indicates a tendency towards some norm, some commonly accepted, normative standard. How do such intensive meanings come about?

Take once again the example of how speech might have arisen. Originally, vocal expressions would have been manifestations of affective intensity—

expressions of feelings—as they are in all primates. Gestural communications would then take place within the context of these intensive expressions as a *means* for achieving a particular purpose. Thus the gestural content becomes meaningful within a pragmatic context. As the hierarchical organization of re-representation develops, vocalizations per se become indicative of content and the intensive aspects of the expressions refer as much to prior stages in hierarchical development (mnemonics of re-representation) as to the affect that initially provided the contextual frame for the communication.

The parts of the brain responsible for the organization of contextual frames are the frontal cortex and related limbic formations (Pribram, 1958, 1960, 1971, 1973). These brain systems are intimately involved not only in regulating the physiological states of the organism but also in relating external stimuli to these states. Excitation whether originating within the body or from sense organs is ordinarily processed by an organization (a representation) of prior similar excitations. Any mismatch between representation and current input is appreciated as "novel" and accompanied by an orienting reaction. Repetition of the excitation produces habituation of the orienting reaction and the excitation now becomes "familiar." Any change in the patterns of repetition or other parameter of the excitation produces dishabituation (i.e., another orienting reaction).

Note that a representation of the excitation is formed by repetition. Irregularities—either temporal or spatial—of repetition produce an orienting reaction. Thus patterns of repetition (i.e., patterns of redundancy, Garner, 1962, 1970; Pribram & McGuinness, 1975) become the essential context in which representations of excitation form. The limbic (Pribram, Lim, Poppen, & Bagshaw, 1966) and frontal (Pribram & Tubbs, 1967; Pribram, Plotkin, Anderson, & Leong, 1977) parts of the brain (and not others) have been shown to be critical to such structuring of redundancy. In audio–vocal communication the structure of redundancy is given by pauses, inflection, and by parsing. Thus INPINETARISINOAKNONEIS makes little sense unless the appropriate pauses are inserted between *in* and *pine* and *tar* and *is* and between *in* and *oak* and *none* and *is*. The pauses and other structuring markers provide the context within which the intended meanings are conveyed. Organization is here achieved through interrupting a continuous string of redundant alphabetical items. Interruptions are produced by placing pauses and by eliminating or delaying what might otherwise have been there. Interruptions are akin to the hole in the doughnut that gives it form; the zero standing for no-thing that nonetheless can become a powerful organizer of magnitudes when properly employed. The syntactic rules of such pragmatic orderings that center on *use* are just coming to be studied by cognitive scientists: the programming of clusters of procedures that can be flexibly switched into ongoing routines in order to handle recurring episodes of experience (Miller & Johnson-Laird, 1976; Schank & Abelson, 1977; Winograd, 1977).

CONCLUSION

Psychological science has come a long way since the early cognitive explorations of the Würzburgers that came aground on the problem of the *act* of thinking. Brentano's (1874) contribution in making explicit the intentional aspects of experience as well as of action were implemented by his pupil Freud in the procedure of "free association." Freud, however, continued to focus on language as the major if not only indicator of cognitive processing. With the rise of Watson's behaviorism, the spectrum of actions investigated was broadened. At the same time however, the intentional and intensional aspects of cognitive processing were not only ignored but considered inappropriate for scientific analysis. Today, as I have outlined previously the breech has been healed: Behavior can be recognized as act with all its intentional and intensional aspects. Not only is it once more respectable to investigate cognition, but a great deal is known about how the brain processes cognitions into perceptions and actions. If this last statement sounds Kantian, it is meant to. More and more evidence accrues to the effect that sensory input becomes processed into its component waveforms by a mechanism in which individual neurons or groups of neurons resonate to specific bandwidths of the frequency of the sensory input. Such resonators, as well as the transducer capacities of the sense organs, place limits on what is sensed as stimulus. At the same time other brain processes operate on the input, often preprocessing it prior to its organization into the mechanisms coordinate with conscious perception. Similar brain processes operate on mnemonic organizations in which are encoded waveforms generated by prior sensory input (the neural hologram). Such operations on the memory store are coordinate with the cognitions. A hierarchy of these brain processes produce the syntactic structures that program behavioral acts. When the programs are organized around sensory stimuli (or their mnemonic derivatives) they provide a referential semantics that can be consensually validated. When the programs are organized around internal physiological stimuli (or their mnemonic derivatives), they provide the pragmatic meaning that forms the context within which the action proceeds. Semantic organizations tend to have a branching structure; pragmatic organizations are more apt to cluster events by interrupting or otherwise bounding and separating them from others. Semantic organizations are formed by neural systems reaching the posterior convexity of the brain; pragmatic organizations devolve from the operation of more medially placed limbic and frontal brain systems. This, I believe is how the relationship between cognition and behavior can be charted today. The chart should prove familiar to philosophers: What is new is the wealth of detailed observation of behavior and of brain frunction that enriches the hitherto sketchy portions of that chart.

REFERENCES

Ashby, W. R. *Design for a brain*. New York: Wiley, 1960.
Barron, F. The psychology of creativity. In *New directions in psychology* (Vol. II). New York: Holt, 1965.
Bernstein, L. *The unanswered question: Six talks at Harvard*. Cambridge, Mass.: Harvard University Press, 1976.
Bernstein, N. *The co-ordination and regulation of movements*. New York: Pergamon Press, 1967.
Brentano, F. *Psychologie vom empirischen Standpunkt*. Leipzig: Meiner, 1874.
Brillouin, L. *Science and information theory*. New York: Academic Press, 1962.
Cannon, W. B. *Bodily changes in pain, hunger, fear and rage*. New York: Appleton, 1929.
Chomsky, N. *Kant lectures*. Stanford, Calif.: Stanford University Press, 1979.
Dowling, J. E. The site of visual adaptation. *Science*, 1967, *155*, 273–279.
Estes, W. K. Theoretical trends and points of controversy. In J. Linhart (Ed.), *Proceedings of the International Conference on Psychology of Human Learning* (Vol. II). Prague: Czech. Academy of Sciences, 1970.
Gabor, D. Information processing with coherent light. *Optia Acta*, 1969, *16*, 519–533.
Gardner, R. A., & Gardner, B. T. Teaching sign language to a chimpanzee. *Science*, 1969, *165*, 664–672.
Garner, W. R. *Uncertainty and structure as psychological concepts*. New York: Wiley, 1962.
Garner, W. R. The stimulus in information processing. *American Psychologist*, 1970, *25*, 350–358.
Gel'fand, I. M., Gurfinkel, V. S., Tsetlin, H. L., & Shik, M. L. Some problems in the analysis of movements. In I. M. Gel'fand, V. S. Fomin, & M. T. Tsetlin (Eds.), *Models of the structural-functional organization of certain biological systems*. Cambridge, Mass: MIT press, 1971.
Granit, R. The functional role of the muscle-spindles: Facts and hypotheses. *Brain*, 1975, *98*, 531–556.
James, W. *Principles of psychology*. New York: Holt, 1890.
Kahneman, D. *Attention and effort*. Englewood Cliffs, N.J.: Prentice-Hall, 1973.
Kolers, P. A. Reading and talking bilingually. *American Journal of Psychology*, 1966, *79*, 357–376.
Kolers, P. A. Bilingualism and information processing. *Scientific American*, 1968, *218*, 78–86.
MacKay, D. M. *Information mechanisms and meaning*. Cambridge, Mass.: MIT press, 1969.
McFarland, D. J. *Feedback mechanisms in animal behavior*. New York: Academic Press, 1971.
Miller, G. A. What is information measurement? *American Psychologist*, 1953, *8*, 3–11.
Miller, G. A., Galanter, E., & Pribram, K. H. *Plans and the structure of behavior*. New York: Holt, 1960.
Miller, G. A., & Johnson-Laird, P. *Language and perception*. Cambridge, Mass.: Harvard Press, 1976.
Mittelstaedt, H. Discussion. In D. P. Kimble (Ed.), *Experience and capacity*. New York: New York Academy of Sciences, 1968.
Mountcastle, V. B., Lynch, J. C., Georgopoulos, A., Sakata, H., & Acuna, C. Posterior parietal association cortex of the monkey: Command functions for operations within extrapersonal space. *Journal of Neurophysiology*, 1975, *38*, 871–908.
Ornstein, R. E. *The psychology of consciousness*. San Francisco: Freeman, 1972.
Ornstein, R. E. *The nature of human consciousness: A book of readings*. San Francisco: Freeman, 1973.
Paivio, A. *Imagery and verbal processes*. San Francisco: Holt, 1971.

Pattee, H. H. Physical theories of biological coordination. *Quarterly Reviews of biophysics,* 1971, *3,* 255–276.

Peirce, C. S. *Collected papers.* Cambridge, Mass.: Harvard University Press, 1934.

Pribram, K. H. Comparative neurology and the evolution of behavior. In G. G. Simpson(Ed.), *Evolution and behavior.* New Haven, Conn.: Yale University Press, 1958.

Pribram, K. H. A review theory in phychological psychology. *Annual Review of Psychology* (Vol. II). 1960.

Pribram, K. H. The neurobehavioral analysis of limbic forebrain mechanisms: Revision and progress report. In D. S. Lehrman, R. A. Hinde, & E. Shaw (Eds.), *Advances in the study of behavior* (Vol. II). New York: Academic Press, 1969.

Pribram, K. H. The biology of mind: Neurobehavioral foundations. In A. R. Gilgen (Ed.), *Scientific psychology: some perspectives.* New York: Academic Press, 1970. (a)

Pribram, K. H. Feelings as monitors. In M. B. Arnold (Ed.), *Feeligns and emotions.* New York: Academic Press, 1970. (b)

Pribram, K. H. *Languages of the brain: Experimental paradoxes and principles in neuropsychology.* Englewood Cliffs, N.J.: Prentice-Hall, 1971.

Pribram, K. H. The primate frontal-cortex executive of the brain. In K. H. Pribram & A. R. Luria (Eds.), *Psychophysiology of the frontal lobes.* New York: Academic Press, 1973.

Pribram, K. H. How is it that sensing so much we can do so little? *The Neurosciences Study Program* (Vol. III). Cambridge, Mass.: MIT Press, 1974.

Pribram, K. H. Holonomy and structure in the oganization of perception. In J. M. Nicholas (Ed.), *Images, perception, and knowledge.* Dordrecht, Holland: Reidel, 1977.

Pribram, K. H. Consciousness and neurophysiology. *Federation Proceedings,* 1978, *37,* 2271–2274. (a)

Pribram, K. H. The linguistic act. In J. H. Smith(Ed.), *Psychiatry and the humanities* (Vol. III): Psychoanalysis and language. New Haven, Conn.: Yale University Press, 1978. (b)

Pribram, K. H. The place of pragmatics in the syntactic and semantic organization of language. *Temporal variables in speech. Studies in honour of Frieda Goldman-Eisler.* Janua Linguarum, The Hague: Mouton, 1979. (a)

Pribram, K. H. Representations. In T. W. Simon (Ed.), *Proceedings of the symposium of language, mind, and brain.* New York: Academic Press, 1979. (b)

Pribram, K. H. Brain mechanisms in music: prolegomena for a theory of the meaning of meaning. *Proceedings of research symposium on the psychology and acoustics of music.* Lawrence, Kans.: University of Kansas press, 1979. (c)

Pribram, K. H., & Gill, M. M. *Freud's "project" reassessed: preface to contemporary cognitive theory and neuropsychology.* New York: Basic Books, 1976.

Pribram, K. H., Lim, H., Poppen, R.,& Bagshaw, M. H. Limbic lesions and the temporal structure of redundancy. *Journal of Comparative and Physiological Psychology,* 1966, *61,* 365–373.

Pribram, K. H., & McGuinness, D. Arousal, activation, and effort in the control of attention. *Psychological Review,* 1975, *82,* 116–149.

Pribram, K. H., Nuwer, M., & Baron, R. The holographic hypothesis of memory structure in brain function and perception. In R. C. Atkinson, D. H. Krantz, R. C. Luce, & P. Suppes (Eds.), *Contemporary developments in mathematical psychology.* San Francisco: Freeman, 1974.

Pribram, K. H., Plotkin, H. C., Anderson, R. M., & Leong, D. Information sources in the delayed alternation task for normal and "frontal" monkeys. *Neuropsychologia,* 1977, *15,* 329–340.

Pribram, K. H., & Tubbs, W. E. Short-term memory, sparsing, and the primate frontal cortex. *Science,* 1967, *156,* 1765–1767.

Reynolds, P. C. Evolution of primate vocal-auditory communication systems. *American Anthropologist,* 1968, *70,* 300–308.

Schank, R. C., & Abelson, R. P. *Scripts, plans, goals, and understanding.* Hillsdale, N.J.: Lawrence Erlbaum Associates, 1977.

Searle, J. R. *Speech acts.* Cambridge, U.K.: Cambridge University Press, 1969.

Tart, C. T. *On being stoned.* Palo Alto, Calif.: Science and Behavior Books, 1971.

Teuber, H. L. Unity and diversity of frontal-lobe functions. In J. Konorski, H. L. Teuber & B. Zerniki (Eds.), *Acta Neurologiae Experimentalis: The Frontal Granular Cortex and Behavior,* 1972, *32,* 615–656.

Teyler, T. *Brain and learning.* Stanford, Conn.: Greylock, 1978.

Turvey, M. T. Periphery and central processes in vision: inferences from an information processing analysis of masking with pattern stimuli. *Psychological Review,* 1973, *80,* 1–52.

Winograd, T. Framework for understanding discourse. *Stanford University Intelligence Monograph,* June, 1977.

8 Thematic Apperceptive Measurement of Motivation in 1950 and 1980

John W. Atkinson
The University of Michigan

This book provides an occasion—none more fitting—for taking stock of the advance in our understanding of thematic apperceptive measurement of motivation. In the spring and summer of 1947, the effects of experimental arousal of hunger (Atkinson & McClelland, 1948) and of motivation to achieve on the content of thematic apperception were discovered (McClelland, Clark, Roby, & Atkinson, 1949). In the winter of 1977, the results of the first computer simulations of thematic apperceptive measurement of motivation were published (Atkinson, Bongort, & Price, 1977). A lot happened in between to establish the general validity of this method of investigating human motivation.

The objectivity, general applicability, and conventional psychometric respectability of the new method of assessing motivation were soon established (Atkinson, 1958a; McClelland, Atkinson, Clark, & Lowell, 1953). The latter question has nevertheless been a particular bone of contention among those unwilling to take the time to achieve expertise in content analysis and background in motivation and among the true believers of traditional test theory. Now, finally, we know that the point of their skepticism and repeated criticism concerning the modest reliability of the method is mistaken (Entwisle, 1972).

Almost immediately, McClelland (1961) began to apply the new method to analysis of the motivational content of literature obtained from different societies and throughout history. At the same time, systematic studies of how individual differences in achievement motivation are expressed in behavior soon yielded an improved version of the old Lewinian conception of the determinants of level of aspiration, a simple theory of achievement

159

motivation (Atkinson & Feather, 1966). This was then extended, elaborated, and made more general by Raynor (1969, 1974). By 1970, the general conceptual framework for analysis of motivation was reconstructed to accommodate a new conception of the basic behavioral problem of motivation that began to emerge in Feather's (1961, 1962) enlightening investigation of persistence. Once accomplished (Atkinson, 1964, Chapter 10; Atkinson & Birch, 1970; Atkinson & Cartwright, 1964), this meant that all the earlier substantive research on achievement-related behavior had to be reconsidered and thought about in a new way (Atkinson & Birch, 1974, 1978). And, given the completeness, precision, and coherence of the new mathematical model of motivation, the dynamics of action, it was possible for a computer program for the theory of motivation to be written (Bongort, 1974; Seltzer, 1973; Seltzer & Sawusch, 1974) and used to analyze problems that were unthinkable 10 years ago (Atkinson & Birch, 1974, 1978; Birch, Atkinson, & Bongort, 1974; Blankenship, 1979; Kuhl & Atkinson, 1979; Kuhl & Blankenship, 1979). A high point in this most recent phase of research at Michigan occurred when the new theory of motivation, developed largely as a result of continued integrative use of thematic apperceptive measurement of motivation in behavioral studies for quarter of a century, was focused on the complexities of the stream of imaginative behavior to advance our comprehension of how motivation is expressed in thematic apperception. The theory of heat explains the expansion and contraction of the mercury that yields the measure called temperature. The theory of motivation explains the variations in time spent imagining achieving (or some other kind of activity) that yields the measure of strength of motivation. And, in so doing, it explains how it would be possible for such a thematic apperceptive measure of strength of motivation to be valid without being at all reliable (i.e., internally consistent) given the conventional meaning of these terms as defined in test theory (Atkinson, Bongort, & Price, 1977).

My aim is to recapture how we thought about thematic apperceptive measurement of motivation around 1950, as a reminder for some and, hopefully, as an introduction to some fundamentally important work for others. Then I describe how we think about thematic apperceptive motivation today to afford a contrast of the old and new views of this diagnostic test.

At the beginning of our research, the issue of establishing the validity of a potentially useful "clinical" method was the primary consideration. This was required to make systematic, empirical studies of individual differences in human motivation possible. Today, having had a few years to savor the fact that thematic apperceptive measurement of motivation now has a very solid theoretical foundation, and to think about the implications of the startling results in computer simulations of thematic apperceptive measurement of motivation, the most important consideration is clearly to get on with the effort to realize the virtually untapped potential of systematic study of the content of imaginative behavior. Until now, general doubts about the psychometric respectability of thematic apperception, anchored in mistaken beliefs concerning the fundamental soundness of traditional test theory, our technological catechism, has deterred even the most venturous scientific investigators. Hopefully, my discussion, will help all to understand that this obstacle to uninhibited scientific study of imagination has been removed.

THE PERSPECTIVE AROUND 1950

Having shown that a "biogenic need," hunger, carefully defined in terms of hours of food privation, influenced the content of imagination (Atkinson & McClelland, 1948), interest immediately turned to the question of whether the arousal of one of Murray's (1938) "psychogenic needs," the kind presumably induced by conditions of "ego involvement," would have a similar effect. If so, as McClelland et al. (1949) have stated: it would "provide evidence for the existence of higher order psychogenic needs which at least function like those at a simpler physiological level [p. 243]." And so a number of different experimental conditions were designed to produce differential arousal of the "need for achievement" immediately before male college students were administered an already standardized "test of creative imagination." It consisted of projecting a series of pictures on a screen, each for 20 seconds, and allowing 4 minutes for a story to be written about each one. Each story was guided by four leading questions spaced at intervals on otherwise blank sheets of paper. The questions, based on Henry Murray's (1937) earlier clinical probes were:

1. What is happening? Who are the persons?
2. What has led up to this situation? That is, what has happened in the past?
3. What is being thought? What is wanted? By Whom?
4. What will happen? What will be done?

The most different of the experimental conditions in this initial experiment were *relaxed,* in which two experimenters were introduced as graduate students interested only in perfecting some tests that were still in an early developmental stage; and *failure,* in which a questionnaire calling for name, high school and college attended, estimated class standing, IQ (if known), and an estimate of general intelligence (above average, average, or below average) preceded instructions that highlighted the importance of doing well on these same tests. The tests allegedly indicated level of general intelligence taken from a set of tests used to select people of high administrative capacity, capacity to organize material, to evaluate critical situations quickly and accurately, to demonstrate whether or not a person was suitable to be a leader, etc. In the latter condition, after completion of all the tests, subjects were given false norms to create the impression that they had performed poorly in comparison with a reference group.

The content analysis of stories written in the motivational states induced by these treatments (and still others reported more fully in McClelland et al., 1953) showed differences that corresponded to those observed in the hunger experiment where the issue of differential motivation among the several treatments was never in doubt. For example, in both studies there were more plots dealing primarily with deprivation of the goal in question (food or success), an increase in the number of times characters in stories were said to want or wish for a goal in question, or to mention instrumental activities that were successful in dealing with need-related problems (McClelland et al., 1949, p. 258). It was possible to identify a number of different kinds of achievement-related imagery that increased significantly when motivation to achieve was presumably experimentally aroused. Later these were carefully defined in a scoring manual (McClelland et al., 1953, Chapter 4, 1958) that has been used ever since.

In addition to *validity,* the first experiments also demonstrated the *objectivity* of the method of content analysis. Two experienced judges working together could agree 91% of the time in the rescoring of individual categories and could produce a rescoring reliability coefficient of .95 for the overall n Achievement score of individuals based on analysis of all the stories each had written. This early and continued concern about the objectivity of the method is expressed in a report by Feld and Smith (1958) of a median total *score coding* reliability of .89 in published studies to that date, and of correlations ranging from .73 to .92 with a median of .87 for 12 novice coders who had just finished using the self-training materials especially prepared by them (Smith & Feld, 1958). A more recent count of coding reliability in other studies collated in Atkinson and Feather (1966) and Atkinson and Raynor (1974) and obtained from recent graduate classes in social motivation at Michigan, where 12 to 20 hours are typically spent learning the technique, showed the median coding reliability for n Achievement ($N = 39$) to be .89 and the lowest quartile at .85 (Atkinson & Raynor, 1974, p. 51). Hopefully, a new generation of investigators reviewing research employing thematic apperceptive measurement of motivation will think to look first at the procedure section to see if this high standard of objectivity has been maintained.

Table 8.1 illustrates how individual differences in achievement motivation are expressed imaginatively. It contains the complete protocols of two male subjects, each of whom wrote eight stories in response to eight different pictures in the very first study of reliability (internal consistency) of thematic apperceptive *n* Achievement score (Atkinson, 1950; reported in McClelland et al., 1953, Chapter 7). The score of each story indicates how many of the various categories of achievement related imagery (shown previously to increase in frequency when motivation is experimentally aroused in a group of subjects) appear in that story. The subject's *n* Achievement score is the total score obtained in response to all the pictures.

The various diagnostic symptoms of achievement motivation, each defined much more fully in the scoring manual (McClelland et al., 1953, 1958), are listed as follows:

Achievement Imagery.   Someone in the story is concerned about performing well in competition with a standard of excellence—an ideal, competitors, or one's own past performance—whatever the nature of the activity.

Need for Achievement.   Someone in the story expresses a desire or intention to accomplish something—to succeed, to be a doctor, to get a good grade on an exam, to finish the invention, etc.

Instrumental Activity.   Some overt or mental activity by one or more of the characters indicates that something is being done to achieve the goal.

Anticipations of Success or Failure.   Someone in the story anticipates or expects a positive outcome or frustration and failure.

Obstacles—Internal or External.   The goal-directed activity is blocked or hindered in some way by some attribute of the individual (e.g., a lack of confidence or ability, a conflict) or something in the environment (e.g., the machine breaks down, the competition is too severe for him).

Nurturant Press.   Some person aids the character who is engaged in achievement-related activity, concretely or with sympathy and encouragement.

Positive and Negative Affective States.   Someone in the stories experiences a positive affective (emotional) state while actively striving to achieve or upon being successful, or a negative affective state when progress is hindered or upon failing.

Achievement Thema.   The concern about achievement is so elaborated that it becomes the single central plot of the story.

TABLE 8.1

Complete Thematic Apperceptive Protocols of Two Male Subjects in Response to Eight Pictures Illustrating Difference Between High and Low *n* Achievement Scores (Data from Atkinson, 1950)

High n Achievement

Boy in a classroom

The young man in the foreground is a student who is preparing for an exam. He appears to be wondering at the moment whether he is going to be able to continue much longer. He is in a library—as indicated by presence of other students.

He has been studying for quite a long time—and is tired of it right about now.

He is wondering if he will get finished in time to have a little free time for a game of bridge or a glass of beer.

He will study a while longer, and finally leave the library in   (0)

Older and younger man

The old man is the employer of the younger man. They are having a business conference—discussing the progress of the young man's work.

The young man has not been doing as well as his boss believes he can do, and realizes the disappointment of his employer.

The young man feels that he really can do better, which is what his employer desires—and feels some pride—because his boss is showing enough interest to show him new ideas and a new approach.

The young man will improve, in order to restore his employer's confidence in him.   **(4)**

Child with a violin

The little boy has a violin lesson to be practiced—but instead, is dreaming of a swim in the creek.

He had planned to go swimming that spring afternoon—but his mother informed him at lunch that the practicing had to be done first.

The little boy is wondering at the ways of adults—wishing he could be in swimming with the rest of the gang—and feeling rather persecuted because he isn't.

He will reluctantly—and half heartedly practice—keeping a close watch on the time—and, after stopping at the short side of an hour, he will happily race from the house, feeling like he has just been released from a dungeon.   (0)

Two men working in an old fashioned shop

These men are partners in a small business. They have been friends for a long time, and are now attempting to perfect a new idea.

They have been making progress on this idea, and are becoming rather impatient to finish it as the end approaches. They have hit a small snag—the man in foreground has stopped to consider the problem as the other tries to work it out with his hands.

The man thinking about the problem is searching for the answer to the detail which is blocking their progress—the other man is also working for a solution but in a less abstract manner.

They will find the correct solution—and have their idea perfected. The man in the foreground is the   **(4)**

Older man handing papers to the younger man

The old man is receiving a report—being submitted by the younger man, who is an employee of the older man.

The young man has spent considerable time and effort in research and fact-finding in order to make the report complete and accurate.

The young man has the feeling of pride, because he feels that his job is well done. The older man is commending him on his work.

(continued)

TABLE 8.1 (*continued*)

Low n Achievement

Boy in a classroom

This student is obviously day dreaming. Thinking about the coming summer vacation which will come about in few week. Himself.

The spring has brought about his day dreaming. Summer approach and he loves the outdoor. Feels confined having to study inside. In winter he doesn't mind being inside.

Thinking about good time in the summer outside fishing, swimming, etc. where school won't be pressing. Wants to be relived of school work.

He'll slack up on his school work, finals won't come as good but he is under pressure of flunking evidently. He goes on his vacation and   (0)

Older and younger man

The man in grey suit is in trouble or has a problem and is asking advice of his father. Father is giving him advice in the nature of helping him to help himself. Laging the facts before him.

The man has had trouble with his wife and she is thinking of divorcing him. This man is somewhat bull headed but he loves his wife and wants to find a solution that he doesn't loose prestige.

He wants a solution from his father but his father isn't telling him what to do only trying to show him what has come about.

The son won't take advice but eventually the father will ask the wife to take him back and she does. They'll have their stiffs but never will be divorced.   (−1)

Child with a violin

This boy has a certain time of the day that his mother makes him study and reluctantly he does. He doesn't enter into it very enthusiastically and has a great sign of relief when its over.

The mother feels that she never had much chance for education and is going to see that her children do. Doing everything possible to see that he gets and enters into education.

The boy is thinking about what he'll do when the study time is up and with home. He wants to get out of the situation. (Boy does)

The boy will wait the time out and enter into something he likes very enthusiastically because of the change. Like getting out of prison.   (0)

Two men working in an old fashioned shop

The men are looking over a heating stove that doesn't seem to work very well. The draft in the stove is poor and the wood won't burn very well Brother-in-laws.

The weather has changed and stove hasn't been used all summer. Nice outside but indoor it is lightly chilly for the women who insist on a fire.

The men are thing those dam women who want a fire at the slightest change of temperature. Fire wanted by their wives.

Eventually they will get the fire going and the men will retire away from it. The women will have sweaters on and will huddle around the stove keeping warm.   (0)

Older man handing papers to younger man

The boss is over inquiring about a story that the young man wrote in the paper. He had claim evidence in a murder trial that didn't actually exist.

Reporter and vice-president.

Reporter reported false evidence and the police have raised quite a stink about. Public opinion is clamering for conviction.

The boss wants reporter to find new evidence which will take pressure off of paper. Reporter is thinking he'll lose job if he doesn't.

(*continued*)

TABLE 8.1 (*continued*)

High in Achievement

When the employer analyses the report, he will be very satisfied with the work of the young man and will remember him as an individual instead of just one part of the office staff.   (4)

Two men talking in well-furnished office

This is a father and a son. The father is an immigrant, and his son has stopped to see his father.

The son has been successful in his business, largely because of the training he received in his home as a child and youth.

The old man is looking with a feeling of pride at his son and feels that he is very fortunate to have many things he himself never had. The son realizes this pride in his father's thoughts.

The son will try to give his father some of the things he gave up in order to educate him.

(8)

Two men in a Colonial American print shop

These two men are owners of a small newspaper in a Colonial town of the early 1700's. They are printing up the first edition of their paper.

They decided there was a need and a place for a newspaper in the town, and have decided to begin publication of one. They have had the printing shop for several years, but have not attempted to publish a newspaper until now.

They are anticipating the completion of the first edition—and its reception by the townspeople. They hope to be successful in their attempt to bring the news to more people faster.

The people in the town will receive the newspaper with great enthusiasm and the business will thrive.   (4)

Boy with vague operation scene behind him

This boy is dreaming of his future, and the day when his ambition to be a doctor is realized. The background figures are part of his dream. He sees himself as the doctor, operating on a soldier— (as evidenced by the presence of the gun at the right of the picture). The other man is an assistant of his.

The boy has read books of the works of doctors. His father is a doctor, also, and he looks to him as his ideal.

The boy has read war stories, too, and believes that life is to be exciting and dangerous.

The boy is thinking of how it will be to live an exciting life. His is a romantic view of his future life as a doctor who will be able to save soldiers' lives in some future war.

The boy will become a doctor.   (3)

Figure 8.1 shows how these various symptoms of achievement motivation appeared significantly more often in imaginative stories produced by persons in a state of experimentally induced achievement motivation than under more relaxed conditions, an exciting fact around 1950. That was the initial evidence of the validity of the method, its sensitivity to situational arousal of motivation. Soon to follow were many studies showing that individuals scoring high in *n* Achievement behaved differently than those scoring low (McClelland et al., 1953). Before long it was possible to state with some precision how personal and situational determinants interacted to influence the strength of achievement motivation that would be expressed in choice, persistence, and performance level in a given setting (Atkinson, 1957; Atkinson & Feather, 1966).

TABLE 8.1 (*continued*)

Low n Achievement

Reporter won't find new evidence but police get a conviction anyway so pressure is off paper. Man doesn't lose job.   (3)

Two men talking in well-furnished office

Young man is being question by his lawyer in connection with his relation to his wife. If they got along allright etc.

This man at the height of frustration shot his wife because of her activities with other men. He came home and caught his wife in bed with another man.

The man is sorry she is dead because he loved her very much but still would be jealous. He wishes he were dead too and doesn't care what the law will do with him.

The man will received some sympathy from the jury and received charges of manslaughter. Will be sentenced to 30 year and wil have broken spirit.   (–1)

Two men in a Colonial American print shop

The man works with clay in England and the man in the back is his boss and the owner of the small pottery factory. Man is-

The man is in his every setup and has been employed for 20 years. The boss is lazy and has taken on aires of being a big shots even though he isn't prosperous.

The man is thinking how nice it would be to have money so you wouldn't have to be another man's slave. His children were going to have every chance to rise up.

The man will go on living as usual. His sons won't fare any better than he and may eventually work for the son of his employer and having same feelings as him.   (0)

Boy with vague operation scene behind him

The doctor is taking out the appendix of the man laying down. Picture of the boy is the doctor's son who died from a similar operation few years ago.

Doctor is reminded of his son as he performed this operation. Man in the picture was working in the steel mill and had an attack two days before operation.

Doc is thinking of his boy and is a little nervous about this ordinary operation because of the rupture. Sons death has brought uncertainty.

The doc will perform the operation very successfully and the man will go back to work. More of these operations will make the sons memory fade from the doc's mind.   (0)

The data had already been collected for the first study of the psychometric properties of the new measure before the initial evidence of its validity was even published (McClelland et al., 1949). To permit identification of effects on thematic apperceptive *n* Achievement that might be attributable to pictures and to the ordinal position of a story, eight different pictures were arranged in eight different ordinal positions for eight groups, each including four randomly assigned subjects. It was a Latin Square design. Stories were written under what had already become the standard *neutral* condition for assessment of individual differences. That is one in which nothing is done either to heighten motivation or to relax people immediately before the writing of imaginative stories. The results of this study (Atkinson, 1950) were published and discussed in the context of the first progress report, *The*

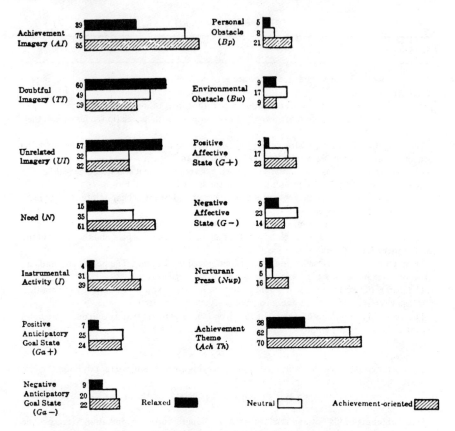

FIG. 8.1. Effect of experimental arousal of achievement motivation on frequency of various achievement-related categories in imaginative stories. Relaxed, neutral, and achievement-oriented conditions. Based on Fig. 5.1 in McClelland, Atkinson, Clark, & Lowell, 1953, p. 141.

Achievement Motive (McClelland et al., 1953, Chapter 7). The several pictures, as described there and in Atkinson (1958) were: (A) Father–son from Murray's TAT; (B) two men ("inventors") in a shop working at a machine; (C) two men, in colonial dress, printing in a shop; (D) "cub reporter" scene: older man handing papers to a younger man; (E) "lawyer's office:" two men talking in a well-furnished office; (F) young boy with a violin from Murray's TAT; (G) boy with vague operation scene in background from Murray's TAT; (H) boy in checked shirt at a desk, an open book in front of him.

The original set of four pictures were B, H, A, G. A new set of four had been selected to be roughtly comparable to them, C, F, E, D.

The results, summarized in Table 8.2, show that stories in response to pictures suggestive of achievement settings (e.g., B, C, F, D) produced

TABLE 8.2

Latin Square Design for Eight Picture Measure of n Achievement Showing Effects Attributable to Pictures, Ordinal Positions, and Particular Sequences of Pictures (n = 32)

Groups of Subjects, or Sequences[a]	Ordinal Position[b] 1	2	3	4	5	6	7	8	Mean
1	3.50F[c]	1.25A	3.25B	4.25E	4.00C	2.50G	2.50H	3.00D	3.03[d]
2	2.75G	3.00D	3.50C	5.75F	1.75A	3.75E	4.75B	2.50H	3.47
3	3.50C	4.25G	3.75D	3.00H	1.00E	3.75B	3.50F	2.00A	3.09
4	2.50D	3.75C	2.50A	4.00G	4.50B	3.25H	2.75E	4.00F	3.41
5	2.75H	5.00E	3.75F	5.50B	5.75D	2.25A	4.00C	3.50G	4.06
6	2.25E	4.25B	5.00H	2.50A	3.50G	5.00F	4.75D	3.75C	3.88
7	5.75B	4.00F	2.75G	5.75D	3.25H	5.25C	1.75A	2.00E	3.81
8	2.25A	5.75H	2.75E	5.00C	3.00F	3.75D	3.25G	6.00B	3.97
Mean	3.16	3.91	3.41	4.47	3.34	3.69	3.41	3.34	3.59

Pictures[c]							
A 2.03	B 4.72	C 4.09	D 4.03	E 2.97	F 4.06	G 3.31	H 3.50

Analysis of Variance

Source	Sums of Squares	df	Variance Estimate	F	P
Ordinal position	161.11	7	23.016	1.797	
Sequences	141.36	7	20.194	1.577	
Pictures	620.36	7	88.623	6.920	.01
Residual	537.91	42	12.807		
Total	1460.74	63			

(From Atkinson (1950) as reported in Table 7.1 in McClelland, Atkinson, Clark, & Lowell, 1953, p. 189).

[a] Rows correspond to eight groups of subjects, four subjects in each row.

[b] Columns correspond to the ordinal position of the pictures.

[c] Latin letters correspond to the picture presented.

[d] Stories were written under Neutral experimental conditions and scored by system C plus a constant of 2 to eliminate negative numbers.

169

significantly more achievement-related imagery than those that were less structured and more ambiguous (e.g., A, E). And though the eye can detect a curious alternation of the average n Achievement score between odd and even ordinal positions, neither *ordinal position* nor *sequence* had a statistically significant effect. The validity of each picture was carefully checked by comparing scores obtained in response to it by those who were above and below the median in total score on all other pictures (McClelland et al., 1953, p. 190). One picture, the boy with a violin (F), had to be discarded because it lacked validity, as here defined. And so instead of two equivalent four picture forms, as planned, the research ended with two equivalent three picture forms: A, B, G (three of the original four) and C, D, E (the three chosen to match them). The product moment correlation between scores obtained on these equivalent forms was .64. And the more general coefficient of internal consistency, *alpha* (Cronbach, 1951), recently calculated from scores listed in the appendix of Atkinson (1950), was .57 (N = 32) for all eight pictures (including the invalid one) and, coincidentally, .64 for the six pictures constituting the equivalent forms (Atkinson, Bongort, & Price, 1977, p. 25).[1]

We were temporally disheartened back in 1950 when Edgar Lowell administered the two equivalent forms to the same group of 40 male college students under neutral conditions with an interim of 1 week between measures and the product moment correlation was only .22. But our spirit improved immeasurably when "experimental judgment" suggested a less pretentious use of the new crude index of motivation. The two forms were found to agree 78.1% in placing subjects above or below the median score when both were administered at the same time (N = 32) and 72.5% when they were administered 1 week apart (both $p < .01$). Thus began our heightened sensitivity to the usually taken for granted presumptions of traditional test theory, including one of having an interval scale to justify product moment correlation, and the need to assume something like "amnesia" or "erasability" to make any psychological sense out of efforts to measure the motivation of the same people repeatedly over periods of time using the same, rather novel method. We began then to appreciate that the new measure might be expected to relate more strongly to other behavioral indicators of motivation (high "validity") than to itself on a second occasion (low retest "reliability"). This argument, advanced particularly by McClelland (et al., 1953, pp. 191–194; 1958; 1971), brings *psychological* insight to the evaluation of methodology, something we can do even more systematically in 1980. Follow up work by French (1955) and Haber and Alpert (1958) reinforced our early impression that thematic apperceptive n Achievement was a relatively crude but valid

---

[1]In a critical appraisal of the method, Entwisle's (1972) estimate of alpha = .37 for the eight stories, based on the published analysis of variance of cell means shown in Table 8.2, substantially underestimated the fact.

measure of individual differences in motivation. Other early studies showing the effect of fear, sex, aggression, n Affiliation and n Power on thematic apperception (Atkinson, 1958) established confidence in the general applicability of the method.

Our primary concern with validity led us to ask whether or not the scores obtained from stories early and late in a series were equally useful. Having identified working alone following achievement-orienting instructions as a setting offering an incentive to achieve but few if any other incentives for task performance (Atkinson & Reitman, 1956), we examined productivity in solving arithmetic problems (the behavioral criterion) by those scoring high (above the median) or low (below the median) in n Achievement on the first and last four stories in a set of eight. The two sets of four pictures (Form A and Form B) were administered A–B to half the subjects and B–A to the other half, so the result would speak to the question of ordinal position and not content of pictures. The result, shown in Table 8.3, shows that the predictive validity of scores obtained from the first four stories (the first 16 minutes) clearly exceeds that of scores obtained from the last four stories (last 16 minutes). The latter did not predict level of performance at all (Reitman & Atkinson, 1958).

This result, until better understood, at least argued for relatively short samples of imaginative behavior in measuring motivation (four to six stories) and, again, ran counter to a major implication of traditional test theory, that increasing the length of a test is a way to enhance the reliability of measurement.

TABLE 8.3

The Effect of the Serial Position of Stories on Prediction of Mean Correct Arithmetic Performance of Male Subjects Working Alone Under Achievement Orientation

| | Serial Position of Pictures | | | |
| | 1st, 2nd, 3rd, 4th | | 5th, 6th, 7th, 8th | |
Achievement Motive	N	M	N	M
High	21	71.57	29	62.24
Low....................	30	55.47	18	61.00
Diff. (H-L).............		16.10		1.24
σdiff.		5.79		6.70
t		2.78		.19
p^a		.005		n.s.

[a]In the predicted direction.
(Based on Table 2 in Reitman & Atkinson, 1958, p. 670.)

The extent to which we tacitly accepted the dictums of traditional test theory (except in the disclaimer about an individual possibly being spoiled for a retest) is already in evidence. But a more fundamental need was already being expressed in the 1950s: to see thematic apperceptive measurement of motives within the context of a theory of motivation. That, in fact was the title of my theoretical summary chapter (Chapter 42) in *Motives in Fantasy, Action, and Society* (1958). Here, following the logic of the primitive theory of motivation then being employed to explain the interaction of personality (motive) and situation (expectancy of an incentive) in behavioral studies showing effects of individual differences in strength of motive (as measured), the level of *n* Achievement expressed in response to particular pictures was explained in similar terms by Atkinson (1958b):

How is the conception of motives as relatively enduring and stable dispositions to be reconciled with the fact that the level of motive-related imagery in thematic apperception, which provides the index of the strength of a motive, is not constant but varies as a function of systematic changes in the situation prior to administration of the test and of the pictures used to elicit stories? How, in other words can the strength of a stable disposition be inferred from the frequency of particular kinds of imaginative responses when the frequency of such responses is known to vary?

These questions can be satisfactorily answered if the distinctions between *motive, expectancy,* and *aroused motivation* which we are forced to make in an analysis of instrumental action are now applied to the imaginative response of the subject to a particular picture. The fact that changes in average level of motivational imagery in stories occur as a result of certain experimental procedures and the idea of a relatively stable strength of motive can be reconciled if imaginative content is thought of as an expression of the *momentary state of aroused motivation* in the person.

According to our theoretical formulation, the momentary state of motivation is a changing thing. It is a joint function of a stable element, the motive, and a transient or changing element, the momentary expectancy of attaining some degree of satisfaction of the motive, which has been aroused by situational cues. When we refer to the total score for a particular kind of motivation (e.g., *n* Achievement score) as obtained from a series of thematic apperceptive stories, we are referring to a summation of the amounts of that kind of motivation which has been expressed in a series of stories *in a particular situation, e.g., under certain experimental conditions.* The strength of motivation aroused by expectancies cued-off by the situation is assumed to remain fairly constant throughout the 20 to 30 minute test period. When, on the other hand, we view the changing level of motive-related imaginative response from picture to picture *within* the test period, we are observing an additional effect on the level of motivation of particular expectancies aroused by the cues of different pictures. Our theoretical task, then, is to define the conditions, both situation-wise and picture-wise, under which the inferring of individual differences in strength of *motive* from observed differences in an index of strength of *motivation* is reasonably valid and to discover the conditions under which inferences about the strength of motive from this motivation score might be very erroneous ...

If we consider the over-all frequency of a particular kind of motivational content in a series of stories to be a measure of the strength of that kind of motivation in the person at the time of writing the stories, the index obtained in the so-called "neutral" or standard situation for assessing individual differences must represent the strength of that kind of motivation which has been aroused in that situation. In experiments dealing with the relationship of individual differences in strength of particular motives to behavior, the thematic apperceptive measure has normally been administered in a college classroom or some similar situation, and stories are written without any attempt by the experimenter either to arouse a particular motive prior to the test or deliberately to relax the subjects. Nevertheless, this so-called "neutral" situation is obviously not neutral with respect to the motives of the individual. The cues of a college classroom should arouse particular kinds of expectancies by virtue of the relatively limited range of kinds of satisfactions that have been experienced by individuals in such a situation.

We have been willing to proceed on the assumption that the kinds of expectancies cued-off in the so-called neutral situation are very similar, i.e., relatively constant, among the individuals tested. It is not too bad an assumption in most cases. There are few situations which can make a greater claim of being illustrative of what is meant by a common or shared learning experience in our society than the average classroom situation. It is the geographic locus of activity of all members of the society for six hours a day, five days a week from age five to sixteen or beyond. To the extent that the assumption is warranted, the state of motivation at the time of writing thematic apperceptive stories, following our theoretical scheme, should be largely a function of the relative strengths of various motives in the individuals. Let us check this assumption, tentatively, as one to be scrutinized carefully a little later on and proceed, for the moment, to a discussion of the instrument itself. The reader who finds it difficult to grant the assumption—even tentatively—may simply imagine an "ideal" standard situation for assessment of motives in a number of individuals. This is one in which the expectancies aroused by the situation cues are the same for all individuals so that differences in the aroused state of a particular kind of motivation can be unambiguously attributed to differences in the strength of motive.

In the neutral situation, or for that matter in any situation, the average score of a group of individuals for a particular kind of motivation varies significantly from picture to picture. Pictures of men working in a shop or of a young man seated at his desk in school, for example, elicit more achievement-related responses than relatively unstructured or obviously nonachievement-related pictures. Similarly, pictures of a group of persons sitting in a clubroom or of two young people apparently conversing are the kinds of pictures which provoke the greatest affiliative response. The pictures which produce the greatest amount of imagery symptomatic of a particular motive are, in other words, pictures of situations which normally arouse expectancies of satisfying that particular motive through some kind of action.

If the situation portrayed in a picture arouses the expectancy that evaluation of performance in terms of standards of excellence is the normal consequence of behavior in that setting, we should expect the achievement motive to be engaged and the motivational content of the imaginative story to contain a variety of associations related to the achievement-directed sequence of behavior. The characters of the story should be trying to achieve something. They should experience feelings of satisfaction when they have performed well and unpleasant feelings when their efforts to accomplish are thwarted in some way. Similarly, if the picture portrays a situation which normally elicits expectancies having to do with the attainment of power, the stories written in response to such a picture should be saturated with associations related to the power-directed sequence of behavior. The motivational content of the story should, in other words, reveal the kinds of motives normally aroused in real-life situations similar to those contained in the picture.

The imaginative story, however, tells us more about the state of motivation than does simple observation of the vigor of acts in a real-life situation; the imaginative story contains specific statements of aim and imagery related to the subtleties of feeling that are never directly observed in action. *The imaginative story defines the motive by describing the kinds of circumstances which produce affective reactions in the characters of the stories.*

If it were plausible to assume that the expectancies aroused by the distinctive cues of a particular picture were the same for all subjects, it would be reasonable to treat differences in the frequency of a particular kind of motivational content appearing in stories written to that picture as a fair index of the strength of the motive in various individuals. If, in other words, the expectancies aroused by a picture were constant for all subjects, then observed differences in a particular kind of motivational content could be directly attributed to differences in the strength of the motive.

We need not make this assumption, however, since the index we use as our estimate of the strength of a motive is the total score obtained from a series of pictures. The total score, you will recall, is a summation of a particular kind of motivational content which appears in *all* the stories the individual has written. To infer differences in the strength of motives from differences in total motivation score, we need only assume that the *average strength* of a particular expectancy (e.g., the expectancy of achievement, or of power, etc.) aroused by *all* of the pictures in the series is approximately equal for all subjects. When such an assumption is warranted, every subject has had a fair opportunity to reveal his motive in the test as a whole.

This condition is likely to be *approximated* when the situations portrayed in the pictures are representative of a wide variety of life situations in which people can satisfy the particular motive. But the "ideal" instrument, and this point is worth repeating, is one in which the average strength of the expectancies of attaining the goal of a particular motive aroused by all of the pictures is equal for all individuals tested. And the "ideal" test situation is one which arouses the same goal expectancies in everyone [pp. 605–610].

THE PERSPECTIVE TODAY (1980)

Between then and now, two important theoretical developments have occurred in the context of the continuing program of research on achievement motivation. Our early adoption of the relatively primitive kind of cognitive theory that Tolman had proposed (Atkinson, 1958b; Tolman, 1955) gave way to a more coherent algebraic conception of the various determinants of achievement motivation (Atkinson & Feather, 1966) that has been elaborated into a more general theory by Raynor (1969, 1974). This development was a product of having integrated the use of diagnostic tests and experimentation in empirical research. It offers a way of thinking about the motivational implications of both immediate and more distant expected future consequences of achievement-related activity within the framework of the motivational model of decision theory (Edwards, 1954). Then in 1970, David Birch and I completed a reconstruction of the theory of motivation, something to replace the traditional, static, episodic theories of the past, both "cognitive" and "mechanistic." *The Dynamics of Action* (1970) took a decade to work out beginning with Feather's conceptual analysis of persistence (Feather, 1961, 1962) and pushed along by a realization of what had been neglected in the traditional episodic theories of motivation (Atkinson, 1964, Chapter 10; Atkinson & Cartwright, 1964).

In order to appreciate the new way of thinking about thematic apperceptive measurement of motivation, one must be familiar with this new conception of motivation. It is presented fully, in simplified form, in the recent revision of Atkinson and Birch (1978). We borrow from synopses of it that are included in an essay about thematic apperception (Atkinson, Bongort, & Price, 1977) and recent overviews of the research on motivation for achievement (Atkinson, 1977; Atkinson & Birch, 1974):

> How can the essentials of a completely new conceptual framework for motivation and action be stated simply and clearly? Traditional theories for motivation, both cognitive (e.g., Cartwright & Festinger, 1943; Edwards, 1954; Lewin, 1938; Tolman, 1955) and within S–R behavior theory (e.g., Hull, 1943; Miller, 1959; Spence, 1956), are stimulus bound. This means that the individual is implicitly viewed as at rest, not doing anything, and unmotivated *to do* anything, until exposed to the stimulus situation of critical interest. The theory of achievement motivation is also like that. It treats the person as if the individual were dead until confronted with the stimulus situation, e.g., a ring-toss game, at which time, as a result of some kind of sudden interaction of personality and environment there occurs—*instantaneously*—a set of competing motivational tendencies of certain magnitudes that control behavior. Life is not like that (Atkinson, 1964, Chapter 10; Atkinson & Cartwright, 1964).

The new dynamics of action exposes the simplistic character of this conventional *episodic* view of behavior, where every new action begins like an event at a track meet with a stimulus situation analogous to the starter's gun. This S-O-R *paradigm* of traditional psychological theory, to use Kuhn's (1962) term, is founded in the Cartesian concept of reflex (1637/1935) that served the new science of physiology so well in the nineteenth century and was a great help to psychology during the first half of this century [From Atkinson, 1977, pp. 74–75].

THE DYNAMICS OF ACTION

The new conception, the dynamics of action, breaks with the traditional mode of thought that has always considered behavioral episodes as isolated events. It begins with a new premise: that an individual is already active in two senses before being exposed to the traditional stimulus situation that in the past has always been assumed to be needed to get things started. First, the individual is already doing something when a scientific observer initially takes notice. Second, the individual is already actively motivated to do many other things before the stimulus situation of traditional interest occurs. This was one of Freud's great insights; that wishes, inclinations, or tendencies, once aroused—whenever—persist until expressed in behavior directly or substitutively, long past the time of direct exposure to their initial instigating stimulus. And it is the idea that Hebb (1949) elaborated in calling attention to the sensory dominance of traditional psychological theory that is incompatible with what is known about an already active brain.

This means, in effect, that we have broken out of the traditional S-O-R mode of thought that considers behavioral episodes as separate, independent, isolated events. We now view the behavioral life of an individual as a continual stream (Barker's concept, 1963) that is characterized by change from one activity to another, even in a constant environment. The emphasis shifts from analysis of the initiation, instrumental striving, and termination of isolated activities to analysis of the continuity of behavior and *the continuity of its underlying motivational structure* as we focus attention on the joint or juncture between activities, a change from one to another (Birch, 1968, 1972; Atkinson, 1969).

In *The Dynamics of Action* (Atkinson & Birch, 1970, 1974, 1978), we conceive the impact on behavior of the immediate environment (or stimulus situation) to be the various instigating and inhibitory forces it produces. These influence the rate of arousal of an individual's tendencies to engage or not to engage in certain activities, including imaginative activities.

If a certain kind of activity has been intrinsically satisfying or previously rewarded in a particular situation, there will be an *instigating force* (F) for that activity, attributable in part to strength of motive in the person and in part to the magnitude of incentive for that activity in that situation. This will cause a more or less rapid arousal and increase in the strength of an inclination to engage in that activity, an *action tendency* (T), depending on the magnitude of the force. If a certain kind of activity has been frustrated or punished in the past, there will be an *inhibitory force (I)* and a more or less rapid growth in the strength of a disinclination to act. This is what we now call a *negaction tendency (N)* and conceive as a tendency *not* to do it. The duration of these forces will determine how strong the action tendency or negaction tendency becomes. The latter, the tendency not to do something, will produce *resistance* to the activity. It opposes, blocks, dampens; that is, it subtracts from the action tendency to determine the *resultant action tendency* ($\bar{T} = T - N$). The resultant action tendency competes with resultant action tendencies for other incompatible activities. The strongest of them is expressed in behavior. The expression of an action tendency in behavior is what reduces it. Engaging in activity produces a *consummatory force (C)*, which depends in part on the *consummatory value (c)* of the particular activity and in part on the strength of tendency being expressed in the activity (i.e., $C = c\bar{T}$). Similarly, the resistance to an action tendency, produced by the opposition of a negaction tendency, constitutes an analogous *force of resistance (R)*, which reduces, in a comparable way, the strength of the negaction tendency. The basic concepts are presented in Table 8.4.

This, very briefly, outlines our conception of the causal factors involved in the continuous rise and decline in strength of tendencies illustrated in Figure 8.2 The changes in strength of competing motivational tendencies in turn account for the changes from one activity to another (*x, y, z* in the behavioral stream of Figure 8.2) and the particular sequence of activities that characterizes an individual's behavior, even in a constant environment.

THEMATIC APPERCEPTION

This sort of thing happens when a person is confronted with a particular picture in the thematic apperceptive test and asked to write an imaginative story. Figure 8.2 is based on one of our earliest computer simulations of what should be expected to happen if an individual were exposed to four instigating forces of different magnitudes with different consummatory values for these incompatible activities in the same environment for a period of time (Seltzer, 1973). One may therefore consider this a simple instance of the kind of thing that happens in our computer simulations of thematic apperception, except that the

TABLE 8.4
Analogous Concepts in the Treatment of Instigation
of Action and Resistance to Action

Instigation of Action	Resistance to Action
Instigating force, F	Inhibitory force, I
Action tendency, T	Negaction tendency, N
Action	Resistance
Consummatory force, C	Force of resistance, R

(From Atkinson and Birch, 1970, p. 207.)

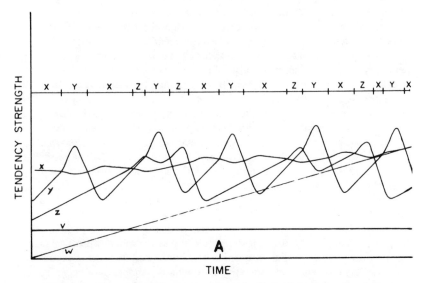

FIG. 8.2.   An example of a stream of imaginative activity (x, y, z) and the systematic changes in strength of tendencies that produced it. Adapted and extended from Seltzer (1973) and Birch, Atkinson, and Bongort (1974).

strength of the several motivational tendencies one sees would carry over and constitute the initial strength of those motivational tendencies when the person is immediately exposed to the next stimulus situation, or picture. It will produce forces that may differ in both kind and strength from those of the first picture, and so on.

The basic concepts of the dynamics of action presented in Table 8.4 should not seem totally unfamiliar to those acquainted with earlier theory of achievement motivation (Atkinson & Feather, 1966). *In the framework of the new dynamics of action, the theory of achievement motivation—as recently elaborated and generalized by Raynor (1969, 1974)—is now to be considered a theory about the determinants of instigating forces to achieve success (F_S) and inhibitory forces to avoid failure (I_F) in various activities and not, as was heretofore assumed, about the determinants of the static strength of the tendencies to achieve success (T_S) and to avoid failure (N_F) in a particular situation* (italics added).

We have made the same general distinction between the arousability (or rate of arousal) of a tendency, calling it the magnitude of force (F), and the level of arousal or strength of that tendency at a particular time (T) that Whalen (1966) proposed in an analysis of sexual motivation.

Considerations of both space and just how far along we are in computer simulations of operant behavior argue for limiting the present discussion to the fate of positive motivational tendencies. So we shall ignore inhibitory force, negaction tendencies, and resistance to action in further discussion, though the theory and its computer program do not. Systematic study of the effect of resistance on thematic apperception is already under way. We cannot conceive of the possibility that this further complication will change the conclusion, already stated, based on even more simple conditions.

THE INTEGRATIVE PRINCIPLE OF A CHANGE IN ACTIVITY

A single and fairly simple principle of change in activity has emerged in our analysis of the question of what is required in a theory to explain a simple change of activity. Several such changes are shown in Figure 8.3 (uncomplicated by inhibitory force, negaction tendency, and resistance).

What causes the change(s) in motivation implied by the observed change in activity in a constant environment? Why does the person stop writing about sex and start writing about achievement?

We began very conservatively, eschewing the idea that action tendencies change in strength spontaneously by mere random oscillation from moment to moment (as presumed in traditional theories). Freud argued that the wish persists until it is expressed. We sharpen that language somewhat. *A behavioral tendency, once aroused, will persist in its present state until acted upon by some psychological force that either increases or decreases its strength.* This explains why all the tendencies in the graphs of Figure 8.3 have some initial (or inertial) strength above zero at the beginning of the interval of observation. The person is

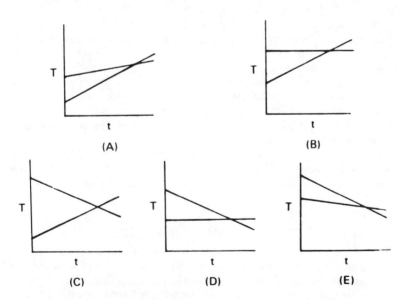

FIG. 8.3.   Various ways in which a change in the relative strength of two tendencies can come about during an interval of time in a constant environment. (From Atkinson & Birch, 1970, 1974.)

active, already doing something (activity A) corresponding to the strongest tendency, and is already actively motivated to do something else (activity B) and certainly many other activities, should we care to complicate both our graphs and introductory discussion with a larger number of initially subordinate tendencies.

The algebraic statement of the principle of a change in activity says simply what the several graphs show. A subordinate tendency will become dominant and a change in activity will occur at a certain time, depending on the initial strength of the subordinate tendency (T_{B_i}); the magnitude of instigating force controlling the rate of arousal or further growth in its strength (F_B), which is attributable in part to strength of motive in the person and in part to the magnitude of incentive in the immediate environment; the strength of the dominant initial tendency (T_A) as it is affected by its instigating force (F_A) and the consummatory force of the activity being expressed, which derives in part from the consummatory value (c_A) of that activity; and, finally, the duration of exposure (t) to these several forces. The mathematical statement of the principle (ignoring resistance), accounting for the time it will take before the change from activity A to activity B occurs, is:

$$t = \frac{T_{A_f} - T_{B_i}}{F_B}, \text{ or } t = \frac{F_A/c_A - T_{B_i}}{F_B}$$

when the ongoing activity has approached the limit of its strength (F_A/c_A) in that situation (see Atkinson & Birch, 1970, Ch. 1; 1974).

Elaboration of the implications of the mathematical statement of the principle and its application to explanation of a sequence of changes in the stream of behavior (Birch, 1972) has yielded hypotheses about how the magnitude of instigating force (and therefore strength of motive, one of its determinants) will influence the initiation of an activity (i.e., latency of response), choice among alternatives, the duration or persistence of a particular activity, the proportion of total time spent in a given activity, the relative frequency of activities, and the operant level or rate of an activity in a given environment.

The dynamics of action purports to be a theory of operant behavior. And it provides the integrative logic or theoretical basis for expecting relationships among various measurable aspects of an activity in the study of personality.

THE STREAM OF BEHAVIOR

In going beyond a simple change in activity to analysis of a sequence of changes in the stream of behavior, we have assumed that there is a temporal lag in the onset and cessation of the full consummatory force of an activity when a change occurs (Atkinson & Birch, 1970, pp. 96–101). The parameters of the lag in our computer programs are its duration and the shape of the ogive-like function that defines the rate of growth to, or decline from, full consummatory force during this interval.

In addition, we have found it meaningful to allow for a certain degree of selectivity in attention to the various cues (or discriminative stimuli) that are the sources of instigating forces for various activities (Atkinson & Birch, 1970, pp. 92–96). It is generally assumed that an individual will be systematically (i.e., constantly) exposed to instigating force for the activity that is occurring. But the degree of attention (or exposure) to cues that produce instigating forces that influence subordinate tendencies is another parameter of interest in simulation of streams of behavior [From Atkinson, Bongort, & Price, 1977, pp. 4–10].

One can see that the major change from the traditional "cognitive" and "mechanistic" models of motivation has to do with continuity versus discontinuity. Molar behavior is viewed as a continuous stream of activity, characterized by change from one to another instead of as a series of discrete and separate episodes, each with a new stimulus situation. Tendencies aroused in one setting are assumed to persist and to carry over to influence behavior in subsequent settings. The impact of the immediate environment is no longer conceived as elicitation of a reaction, whether mediated by cognitive expectations about the consequences of an action or not. Exposure to the stimulus situation is considered the cause of continuous arousal (i.e., strengthening of tendencies to act or not to act, the rate of arousal depending on prior life experience of the individual in that setting [e.g., learning]). And the new conception deemphasizes the relative importance of the immediate stimulus situation in another way. It gives the response or, more appropriately, the expression of a tendency in an activity, an equivalent motivational significance—that of reducing the strength of the tendency motivating it. The concept of consummatory force of an activity turns the traditional qualitative distinction between so-called preparatory or instrumental activities and consummatory or goal activities into a quantitative one in presuming that *all* activities have some consummatory value, it being a matter of degree. The treatment of resistance involves the supposition of an analogous continuous process of arousal of a tendency *not* to act (negation tendency) by exposure to inhibitory force and an analogous process of diminution of the tendency by the force of resistance when the negation tendency does its work in blocking (e.g., suppressing) the expression of an action tendency.

As we turn now to thinking about the motivational determinants of the stream of imaginative behavior in terms of this new conception, the reader is reminded that it was not especially developed just to explain thematic apperceptive measurement of motivation. Rather, it evolved in the natural course of research using that method of measuring individual differences in motivation to explain the interrelatedness of persistence of an activity and initiation of an activity, two aspects of a single behavioral problem—a change in activity. And the principles of the dynamics of action have already been used in computer simulation of other motivational problems such as operant behavior, to explain the allocation of time among different activities

(Atkinson & Birch, 1978, Chapter 8); cognitive control of action, to explain conscious volition (Birch, Atkinson & Bongort, 1974); the effect of the consummatory value of success of tasks that differ in difficulty (Blankenship, 1979; Kuhl & Blankenship, 1979), and the motivational determinants of decision time (Kuhl & Atkinson, 1979). Now, with this rather broad basis for confidence in what we are doing, we see what light has been thrown on the psychometric questions arising in thematic apperceptive measurement of motivation.

The traditional episodic conception of motivation makes us think of a series of imaginative stories in response to pictures as a set of separate and discrete incidents as in 1950. Each begins with presentation of the stimulus (picture) that calls forth a reaction (the story) expressing the motivational tendencies of an individual. In each case, the strength of tendency to achieve, for example, is thought to depend on the interaction of cognitive expectations about a goal to be attained, an incentive, aroused by the picture cue and the strength of motive to achieve within the individual. When, as was generally assumed, these cognitive expectations are reasonably equivalent for all individuals tested (Atkinson, 1958b), variations among individuals in achievement-related imaginative reaction should, except for *random error,* express variations among individuals in the strength of achievement motive, the attribute of personality presumably being measured. The argument is repeated for every picture and story, each taken as a discrete diagnostic test of strength of achievement motive. The logic of traditional test theory, viz., obtained score = true score ± random error, is applied to determine the reliability (internal consistency) of the total n Achievement score. The reliability, as traditionally conceived, supposedly sets an upper limit for validity, and so reliability is considered the basic prerequisite for fruitful scientific research (Entwisle, 1972).

Today, however, we take the old cognitive theory of achievement motivation (e.g., $T_s = M_s \cdot P_s \cdot I_s$ in the simplest case) to be an hypothesis about the determinants of instigating force (e.g., $F_s = M_s \cdot P_s \cdot I_s$). This refers to the arousability or rate of growth in strength of tendency to achieve when exposed to the stimulus situation and not the static strength of the tendency elicited by that stimulus situation. This is illustrated in the initial slopes of curves y and z in Fig. 8.2. More generally, the components of traditional cognitive theory, Expectancy × Value, are taken to be the determinants of instigating or inhibitory forces in the new dynamics of action (Atkinson & Birch, 1970, Chapter 6).

Consider Fig. 8.2 an illustration of what might be expected in the stream of imaginative behavior *emitted* as a result of exposure to the first picture in a thematic apperceptive test of strength of achievement motive. Let Y represent "concern about achieving."

To begin with, we note that T_X, T_Y, T_Z, and T_V are assumed to be already aroused even before the individual is exposed to the picture stimulus. Only T_W, which begins at zero strength, reminds us of the traditional assumption of an organism at rest awaiting the stimulus as a goad to react. All this is shown at the extreme left side of the graph that corresponds to the instant when the first picture is presented.

Now turn to the extreme right side of the graph. This describes the underlying structure of the motivational state of the person at the end of the first story. The strengths of T_V, T_W, T_X, T_Y, and T_Z persist to influence the next event that begins immediately as the second picture is shown. The strengths of these tendencies differ *systematically* from what they were at the outset of the first story. The second picture has its own motivational properties. The incentives for different kinds of activity in the setting portrayed in it are different. Perhaps the next picture produces an instigating force for activity V, a tendency for which has persisted unchanged throughout the whole interval of the first story because it was neither instigated nor expressed in behavior. Perhaps there is no incentive for activity Z, and so T_Z persists unchanged and never is expressed throughout the whole interval of the second story.

It is obvious that T_W, instigated throughout the whole 4 minute interval of the first story but not expressed because it never became the strongest tendency during that interval, should become dominant and be expressed very early in the second story even if the subsequent magnitude of instigating force (F_W), providing for further increase in its strength, is quite weak.

The changing content of imaginative thought in the first story is depicted by the segments of the line x, y, x, z, etc., at the top of the graph. The changes in content of thought represent expression of the strongest or dominant tendency at each point in time.

The total amount of time spent expressing the tendency to achieve (T_Y) is represented by a summation of the line segments y. The percentage of time spent thinking about achievement is represented by this total time thinking about y divided by the total time spent thinking about x, y, and z, all the activities that occurred during the whole time interval of the first story.

In this case, about 37% of the total time was spent thinking about achievement (Y). One can imagine that if the instigating force (F_Y) had been weaker and the initial slope of curve Y less steep than shown in the figure (more like that of Z), the initial expression of Y in the stream of thought would have been delayed, each occurrence would probably have been of shorter duration, and these occurrences probably would have been less frequent. In sum, the percentage of time thinking about achievement (Y) would have been less. This would be expected if the strength of achievement motive in the person, one of the determinants of F_Y, had been weaker. And, in contrast, we can visualize the effect of a stronger motive to achieve as a determinant of F_Y in Fig. 8.2. The initial slope of T_Y would be steeper, describing a more rapid arousal of the tendency. The latency of the initial achievement-related activity would be shorter than shown. The average duration of that and all subsequent occurrences would be longer, and the occurrences of activity Y more frequent. In sum, a greater percentage of time would be spent thinking about achievement.

Look again at the initial and final strengths of the competing motivational tendencies in Fig. 8.2. At the end of the first story, and therefore at the very beginning of the second story, T_X is stronger than it was at the beginning of the first story. So are T_Z, T_Y, and particularly T_W. The rank order of the strengths of tendencies was T_X, T_Y, T_Z, T_V, T_W, at the outset of the first story. But it is $T_X = T_W$, T_Z, T_Y, T_V when the picture for the second story is presented. So even if that picture were exacty equivalent to the first one in its motivational properties, so that in interaction with the personality of the same subject it produced exactly the same magnitudes of instigating forces for V, W, X, Y, and Z as the first picture, the content of the stream of imaginative behavior would nevertheless be different. The most noticeable difference would be the early and repeated expressions of activity W that didn't occur at all in the first story. Here, both determinants of the instigating forces, personal (motives) and environmental (incentives), are presumed constant; but the expected imaginative behavior is different. In other words, the assumption of constancy (or stability) in personality throughout the temporal interval of two imaginative stories does not imply equivalent constancy in the expected behavior even if the picture stimuli are identical. This *expected behavior* corresponds to the *true score* in the equation of traditional test theory: Obtained score = True score ± Error.

The very same point is made if one divides Fig. 8.2 in half at point A on the abscissa, as if this corresponded to the end of the first story and the beginning of a second story to an equivalent picture stimulus. The time spent thinking about Y (achievement) in the second story is here *expected to be* 40% greater than in the first story, though the personality disposition and the picture influencing F_Y (the arousal of T_Y) have both remained constant.

Here then, is the main point of the results of 25 computer simulations of thematic apperceptive measurement of individual differences in strength of achievement motive, as stated by Atkinson, Bongort, and Price (1977):

> The theory of motivation specifies how a *stable* personality disposition, strength of motive, will be expressed behaviorally in *variable* amounts of times spent thinking and/or writing about achievement. It tells us specifically how, under various conditions, the "truly expected" time spent expressing the tendency to achieve will vary in a sequence of consecutive incidents....
>
> Basic theory about the underlying psychological process is logically prior to any application of traditional test theory. One must, in other words, have some

sound theoretical basis for expecting a certain "true score" on a given test before one introduces the whole logic of test theory, which has to do with the implications of random error in the effort to measure accurately. With thematic apperception, it has been a mistake to assume that the "true score" (some behavioral manifestation) should be constant just because the strength of the underlying trait (motive) is presumed constant. One needs a theory to get from personality to someting measurable, viz., behavior [p. 24].

This is what traditional test theory has lacked—a psychological theory to get from individual differences in personality, which presumably remain constant through the temporal interval of a diagnostic test, to the expected individual differences in behavior. And so mental testers (and unfortunately many personologists) have just gone ahead and assumed that if the magnitude of differences in personality were of the order 8, 7, 6, on some attribute, the expected differences in behavior (true scores) should also be of the order 8, 7, 6, except as they are made spuriously high or low on each of several repeated occasions by errors assumed to be independent, identically and normally distributed, with mean zero.

Using departure (±) from seven in the sum of the points rolled on two dice to generate independent, random errors of ±1 to 5, I obtained the scores shown in Table 8.5 to provide a simplified simulation of thematic apperceptive measurement of motives for three persons guided by the traditional *statistical* logic of test theory as in 1950.

Given the dynamics of action, a psychological theory about the motivational process underlying the stream of imaginative behavior, one is led to expect *systematic* variations in time spent thinking about achievement on consecutive diagnostic tests. These are the theoretically deduced true scores (behavioral manifestations) presuming constancy in the attribute of personality (motive) being expressed, even before confronting the effects of variations attributable to random errors in measurement.

TABLE 8.5

Simulation of Thematic Apperceptive Measurement of Individual Differences in Strength of Motive Guided by Statistical Logic of Traditional Test Theory: Obtained Score=True Score ± Error

	Stories in Response to Pictures				
Strength of Motive	Story 1	Story 2	Story 3	Story 4	Total
8	11	7	5	8	31
7	8	6	7	5	26
6	8	5	8	3	24

Note: For simplicity, it is assumed that the incentive provided by each picture equals 1. Random error simulated by ± deviation from a sum of seven in independent rolls of two dice.

Given the arbitrary presumption of traditional test theory, that a constant strength of motive in the person implies a similar constancy in the true scores on consecutive diagnostic tests, *the truly expected internal consistency,* unmarred by any errors of measurement, should be 1.00; that is, all the subparts of the test as a whole, including all possible halves of the test, should yield scores that are correlated 1.00 if there were no error of measurement.

Given, now, a theoretical basis for expecting something less than perfect internal consistency in an errorless test, the important question becomes— how does this affect the validity of the measure of motive strength obtained from the test as a whole? That is the question that a series of 25 computer simulations of thematic apperceptive measurement of achievement motivation were designed to answer. The answer forthcoming was unambiguous, as stated in Atkinson, Bongort, and Price (1977):

> *Simulation of conditions that exist when people who differ in strength of achievement motive write imaginative stories in response to a sequence of pictures shows that construct validity does not require internal consistency as traditionally supposed. The theoretically deduced differences in total time spent imagining achieving (instead of something else) can postdict input differences in motive strength (i.e., construct validity) even when there is little or no internal consistency reliability as indicated by Cronbach's (1951) alpha computed from theoretically deduced time spent imagining achievement in response to particular pictures* [p. 1].

The pattern of 25 computer simulations involving, in each case, 18 to 30 hypothetical subjects who differed in strength of motive was quite simple. The hypothetical individuals differing in strength of motive to achieve (one determinant of instigating force to achieve) were confronted with a hypothetical picture producing an incentive to achieve (another determinant of the instigating force to achieve) and also instigating forces for other competing activities. The time spent engaging in achievement and other imaginative activities is generated, as in Fig. 8.2. Then, after an arbitrary interval of 100 units of time (corresponding to a 4 minute story), these hypothetical individuals who continue to differ in personality (motive) were immediately confronted with a new picture that presented more or less incentive to achieve than the first one and variations in the incentives that influenced the competing tendencies. We assumed, quite simply, that the product of motive (personality) and incentive (situation) determined the magnitude of instigating force for each of the several different activities. What happens, we asked, when after another 100 time units a third picture is presented and later still a 4th, 5th, and so on.

The computer program applies the principle of a change in activity continuously given the strength of a set of competing tendencies in the individual and the forces produced by the first picture, as in Fig. 8.2. Then, at the end of 100 time units, it applies the principle again but now with a different set of forces operating on tendencies that have changed in strength but persisted to influence what happens in the second interval of 100 units of time. This continues to happen for consecutive intervals of 100 time units until all the hypothetical pictures have been presented.

At the end of each 100 units of time, the computer printout tells how much time was spent imagining achievement in that story by each hypothetical subject. This corresponds to the theoretically expected or *true n* Achievement score for that subject, as if we had an empirical measure that corresponded to a perfect clock. Treating each story as a separate test or item as Entwisle (1972) did, Cronbach's alpha was calculated to ascertain the theoretically expected average split-half reliability. And the total times spent thinking about achievement in all the stories, corresponding to the theoretically expected total *n* Achievement scores of different individuals, was correlated with the strength of achievement motive that had been fed into the computer as input descriptive of how the hypothetical subjects differed in personality.

In some studies, the pictures were presented in Latin Square Designs following the plan of the earliest empirical study of reliability (Atkinson, 1950; McClelland et al., 1953, Chapter 7). In others, the pictures were presented in a fixed order as by Haber and Alpert (1958) and in most all studies of behavioral effects of individual differences in motivation.

The results for the set of studies, each with a hypothetical sample of 18 to 30 individuals and concerned with the effects of variation in such parameters as selective attention, consummatory lag, strength of force to achieve relative to number and strength of forces for alternative activities, etc., are presented simply in Fig. 8.4. It shows, rather definitively, that the construct validity of the total score does not require reliability (internal consistency) as traditionally conceived. Details of the various simulations are described elsewhere (Atkinson, Bongort, & Price, 1977). Here it is sufficient to note that our thinking about thematic apperceptive measurement of motivation need no longer be constrained by mistaken myths of measurement.

Correspondence with Earlier Empirical Evidence

We were amazed at the degree of correspondence between the results in some of these computer simulations of thematic apperception and earlier empirical evidence. For example, in a simple preliminary simulation with a particular Latin Square involving five pictures, five sequences and 15 subjects, one was arbitrarily designated high (3), another mid (2), and another low (1) in strength of achievement motive for each sequence of pictures. Incentives to achieve for these five pictures were designated 2, 3, 4, 6, and 8, following the logic of Jacobs' (1958) method for varying cue strength of pictures. The product of motive (person) and incentive (picture) yielded a range of

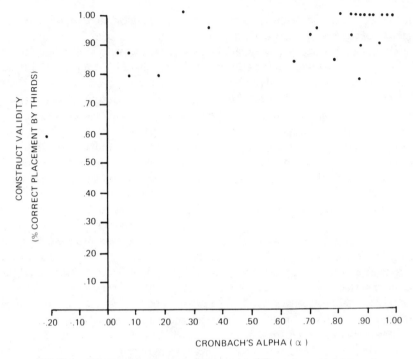

FIG. 8.4. Relationship of expected construct validity and expected internal consistency (alpha) in 25 simulations of thematic apperceptive measurement of individual differences in strength of achievement motive. Construct validity refers to percentage of subjects correctly placed by total time in achievement activity into rank-ordered thirds of motive strength defined by computer input. (Based on Figure 4 in Atkinson, Bongort, & Price, 1977, p. 14.)

magnitudes of instigating force to achieve (2 to 24) that were pitted in each story against instigating forces for three incompatible activities having magnitudes of 12. Coefficient alpha was .42 ($N = 15$) and the ordinal position effect for the five subjects classified Low (1) in achievement motive showed the odd–even oscillation or "sawtooth" effect first noted in 1950 (Table 8.2) and given some emphasis by Reitman and Atkinson (1958). The initial correspondence with something already familiar influenced our selection of parameter values for the more systematic studies that followed.

The following study by Mary M. Moffett from our research group was a balanced Latin Square involving 10 sequences of five pictures, each presented to three hypothetical subjects designated *high* (1.5), *mid* (1.0), and *low* (0.5) in achievement motive with other parameters as already described. It yielded an alpha = .08 ($N = 30$) indicating no "reliability." Yet 86.7% of the subjects were correctly placed into thirds by total scores and the product moment correlation between motive strength and total time spent thinking about achievement was .85 (construct validity).

The odd–even oscillation was lost in the results for ordinal position in this balanced Latin Square as it had been lost in an early follow up study by Birney (1958) using different sets of pictures. Apparently it depends on a fortuitous ordering of pictures in a Latin Square design. But other familiar things appeared. The more strongly cued pictures produced more time spent in achievement activity than those less strongly cued (Haber & Alpert, 1958). More important, scores based on stories early in the series were found to have greater validity than those based on stories later in the series. In Study 1 by Moffett, 73.3% of the cases (N = 30) were correctly ordered in high, mid, low thirds on motive strength defined by computer input on the basis of total time spent "achieving" on the first two of the five stories, but only 33% (the chance probability) were correctly placed on the basis of time spent "achieving" on the last two of the five stories. Here is more than a strong hint of correspondence with the early empirical research on predictive validity of the n Achievement score based on stories early and late in a series of eight shown earlier in Table 8.3.

A later analysis of the comparative reliability (internal consistency) and validity of simulated time spent "achieving" in the first six stories and last six in a set of twelve, in which order of six pictures was repeated, showed two things. When the cue strength of pictures for achievement was weakened relative to that for competing activities in the test as a whole, the percentage of total time spent "thinking about achievement" was reduced from 39% to about 15%. Corresponding to this reduction in percentage of time spent engaging in the critical activity is a reduction in the internal consistency, from .68 to .35 when the coefficient is based on the first six pictures, and from .76 to .52 when it is based on the last six pictures. The former (scores from the first six pictures) corresponds more to the typical length of test used in empirical research. Despite the decreased internal consistency, the percentage of persons correctly placed into ordered thirds on motive strength on the basis of total time for the first six pictures never fell below 75%, indicating substantial validity. But this indicator of construct validity dropped to 41.7% for *the second six pictures* when the cue strength of the pictures (and internal consistency reliability) was lowest (Atkinson, Bongort, & Price, 1977, pp. 21–22). Here again is a simulated confirmation of early empirical research that showed the predictive validity of n Achievement scores based on the first four stories but not the last four in a set of eight (Table 8.3).

This should be enough to indicate the promise of computer simulation of thematic apperception, grounded in contemporary theory of motivation, to advance our comprehension of what is being measured and how well. The obvious confrontation between motivational psychology and traditional test theory has begun in this work and is also under discussion elsewhere

(Atkinson & Birch, 1978, Chapter 8). Entwisle (1972), echoing an argument we have heard repeatedly in the past quarter of a century, was moved "to dispel fantasies about fantasy-based measures of achievement motivation" in light of estimating the reliability to be about .30 to .40, rather too modest, it was argued, to claim much validity. Now we see that substantial validity is possible even when reliability (internal consistency) is nil. But there remain important cautions about the optimal length of a test and the relative merits of strongly cued versus weakly cued pictures, both in the earliest empirical methodological research and now in the contemporary theoretical analysis involving computer simulation. The latter, which we have been discussing, tells what might be expected given the theory of motivation, if we imagine that time spent thinking about achievement in a story had been measured by a perfect clock. We must acknowledge that the 30-year-old experimentally validated n Achievement score, even when obtained by expert coders whose scoring reliability is .90 or above, must yield a relatively crude indication of what that perfect clock would say. So the modest indices of internal consistency noted by critics of the method must be considered degraded versions of some higher theoretically expected value of alpha. It is timely, now, to recognize the need to improve our estimate of real time spent thinking about achievement in thematic apperception. A first exploratory step has been taken by Shapiro (1978). More important still is to recognize the virtually untapped promise of content analysis of imaginative thought as a resource for future development of social psychology generally, now that the stream of imaginative behavior has a sound theoretical foundation, something it lacked in 1950. The every day stream of overt operant behavior is characterized by change from one activity to another. This is also characteristic of *the content* of the covert stream of imaginative thought. The individual in a laboratory, when invited to exercise imagination, has the ability to change, when so inclined, from thinking about one thing to thinking about another. The content of imaginative thought can encompass anything that one is inclined to think about. The challenge of the future is to bring experimental skill, breadth of background, and theoretical insight that is commensurate with the promise of the method to the task of exploiting it. One hopes that social psychology can recover what it has lost in its thrust to become an experimental, *cognitive* social psychology; that is an understanding and appreciation of the fundamentally important implications, both theoretical and methodological, in the work of Sigmund Freud and the clinical tradition. Both are expressed here, in the dynamic theory of motivation and in the sustained interest in an indirect, projective method of studying human motivation in preference to the ever popular, easily administered self-descriptive test. Hopefully the recovery of unconscious processes by Nisbett and Wilson (1977) within the mainstream of cognitive social psychology may herald a rebirth of interest in basic insights and guiding hypotheses that were part of an earlier, heuristic consensus.

In the final chapter of *The achievement motive* (1953), McClelland, mainly responsible for composing that chapter, speculated about the great promise of the new method of "thought sampling" that we had gotten into in the early research on hunger and achievement motivation. He estimated that the average person must produce about 8 to 12 identifiable thoughts a minute, as we were coding them. "At this rate he would produce about 600 an hour, up to 10,000 a day, between 3 and 4 million a year, or 250 million in a lifetime [p. 321]." Then the argument went on to consider the total population of the earth and the order of the number of thoughts, covert activities, that were out there to be studied by the new objective method, in order to close the gap between a psychology of "experience" and of "behavior." A few years later, now 25 years ago, McClelland (1955) wrote an essay entitled "The psychology of mental content reconsidered." In it he argued again and more extensively that the very high degree of objectivity (i.e., coding reliability) and experimental validity that had been achieved in content analysis of imaginative behavior provided a new, scientifically sound basis for bringing analysis of thought content back into the mainstream of psychology. Since then, the heyday of S–R behavior theory, psychology has obviously become much more cognitive. As Heckhausen and Weiner (1972) have said: It has been "regaining its mind [p. 126]." But most "cognitive psychologists," whether for reasons of expediency (it takes time to employ thematic apperception) or because of the continual harping criticism of psychometricians who have always put their conception of reliability, deduced from a set of questionable basic premises, ahead of validity that the eye can see, have tended to shy away from the richness of imaginative thought long favored by those reared in the clinical tradition. Hopefully, the mistaken criticism of thematic apperception—an obstacle to progress—has been laid to rest. There remains, now, only the matter of expediency.

The Meaning of Thematic Apperceptive *n* Achievement Score

Perhaps the most important generalization to come from the new dynamics of action is one that supports its claim of being a theory of operant behavior (Atkinson & Birch, 1978, pp. 306–311 and Chapter 8). The generalization has to do with time allocation among competing activities in a given setting. Initially developed in reference to the simple case of two competing activities (Atkinson & Birch, 1970, pp. 101–107), extended to the case of multiple alternatives (Sawusch, 1974) and supported by the results of computer simulations (Atkinson & Birch, 1978, pp. 145–146 and 364–366; Atkinson, Bongort, & Price, 1977, p. 177), the generalization is stated:

$$\% \text{ time spent in Activity } A = \frac{F_A/c_A}{(F_A/c_A) + (F_B/c_B) + \cdots + (F_N/c_N),}$$

where $F_A, F_B, \ldots, F_N$ refer to the magnitudes of the instigating forces for activities $A, B \ldots N$, $c_A, c_B, \ldots, c_N$ refer to the consummatory values of those activities, and $F_A/c_A + F_B/c_B + \cdots + F_N/c_N$ refer to the asymptotic strengths of the competing tendencies, $T_A, T_B, \ldots, T_N$, in a given setting. It follows from the principles of the dynamics of action that in any situation an action tendency increases or decreases in strength when it is expressed in behavior, depending on the relative strengths of the instigating and consummatory forces. In time, the strength of the tendency becomes relatively stable as it approaches a level corresponding to the ratio of the magnitude of instigating force (F) to the consummatory value (c) of the activity as exemplified by the initial level of T_X in Fig. 8.2. This theoretical generalization concerning time allocation corresponds in form to the Matching Law in operant behavior (de Villiers & Herrnstein, 1976), according to which the relative frequency of a particular response (when there are multiple alternatives) equals, or matches, its relative frequency of reinforcement. The consummatory values of various activities in animal studies of operant conditioning are so similar that one might assume they would cancel out in the time allocation generalization leaving, as a vitally important implication, the hypothesis that the magnitude of instigating force for an activity depends on the frequency of prior reinforcement of that activity.

The same principle of time allocation accounts for the time spent thinking about achievement (or anything else) in thematic apperception. We now view the earlier theory of achievement motivation (Atkinson & Feather, 1966; Raynor, 1969, 1974) to be an hypothesis about the components or determinants of instigating force (i.e., $F_S = M_S \cdot P_S \cdot I_S$ in the simplest case). If one presumes that the consummatory values of different kinds of imaginative activity are reasonably equivalent, the time allocation rule may be simplified to read:

$$\% \text{ time spent in Activity } A = \frac{F_A}{F_A + F_B + \cdots F_N}.$$

Kawamura-Reynolds (1977) employed this logic in studying the expression of motivation in thematic apperception immediately following working alone and working in the presence of an audience. She replicated the experimental conditions employed in recent studies of social facilitation and impairment of performance (Cottrell, 1972; Zajonc, 1965). She then compared the effect on TAT n Achievement and TAT n Affiliation (often taken as a measure of need for social approval) when working alone, with a substantial incentive to achieve, and with both that and additional incentive for social approval provided by having an audience.

Intuition suggests that average n Achievement score should be rather high and constant, but that average n Affiliation score should increase with the audience. The principle of time allocation (mentioned earlier), which takes into account the strength of instigating force for achievement (or affiliation), the numerator, relative to the sum of all instigating forces attributable to incentives in the situation, the denominator, implies something different: the effect of an audience should be to increase time spent thinking about approval (n Affiliation) and to decrease time spent thinking about achievement (n Achievement) in comparison with the alone condition. Both trends occurred, as predicted, and the combined effect was statistically significant.

Finally, if one were to continue to assume, as we have before (Atkinson, 1958b), that other determinants of instigating forces to achieve, to affiliate, to gain power, etc.,... produced by a particular picture in thematic apperception are also reasonably equivalent among different subjects, one might rewrite the generalization so that it refers only to the systematic effect of strength of motives as determinants of differences among people in the magnitude of various instigating forces:

$$\% \text{ time spent in Activity } A = \frac{M_A}{M_A + M_B + \cdots M_N}.$$

Obviously, these are very strong and probably unwarranted assumptions given the number of different variables that can influence the magnitude of instigating force (e.g., probability of attaining the goal, incentive value of the goal, future orientation, etc.). I make them here to simplify the discussion of the new insight we have achieved concerning the meaning of n Achievement score (taken as an indicator of time spent thinking about achievement).

It is clear that the time spent thinking about achievement depends almost as much on the number of competing motives within a person, and their strengths, as it does on the strength of achievement motive. In the past, we have rather glibly taken variations in n Achievement score to mean variations among individuals in absolute strength of motive to achieve. Now we see that the theoretically sound inference is that we have measured the strength of achievement motive relative to the number and strength of competing motives within the individual. We are dealing with the conjectured hierarchy of motives suggested earlier by Murray (1938), McClelland (1951), and popularized by Maslow (1954). This measure should always provide a useful basis for predicting other differences in behavior that also depend on the *relative* strength of achievement motive within an individual (e.g., initiation of activities, preference among different kinds, persistence, time allocation among activities, etc.) but not necessarily differences in behavior that depend on differences in the *absolute* strength of motive (e.g., choice among alternative *achievement-related* activities [Hamilton, 1974; Schneider, 1978], the levels of performance on an *achievement-related* task engaged in constantly for a period of time [Atkinson & Reitman, 1956]). Two individuals who differ greatly in absolute strength of achievement motive (the numerator) might, nevertheless, obtain the same thematic apperceptive n Achievement score *if they also differ in a certain way in number and/or strength of competing motives* (the denominator). For example, the ratio of $1/(1 + 1 + 1)$ is equivalent to $3/(3 + 3 + 3)$ is equivalent to $2/(1 + 2 + 2 + 1)$. All equal $1/3$ and imply the same percentage of time spent thinking about achievement, yet the strengths of achievement motive are 1, 2, and 3.

In light of this, it is important to note that to derive the repeatedly obtained relationships between thematic apperceptive *n* Achievement score and preference for moderately difficult tasks (in the simplest case), and the differences in level of performance at a task engaged in for a period of time under appropriate conditions, requires the assumption (or conclusion) that differences in *n* Achievement score *do* express differences among individuals in absolute strength of the motive (see Atkinson & Birch, 1970, pp. 187–189, 1974, 284–287, 1978, 130–131 for the derivations). These repeatedly obtained behavioral results could occur, given the dynamics of action as the theoretical foundation, only if variation among individuals in strength of achievement motive were not very highly correlated with the sum of the strengths of all competing motives. Given the time allocation principle, it must be concluded that variations in the numerator of the equation must not be counteracted or compensated for by correlated variations among individuals in the denominator. Here is a new inference which raises many new and interesting questions, another product of the kind of continuing dialogue between experimental fact and theoretical conception that characterizes fruitful scientific work.

TABLE 8.6

The Expected Effect of the Strength of Achievement Motive (and Others) on Idealized Thematic Apperceptive *n* Achievement Score Deduced from Generalization About Time Allocation Based on the Dynamics of Action

Motives	1	2	3	4	Idealized *n* Achievement Score
Assuming independence of motives (N = 50)					
A. 1. Achievement	1.00	.01	.04	.04	.86
2. Power		1.00	.06	.00	−.26
3. Affiliation			1.00	.04	−.26
4. Sex				1.00	−.20
B. 1. Achievement	1.00	.01	.04	−1.00	.92
2. Power		1.00	.06	−.01	−.25
3. Affiliation			1.00	−.04	−.22
4. Sex				1.00	−.92
C. 1. Achievement	1.00	.01	.04	1.00	.82
2. Power		1.00	.06	.01	−.35
3. Affiliation			1.00	.04	−.34
4. Sex				1.00	.82

Note: This table contributed by Dr. Virginia Blankenship.

To engage the interest of a new generation of specialists in psychological measurement even more, let us consider Table 8.6. Assuming only four different motives (achievement, power, affiliation, and sex) as common characteristics of 50 hypothetical personalities, Blankenship determined the strength of each motive randomly from a normal distribution of values ranging from 1 to 10. Then, using the time allocation principle, as stated in reference to strength of achievement motive relative to the sum of the strengths of all motives in a person, the percentage time spent imagining achievement was deduced. We treat the latter as an idealized n Achievement score. Linear correlations between the strengths of each motive and each with the idealized n Achievement score are shown in Section A of Table 8.6.

When the strengths of all the motives are assumed to be independent within the fifty hypothetical persons, the strength of achievement motive is correlated .86 with the idealized n Achievement score. Here, 73% of variance in simulated n Achievement score is attributable to differences in achievement motive. The residual 27% of the variance is attributable to the sum of the strengths of all other motives within individuals.[2]

When a perfect negative correlation is assumed between achievement and sexual motives (B in Table 8.6), the correlation between achievement motive and errorless n Achievement score is higher, .92. This indicates the direction of things if the relationship among various motives within people tends to be complementary or compensatory. In this case, the absence of concern about achievement becomes an excellent indicator of strength of sexual motive.

When a perfect positive correlation is assumed between these same two motives (C in Table 8.6), the correlation between strength of achievement motive and idealized n Achievement score is lower, .82, than when they are independent. This indicates the direction of things when strength of motives within people tend to be positively correlated.

Here is a guide for future psychological measurement firmly anchored in theory about the basic underlying behavioral processes. We may anticipate a richer and more enlightened dialogue between empirical inquiry and theoretical analysis, certainly a quickened pace, when more psychologists come to realize that we can leave behind our old crutch—the stale, sterile, statistical logic of the normal curve expressed in traditional test theory that has helped us merely to limp along. Today we can step boldly into an era in which our most heuristic tool is the computer's capacity to spell out the implications of simple principles about basic processes applied to complex conditions.

---

[2]Note that strength of achievement motive is represented in the sum of the strength of all motives. In this particular analysis, it is responsible for 25% of the variance among individuals in that sum. If the number of other independent motives is increased, the variance in simulated n Achievement score that is attributable to their sum diminishes.

REFERENCES

Atkinson, J. W. *Studies in projective measurement of achievement motivation.* (Doctoral thesis, University of Michigan, 1950). Ann Arbor (University Microfilms Publication #1945, 145); also: Ann Arbor (Microfilm Abstract, 10–14, 1950, 290–291).

Atkinson, J. W. Motivational determinants of risk-taking behavior. *Psychological Review,* 1957, *64,* 359–372.

Atkinson, J. W. (Ed.). *Motives in fantasy, action, and society.* Princeton, N.J.: Van Nostrand, 1958. (a)

Atkinson, J. W. Thematic apperceptive measurement of motives within the context of a theory of motivation. In J. W. Atkinson (Ed.), *Motives in fantasy, action, and society.* Princeton, N.J.: Van Nostrand, 1958. (b)

Atkinson, J. W. *An introduction to motivation.* Princeton, N.J.: Van Nostrand, 1964.

Atkinson, J. W. Change of activity: A new focus for the theory of motivation. In T. Mischel (Ed.), *Human action.* New York: Academic Press, 1969.

Atkinson, J. W. Motivation for achievement. In T. Blass (Ed.), *Personality variables in social behavior.* Hillsdale, N.J.: Lawrence Erlbaum Associates, 1977.

Atkinson, J. W., & Birch, D. *The dynamics of action.* New York: Wiley, 1970.

Atkinson, J. W., & Birch, D. The dynamics of achievement-oriented activity. In J. W. Atkinson & J. O. Raynor (Eds.), *Motivation and achievement.* Washington, D.C.: Winston, 1974.

Atkinson, J. W., & Birch, D. *An introduction to motivation (rev. ed.).* New York: Van Nostrand, 1978.

Atkinson, J. W., Bongort, K., & Price, L. H. Explorations using computer simulation to comprehend thematic apperceptive measurement of motivation. *Motivation and Emotion,* 1977, *1,* 1–27.

Atkinson, J. W., & Cartwright, D. Some neglected variables in contemporary conceptions of decision and performance. *Psychological Reports,* 1964, *14,* 575–590.

Atkinson, J. W., & Feather, N. T. (Eds.). *A theory of achievement motivation.* New York: Wiley, 1966.

Atkinson, J. W., & McClelland, D. C. The projective expression of needs. II. The effect of different intensities of the hunger drive on thematic apperception. *Journal of Experimental Psychology,* 1948, *38,* 643–658.

Atkinson, J. W., & Raynor, J. O. (Eds.). *Motivation and achievement.* Washington, D.C.: Winston, 1974. Abridged version, *Personality, motivation, and achievement.* Washington, D.C.: Hemisphere, 1978.

Atkinson, J. W., & Reitman, W. R. Performance as a function of motive strength and expectancy of goal attainment. *Journal of Abnormal and Social Psychology,* 1956, *53,* 361–366.

Barker, R. G. *The stream of behavior.* New York: Appleton-Century-Crofts, 1963.

Birch, D. Shift in activity and the concept of persisting tendency. In K. W. Spence & J. T. Spence (Eds.), *The psychology of learning and motivation: Advances in research and theory* (Vol. II). New York: Academic Press, 1968.

Birch, D. Measuring the stream of activity. *Michigan Mathematical Psychology Publication,* MMPP 72-2, Michigan Mathematical Psychology Program, Ann Arbor: University of Michigan, 1972.

Birch, D., Atkinson, J. W., & Bongort, K. Cognitive control of action. In B. Weiner (Ed.), *Cognitive views of human motivation.* New York: Academic Press, 1974.

Birney, R. C. Thematic content and the cue characteristics of pictures. In J. W. Atkinson (Ed.), *Motives in fantasy, action, and society.* Princeton, N.J.: Van Nostrand, 1958.

Blankenship. V. *Consummatory value of success, task difficulty, and substitution.* Unpublished doctoral dissertation, University of Michigan, 1979.

Bongort, K. *Revision of program by Seltzer and Sawusch: Computer program written to simulate the dynamics of action.* Unpublished program, University of Michigan, September 4, 1974.

Cartwright, D., & Festinger, L. A quantitative theory of decision. *Psychological Review,* 1943, *50,* 595–621.

Cottrell, N. Social facilitation. In C. McClintock (Ed.), *Experimental social psychology.* New York: Holt, Rinehart & Winston, 1972.

Cronbach, L. J. Coefficient alpha and the internal structure of tests. *Psychometrika,* 1951, *16,* 297–334.

Descartes, R. Discourse on method [1637]. In J. Veitch (trans.), *Religion of Science Library No. 38.* Chicago: Open Court publishing, 1935.

deVilliers, P. A., & Herrnstein, R. J. Toward a law of response strength. *Psychological Bulletin,* 1976, *83,* 1131–1153.

Edwards, W. The theory of decision making. *Psychological Bulletin,* 1954, *51,* 380–417.

Entwisle, D. R. To dispel fantasies about fantasy-based measures of achievement motivation. *Psychological Bulletin,* 1972, *77,* 377–391.

Feather, N. T. The relationship of persistence at a task to expectation of success and achievement related motives. *Journal of Abnormal and Social Psychology,* 1961, *63,* 552–561.

Feather, N. T. The study of persistence. *Psychological Bulletin,* 1962, *59,* 94–115.

Feld, S., & Smith, C. P. An evaluation of the objectivity of the method of content analysis. In J. W. Atkinson (Ed.), *Motives in fantasy, action and society.* Princeton, N.J.: Van Nostrand, 1958.

French, E. G. Some characteristics of achievement motivation. *Journal of Experimental Psychology,* 1955, *50,* 232–236.

Haber, R. N., & Alpert, R. The role of situation and picture cues in projective measurement of the achievement motive. In J. W. Atkinson (Ed.), *Motives in fantasy, action and society.* Princeton, N.J.: Van Nostrand, 1958.

Hamilton, J. O. Motivation and risk taking behavior: A test of Atkinson's theory. *Journal of Personality and Social Psychology,* 1974, *29,* 856–864.

Hebb, D. O. *The organization of behavior.* New York: Wiley, 1949.

Heckhausen, H., & Weiner, B. The emergence of a cognitive psychology of motivation. In P. C. Dodwell (Ed.), *New Horizons in Psychology, 2.* Middlesex, England: Penguin Books, 1972.

Hull, C. L. *Principles of behavior.* New York: Appleton-Century-Crofts, 1943.

Jacobs, B. A method for investigating the cue characteristics of pictures. In J. W. Atkinson (Ed.), *Motives in fantasy, action and society.* Princeton, N.J.: Van Nostrand, 1958.

Kawamura-Reynolds, M. Motivational effects of an audience in the content of imaginative thought. *Journal of Personality and Social Psychology,* 1977, *35,* 912–919.

Kuhl, J., & Atkinson, J. W. *Motivational determinants of decision time: An application of the dynamics of action.* Unpublished manuscript, University of Michigan, 1979.

Kuhl, J., & Blankenship, V. The dynamic theory of achievement motivation: From episodic to dynamic thinking. *Psychological Review,* 1979, *86,* 141–151.

Kuhn, T. S. *The structure of scientific revolutions.* Chicago: University of Chicago Press, 1962.

Lewin, K. *Conceptual representation and measurement of psychological forces.* Durham, N.C.: Duke University Press, 1938.

Maslow, A. H. *Motivation and personality.* New York: Harper & Row, 1954.

McClelland, D. C. *Personality.* New York: Sloane, 1951.

McClelland, D. C. The psychology of mental content reconsidered. *Psychological Review,* 1955, *62,* 297–302.

McClelland, D. C. Methods of measuring human motivation. In J. W. Atkinson (Ed.), *Motives in fantasy, action, and society.* Princeton, N.J.: Van Nostrand, 1958.

McClelland, D. C. *The achieving society.* Princeton, N.J.: Van Nostrand, 1961. (Reissue New York: Irvington, 1976.)

McClelland, D. C. *Assessing human motivation.* Morristown, N.J.: General Learning Press, 1971.

McClelland, D. C., Atkinson, J. W., Clark, R. A., & Lowell, E. L. *The achievement motive.* New York: Appleton-Century-Crofts, 1953.(Reissue New York: Irvington, 1976.)

McClelland, D. C., Atkinson, J. W., Clark, R. A., & Lowell, E. L. A scoring manual for the achievement motive. In J. W. Atkinson (Ed.), *Motives in fantasy, action, and society.* New York: Van Nostrand, 1958.

McClelland, D. C., Clark, R. A., Roby, T. B., & Atkinson, J. W. The projective expression of needs. IV. The effect of need for achievement on thematic apperception. *Journal of Experimental Psychology,* 1949, *39,* 242–255.

Miller, N. E. Liberalization of basic S–R concepts: Extensions to conflict behavior, motivation, and social learning. In S. Koch (Ed.), *Psychology: A study of a science* (Vol. 2). New York: McGraw-Hill, 1959.

Murray, H. A. Techniques for a systematic investigation of fantasy. *Journal of Psychology,* 1937, *3,* 115–143.

Murray, H. A. *Explorations in personality.* New York: Oxford University Press, 1938.

Nisbett, R. E., & Wilson, T. D. Telling more than we can know: Verbal reports on mental processes. *Psychological Review,* 1977, *84,* 231–259.

Raynor, J. O. Future orientations and motivation of immediate activity: An elaboration of the theory of achievement motivation. *Psychological Review,* 1969, *76,* 606–610.

Raynor, J. O. Future orientation in the study of achievement motivation. In J. W. Atkinson, & J. O. Raynor, *Motivation and achievement.* Washington, D.C.: Winston, 1974.

Reitman, W. R., & Atkinson, J. W. Some methodological problems in the use of thematic apperceptive measures of human motives. In J. W. Atkinson (Ed.), *Motives in fantasy, action, and society.* New York: Van Nostrand, 1958.

Sawusch, J. R. Computer simulation of the influence of ability and motivation on test performance and cumulative achievement and the relation between them. In J. W. Atkinson, & J. O. Raynor (Eds.), *Motivation and achievement.* Washington, D.C.: Winston, 1974.

Schneider, K. Atkinson's "Risk Preference" Model: Should it be revised? *Motivation and Emotion,* 1978, *2,* 333–344.

Seltzer, R. A. Simulation of the dynamics of action. *Psychological Reports,* 1973, *32,* 859–872.

Seltzer, R. A., & Sawusch, J. R. A program for computer simulation of the dynamics of action. In J. W. Atkinson, & J. O. Raynor (Eds.), *Motivation and achievement.* Washington, D.C.: Winston, 1974.

Shapiro, J. P. A new format for thematic apperceptive measurement of motivation. *Perceptual and Motor Skills,* 1978, *47,* 744–746.

Smith, C. P., & Feld, S. How to learn the method of content analysis for *n* achievement, *n* affiliation, and *n* power. In J. W. Atkinson (Ed.), *Motives in fantasy, action, and society.* Princeton, N.J.: Van Nostrand, 1958.

Spence, K. W. *Behavior theory and conditioning.* New Haven, Conn.: Yale University Press, 1956.

Tolman, E. C. Principles of performance. *Psychological Review,* 1955, *62,* 315–326.

Whalen, R. E. Sexual motivation. *Psychological Review,* 1966, *73,* 151–163.

Zajonc, R. B. Social facilitation. *Science,* 1965, *149,* 269–274.

9

Future Orientation and Achievement Motivation: Toward a Theory of Personality Functioning and Change

Joel O. Raynor
State University of New York at Buffalo

OVERVIEW

This program of research has been guided by the premise that the cognitive structure of the individual, representing opportunities for action as steps along a path to a goal, interacts with relatively stable dispositions of the individual to affectively react to the possible outcomes of those actions (e.g., motives), to determine the amount of motivation (tendency) aroused for a particular immediate activity faced by the individual. At the onset, we were primarily concerned with cognitive representations of the anticipated future consequences of immediate activity. Theory of achievement motivation was elaborated to take into account the impact of these distant future goals on motivation of immediate achievement-oriented activity. We became concerned with the distinctions between immediate success as "earning the opportunity to continue" along a contingent path where continuation required that success, immediate success as indicating a "personal accomplishment" independent of "moving on," and immediate success as "evaluating the degree of possession" of prerequisite competences that are believed to be needed for future striving and success along the path. Thus the *meaning of success to the individual* came to be viewed in terms of these three distinct possibilities. We began to conceptualize the motivational effect of the *immediate present* primarily in terms of this "diagnostic testing" based on the outcomes of immediate skill-demanding activity. Most recently, we have become concerned with the possible effects of the *retrospected past* on motivation of immediate activity. These ideas and relevant research findings have led to the formulation of a motivational theory of personality

199

POINT LOMA COLLEGE
RYAN LIBRARY

functioning and change that builds on an expectancy × value approach to conceptualize the effects of the anticipated future, the retrospected past, and the evaluated present, on motivation of immediate activity—as well as on the person's perception of his own self-identity and self-worth as related to that immediate activity. The concept of "psychological career" has been introduced as representing *opportunities for action that define self-identity* and various sources of value that motivate immediate activity and provide self-esteem as a basis for psychological morale. The theoretical perspective represented here can best be viewed as an elaboration, extension, and specification of the approaches of Lewin (1938), McClelland (1951, 1961), and Atkinson (1957) to the study of the determinants of action/cognitive reorganization, as accomplished through the systematic study of achievement-oriented activity. The theory of personality functioning and change outlined here is meant to be a general theory that builds on and extends the earlier work in the area of achievement motivation.

The basic strategy for this program has been to: (1) specify and then assess and/or experimentally induce the cognitive structure of the individual that provides a representation of the future/present/past consequences of immediate activity; (2) indicate how this cognitive structure is expected to interact with previously specified and assessed individual differences in relatively stable motive dispositions of the individual; (3) use some behavioral measure of choice, intensity, or persistence of immediate action, or some self-report measure of interest, affect, or involvement, as a measure of the resultant amount of motivation aroused by the interaction between motives and cognitive structure; (4) extend, modify, or delete theoretical assumptions when they are consistently at odds with the data; and, finally, (5) add new assumptions to theory when either data or logical analysis suggest that present theory is inadequate to account for some behavior or phenomenological data or problem.

FUTURE ORIENTATION

The early research in this program was based on a more general statement (Raynor, 1968a, 1969, 1974a) of an initial expectancy × value theory of achievement motivation (Atkinson, 1957, 1958, 1964; Atkinson & Feather, 1966), which itself refined resultant valence theory of level of aspiration (Lewin et al., 1944) to specify: (1) the function of relatively stable motives that influence valence (value to the individual) of success and failure; and (2) the particular mathematical statement of the relationship between subjective probability of success and failure (expectancy) and the incentive value of success and failure.

In the initial theory of achievement motivation (Atkinson & Feather, 1966), tendency to achieve success (Ts) was taken to be the product of the motive to achieve success (Ms), the subjective probability of success (Ps), and the incentive value of success; $Ts = Ms \times Ps \times Is$. The incentive value of success was assumed equal to the inverse of the subjective probability of success; $Is = 1 - Ps$. Tendency to avoid failure (Tf) was represented as the product of the motive to avoid failure (Mf), the subjective probability of failure (Pf), and the negative incentive value of failure ($-If$), with $If = 1 -Pf$. The difference between the tendencies to achieve success and to avoid failure ($Ts - Tf$) yields the resultant tendency to achieve (Tr), so that achievement motivation is here viewed as the resultant of a conflict between the impulses to "do it" in order to succeed and "don't do it" in order not to fail. A useful summary statement of the initial theory is $Tr = (Ms - Mf) (Ps \times (1 - Ps))$, indicating that resultant achievement is influenced by an individual difference factor ($Ms - Mf$) and a situational factor specified completely by expectancy of success (Ps). Strength of tendency (Ta) is also influenced by other positive "extrinsic" motivation; $Ta = Tr + Text$. Hypotheses and evidence concerning this theory are found in detail in a series of research reports (Atkinson, 1958; Atkinson & Feather, 1966; Atkinson & Raynor, 1974).

Initial theory of achievement motivation can be viewed as the simplest case of the more general theory (Atkinson & Birch, 1978; Raynor, 1974a). The more general theory uses the assumptions of a general expectancy × value approach, in which action tendency is taken as the product of the strength of expectancy that action produces an outcome, and the value of that outcome to the person, summed over each expected outcome of that action. It represents an activity as the immediate next step of a path consisting of a series of steps, where each step has two components, activity and its anticipated outcome(s). The person's knowledge or beliefs concerning the order and kinds of steps in a path is taken to specify the length of that path. Component tendencies to achieve success and to avoid failure aroused by each anticipated step of a *contingent path* combine to determine total achievement motivation for the immediate activity of that path, where each component is a product of motive (M), subjective probability (P), and incentive value (I). A contingent path is defined as a series of steps where immediate success is believed a requirement in order to insure the chance to try for success in later steps of the path, whereas immediate failure is believed to guarantee loss of the chance to move on. In a contingent path, the product of the anticipated subjective probabilities of success at each step of the path between the individual and some success is assumed to determine the subjective probability that immediate action results in that success, whereas the incentive value of that success is taken as the inverse of that subjective probability of success. These assumptions yield a more general statement of the initial theory;

$$Tr = (Ms - Mf) \sum_{n=1}^{N}(P_1s_n \times Is_n),$$

where P_1s_n is equal to

$$\prod_{i=1}^{n}(P_is_i), \quad \text{and} \quad Is_n = 1 - P_1s_n.$$

Contingent Versus Noncontingent Paths of Equal Length

Research has been concerned with the effects of a contingent path on motivation of immediate activity. The more general theory derives that each anticipated step of a *contingent path* adds a component of resultant achievement motivation (*Tr*) for immediate activity. A *noncontingent path* consists of a series of steps where immediate success/failure has no bearing on the opportunity to continue and is not expected to augment motivation for the first step. Therefore, when path length is held constant, resultant achievement motivation for the first step of a contingent path should always be larger than that for the first step of a noncontingent path, when subjective probabilities of success along the paths are held constant. If $Ms > Mf$, Tr should be more positive, but if $Mf > Ms$, Tr should be more negative, in immediate activity of a contingent than a noncontingent path, whereas if $Ms = Mf$, Tr should be the same regardless of path. If performance is directly related to Tr, those with $Ms > Mf$ should do better, but those with $Mf > Ms$ should do worse, in immediate activity of a contingent than a noncontingent path, whereas those with $Ms = Mf$ should perform at the same level regardless of kind of path.

Two early studies employed the same performance task (complex 3-step arithmetic, Wendt, 1955) known to be sensitive to differences in achievement motivation, but they used different: (1) subject samples; (2) procedures to create paths; (3) probabilities of success; and (4) means of obtaining motive groups. The second (Entin & Raynor, 1973) used a design to eliminate possible alternative explanations that might account for the results of the first (Raynor & Rubin, 1971). In both studies the n Achievement score (Atkinson, 1958, Chapter 12 and Appendix III; McClelland et al., 1953) was used to assess strength of the motive to achieve success (*Ms*) and the first third of the Text Anxiety Questionnaire (Mandler & Sarason, 1952) was used to assess strength of the motive to avoid failure (*Mf*). Those relatively high on n Achievement and relatively low on Test Anxiety were assumed to have $Ms > Mf$ (called *success oriented*), those low on n Achievement and high on

TABLE 9.1

Mean Number of 3-Step Arithmetic Problems Attempted and Solved (for Males) as a Function of Motive Groups and Experimental Conditions (after Raynor & Rubin, 1971, with permission of the authors and of the publisher, the American Psychological Association)

				Condition		
		Noncontingent			Contingent	
Motive Group[1]	N	Attempted	Solved	N	Attempted	Solved
High–Low	8	15.63	13.00	7	18.43	17.43
High–High	6	11.67	8.83	6	14.17	12.00
Low–Low	10	14.40	12.70	6	12.67	11.33
Low–High	7	14.14	11.86	8	8.38	7.00

[1]n Achievement-Test Anxiety, based on median breaks.

Test Anxiety were assumed to have $Mf > Ms$ (called *failure threatened*), and those relatively strong or weak on both were assumed to have $Ms = Mf$ (called *achievement indifferent* or moderate in achievement motivation). Data for both studies (Tables 9.1 and 9.2) supported all but one of the predictions of the more general theory: Success-oriented subjects had higher performance, whereas failure-threatened subjects had lower performance, in the first step of the contingent than the noncontingent condition. Within the

TABLE 9.2

Mean Number of Problems Solved Correctly[a] (for Males) on the Complex (three-Step) Arithmetic Task as a Function of Motive Groups and Experimental Conditions (from Entin & Raynor, 1973, with permission of the authors and of the publisher)

			Condition	
		Noncontingent		Contingent
Resultant achievement motivation[b]	N	Mean	N	Mean
High	18	31.78	17	36.41
Moderate	19	31.53	15	32.28
Low	22	29.64	12	26.41

[a]Results were almost identical for problems attempted and therefore were not reported.

[b]Obtained by subtracting the standard score on Test Anxiety from the standard score on n Achievement and breaking the distribution into thirds.

contingent condition, success-oriented subjects outperformed failure-threatened subjects, with the intermediate motive groups falling between these extremes. Only within the noncontingent condition was there failure to find the expected higher performance of the success-oriented over the failure-threatened subjects; the difference was small in the predicted direction and not statistically significant in both studies. This general pattern of interaction—consisting of an increment in performance for the success-oriented group coupled with a decrement for the failure-threatened group, from noncontingent to contingent conditions—has been replicated several additional times (Entin, 1981; Entin & Feather, 1981; Raynor & Entin, 1981a, 1981b), although the pattern of interaction sometimes reverses unexpected higher performance of failure-threatened over success-oriented subjects in the noncontingent condition rather than producing superior performance of the success-oriented over failure-threatened subjects in the contingent condition.

Academic Motivation in Presumed Contingent and Noncontingent Paths

Experimental research comparing immediate performance in contingent and noncontingent paths had been preceded by studies in which n Achievement and Test Anxiety had been used to obtain motive groups, whereas ratings of the perceived instrumentality (helpfulness/importance) of grades for future success had been used to infer whether the person faced a contingent path (high importance/perceived instrumentality) or a noncontingent path (low importance/perceived instrumentality), relating immediate academic performance to future career goals. In the first study (Raynor, 1968a, also reported in Raynor, 1970 as Study I), the high-low n Achievement–Test Anxiety group received higher grades, whereas the low–high n Achievement–Test Anxiety group received lower grades when the course grade was rated as high in perceived instrumentality than when it was rated as low. Within the high perceived instrumentality group the high-low n Achievement–Text Anxiety subjects received highest grades, the low–high group lowest grades, with the high–high and low–low groups falling intermediate between these extremes. An increase in grades for the success-oriented group coupled with a decrease for the failure-threatened group from low to high importance, with less change for the middle group, is the pattern of interaction now predicted by theory. This pattern was found for both men and women separately, and for both n Achievement and Test Anxiety separately (these data are reported by sex and motive measure separately in Raynor, 1968a but were shown for sex combined and motive measures combined in Raynor, 1970, Study I). This particular pattern of results was first reported by Isaacson and Raynor (1966) using anxiety scores only to infer motive groups. The original data obtained by Isaacson and Raynor

(1966) served as the basis for development of the more general theory of achievement motivation so as to derive accentuation of aroused achievement motivation due to future (contingent) orientation.

Atkinson (1966) reported an early extension of the Isaacson and Raynor (1966) research that is described in greater detail in Raynor, Atkinson, and Brown (1974). n Achievement and Test Anxiety scores were obtained early in a college course, and ratings of perceived instrumentality at the end, just prior to the final examination. Subjective reactions of the students about to take the final were also assessed. Concern about doing well and reported anxiety were coded from the subjective reactions. A resultant motivation score was calculated so that the more positive the score, the greater the concern over doing well relative to anxiety. There was an accentuation from low to moderate to high perceived instrumentality, so that the high–low n Achievement–Test Anxiety group showed a more positive reaction, whereas the low–high group showed a more negative reaction. This interaction effect resembles that found by Isaacson and Raynor (1966), and Raynor (1968a, 1970, Study I) and reflects the accentuation predicted by the more general theory when contingent and noncontingent immediate performance is viewed—and when extrinsic motivation is assumed relatively small.

A second pattern of result reported by Raynor (1968a, 1970, Study II) showed that students received higher grades when grades were seen as helpful/important to attain future goal, regardless of motive standing. Subsequent research has continued to show these two differing patterns of results. One study (Raynor, 1968b) related n Achievement, Test Anxiety, and perceived instrumentality scores included in the Bachman et al. (1967) national survey of high-school boys to reports of high-school grades. Main effects due to both achievement-related motives and to perceived instrumentality were obtained with little interaction found between them: Reported grades were significantly higher for the high n Achievement–low Text Anxiety than the low–high group and were significantly higher for high than for low perceived instrumentality. Three years later these same students were contacted to determine which had obtained some form of post-high-school education (Atkinson, Lens, & O'Malley, 1976). The results again showed main effects of motives and perceived instrumentality on post-high-school education, with little interaction between the two; the success-oriented group was more likely to go on to further schooling, and so were those high in perceived instrumentality of high-school grades. This main effect of contingent future orientation is now expected to occur when positive incentives other than those that arouse achievement motivation are relatively strong, but this was not predicted beforehand in this study. Further research must specify a priori the level of positive extrinsic motivation, so that it is possible to predict (rather than explain after the fact) whether motives and contingent future orientation: (1) interact to accentuate motive group differences; or (2) produce higher overall positive motivation for all individuals.

Another study viewed the effects of both future importance and self-importance on grades (Mitchell, 1974, reported by Raynor, 1974b). n Achievement, Test Anxiety, and the rated necessity of getting a B or better grade for: (1) future plans to work out; and (2) self-esteem (feeling good about yourself) were assessed at the beginning of a course, while final grades were obtained 4 months later. Data for the male students showed the accentuation of motive group differences within high importance for future goals (and within high importance for self-evaluation), whereas the data for women did not.

Contingent and Noncontingent Paths:
An Overmotivation Effect?

Sorrentino (1971, 1973, 1974) viewed both achievement-related and affiliative motives (the latter an explicit "extrinsic" motivation factor for skill activity) in predicting level of performance. The group setting may have produced higher levels of total positive motivation than often found when subjects work individually. The task required rather complicated problem-solving strategies, far more so than is usually the case for tasks employed in this research. These two factors may have combined to produce apparent reversals of predicted effects that were eventually interpreted in terms of so-called "overmotivation effects" expected for performance on complex as opposed to simple tasks (Atkinson, 1967, 1974). Groups of four subjects preselected to sample appropriate motive groups were presented with three-step contingent or three-step noncontingent conditions. They then worked individually for several "practice trials." Subjects low in n Affiliation yield the expected pattern of interaction found in previous experimental work (Entin & Raynor, 1973; Raynor & Rubin, 1971), with the high–low n Achievement–Test Anxiety group performing better, but the low–high group performing worse on the practice trials of the contingent than the noncontingent condition, so that within the contingent condition, the high–low group did better than the low–high group. However, subjects high in n Affiliation reverse this pattern: There is a performance decrement for the high–low subjects and a performance increment for the low–high subjects from noncontingent to contingent conditions, yielding higher performance of the low–high than the high–low motive group. This produces the exact opposite pattern of interaction between motives and kind of path than is predicted by theory. Why?

A speculative argument with independent supportive evidence drawn from additional data obtained in the study suggests that the contingent path accentuated resultant achievement motivation as expected by the more general theory, but the additional factor of high n Affiliation in the group setting produced too much positive motivation for the high–low *n* Achievement–Test Anxiety group to perform optimally, and, paradoxically, the high *n* Affiliation motivation produced more optimal performance efficiency of the low–high *n* Achievement–Test Anxiety group, because it dampened excessive positive motivation that would ordinarily lead to the overmotivation effect purported for the high–low motive group (see Atkinson, 1974; Sorrentino, 1974, for further details of this kind of explanation). Independent assessment of aroused motivation by use of ratings of "anticipated interest" obtained before practice performance is consistent with the argument as far as aroused motivation is concerned. For those high in *n* Affiliation, positive motivation as inferred from anticipated interest increased for the high–low *n* Achievement–Test Anxiety group but decreased for the low–high *n* Achievement–Test Anxiety group from noncontingent to contingent conditions, whereas the performance trends within motive groups across conditions are in the opposite directions. Within the low *n* Affiliation—noncontingent condition subjects, the low–high *n* Achievement–Test Anxiety group outperformed the high–low *n* Achievement–Test Anxiety group. This provides independent suggestive evidence that this failure-threatened group was in fact sufficiently positively motivated to start with, so that increased inhibition for those also high in *n* Affiliation in the contingent condition could dampen *too much* positive motivation. All the conditions specified by Atkinson (1974) for such effects to completely account for the data are fulfilled, but for the first time with *contingent future orientation* providing the sources of additional motivation as well as *n* Affiliation in a group setting.

This attempt to account for the Sorrentino (1971) results assumes that predictions were not supported for those high in *n* Affiliation due to failure to take seriously the possibility that total positive motivation and performance efficiency are *curvilinear related in certain kinds of relatively complex performance tasks.* This possibility suggests caution concerning the expected impact of contingent paths on immediate actual performance rather than on aroused resultant motivation (as assessed by, for example, persistence or affective reactions), particularly when levels of extrinsic motivation are unknown. Surprisingly, little evidence is found for such an overmotivational effect on grades in studies of academic motivation reviewed previously. But perhaps we have not looked closely enough for it. The role of extrinsic incentives remains an unresolved issue requiring a priori specification and prediction.

Motivation in Contingent Paths That Differ in Length: Task Versus Time Effects

Comparison of motivation in immediate activity of contingent paths that differ in the number of anticipated future steps is based on the derivation that the greater the number of steps, the larger the number of components of resultant achievement motivation that determine total motivation for the first step. This resultant achievement motivation should be greater in the first step, for example, of a four-step contingent path than a two-step contingent path, other things equal.

Psychological distance in this theory was initially viewed in terms of a contingent path as the *number of anticipated tasks* intervening between the individual and some future success of the path, or the final step of the path. Psychological distance, as time in a contingent path, can be viewed as the anticipated amount of time to elapse prior to success in the final step of the path but was ignored in the earlier conception of the more general theory (Raynor, 1968a), although noting its possible role in "discounting value" of success and/or failure to the individual. Rather, we concentrated theory and research efforts on the "task hierarchy" (rather than the "time hierarchy").

The "goal gradient as time" suggests that the greater the closeness in time to a goal, the greater the amounts of aroused achievement motivation. However, greater closeness in time suggests *fewer* tasks in the anticipated contingent sequence, and the more general theory predicts *lesser* amounts of aroused achievement motivation with fewer steps in a contingent path. Thus the two meanings of psychological distance are not only systematically confounded in most life situations, but their predicted effects on achievement motivation sustaining immediate activity are expected to be the exact opposite—and might cancel each other when of equal strength. In addition, results reported by Gjesme (1974) clarified the role of time in the arousal of achievement motivation by showing that closeness in time to a real examination heightened both positive motivation of success-oriented subjects and negative motivation of failure-threatened subjects. This suggested that unsuccessful attempts by Brecher (1972, 1975) to replicate an early study concerning the effects of length of contingent path (Raynor, Entin, & Raynor, 1972) failed to show the predicted accentuation of motivation of immediate activity with an increased length of contingent path because of the confounding of the time and task hierarchies.

In Pearlson's (1979) doctoral research (reported in Raynor & Entin, 1981c), time and task hierarchies were systematically torn apart. Two and 4-step contingent paths were induced, holding time to complete the total path constant, using both a "short" (20 minute) and "long" (40 minute) total amount of time. For the short time condition, the 4-step path consisted of four tasks with 5 minutes to work on each, whereas for the 2-step path, the first task was to be worked for 5 minutes, followed by a second task to be worked for 15 minutes. For the long time condition, the 4-step path consisted of four 10 minute tasks, whereas the 2-step path had a first step to be worked for 10 minutes, to be followed by the second task to be worked for 30 minutes. Thus the design allows for the complete unconfounding of number of tasks and time to complete the path. To avoid possible pacing effects and to obtain a comparable performance measure, subjects (male college students) faced with a first step of 10 minutes (the long time conditions) were told that they would be given a short rest period after 5 minutes and that they therefore should not pace their effort. Performance on the first 5 minutes of a digit–symbol substitution task was taken as a measure of aroused achievement motivation. Just prior to beginning work, subjects completed a series of mood adjective ratings in which were embedded three positive and three negative affect words. A resultant affect measure (positive affect rating minus negative affect rating) was taken as a second measure of aroused achievement motivation. Individual differences in achievement-related motives were inferred from a combined measure consisting of the difference in standing on the Mehrabian (1968, 1969) measure of resultant achievement motivation and the Test Anxiety Questionnaire (Mandler & Sarason, 1952).

The pattern of results was, in general, similar for both digit–symbol performance and resultant affective ratings. It showed the predicted motive × task interaction: Success-oriented subjects (the top third of the Z Mehrabian – Z Test Anxiety distribution) were more positively motivated (e.g., performed better and reported more positive affect) in the 4-step than the 2-step paths, whereas the failure-threatened subjects (bottom third on Z Meh. – Z TAQ) were more negatively motivated (e.g., performed worse and reported more negative affect) in the 4-step than the 2-step path. A predicted motive × time interaction was found: Success-oriented subjects were more positively motivated in the short than in the long time condition, although failure-threatened subjects were more negatively motivated in the short than in the long time condition. In addition, and most importantly, a predicted triple-order interaction was obtained between motives, path length, and time to complete the path. The specific nature of this three-factor interaction was as follows. Within the short time condition, the predicted interaction between motives and length of contingent path was obtained: There was an increment in a positive motivation (higher performance and more positive affect) for the success-oriented subjects coupled with increment in negative motivation (lower performance and more negative affect) for the failure-threatened subjects, from the 2-step to 4-step conditions, resulting in higher performance and greater positive affect of the success-oriented over the failure-threatened group within the 4-step condition. However, within the long time period, these patterns were reversed, so that predictions from theory about steps held only for the short time period. The data suggest that maximum positive motivation of success-oriented individuals and maximum negative motivation of failure-threatened individuals is obtained when a path with a great number of contingent steps is presented in a relatively short time interval.

Theoretical interpretation of these results first assumes that total time for activity in the path represents the path as a single step with regard to the amount of time the individual perceives himself faced with between immediate activity and the last goal of the path, which in the present research may either be success in the last step or "making it through the path," or both. Thus the data are consistent with previous theory and research concerning the interaction between motives and time (Gjesme, 1974): The greater the elapsed time between activity and a goal, the less its impact on motivation sustaining immediate activity. Further research is needed to determine whether increased time decreases the incentive value of the goal or decreases the subjective probability of attaining the goal, or both, and whether such an effect is consistent with an inverse relationship between the two.

Contingent Paths That Differ in Subjective Probability of Success

In the more general theory of achievement motivation, it was assumed that the subjective probability that action of the individual in step one of a contingent path might result in success in, for example, step four of the path, was represented by product of the subjective probabilities of success at each step between the individual and that success; $P_{1}s_4 = P_{1}s_1 \times P_{2}s_2 \times P_{3}s_3 \times P_{4}s_4$, where $P_{1}s_4$ is the strength of expectancy that step-one activity produces step-four success, and $P_{2}s_2$, $P_{3}s_3$, etc., are the strengths of subjective probability that action in that step produces its own immediate success, as viewed by the individual facing step one of the path. Incentive value of a success as viewed at step one was assumed to equal one minus the expectancy that immediate action would produce that success ($Is_4 = 1 - P_{1}s_4$, for example, in the case of success in step four).

Derivations using these assumptions are different than those for a single activity. For long contingent paths, a series of *easy* steps is expected to produce greatest arousal of resultant achievement motivation (Raynor, 1974a; Raynor & Entin, 1981c), whereas derivations for the one-step (isolated activity) case are that motivation is greatest when *Ps* is intermediate (.5) and smaller for both easy and difficult tasks (Atkinson & Feather, 1966). Note that as path length decreases, predictions for a contingent path and a one-step path become increasingly more similar. For example, for a path of two steps, the greatest amount of resultant achievement motivation is still predicted for an intermediate *Ps* series (.5 .5), but as path length increases, the point of maximum arousal of achievement motivation moves from an intermediate series to an increasingly easier series (.6 .6 .6, and then .7 .7 .7 .7, etc.). By 15 steps, the difference between an intermediate series and an easy one is quite substantial. Therefore the general theory derives the initial theory as a special case, the simplest one, when $N = 1$ (see Raynor, 1978, and Raynor & Entin, 1981b, for calculation of these derivations).

Two studies were initially conducted (Raynor & Sorrentino, 1972) where values of *Ps* were varied in contingent paths of equal length. Within a given path, the same *Ps* value was used for each step (i.e., .9 .9 .9 .9 for a four-step path). Resultant achievement motivation should be greatest for immediate activity in contingent paths consisting of an easy series, smallest for one consisting of a difficult series, and intermediate for a moderately difficult series. Data (reported in Raynor & Entin, 1981d) for the first study showed that only in the first task of the easy series did success-oriented subjects (high *n* Achievement–high Test anxiety) significantly outperform (on the complex arithmetic task) failure-threatened subjects (low *n* Achievement–High Test anxiety), while this difference was smaller for the moderate series and in the opposite direction for the difficult series. The predicted pattern of interaction was obtained, with success-oriented subjects tending to score higher from the difficult to the moderate to the easy series, whereas the opposite trend was found for the failure-threatened subjects. Results of the second study, where different values of *Ps,* path lengths, and instructions to create contingent paths were used, are very similar to the first for groups low (success oriented) and high (failure threatened) in Test Anxiety, but differences for *n* Achievement were small and nonsignificant. For both studies the levels of significance for the predicted interaction effect were of marginal significance.

   Recent findings by Sorrentino, Short, and Raynor (1979) suggest one reason why stronger evidence was not found in the two studies just described. They show that uncertainty-related motivation (using a projective measure of *n* Uncertainty and the Byrne and Lamberth [1971] measure of authoritarianism) is also aroused in contingent paths and that behavior is more complexly determined than currently conceptualized by the more general theory. Their data may mean that effects now expected occur only for success-oriented individuals who are also positively motivated to seek out uncertainty of success, and only among failure-threatened individuals who are motivated to avoid a great deal of total uncertainty of success. The general suggestion of the series of studies reported by Sorrentino et al. (1979) is that uncertainty-related motivation as well as achievement motivation are both routinely aroused when *Ps* varies between zero and 1. If this turns out to be the case, theory has to be revised to take account of both kinds of motivation in skill-demanding activity.

Decreasing and Increasing Probability Contingent Paths

Subjective probability of success can be varied from one step to another within a given contingent path. Raynor and Harris (unpublished data reported by Raynor & Entin, 1981d) created decreasing and increasing probability contingent paths by manipulating the subjects' chances of moving on from one step to another of the path. Subjects were told that the percentile ranking of performance scores would determine who moved on and who did not. Instructions indicated that for the decreasing probability path, those in the top 95% in Test 1 would be permitted to take Test 2, those in the top 65% on Test 2 would be permitted to take Test 3, those in the top 35% would be permitted to take Test 4, and those in the top 5% would be permitted to take Test 5. These probabilities of moving on were reversed for the increasing probability series. Resultant achievement motivation is derived (see Raynor, 1978 and Raynor & Entin, 1981d, for calculations showing this derivation) to be much greater for step one of this decreasing path (.9 .7 .5 .3 .1) than for the first step of this increasing path (.1 .3 .5 .7 .9). It was expected that if motivation is a linear determinant of performance, success-oriented subjects would perform at a higher level but failure-threatened subjects at a lower level in immediate activity of the decreasing than the increasing probability contingent path. The pattern of results (Raynor & Entin, 1981d) obtained for three-step arithmetic performance was as predicted: The positive motive group (above the median on $Z n$ Achievement - Z Test Anxiety) performed better in the decreasing than the increasing path and performed better than the negative motive group (below the median on $Z n$ Achievement - Z Test Anxiety) within the decreasing path. When reported ability was controlled, the pattern of results did not change, but statistical significance becomes marginal for the overall interaction effect, although the difference within the decreasing path remains statistically significant.

Replication of this study using a larger sample allowed for viewing possible overmotivation effects due to large positive achievement motivation per se rather than to achievement plus extrinsic motivation as in previous research (Sorrentino, 1971, 1973, 1974). With extreme motive scores, those very low on n Achievement but very high on Test Anxiety (failure threatened) should do even worse than a less extreme failure-threatened group, but more so in immediate activity of the decreasing than the increasing probability path. However, if optimally efficient performance is produced by moderate levels of positive achievement motivation, but even greater positive achievement motivation produces "trying too hard" and less efficient (lower) performance, then the very high n Achievement–very low Test Anxiety group should perform worse than a less extreme success-oriented group, and the more so in immediate activity in the decreasing than the increasing probability path. Results of the second study (Raynor & Entin, 1981d) are consistent with this set of arguments, but again, were not predicted a priori but rather in the course of data analysis when comparisons using more and less extreme (positive or negative) motive groups failed to replicate the pattern of results obtained in the first study. Significant or near significant differences described earlier were obtained within the decreasing probability path, and across paths for the different motive groups, but differences within the increasing probability path were very small and did not begin to approach statistical significance. However, the problem remains of being able to predict such (purported) overmotivation effects prior to data analysis rather than after the fact. It appears that more times than not, when very positive motivation is suspected to be aroused and sufficient sample size allows for viewing extreme motivation groups, such effects become apparent.

Motivation for Successive Steps of a Contingent Path

The more general theory of achievement motivation can also be used to make predictions for motivation in each next step of a contingent path as prior success (in earlier steps) allows a person to go through the successive steps of the path. If such successive movement is correlated with age and aging, the theory becomes able to address data concerning motivational trends over time. If we consider a *closed* contingent path, where no new chances for future striving are perceived to add to the end of the original contingent path as a function of success along that path, then motivation for each new step of the contingent path changes in systematic ways that can be calculated if assumptions about values of Ps for remaining steps are made (see Raynor & Entin, 1981d, for such calculations for a variety of possible path situations). It has been derived that a decrease in resultant achievement motivation for each successive new step always occurs when values of Ps are the same for each anticipated step of a contingent path and remain unchanged as a function of successive successes along the path. But predictions differ when success moves a person through, for example, increasing and decreasing probability contingent paths. If initial values of Ps remain unchanged or increase as a function of prior success and one step of the path is lost for each success, motivation for each new immediate activity of the remaining path of the increasing probability series is predicted to rise and then drop but is predicted to drop regularly for the decreasing probability path—so long as for the decreasing probability path the prior successes do not increase later values of Ps. Resultant achievement motivation in the first step of this decreasing path (.9 .7 .5 .3 .1) is predicted to be initially greater than that in the first step of this increasing probability path (.1 .3 .5 .7 .9), but by the time that two prior successes have occurred so that the remaining closed paths are now .5 .3 .1 and .5 .7 .9, resultant achievement motivation in the first step of the remaining decreasing path (.5 .3 .1) is less than that for the first step of the remaining increasing path (.5 .7 .9).

In general, for changes in resultant achievement motivation in the first step of closed contingent paths as a function of prior successes, an increasing probability contingent path by itself (.1 .3 .5 .7 .9) or an increasing path coupled with a constant probability or decreasing probability path (e.g., .1 .3 .5 .7 .9 .9 .9 .9 or .1 .3 .5 .7 .9 .7 .5 .3 .1, respectively) produces a rise followed by a decline, whereas either a constant probability path (.9 .9 .9 .9 .9 or .6 .6 .6 .6, etc.) or a decreasing-probability path (.9 .7 .5 .3 .1) produces a steady decline (see Raynor & Entin, 1981d, for a complete set of calculations that lead to these conclusions).

Atkinson (1977) has viewed the data from the Lehman (1953) study of productivity as a function of age, and the data from the Veroff, Atkinson, Feld, and Gurin (1960) national-survey study of motivation as a function of age (see Fig. 9.1) and has suggested the possibility that predictions of the more general theory are consistent with these results. Both the Lehman (1953) data for creative contributions and the Veroff et al. (1960) data for the *n*

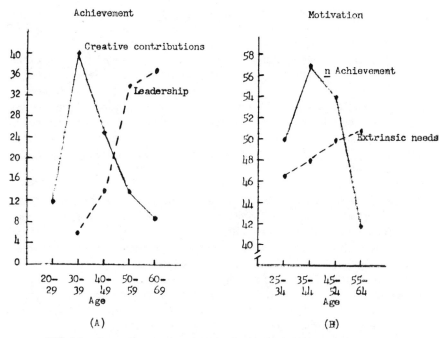

FIG. 9.1. Age, achievement, and motivation to achieve. In (A) the curves for creative contributions and leadership are based on medians of fairly recent work in fifteen fields of creative endeavor and in ten fields of governmental, judicial, and military leadership, respectively. (Redrawn after Tables 42 and 43 in Harvey C. Lehman, *Age and achievement,* published by the Princeton University Press, copyright 1953 by the American Philosophical Society, pp. 250-251. Reprinted by permission of Princeton University Press.) In (B), the curves for TAT *n* Achievement and extrinsic needs (the average of *n* Power and *n* Affiliation) are based on results from a representative sample of males in the United States in 1957. (From Veroff, J., Atkinson, J. W., Feld, S., & Gurin, G. The use of thematic apperception to assess motivation in a nationwide interview study. *Psychological Monographs,* 1960, *74,* 12, Whole No. 499. Copyright 1960 by the American Psychological Association. Reprinted by permission.)

Achievement score show an increase followed by a decrease as a function of age. If assumptions concerning values of *Ps* and the nature of the path faced by individuals in their occupational careers that derive this bell-shaped curve for positive motivation as a function of success correspond to those (unmeasured) values operative for these individuals—and we feel that the required assumptions of: (1) success orientation; (2) increasing probabilities followed by constant or decreasing ones; and (3) facing an eventual closed path, are reasonable ones for the majority of individuals continually making contributions in an occupational area—then we can claim that the more general theory can successfully postdict both sets of data. But if a group of individuals were identified for which different assumptions are required, then we would no longer expect a rise followed by a decline in achievement motivation, and the particular prediction would depend on the particular assumptions used to calculate resultant achievement motivation as a function of continued success.

The implications of the more general theory for positive extrinsic motivation along a closed contingent career path have been derived (Raynor & Entin, 1981d) and suggest that it generally (but not always) increases as one approaches the final goal of a closed contingent path but sooner or later also starts to drop off. Such a decline occurs at a later step than the comparable one for achievement motivation, for equivalent values of *Ps* along the path, and for the number of steps remaining in the path, etc. It is worth noting that both the Lehman (1953) data for leadership contributions and the Veroff et al. (1960) data for "extrinsic motives" (*n* affiliation plus *n* power) show such an increasing linear trend as a function of age (see Fig. 9.1). Again, this postdiction is suggestive. Taken together, predictions for achievement and extrinsic motivation are sufficiently consistent with data to merit serious consideration in further research concerning motivational trends over time as a function of success (e.g., aging).

EVALUATION OF COMPETENCE

The present view of evaluation of competence evolved from our use of Weiner's (1972, 1974) early work on attribution and achievement motivation within a motivational rather than a social–psychological perspective (e.g., the study of self-attribution and its effects on behavior rather than attribution to others concerning the causes of their success/failure), and from work reported by Raynor, Atkinson, and Brown (1974) in which a positive relationship was found between ratings of the future relatedness of a course examination and the relatedness of that exam for the student's own positive self-evaluation. Perceived possession of ability (along with task difficulty, effort, and luck being the four factors first dealt with by Weiner) was also found by Raynor and English (1981) to be positively related to both future importance and self-importance. An attempt was then made to account for these positive associations as well as for the functional significance of future importance and self-importance in determining motivation of immediate activity. We became concerned with the situation where success/failure could be used by the subject to assess his degree of possession of an ability believed to be required for success on a task (e.g., with anticipated internal attribution to ability as a function of success on a diagnostic test). This led to consideration of the arousal of motivation for *finding out about oneself* as well as for *doing well on* achievement-oriented activity.

Future Importance, Self-Importance, and Self-Possession

Raynor and English (1981) were guided by extension of the attribution approach to the study of achievement motivation (Weiner, 1972, 1974) to view the relationship between self-attribution of various descriptors (hard working, competent, and lucky based on Weiner's work, and competitive, popular, and influential, as some other possible self-descriptors) and the importance of possessing that attribute for both self-evaluation and attaining future goals. Questions were asked about each of the six self-descriptions: To what extent do you see yourself as ... (self-possession)?; how important is seeing yourself as ... for your own positive self-evaluation (self-importance)?; how important to you is being ... for achievement of your own future goals (future importance)? A positive correlation was found between each of these and the other two for most of the six self-descriptions (except lucky), even when corrected for possible effects of response sets and/or response keying of the items. These data replicate and extend earlier findings to include self-possession as well as future importance and self-importance, this time for personality attributes.

In the Raynor and English (1981) study, subjects were later presented with a two-step contingent path involving complex arithmetic performance. Positive correlations were found for the rated importance of these tests (and for doing well on them) for both achieving future goals and for positive self-evaluation, *even though subjects (college students) most probably realized that status for continuation in school or in any other life activity was noncontingently related to performance scores during the laboratory session.* We return to this point shortly, when viewing the Weinberg (1975) doctoral research.

Gazzo (1974) also found a positive correlation between degree of self-possession of an attribute (competence or nurturance) and degree of perceived necessity of possessing that attribute for future success. Both interest and willingness to volunteer for a tutorial program described as requiring either competence or nurturance was positively related to ratings of both self-possession and future importance of that attribute.

The Raynor and Mitchell data referred to earlier (first reported for men in Raynor, 1974b, and for both men and women in Raynor, 1981a) also show a positive relationship between the necessity of doing well for achieving future goals and for positive self-evaluation for men, but not for women, college students. Recall that results (described earlier) showed that both self-importance and future importance interacted with motives in an equivalent manner; for men, each accentuating predicted effects for success-oriented and failure-threatened motive groups, whereas for women, both producing an increment in grades for success-oriented students but not a decrement in grades for the failure-threatened ones.

Evaluation of Competences in Skill-Demanding Activity

Findings concerning the positive association between self-importance, future importance, and self-possession imply that arousal of achievement motivation depends on the meaning of immediate activity: (1) for earning the opportunity to continue on; (2) for a person's positive self-esteem; and (3) for assessment of competences believed to be required by the immediate activity faced by the person. Recall that in the Raynor and English (1981) study, performance was seen as important for both achieving future goals and for positive self-evaluation, even though no obvious contingent path linked test performance to students' own life activity or future goals. Although the two-step contingent path induced by the experimenter may have produced such perceived importance, this does not seem plausible.

Weinberg's (1975) doctoral research provides more direct evidence concerning perceived importance influencing assessment of competence. In this study, a pursuit rotor task was worked by college athletes and nonathletes in relaxed and achievement-oriented conditions. The Mehrabian (1968, 1969) measure of resultant achievement motivation was used to infer motive standing. Self-importance and future importance were assessed after task performance. Again, both measures were positively correlated, with mean ratings on both significantly higher under achievement oriented than relaxed conditions. Athletes rated both self-importance and future-importance significantly higher for the pursuit rotor task than did nonathletes, but ratings for verbal performance did not differ significantly for athletes and nonathletes. Success-oriented athletes did best, whereas failure-threatened athletes did worst, with both motive groups of nonathletes intermediate in performance on the pursuit rotor task under achievement-oriented conditions. When high and low groups on future and self-importance are obtained and data collapsed across arousal conditions and kind of student, pursuit rotor performance increases regularly for success-oriented subjects high in self- and/or future importance, whereas it decreases regularly for failure-threatened subjects high in one and/or the other.

Arousal of Achievement Motivation in Competence Testing

Because of the distinctions made between athletes and nonathletes, use of an obvious task involving physical coordination and comparison of performance under relaxed versus achievement conditions, the Weinberg (1975) data is clear in suggesting that anticipated diagnostic assessment of an attribute (physical coordination?) relevant to life future goals (athletic success?) and to seeing oneself in a certain way (as an "athlete"?) arouses achievement motivation for performance on it that depends on strength of achievement-related motives. And even though no contingent path is created linking immediate performance to future goals, performance is seen as tied to future success. We believe this is so because the skill involved in pursuit rotor performance is seen as a necessary (prerequisite) competence for attainment in an athletic career (the future goal) and for continuing to see oneself as an athlete (self-image). Thus pursuit rotor performance was more "ego involving" for the athletes than the nonathletes, and achievement-related motives predicted performance more reliably for athletes than nonathletes. Once constrained to work on such an obvious test of athletic ability, arousal of achievement motivation due to future importance and self-importance "turned on" the success-oriented athlete but "inhibited" the failure-threatened athlete—just as in previous research, when the rated importance of a course grade for future success influenced immediate action in both life activity as academic performance (Raynor, 1968a, 1974b, 1981a) and as task output in experimentally induced contingent paths in the laboratory (Entin & Raynor, 1973; Raynor & Rubin, 1971).

If the previous interpretation is correct, the more general theory of achievement motivation should apply when concern about doing well/not doing poorly is aroused by constrained performance on an ability test but not necessarily prior to or in choice of tasks. In the latter situation, an individual is seeking information about himself based on anticipated use of task outcomes to infer degree of possession of an attribute that is positively valued by him. Choice of a diagnostic test and/or willingness to undertake or resist undertaking a diagnostic test, and motivation aroused when performance is undertaken on such a test, are now seen as requiring separate conceptual treatment (Raynor, 1981a). Previous research on achievement motivation has successfully predicted constrained task performance on obvious tests of ability (Atkinson, 1958; Atkinson & Feather, 1966; Atkinson & Raynor, 1974). We would now argue that an actual and/or anticipated increment in perceived possession of an ability or a decrease in perceived task difficulty, or both, can produce an increase in subjective probability in steps along a contingent path and hence accentuate differences in aroused achievement motivation sustaining immediate activity. In addition, such upward evaluation of ability and/or task ease is derived to heighten a person's extent of future orientation by shifting the phenomenal goal and/or threat of immediate activity to a more distant step along the contingent path (Raynor, 1974a). Thus findings concerning the correlation between self-possession and future importance can be accounted for by existing theory if the additional (reasonable) assumption is made that upward evaluation of competence raises Ps for subsequent activity seen as requiring that competence for successful performance.

We now also believe that only attributes that in a given culture are seen as desirable ones to possess, holding constant their perceived instrumental value for attaining future goals—so that one can positively evaluate oneself when using that competence as a means of self-identification—the more so the greater its perceived possession—are expected to arouse motivation to seek information concerning degree of its possession. Thus "intelligence" is more or less positively valued by many (but not all) members of Western culture. Information seeking in skill-demanding activity perceived to be a valid diagnosis of "intelligence" is expected to attract the greatest number of individuals so that for the great majority we can obtain psychologically constrained (e.g., "ego involving") performance on such tasks and accentuate characteristic differences in achievement-related motivation. When other valued attributes are also perceived to be validly assessible through performance on skill-demanding activity, such constrained performance also arouses achievement motivation. "Trivial" as opposed to "important" activity as seen by the individual involves performance on tasks that: (1) do not require highly culturally valued skills to do well on them; (2) are not perceived as valid diagnostic tests of highly valued competences; (3) are not contingently related to achievement of (important) future goals; and/or (4) do not bear on positive self-evaluation. Thus task difficulty per se can arouse resultant achievement motivation in a one-step activity, but the amounts of motivation so aroused are substantially smaller when any of the aforementioned conditions are also met.

A THEORY OF PERSONALITY FUNCTIONING AND CHANGE

This theory developed initially from use of the more general theory of achievement motivation to understand behavior in societal contingent paths where a series of prior successes permit further activity in an occupational career (Raynor, 1978) and/or to understand behavior when success is anticipated to lead to upward evaluation of competences that are seen as prerequisites for eventual career success (Raynor, 1974a). These developments have been referred to in preceding sections of this chapter.

Inclusion of a "future self-image" or "future sense of self," attainment of which depends on ultimate success in a career path, then linked future goal striving to "feeling good about oneself" (Raynor, 1978). Evidence of a positive correlation between future importance and self-importance (as defined earlier) implied that earning the opportunity to continue was important for positive self-evaluation. When self-possession was also found to be related to future and self-importance, attention was focused on changes in competence judgments linked to contingent path striving and positive self-evaluation. We began to conceptualize a person *before* diagnostic assessment, *at the time* when performance was undertaken, and then *after* some number of successful steps of a path had been taken. It appeared that a person might then be striving to *maintain* the positive value of past success(es) as well as striving to attain the positive value of future success(es) as a means of feeling good about himself/herself—whether that success was related to diagnostic assessment, or successful movement along a contingent path, or both. The budding conceptual analysis was then extended to include all three possible time-linked self-images (past, present, and future) to define a self-system providing both esteem-income to the individual and additional sources of motivation of immediate activity. We now consider an individual's past, present, and/or future sense(s) of self as potent influences on the direction, vigor, and persistence of immediate activity when pursuing a psychological career—where *the outcomes of opportunities for action serve as a means of self-identity*. Finally, individual cultural value was added as a variable to account for why some goals and/or self-images provide more valued outcomes and/or self-identities than others.

We now derive that striving to know and to feel good about oneself can be a primary goal of adult life when a self-image provides substantial amounts of positive value to the individual. This provides the underlying motivational basis for a theory of adult personality functioning and change that combines the study of personality and motivation as did Maslow (1954), but with more explicit theoretical assumptions and more explicitly derivable and testable hypotheses. The focus here is on important (as seen by the individual) behaviors as they relate to self-identity in life activity over time. The resulting conceptual analysis (Raynor, 1981b) is both a further extension of theory of achievement motivation and a general theory of personality functioning and change in its own right. No longer restricted to occupational–educational career striving, it uses the concept of "psychological career" in any substantive area (family, sexual, leisure, etc.) to relate opportunities for action to means for self-identity.

We assume that a person is motivated to maximize positive value and to minimize negative value. Several distinctions are made concerning kinds and sources of value; affective (feeling) versus information (knowing) value (Feather, 1967); intrinsic (Deci, 1975), difficulty (Atkinson, 1957);

instrumental (Raynor, 1974a); extrinsic (Atkinson & Feather, 1966), and cultural value; and time-linked sources of value (past, present, future). The external and internal viewpoints in analyzing sources of value are distinguished, as are the kinds of path (contingent, partial, noncontingent, and one-step) that provide value, and the behavioral versus the self-systems as sources of value.

Sources of Value and Steps in a Path

Outcomes of activity can provide value. Activity and its outcomes represent a step, a sequence of which can form a path. We can view a person moving from one step to another of a path (external viewpoint), or we can assess the anticipated future steps, the remembered (retrospected) past steps, and the immediate present step of the path as perceived by the individual at a given point along a path (internal viewpoint). Contingent, noncontingent, partial, and one-step paths are distinguished as in previous theory, but paths are no longer restricted to future orientation. A past contingent path exists when some past success(es) is seen by the individual to have provided the chance to continue on along the path to some number of later steps, and it is believed that a past failure along that path would have resulted in loss of the opportunity to continue on to the present step of the path. In a *closed* path, the final (future) goal or past success remains fixed as the individual moves from step to step. For a closed future path, the final goal remains unchanged as the individual moves toward it, so that fewer steps remain as possible sources of value in the anticipated future as a function of successful movement toward that goal. The final goal of an (future) *open* path is continually changing when moving through steps of the path, so that an old final goal is replaced by a new one and is now just another goal along the path. Open and closed (future and past) *contingent* paths are important in that all anticipated future steps and all retrospected past steps of the path are assumed to produce motivation sustaining immediate activity along that path, the amount contributed by each step being determined by the difference between the product of the positive value of the step and its subjective probability of occurrence, and the product of the negative value of each step and its subjective probability of occurrence.

The Behavioral and Self-Systems.   Each outcome of action is assumed to have the potential for providing self-identity through definition of a self-image, which in turn is time linked to that (past, present, future) outcome and can serve as an additional source of positive and/or negative value. The behavioral system refers to action, evaluative standards defining outcomes, and the magnitudes of value of those outcomes, termed *valence* (Lewin, 1938). The self-system refers to action and outcomes that define self-images, the standards of self-evaluation that determine fulfillment or not of self-images, and the magnitudes of positive and negative value of these self-images, termed *self-esteem* or *esteem-income* (Maslow, 1957; Rogers, 1959). When the self-system emerges in a substantive area of activity, the person's self-identity and self-worth are judged by that person to be evaluated by the outcomes of activity in that area, and greater positive and negative motivation is aroused to determine immediate activity. Components of motivation determined by the product of expectancy of occurrence of the self-image and its value to the individual determine the magnitude of the additional motivational impetus contributed by the self-system to motivation of immediate activity. Thus when the self-system is aroused so that outcomes of action define an answer to the question "Who am I?," net esteem-income (the difference between positive and negative value in the self-system) determines the individual's psychological morale for that psychological career. A psychological career is defined by the substantive activity in question and the self-image(s) that can be attained (in the future), assessed (in the present), and/or maintained (from the past) by that action.

Psychological Careers

"Psychological career" as a theoretical construct relates time-linked senses of self to action through the possible outcomes of that action. A psychological career is jointly determined by a person's self-image and a particular opportunity for action and links the internal view of self and the external view of role (as seen by others) so that *a psychological career provides behavioral opportunities for self-identity.*

Psychological careers are tied to substantive areas of activity in a society. Occupational, sexual, family, leisure, etc. activity can simultaneously be aroused to define different substantive self-identities for an individual involved in these different areas. Any substantive activity can define a psychological career when a self-image having substantial positive value is linked to the outcomes of action in that activity.

Kind of Value

Intrinsic value refers to the value of the outcome of activity that is defined by the inherent properties of that activity for a particular individual in question and may be innately determined or acquired through experience. Intrinsic value to the individual as a construct permits the situation where what is positively valued to some greater or lesser extent by one person may be negatively valued to some greater or lesser extent by another.

The attractiveness/repulsiveness that derives from a person's perceived chances of attaining that outcome is referred to as *difficulty value* and is similar to incentive value in theory of achievement motivation (Atkinson, 1957). We use difficulty value in a more general way so that, for example, the greater the scarcity of occurrence of certain attributes of individuals, the greater the positive/negative difficulty value they are perceived to have.

The number of opportunities for subsequent action that the attainment of an outcome, or possession of some competence, is believed to guarantee (in the future) or to have guaranteed (in the past), defines magnitude of *instrumental value*. The future instrumental value of immediate success is greater, the greater the number of steps in a contingent path. Past instrumental value of success increases as a function of success along a contingent path. It increases when some immediate success is seen to have been able to insure the value of an increasingly larger number of past successes that resulted from past earned opportunities.

Sources of value that derive from rewards and punishments that are contingent upon outcomes of action (or self-image tied to those outcomes) but do not relate to the difficulty value or the intrinsic value of the outcome per se are referred to as *extrinsic value*. Money, approval, power, security, etc., are common sources of positive extrinsic value. They are assumed to function to provide positive motivation when perceived to be appropriate and/or usual outcomes of that activity. Negative extrinsic value provides inhibitory motivation that dampens intensity of immediate activity.

Extent of *individual cultural value* refers to the belief that attainment of an outcome is good/bad or right/wrong or proper/improper in that cultural context, or to how good or bad a person the attainment of that skill, outcome, or self-image makes the individual. It implicates a moral-evaluative source of value. The *consensual cultural value* associated with *success* is most often positive in our culture, and for many individuals in our culture their *individual culture valuation* of success is also positive. A "successful person" is believed to be a "good" person; so is an "intelligent" person. Individual cultural value may also be negative, as might be the case for "failure" and "alcoholic," etc. Individual cultural value is most often potently aroused when a person strives to attain/maintain/evaluate time-linked self-images that define "who I am." The cultural value of a self-image indicates how good or bad a person I am when I see myself in terms of that self-image. Senses of self that define self-identity for a person provide substantial cultural value to the individual.

An individual may have one or more simultaneous psychological careers in different substantive areas, or may have only one or even none, or he may have only one or two time-linked sources of value in the self-system for any of these, and any of the five sources of value (positive and/or negative) may provide large or small amounts of that particular value. An individual may have no clear-cut sense of self tied to any substantive activity, so that the self-system is not aroused and a psychological career does not exist for that area.

Activity can still be sustained by value in the behavioral system that is aroused for that activity, so that predictions concerning action do not require that self-evaluation and self-worth be at stake for every human activity. Only those activities that arouse substantive positive value (particularly but not exclusively cultural value) are expected to become linked to self-identity and require use of the concept of psychological career.

Stages of Striving

By using time-linked sources of value, we can derive differences in both quality and quantity of motivation at various stages of striving along a closed contingent path. Earlier theory dealt with differences due to the anticipated future aroused in the behavioral system. We now can refer additionally to effects aroused by the self-system and to those produced by the retrospected past as well as the anticipated future. The *initial stage* of career striving is characterized by an individual facing the first step of an anticipated contingent path (termed *becoming*) where the final goal defines "the person I am striving to become." Possible sources of value exist from the anticipated future and evaluation of present competence, and not from the retrospected past. The *final stage* of career striving is characterized by prior successful movement so that the individual faces the last step of a retrospected contingent path (termed *having been*) where past successes define "the person who I have become." Possible sources of value exist from the retrospected past and evaluated present, but not from the anticipated future. All three time-linked sources of value (esteem–income) can contribute motivation at some *middle stage* of career striving. Differences in motivation and esteem income between individuals who are "psychologically young" (becoming) and "psychologically old" (having been), and those in the middle stage of striving, become apparent from the qualitative differences in time-linked source of value and the difference between action versus cognitive work that can attain versus maintain value. We expect a rough correlation between psychological and chronological age, but the exceptions are of great interest—the older person faced with initial striving and the younger person faced with terminal striving in a given substantive area.

The Self-System as a Source of Value

In order for value in the self-system to emerge, the person must be able to meaningfully ask the question "Who am I?" and to be able to answer it in terms of potential outcome of action in the real world. Only then does a psychological career emerge in a substantive area of activity. The greater the value of an outcome (behavioral system) the more likely it can serve as a source of self-identity to define self-worth (self-system) and the more probable will be the interaction between the self-system and behavioral system to define a psychological career. This implies that the self-system may provide value without being tied to action (as when young children "make believe" they "are" doctors), that action may occur without being tied to the self-system (as when young children do things without seeing themselves in terms of outcomes of those things), and that the emergence of the self-system in a substantive area substantially increases both self-evaluation tied to that activity (both positive and negative) and motivation sustaining it. Thus although it is possible for a very young child to see himself as "becoming a doctor" by going through the various educational–occupational steps (of grade school, high school, medical school, internship, residency), motivation of action of young children is more often expected as a function only of arousal in the behavioral system. This would explain the general difficulty in motivating some children for long periods of time in life activity of a society, as opposed to play activity where self-identity (in fantasy, play, and daydreams) is not tied to outcomes of real-world activity. When time-linked self-images become tied to real-world action, they then can come to contribute motivational impetus sustaining that activity, as when "becoming a doctor" is seen as tied to successfully moving through contingent steps (listed earlier) and more than merely "graduating from medical school" is the goal—becoming a particular kind of (culturally valued) individual is also an ultimate goal. Analogously, we believe that psychological retirement, often seen in elderly individuals but not exclusively limited to them, occurs when the individual no longer defines himself in terms of real-world outcomes along a societal contingent path, so that he is perceived by others as "childlike" because in fact, like children, only the behavioral system sustains immediate activity and fantasy outcomes rather than world outcomes serve as sources of esteem-income. For more (psychologically) middle-aged individuals, both the behavioral and self-systems more often (but certainly not always) contribute value, and immediate activity is perceived as important to future goals, past accomplishments, self-evaluation, and self-possession when all three time-linked sources of value in the self- and behavioral systems contribute motivation sustaining immediate action.

Striving in an Open Path

An open path exists when immediate success or some situational factor suggests one or more new goals that become part of the path so that an initial "final" goal becomes just another goal along the path whose length has now remained the same or even increased (Raynor, 1974a). In an open path there is no decrease in "becoming" as value from "having been" increases. Here the individual can accumulate sources of positive esteem-income through past successes along that path although still retaining the initial impetus of "becoming" through striving for newer future goals. In open path striving there is no "final stage," because a final fixed goal does not exist for long as a target whose attainment indicates the end of "becoming." This has important implications for life striving of success-oriented individuals (now referred to as positively motivated individuals for the substantive career in question) in that we can see the difference between those who remain psychologically young through continued "becoming" and those who become psychologically old through exclusive dependence on "having been" to feel good about themselves. Paradoxically, for life striving of failure-threatened individuals (now referred to as negatively motivated individuals for the substantive career in question), the psychologically young person is inhibited by "becoming" through his anticipated future failure as the dominant outcome, so that successful movement along a contingent path from a psychologically young to a psychologically old person in that career should reduce inhibition, dread, and negative-self-evaluation (rather than reduce excitation, enthusiasm, and positive self-evaluation as predicted for the positively motivated individual). Thus positively motivated individuals faced with final steps of closed contingent careers are expected to be restless, bored, and "lost," although appearing very successful to others, but when faced with open paths are still able to maintain their enthusiasm and "drive" for further success. Conversely, negatively motivated individuals faced with final steps of a closed contingent career are expected to be relieved, less inhibited, and more content with the immediate situation and relatively more positively motivated than earlier, although they remain inhibited, worried, and concerned about negative self-evaluation in open contingent career paths. Thus the effects of psychological aging (due to success along a contingent path) are expected to differ depending on the open–closed nature of the path and the resultant motivational disposition of the individual for that substantive area. The "identity-crisis" (Erikson, 1968) of the positively motivated individual in a closed path is tied to his previous definition of self in terms of becoming when he can no longer look forward to continued becoming. No identity crisis would occur if self-identity were seen in terms of past accomplishments ("having been") along that very same path. On the other hand, the negatively motivated individual might just be "finding himself" in terms of a positive self-image tied to "having been successful" along the closed path, which might be lost when open path striving renews the dread of future career failure through more contingent opportunities in which failure can occur.

Sooner or later, in usual life striving, we can expect an open path to become a closed one, either because the situation defines some final goal not initially seen, or because limited competences are seen to set limits to realistic prospects for advancement in that area not original appreciated. Also, a closed path may become an open one in that later successes or a changed situation might begin to suggest new future goals that were not apparent in earlier path striving. Thus open and closed paths should not be conceptualized as fixed for a given individual or a given situation. If and when such changes are perceived, they provide for predictable motivational consequences that are of crucial importance in adult personality functioning. These are in fact the rather common changes that are determinants of motivation for second careers, retirement careers, and identity crises. In this theory the consequences of closed–open and open–closed path changes are tied to differences in time-linked sources of value as a function of stage of striving and to differences in basic motivation dispositions for that substantive area of activity.

Maintaining Versus Attaining as Determinants of Immediate Action

Achievement of future goals is the primary source of esteem-income and motivation of immediate activity in *initial stages* of closed path striving. Previous expectancy × value theory of action is best suited for prediction under these circumstances. Retrospection about past successes and maintenance of past value is the primary source of esteem-income and motivation of immediate activity in *final stages* of closed path striving. Theories dealing with cognitive work are best suited for prediction under these circumstances, whereas contemporary expectancy × value theory did not take such factors into account, despite the fact that Lewinian (1938) theory considered both "locomotion in the life space" and "cognitive reorganization" as alternative means of reducing "tension" in a person. Both anticipated future and retrospected past sources of value influence esteem-income and motivation of immediate activity in *middle stages* of career striving, as do concerns about evaluation of prerequisite abilities for that substantive career. Theory dealing with attaining, maintaining, and evaluating sources of value are all needed, but each if used alone is of limited predictive utility because all three time-linked processes occur in middle-stage striving. The present emphasis on the interrelationship between time-linked sources of value, coupled with systematic use of expectancy × value theory to derive effects on motivation and self-evaluation, is believed to be consistent with the implications of existing empirical findings in all three time-linked domains.

We also expect that attitudes toward sources of value are time linked, so that individuals at different stages of striving are favorably or unfavorably disposed to the source of value to the extent to which that source of value can provide positive and/or negative self-evaluation (Peak, 1955). Success-oriented individuals should be more favorably disposed toward prerequisite hierarchies that define future striving in initial stages but more favorably disposed toward defense of the past record of accomplishment in the final stages, whereas failure-threatened individuals should be less negatively disposed toward contingent hierarchies when they no longer face them at the final stages of striving and less negatively disposed toward avoiding definition in terms of the past record of activity at the early stages of striving (when no such record exists to be interpreted in terms of past failure). In a psychological career, the primary goal is to know and feel good about oneself, however this can be brought about, and individual differences in personality, the nature of the path faced by the individual, and the stage of striving are all relevant to prediction of quality and quantity of value and motivation.

REFERENCES

Atkinson, J. W. Motivational determinants of risk-taking behavior. *Psychological Review,* 1957, *64,* 359–372.

Atkinson, J. W. (Ed.) *Motives in fantasy, action, and society.* Princeton, N.J.: Van Nostrand, 1958.

Atkinson, J. W. *An introduction to motivation.* Princeton, N.J.: Van Nostrand, 1964.

Atkinson, J. W. An approach to the study of subjective aspects of achievement motivation. In J. Nuttin (Ed.), *Motives and consciousness in man.* Proceedings of the 18th International Congress in Psychology, Symposium 13, Moscow, 1966.

Atkinson, J. W. *Strength of motivation and efficiency of performance: An old unresolved problem.* Paper presented at the meetings of the American Psychological Association, Washington, D.C., September, 1967.

Atkinson, J. W. Strength of motivation and efficiency of performance. In J. W. Atkinson & J. O. Raynor (Eds.), *Motivation and achievement.* Washington, D.C.: Winston, 1974.

Atkinson, J. W. Motivation for achievement. In T. Blass (Ed.), *Personality variables in social behavior.* Hillsdale, N.J.: Lawrence Erlbaum Associates, 1977.

Atkinson, J. W., & Birch, D. *Introduction to motivation.* Princeton, N.J.: D. Van Nostrand, 1978.

Atkinson, J. W., & Feather, N. T. (Eds.) *A theory of achievement motivation.* New York: Wiley, 1966.

Atkinson, J. W., Lens, W., & O'Malley, P. M. Motivation and ability: Interactive psychological determinants of intellective performance, educational achievement, and each other. In W. H. Sewell, R. M. Hauser, & D. L. Featherman (Eds.), *Schooling and achievement in American society.* New York: Academic Press, 1976.

Atkinson, J. W., & Raynor, J. O. (Eds.). *Motivation and achievement.* Washington, D.C.: Winston, 1974.

Bachman, J. B., Kahn, R. L., Mednick, M. T., Davidson, T. N., & Johnson, L. D. Youth in transition (Vol. 1). *Blueprint for a longitudinal study of adolescent boys.* Ann Arbor, Mich.: Survey Research Center, Institute for Social Research, 1967.

Brecher, P. J. *Examination of achievement-oriented performance decrement in contingent pathways.* Unpublished masters thesis, Ohio University, 1972.

Brecher, P. J. *The effect of extrinsic incentives on achievement-oriented performance in contingent paths.* Unpublished doctoral dissertation, Ohio University, 1975.

Byrne, D., & Lamberth, J. The effect of erotic stimuli on sex arousal, evaluative responses, and subsequent behavior. *Technical Reports of the Commission on Obscenity and Pornography* (Vol. 8). Washington, D.C.: U.S. Government Printing Office, 1971.

Deci, E. L. *Intrinsic motivation.* New York: Plenum Press, 1975.

Entin, E. E. Achievement motivation, future orientation, and acquisition. In J. O. Raynor & E. E. Entin (Eds.), *Motivation, career striving, and aging.* Washington, D.C.: Hemisphere Publishing Corp., 1981.

Entin, E. E., & Feather, N. T. Attributions to success and failure in contingent and noncontingent paths. In J. O. Raynor & E. E. Entin (Eds.), *Motivation, career striving, and aging.* Washington, D.C.: Hemisphere Publishing Corp., 1981.

Entin, E. E., & Raynor, J. O. Effects of contingent future orientation and achievement motivation on performance in two kinds of task. *Journal of Experimental Research in Personality,* 1973, *6,* 314–320.

Erikson, E. H. *Identity, youth and crisis.* New York: W. W. Norton, 1968.

Feather, N. T. An expectancy-value model of information-seeking behavior. *Psychological Review,* 1967, *74,* 342–360.

Festinger, L. A theoretical interpretation of shifts in level of aspiration. *Psychological Review,* 1942, *49,* 235–250.

Festinger, L. A theory of social comparison processes. *Human Relations,* 1954, *7,* 117–140.

Gazzo, B. *The effects of achievement motivation, self-future orientation, and competent versus nurturant role descriptions on interest and expectancy of success in a tutorial program.* Unpublished honors thesis, State University of New York at Buffalo, 1974.

Gjesme, T. Goal distance in time and its effect on the relations between achievement motives and performance. *Journal of Research in Personality,* 1974, *8,* 161–171.

Isaacson, R. L., & Raynor, J. O. *Achievement-related motivation and perceived instrumentality of grades to future career success.* Unpublished paper, University of Michigan, 1966.

Lehman, H. C. *Age and achievement.* Princeton, N.J.: Princeton University Press, 1953.

Lewin, K. *Conceptual representation and measurement of psychological forces.* Durham, N.C.: Duke University Press, 1938.

Lewin, K., Dembo, T., Festinger, L., & Sears, P. S. Level of aspiration. In J. McV. Hunt (Ed.), *Personality and the behavior disorders* (Vol. 1). New York: Ronald Press, 1944.

Mandler, G., & Sarason, S. B. A study of anxiety and learning. *Journal of Abnormal and Social Psychology,* 1952, *47,* 166–173.

Maslow, A. H. *Motivation and personality.* New York: Harper & Row, 1954.

McClelland, D. C. *Personality.* New York: Wm. Sloane Associates, 1951.

McClelland, D. C. *The achieving society.* Princeton, N.J.: Van Nostrand, 1961.

McClelland, D. C., Atkinson, J. W., Clark, R. A., & Lowell, E. L. *The achievement motive.* New York: Appleton-Century-Crofts, 1953.

Mehrabian, A. Male and female scales of tendency to achieve. *Educational and Psychological Measurement,* 1968, *28,* 493–502.

Mehrabian, A. Measures of achieving tendency. *Educational and Psychological Measurement,* 1969, *29,* 445–451.

Mitchell, J. S. *Relationships between achievement motivation, contingent future orientation, and subjective probability of success.* Unpublished honors paper, Department of Psychology, State University of New York at Buffalo, 1974.

Peak, H. Attitude and motivation. In M. R. Jones (Ed.), *Nebraska symposium on motivation.* Lincoln, Nebr.: University of Nebraska Press, 1955.

Pearlson, H. B. *Effects of temporal distance from a goal and number of tasks required for goal attainment on achievement-related behavior.* Unpublished doctoral dissertation, State University of New York at Buffalo, 1979. Also in J. O. Raynor & E. E. Entin (Eds.), *Motivation, career striving, and aging.* Washington, D.C.: Hemisphere Publishing Corp., 1981.

Raynor, J. O. *The relationship between distant future goals and achievement motivation.* Unpublished doctoral dissertation, University of Michigan, 1968. (a)

Raynor, J. O. *Achievement motivation, grades, and instrumentality.* Paper presented at the meetings of the American Psychological Association, San Francisco, September 1968. (b)

Raynor, J. O. Future orientation and motivation of immediate activity: An elaboration of the theory of achievement motivation. *Psychological Review,* 1969, *76,* 606–610.

Raynor, J. O. Relationships between achievement-related motives, future orientation, and academic performance. *Journal of Personality and Social Psychology,* 1970, *15,* 28–33.

Raynor, J. O. Future orientation in the study of achievement motivation. In J. W. Atkinson & J. O. Raynor (Eds.), *Motivation and achievement,* Washington, D.C.: Winston, 1974. (a)

Raynor, J. O. *The engagement of achievement-related motives: Achievement arousal versus contingent future orientation.* Paper presented at the meetings of the American Psychological Association, New Orleans, La., September, 1974. (b)

Raynor, J. O. Motivation and career striving. In J. W. Atkinson & J. O. Raynor (Eds.), *Personality, motivation, and achievement.* Washington, D.C.: Hemisphere Publishing Corp., 1978.

Raynor, J. O. Self-possession of attributes, self-evaluation, and future orientation: A theory of adult competence motivation. In J. O. Raynor & E. E. Entin (Eds.), *Motivation, career striving, and aging.* Washington, D.C.: Hemisphere Publishing Corp., 1981. (a)

Raynor, J. O. A theory of personality functioning and change. In J. O. Raynor & E. E. Entin (Eds.), *Motivation, career striving, and aging.* Washington, D.C.: Hemisphere Publishing Corp., 1981. (b)

Raynor, J. O., Atkinson, J. W., & Brown, M. Subjective aspects of achievement motivation immediately before an examination. In J. W. Atkinson & J. O. Raynor (Eds.), *Motivation and achievement.* Washington, D.C.: Winston, 1974.

Raynor, J. O., & English, L. D. Relationships between self-importance, future importance, and self-possession of personality attributes. In J. O. Raynor & E. E. Entin (Eds.), *Motivation, career striving, and aging.* Washington, D.C.: Hemisphere Publishing Corp., 1981.

Raynor, J. O., & Entin, E. E. Achievement motivation as a determinant of persistence in contingent and noncontingent paths. In J. O. Raynor & E. E. Entin (Eds.), *Motivation, career striving, and aging.* Washington, D.C.: Hemisphere Publishing Corp., 1981. (a)

Raynor, J. O., & Entin, E. E. Effects of high versus low achievement arousal on level of performance in contingent and noncontingent paths. In J. O. Raynor & E. E. Entin (Eds.), *Motivation, career striving, and aging.* Washington, D.C.: Hemisphere Publishing Corp., 1981. (b)

Raynor, J. O., & Entin, E. E. (Eds.) *Motivation, career striving, and aging.* Washington, D.C.: Hemisphere Publishing Corp., 1981. (c)

Raynor, J. O., & Entin, E. E. Theory and research on future orientation and achievement motivation. In J. O. Raynor & E. E. Entin (Eds.), *Motivation, career striving, and aging.* Washington, D.C.: Hemisphere Publishing Corp., 1981. (d)

Raynor, J. O., Entin, E. E., & Raynor, D. *Effect of n Achievement, Test Anxiety, and length of contingent path on performance of grade-school children.* Unpublished paper, State University of New York at Buffalo, 1972.

Raynor, J. O., & Rubin, I. S. Effects of achievement motivation and future orientation on level of performance. *Journal of Personality and Social Psychology,* 1971, *17,* 36–41.

Raynor, J. O., & Sorrentino, R. M. *Effects of achievement motivation and task difficulty on immediate performance in contingent paths.* Unpublished paper, State University of New York at Buffalo, 1972.

Rogers, C. R. A theory of therapy, personality and interpersonal relationships, as developed in the client-centered framework. In S. Koch (Ed.), *Psychology: A study of a science* (Vol. 3). New York: McGraw-Hill, 1959.

Sorrentino, R. M. *An extension of theory of achievement motivation to the study of emergent leadership.* Unpublished doctoral dissertation, State University of New York at Buffalo, 1971.

Sorrentino, R. M. An extension of theory of achievement motivation to the study of emergent leadership. *Journal of Personality and Social Psychology,* 1973, *26,* 356–368.

Sorrentino, R. M. Extending theory of achievement motivation to the study of group processes. In J. W. Atkinson & J. O. Raynor (Eds.), *Motivation and achievement.* Washington, D.C.: Winston, 1974.

Sorrentino, R. M., Short, J. C., & Raynor, J. O. *Uncertainty motivation: Implications for a general theory of human motivation.* Unpublished manuscript, 1979.

Veroff, J., Atkinson, J. W., Feld, S., & Gurin, G. The use of thematic apperception to assess motivation in a nationwide interview study. *Psychological Monographs,* 1960, *74* (12, Whole No. 499).

Weinberg, W. T. *Perceived instrumentality as a determinant of achievement-related performance for groups of athletes and nonathletes.* Unpublished doctoral dissertation, University of Maryland, 1975.

Weiner, B. *Theories of motivation.* Chicago: Rand-McNally, 1972.

Weiner, B. *Achievement motivation and attribution theory.* Morristown, N.J.: General Learning Press, 1974.

Wendt, H. W. Motivation, effort, and performance. In D. C. McClelland (Ed.), *Studies in motivation.* New York: Appleton-Century-Crofts, 1955.

10 Cognition of Time in Human Activity

Paul Fraisse
Université René-Descartes,
Ecole Pratique des Hautes Etudes, Paris

Time? There is time of the cosmos, of the earth, of the living, and of man. All these times are made of successions that men have sought to quantify with unities whose dimensions vary from million years to the nanosecond. But even from the point of view of the physician or biologist, time is not homogeneous. There are periods where change is slow and then there are events such as stellar explosions, earthquakes, the emergence of life, and of man. There is thus succession but there is also a duration stretching between events and a duration of the event itself. In a day of 24 hours there are two fundamental events that determine the duration of day and night, the rising and setting of the sun. This physicist's description is also that of a man who regards reality and distinguishes therein, in an incessant succession, present or past periods, some where changes are only slightly discernable (and we then speak of duration), and others that are outstanding events.

Each person has a unique experience of time, because he/she appears at a moment in the history of the world that he/she apprehends from what happens to him/her and from what other people make him/her discover about the past, the present and even the possibilities of the future. There is a distance between the "time" of the world and the time that I apprehend. I am not living only in the present. The instants succeed one another and I construct their succession by discerning in it durations and changes or events: I transform the succession of my experiences with an actual representation that permits me to take into consideration changes in the present as well as those of the past or future.

In any case, man must handle temporal information. History teaches us that the Ancients were first preoccupied with knowing if their "idea" of time corresponded to the reality of the world: a model of eternity unfolding in a world dominated by a recurrence of changes (Plato); history of a world created with a time where the drama of the Fall and Redemption is played out to an eschatology in which time returns to eternity in the City of God (Judeo–Christianity); and place of indefinite progress according to the laws of evolution and to the progress of science and technology (Darwin and the socialist thinkers). But modern man, since Descartes, passing from Kant to Piaget, has put into question his "idea" of time and the conditions behind its genesis. It then became apparent that time is a concept resulting from a cognitive activity that organizes the changes that confront us.

This critical reflection led into a psychology of time. Time is not a stimulus like light. It is only given to us through our experience of the relative permanence and succession of changes. The psychology of time is that of the treatment of temporal information, a treatment motivated by the need to understand the changes of the world that surrounds us and our own transformations.

Psychologists first compared the direct estimations of time to the durations measured by physics. Psychophysical problems were attacked first. What is the lower limit of perception of succession (Exner, 1875)? What is the precision of our estimation of brief durations (Vierordt, 1868)? Is there a privileged interval (Bolton, 1894; Höring, 1864)? What is the duration or the span of apprehension in which successive elements are made present, as things are seen in the field of a glance (Wundt, 1874)? We are trying to refer in these pages to those who seem to have opened new perspectives of research, without being ignorant of the fact that since the days of yore pertinent observations have been made by philosophers and naturalists.

Then came other questions. Mach (1865) thought that we have a sense of time in relation to audition. Guyau (1890) believed that the origin of our experience of duration lay in the distance that exists between a desire and its achievement, and also in the effort that multiplies images and affects. Janet (1928) was primarily concerned with the feeling of duration, which he saw as assuring the regulation of actions directed to adaptation to irreversible changes. In all studies, psychologists have found discrepancies between the time measured by chronometers and the time that we estimate. Duration appears shorter in some cases, longer in others. Hence the numerous experiments trying to find the laws behind our systematic errors (for a summary of these studies, see Doob, 1971; Fraisse, 1963; Wallace & Rabin, 1960).

The results are complex and it soon became apparent that they are related not only to the content of the task but also to the attitudes and motivations of the subject. Furthermore, they depend on the methods employed (metric or parametric estimation, production, reproduction, comparison, and discrimination). All authors admit to finding themselves facing a Tower of Babel where the voices of psychiatrists also make themselves heard, observing considerable distortions of time as lived by depressives, schizophrenics, mental retardates, and so on (Israeli, 1932; Jaspers, 1913; Kleist, 1934; Minkowski, 1933). Psychophysiologists add their observations on the conditioning of time in the animal (Pavlov's school; Feokritova, 1912), the influence of metabolic factors (François, 1927; Hoagland, 1933), the adaptive capacities of the animal (Anderson, 1932; Hunter, 1913), and the physiological regulations of the organism and in particular circadian rhythms (Aschoff, 1965; Bunning, 1964).

In the more recent past, psychologists, all the while multiplying their observations and precise experiments, have sought to establish models of the treatment of temporal information. Piaget opened the way in 1946 by proposing a model of the development of the child's modes of adaptation to time (Piaget, 1946). Drawing inspiration from his works on the development of intelligence, Piaget distinguished the stages through which the child confronted with successions and durations passes: sensorimotor, concrete operations, then formal operations.

Fraisse (1957) proposed to distinguish three modes of adaptation to time: on the one hand a biological system manifested in periodic changes and conditioning to duration; on the other hand two cognitive systems, a perceptual system for brief durations and a symbolic system that permits us to master time. With his representations, man constructs a time that opens to him a temporal horizon stretching from past to future and that allows him to estimate duration according to the number of changes perceived and memorized. Frankenhaeuser (1959) and later Michon (1975, 1979) distinguished two levels of the estimation of time that correspond to the last two levels proposed by Fraisse. Michon is the first to make explicit reference to information processing to integrate short and long time experiences as dependent on the content of short-term storage. Ornstein (1969) adds a dimension to this analysis, proposing what he himself calls a metaphor borrowed from computer usage: The estimations of time depend on the manner in which information has been treated at the moment of perception and on the "storage size" that the information occupies afterward in memory.

Our present contribution follows this line in seeking to present a two-level model that accounts for the numerous and sometimes contradictory results that we have recalled here. In the domain of time, it is less a question of knowing if the models are accounting for what we do in life than of seeing if the numerous established facts allow us to construct a model that brings coherence to them.

TWO MODES OF KNOWLEDGE OF TIME

A clear distinction between two modes of our cognitive relations with the environment is essential to avoid confusion: on the one hand, the perception of time; on the other hand, the representation of time. This distinction was proposed as early as 1890 by W. James (1890). We have a perception of the present (he calls this a "specious present" to distinguish it from an instantaneous present that is a philosophic abstraction) that lasts several seconds; beyond that, the duration ceases to be a perception and becomes a symbolic construction.

Our first objective is to elaborate this distinction that received little attention. Within the range of a few seconds, we perceive a succession of events as relatively simultaneous. Such events are ordered and perceived as unities: a telephone number, a rhythmic structure, a melodic theme, or a simple sentence (subject–verb–object). In this case we speak of a *perception of time* and refer to this as "perceived present." The existence of this present has been recognized by many authors under similar names: "field of internal regard" (Wundt, 1874); "psychic present" (Stern, 1897); "mental present" (Piéron, 1923), and "actual present" (Koffka, 1935).

Immediately beyond this limit we apprehend changes only through our capacity to stock in memory those events lived or known through the experiences of others. Thus we arrive at a *representation of time,* that is to say a representation of changes that constitute physical time, biological time, historical time, and the time of our own existence. This representation is clearly not a copy of reality but a construction growing from memories or knowledge continuously compared to the time measured by clocks and calendars.

These constructions, all based on the same principle, are situated on different scales (own life, own family, own nation, the historical man, etc.). They are at the base of several forms of our relations with time. They permit to *estimate* a duration in the immediate past (e.g., I have probably been writing now for an hour) or more distant past (e.g., yesterday I probably wrote for 5 hours), to orient myself in time (e.g., it must be lunchtime), and above all to place myself in time via the temporal perspectives opened by these representations. I exist in an actual present where according to my whim I can encompass a period more or less long: The present hour, the present day, etc... In relation to this present, I order both past events and a future whose events I attempt to foresee (those of tomorrow, next week, etc.).

The difference between these two modes of treatment of temporal information has been masked by the fact that research has been directed above all toward the estimation of a duration. Indeed, one can use the same methods to evaluate a perceived duration or a memorized duration. All these methods involve biases that have to some extent concealed the specificity of the two modes of time treatment.

Perceived present should not be reduced to the sensory register investigated by Sperling (1967). The latter corresponds only to a trace whose information can be used during at most 250 msec. Perceived present and short-term memory are also often confused (Ornstein, 1969). Reasoning in the abstract, one could say that the perception of a succession or a duration always implies that memory has been put into play. When someone informs me of a telephone number, for example 325-5426, it might be said that when I hear 26, 325 is already in my memory. Perception, however, is not condemned to such instantaneity. If it were, I wouldn't perceive even the 26 but a series of phonemes of which only one would be present at a time. Gibson (1966) puts it nicely: "Perception is an activity, not an instantaneous event." As we see, perceived present can attain a duration of 3 to 4 sec, whereas short-term memory lasts from 20 to 30 sec. Short-term memory degrades rapidly in time, as one notices for instance in utilizing the paradigm of Peterson and Peterson (1959).

What is perceived (for example, a short sentence that I can repeat immediately) enters short-term memory where it undergoes erosion. Certain elements disappear or are integrated with earlier memories or with the perceptions that follow. From the point of view of the apprehension of time, representations of short-term and long-term memory can hardly be differentiated, except that perceptual data aren't organized in the two memories according to the same processes (e.g., disappearance of the effects of recency and a decrease of the effects of primacy at the end of a certain time interval [Craik, 1970]).

The first representations of time in the child don't appear until around two years, at the moment when he begins to use the rudiments of language. These words of a 2.1-year-old child, reported by Decroly and Degand (1913), are quite revealing in their simplicity. "Milk gone, Mariette" that, in the context, meant: "I drank my milk. I'm going to Mariette's." A representation of time is sketched out in these words, a time in which the child locates himself through reference to a near past and an immediate future. In contrast, recent research (Demany, McKenzie, & Vurpillot, 1977) shows that the infant of 2 months can discriminate brief durations, indicating that he already perceives them. This heterochrony is found later in reproduction tests. A 2-year old can reproduce brief "ahs" of different durations (durations less than 2 sec) said in front of him, but he can't directly estimate longer durations. At 6 years, the child is capable of reproducing a duration of 1 sec as precisely as an adult (with a greater variability), but the reproduction of an empty duration or filled duration of 20 sec is difficult for him. When he is asked to reproduce an empty duration defined by two sounds, the child often reproduces only one sound or a fairly rapid succession of two sounds, which indicates that he has registered the succession but not the duration. If the duration is filled (a continuous sound), the child is more successful on the average, but with considerable variability. It is as though he had registered that the event was lasting, but without having estimated its duration: The response has an indeterminate duration (Fraisse, 1948). Through practice, however, the child of this age is capable of taking succession and duration into account (Fraisse, 1963).

PERCEPTION OF TIME

The Physiological Limits of the Perceived Present

Cases of perceived present involving one, two, or several stimuli are distinguished, as each entails a specific problem.

One Stimulus: The Threshold of the Lasting.   A very brief stimulation (a fraction of a millisecond), if very intense, is perceived with a character of instantaneity. An average intensity stimulation poses the question of how long the duration must be before it is perceived as a duration. The most recent work (Servière, 1979) confirms the oldest theory: The threshold of the lasting is around 100 msec.

Two Stimuli: Simultaneity and Threshold of Succession.   When there are two stimulations, the problem is to discover the perceptual threshold of their succession, or "temporal acuity" (Oostenbrug, Horst, & Kniper, 1978). Although these values vary slightly from one author to another, they cluster around a duration of 50 msec, if one takes as a criterion not the variation of intensity of a stimulus as in the flicker situation but rather the separation and ordering of two distinct and successive stimulations.

The problem can be treated by considering the nonsuccession or simultaneity that has a practical importance in daily life. Within what limits are two or more stimulations perceived as simultaneous? As early as 1903, Hylan (1903) had found that six letters forming a word presented successively were perceived as simultaneous provided that the total duration of presentation did not exceed 86 msec. Similar results have been obtained with different paradigms: for example, perception of the simultaneity of the four apexes of a diamond (Lichtenstein, 1961), of two words in one (Fraisse, 1966b), and of two groups of points whose integration forms a syllable (Eriksen & Collins, 1967). The upper limit of perception of the simultaneity is always between 50 msec and 100 msec.

Several Stimuli: The Upper Limit of Perceived Present.   This upper limit is measured by the duration during which a sequence of stimuli can be perceived as a unity: a sequence that may be a series of figures, a sentence, a rhythmic structure, etc. This limit is dependent on the interstimulus interval and temporal proximity.

In the case of two identical stimuli such as the tick-tock of a metronome, the unity disappears when the interval between the tick and the tock reaches 1800 msec. Reduction of the interval increases the number of elements perceived as a unity. Subjects asked to produce rhythmic groups of 2, 4, or 6 taps spontaneously reduce the duration of the intervals between taps as a function of the number of taps. The duration of a group of 4 taps is 1.8 times as long as the duration of a group of 2 taps, whereas a group of 6 taps lasts 2.2 times longer than a group of 2 taps (MacDougall, 1903).

Temporal proximity facilitates perceptual grouping. Thus we may perceive more sounds as a perceptual unity if they are grouped in substructures. Subjects are able to perceive (without counting) from four to five groups of five sounds with an interval of 340 msec between groups and 180 msec between sounds (Fraisse & Fraisse, 1937). This means that 20 to 25 elements are perceived in approximately 5 sec. Dietze (1885) had found that subjects could perceive no more than 24 elements during presentation of grouped sounds. This result is particularly interesting in light of Aristoxene de Tarente's conclusion that a rhythmic measure can't exceed 25 brief beats (Laloy, 1904).

All types of organization other than proximity favor the extension of perceived present, whether the grouping of phonemes into words, words into sentences, etc. Binet (1911) asked 15-years-olds to repeat a sentence of 26 syllables whose pronunciation at a normal reading speed lasted approximately 5 sec. Perceived present is limited both by the number of items in the field and by the total duration of their presentation. The *duration* of the perceived present, insofar as it can be measured by laboratory techniques, should be compared with the practices of those rhythmic arts using successions of perceptual unities each of which must be registered in a perceived present. The average duration of an English verse is 2.9 sec (extremes vary from 0.89 to 5 sec [Wallin, 1901]). According to the examples given by Vos (1976), musical measures last between 1.75 and 4.8 sec.

Perceptual Treatment of Temporal Information

The estimation of perceived duration in ordinary life is almost useless. In contrast, we must constantly take this duration into account in the sensori-motor regulations of our activities. This perception depends on two factors: the *durations* themselves because we can discriminate the durations of two identical stimuli and their *contents,* that is to say, *what* is lasting.

Duration of Perceptions.   The range of perceived durations from 50 to 1800 msec is not homogeneous from a perceptual point of view. The shortest durations are overestimated whereas the longest durations are under-estimated. The optimum interval, the so-called interval of indifference, lies around 700 msec. It is noteworthy that the relative differential threshold is minimum (8%) around 700 msec; it reaches 25% for 100 msec and 10% for 2000 msec. According to Vierordt's (1868) law, the larger interval within a given series of stimulus intervals tends to be underestimated whereas the shorter interval tends to be overestimated. In general, these systematic errors correspond to the centralizing tendency of judgment (Hollingworth, 1910), but they are founded *only* when the subject has to make evaluations of a series of intervals. However, *Ss* show a centralizing tendency in the *perception* of short intervals even when they have only a single interval to reproduce. Because of lack of differentiation between perception and estimation of duration, the literature is full of misunderstandings about the "indifference interval" (Woodrow, 1934).

Within the range of perceived time, discrimination sensitivity may be evaluated by the number of stimuli correctly identified in a set, using the method of absolute judgments. Research shows that at most three different durations can be discriminated. This corresponds, in terms of information theory, to a channel capacity between approximately 1.5 and 1.6 bits. This result is important because it explains—a posteriori—why the Morse alphabet based on the discrimination of durations was constructed using only two durations (dots and dashes) and why musical melodies are also based principally on the interplay between two durations (Fraisse, 1956, 1974).

The Nature and Content of Stimulation.   The duration of our perceptions depends partly on what is perceived. More precisely, this dependency rests on:

1. The physical nature: An auditory stimulation seems longer than a visual one of the same duration. More intense stimuli seem longer than less intense ones, etc.

2. The physical context: The perception of a duration depends on the sequence of durations to be perceived. If we have to perceive a duration stretching between two spatially distinct visual stimulations, the larger the distance between them, the longer the duration appears (Kappa effect). If the distance is multiplied by 10, the increase of the perceived duration is only 12%, however. Further, divided durations are perceived as longer than empty durations.

3. Informative content: If we take into account not only the duration of simple stimuli but stimulations with an informative content, it becomes apparent that perceived duration depends on the coding process put into play. It is necessary, from this point of view, to distinguish the coding of the stimulus at the input from the coding of the response at the output:

   a. Coding of the stimulus: For brief stimuli, the more simple the information to be coded the briefer the perceived duration is with equal durations (40 or 80 msec), an empty interval appears shorter than an interval filled with a three letter syllable (Thomas & Weaver, 1975). The presentation duration of a familiar stimulus (30 msec) appears shorter than that of an unfamiliar stimulus (Avant, Lyman & Antes, 1975). For 500 msec, Mo (1971, 1974) found that when two stimuli are presented the stimuli with fewer dots (one or three as opposed to five) seem briefer. This result can be explained in terms of coding difficulty, and the latter can be demonstrated by measuring the recognition threshold.

b. Encoding of the response: Response encoding requires the ability to name the stimulus. For a given stimulus category, response latency is proportional to the number of responses (Fraisse, 1977; Fraisse & Smirnov, 1976). But the absolute value of the latency depends on the relation between stimulus and response. The latency of the verbal response to a written word (reading material) is shorter than the latency for the labeling of a geometric figure or object (Fraisse, 1964, 1969). In other words, encoding in labeling is more difficult than encoding in reading. This difference had an effect on the estimation of response durations. In one of our experiments, the subjects were asked to read series of 48 items composed of four names of simple geometric figures randomly presented and to name 48 items composed of the four corresponding geometric figures. The task, in both cases, was to give responses at 1-sec intervals. This standard was made concrete for the subject before each series of responses by the presentation of 30 clicks at the rate of 1 per sec. Response intervals in the reading conditions proved to be 937 msec whereas in the labeling condition they were 1073 msec. Thus, one can conclude that 973 msec in reading equals 1073 msec in labeling. When response times are equal, the reading response would be judged longer than the labeling response, an effect opposite to that found in stimulus coding at the input. Perceived duration of a response depends on the required type of coding. The more difficult the coding involved, the shorter the duration appears to be.

Effects of Attitude and Attention.   The roles of attitude and attention in perception are well known. Both increase in importance as a function of stimulus ambiguity. This is precisely the case in the perception of time. In the complication experiment intended to study the so-called factor of the personal equation, which is at the source of much nineteenth-century research, Wundt (1874) found that of the two simultaneous stimuli the one to which the subject attends appears to precede the other. This error, resulting simply from attention, is approximately 50 msec.

More generally, it has been shown that the more attention that is focused on a duration the longer it appears (Benussi, 1913). This law applies both to the range of perceived durations and to the estimation of longer durations.

Interpretations.   The following interpretations tried to account for the fundamental observations made so far:

1. The duration of the stimulus is perceived with relative precision. The most current hypothesis argues that we possess a *biological clock*. However, attempts to connect perception of duration to heartbeat rate or α waves have failed. Biologists lack hypotheses concerning perceived durations, but partisans of the biological clock are reinforced in their conviction by the fact that perceived durations are influenced by metabolic changes. Tapping at a rate of one tap per second with a subjective standard is more rapid when body temperature is raised by diathermy or sickness (Hoagland, 1933). Research with drugs points in the same direction (Doob, 1971, p. 312–316). Amphetamine–type stimulants accelerate tapping set to a rhythm of one tap per second and consequently extend the apparent duration of each second. Depressants produce the opposite effect. Psychologists such as Creelman (1962), without referring to an explicit biological mechanism, postulate the existence of a counter drawing on a large number of pulse sources, each with a fixed probability of firing at any given moment. This counter would provide a model capable of explaining threshold variations in the detection of duration differences between two intervals.

Other authors focus instead on the possible unities of time. Several have proposed durations between 50 and 100 msec (the "psychological moment" of James [1890], Stroud's [1956] "quantum of time," the "perceived chronon" of Fraser [1978]) that could correspond to the threshold of the lasting, or the threshold of succession, or the time necessary to switch attention from one stimulus to another (Kristofferson & Allan, 1973).

We think there is a neuropsychology of perceived time, not of the clock type but rather one that would correspond to cerebral processes set off by stimulation. One stimulation sets off a lasting process of an electro-physiological nature. Its duration would explain the attributes of duration perception and could be investigated using the techniques of electro-physiology.

a. *The duration necessary for the formation of a percept is approximately 50 to 100 msec.* A briefer stimulus of sufficient intensity is perceived but doesn't appear lasting and above all can't be isolated from other stimulations occurring during the same duration.

b. *Using a brief stimulus, sensation rapidly diminishes and becomes infraliminary (Békésy, 1933).* The physiological repercussion, however, is prolonged for several hundred msec, as is demonstrated by the work done on evoked potentials. Without going into technical details, numerous studies have shown that modifications of evoked potentials are prolonged at least 500–600 msec beyond the first N and P waves (Picton & Hillyard, 1974; Picton, Hillyard, Krausz, & Galambos, 1974) and that they depend on the information content and task. We hypothesize that the indifference interval of 700 msec corresponds to the duration physiologically necessary to achieve the termination of a perceptual process. This neurological base would also explain why spontaneous tempo and preferred tempo usually have the same value. When stimuli succeed one another at an interval larger than 100 msec and less than 700 msec, the overlapping of the two perceptual processes involves an overestimation of the interval that results in some way, from the effort to distinguish them. Inversely, when the interval between two stimulations is greater than 700 msec, the effort to group them involves an underestimation of the interval.

c. The maximum duration of the perceived present can be related to the temporal path of evoked potentials. Gjerdingen and Tomsic (1970), for example, have established that when there are two successive stimulations (auditory, visual, or tactile) the $N1$ and $P2$ amplitudes of the evoked potential of the second increase as the interval between stimuli is increased. This increase continues up to 2 sec, and beyond for some subjects and situations. The most recent research reveals interactions between on and off effects of auditory stimuli when durations are shorter than 5 sec (Hillyard & Picton, 1978).

These facts might explain the duration during which successive stimuli can be organized, but the maximum number of stimuli perceivable during a particular duration would depend more on the evocative capacity or, in current terminology, buffer or response generator capacity.

2. Perceived duration depends on information processing. A certain number of facts assembled here prove it: generally speaking, the more difficult and complex the process, the longer the perceived duration is. However, this effect is always relatively minimal, which may explain sometimes contradictory results.

Thus, the duration effectively perceived depends both on a process of direct estimation of the duration and on the repercussions of the complexity of the treatment of the information.

The most elaborate hypothesis combining the two processes is still that of Thomas and Weaver (1975). It consists of relating processing time and perceived duration. "The key assumptions of this theory are that (1) in general temporal information is obtained from a timer (f processor) and a visual information (g processor). (2) Attention is shared between the f and g processors such as the output of the f processor becomes less reliable as the g processor captures more attention [p. 366]." The authors also assume that the ratios between the processors are dependent on the range of durations. It is probable that the g processor plays a larger role when perceived duration is short.

This hypothesis holds up well as long as it is emphasized that the f processor, when it is a question of perceived duration, plays a more important role than the g processor, which only modulates the duration picked up by the f processor. Finally, from this author's point of view, it would not be necessary to equate the "timer" with a biological clock stricto sensu.

REPRESENTATION OF TIME

The Events

Time is tied to memory. Block (1974) recalls Aristotle's proposition: "Only the animals who perceive time remember, and the organ whereby they perceive time is also that whereby they remember." Today, the majority of psychologists accept the thesis outlined by Guyau (1890), developed by Fraisse (1957, 1963) and Frankenhaeuser (1959), and finally systematized by Ornstein (1969). Our estimations of durations depend on the number of events that we are remembering. The criticism most frequently presented against this thesis is that no precise definitions for the terms *events* or *changes* have been given. Let us try to contribute to the resolution of this difficult problem by anticipating some of our ideas concerning the estimation of duration, a subject we discuss in more detail later.

Ornstein (1969), speaking of the space that events occupy in memory, says: "the size of the storage space would depend on two factors: the amount of information or number of occurrences in the interval which reach awareness and the way in which the information was "chunked" and "stored [p. 104]." An event is what arouses my memory through evocation: one or several images of scenes I've lived; a "word" or a sentence heard, or semantic constructions where verbalization holds an important place (e.g., the recital of a conversation or an adventure). Memory is mostly constructed with language. Consider the following two factors proposed by Ornstein, 1969:

1. The amount of information. It depends on both its origins (more or less frequent stimulations or tasks whose parts are more or less evenly broken up throughout the duration) and also on what exactly has been memorized. The two possible aspects of events are illustrated by some recent research done by Block (1974). In a first experiment, a duration of 180 sec is filled either with 30 words at a rhythm of one every 6 seconds or with 60 words at a rhythm of one every 3 seconds. Subjects perceive that the number of words presented is larger in the second situation than in the first. We would say that there are more events in the second situation than in the first. In immediate memory subjects remember approximately the same number of words after the two series. Thus, there are two possible systems for evaluating the number of events, one originating in perception, the other in memory. Results show that in this case subjects estimate the duration according to the number of perceived events (the larger the number of perceived words, the longer the duration).

Block's second experiment gave inverse results. Eighty words belonging to 20 different categories (four of each) were presented during a duration of 120 sec. The words were presented in blocks of four on the same slide but for one group of subjects, four words belonging to the same category appeared together, whereas for the other group the words were randomly mixed on each slide. Subjects estimated (with reason) that the number of stimuli presented was the same in both cases, but the number of words memorized was 16.7 with blocked stimulus, as opposed to 9.1 with mixed stimulus. The duration with blocked stimulus was judged to be longer than the mixed-stimulus duration. These results suggest that subjects in this situation based their estimation of time on the number of events memorized.

The number of events that can serve as the basis for temporal estimation can thus be related to either the conditions of their perception or what remains of them in memory. The distinction of perceived events may depend on the discontinuity of physical stimulations, but in continuous activity it is achieved by the subject's attention. One can predict with confidence that the number of events perceived is smaller in an automatic activity than in a monitored activity. Let us take an example from everyday life: suppose I must go, for the first time, from place A to place B in an unknown city. All the reference marks of the environment and all the switches in direction are important. If I pass this way several times however, my driving becomes automatic and I no longer notice the details of the path. There are more events perceived in a new task than in a habitual one. Correlatively, we know that the duration of a new task appears longer than that of a routine task.

All that renders a task more difficult, either by its nature or by the importance we attach to it, multiplies the number of events. I believe that such analysis explains classical results in time estimation. Thus, Harton (1939) used a maze in which alleys could be modified without the subject's knowledge. In one case, subjects were able to succeed and during the course of the trial it was pointed out to them that they were on the right track. In the other case, subjects could not succeed; the experimenter multiplied the number of remarks and subjects were led to suspect their upcoming failure. Fifty-two out of 57 subjects estimated that the task that attracted more attention to the particular segments of the maze, that is to say the more difficult, was the longer of the two (though the durations were actually equal). Meade (1960) compared the evaluations of a duration of 5 min where the task was to construct a puzzle (in reality not solvable) presented as an intelligence test. One group of subjects were led to believe that they would succeed, as the experimenter said "good" 10 times during the task. The other group was given no information. The first group estimated the duration at 3 min 4 sec, the second group had a mean estimation of 5 min 5 sec.

The number of perceived events may play an important role when estimation immediately follows action (see Section titled "Immediate Estimations"); when estimation intervenes sharply after an action then belonging to the past (see Section titled "Estimations of Past Durations"), the events are obviously those that the subject is capable of evoking.

Experiments on sensory deprivation (Vernon & McGill, 1963) as well as "out of time" experiments (Siffre, 1963) in which the subject remains several weeks or even several months in an enclosed place without any temporal information, may be considered as situations in which the number of events to be perceived and thus to be memorized is quite small. This might explain why in these situations, however wearisome, subjects make evaluations of the duration of their action and of their stay substantially inferior to the actual duration.

2. Number of Events and Treatment of Information.   Ornstein (1969) emphasizes that the number of events depends not only on the situation, which we too have tried to emphasize earlier, but also on the manner in which, through his activity, the subject is capable of creating chunks, that is to say to assemble in one unity several stimuli or activities. Axel (1924) spoke of the unity of the task as a temporal cue. To do *one* multiplication is *one* event, whereas to write a series of figures is a divided task (Loehlin, 1959). Ornstein showed that storage size was less important for the spectator watching a dancer if that spectator is capable of integrating several successive movements into the unity of a form than if he is naive.

Obviously, these interpretations of storage size have been made from estimations of duration, leaving them open to the criticism of circular reasoning, but here we are seeking only to clarify what can be called *events* and *number of events*.

Temporal Information

Besides the memory of events, our representation of time is constituted through information of a strictly temporal nature, furnished by our bodies, the cosmic environment, and all the means invented by man to measure time: Watches, clocks, and calendars. Let us quickly outline the information provided by these three important sources.

Biological Information.   If, within the range of a few seconds, we have not found any indication of the existence of biological clock, this is not the case for durations in the order of hours. Our body possesses a true circadian clock that functions on a period of approximately 24 hours, even when man is deprived of all other sources of information. Fraisse, Siffre, Oléron, & Zuili (1968) showed that a man deprived of all temporal cues during 174 days woke regularly at 24-hour intervals (± approximately 6 hours) even though he had confounded night sleeping with day napping, believing that he was living 24-hour "days" actually lasting twice that long. The rhythm of his temperature was also on an approximately 24-hour schedule.

But there is no need to look for such extreme examples. Our body alerts us to an approaching mealtime. "It must be close to noon" we say ordinarily though having no other information. We are also alerted to the time by fatigue or drowsiness. Developmental or involutional processes are also information sources in our lives. Chidren first compare their age by their height (taller = older) and the physical limitations of age inform us of the multiplications of our years.

More subtly, we are conditioned to time intervals in the Pavlovian or Skinnerian sense. Animals use the same cues as we do at the level of conditioning as well as circadian cycles. The role of these cues is even more evident in the animal, who has no other temporal cues.

Information Provided by the Cosmic Environment. The succession of days and nights, of seasons, and of the annual return of the cycle of seasons were man's first temporal cues. We are still using them: "The sun is coming up, it must be 7"; "when the leaves fall, it is autumn."

Clocks and Calendars. To organize social life or develop science, men need more precise temporal references. They have therefore invented ways to measure time. Without going into scientific details, we know the importance in daily life of watches, and the role in our lives and in the life of humanity of calendars and dates.

Estimation of Duration

The Double System of Estimations. We speak, in general, of the estimation of a duration when chronometric methods are not available. Even in this case our estimations of time, if they depend on the amount of perceived and/or memorized information—as we have let it be understood—always depend also on our knowledge of time (the duration necessary to accomplish one action) or on parachronometric references provided by the action itself (the space crossed, or the number of pieces fabricated, etc.). Our estimations, according to the situation and also according to our attitude, depend simultaneously on memorized and on more temporal information. We have thus a double system of estimations that are far from always coinciding.

Sometimes we are aware of this and sometimes we rely on a single type of information.

The distinction between two systems of evaluation has been made by other authors in slightly different terms. Doob (1971) distinguishes two levels of judgment: primary-judgment potential and secondary-judgment potential. He considers primary judgment to be all that is based on subjective intuitions, direct estimations of time as well as temporal information, whereas secondary judgments relate to measures of time and to corrections based on primary judgments.

Michon (1979) proposes the principle of a double strategy of estimation, an "impressionist" strategy that is adopted by the subject when he considers the number of events that he is remembering to be effectively representative of time elapsed; and an "analytic" strategy adopted when the subject transforms his temporal estimations with a cognitive treatment based specifically on the notion of conventional time [p. 278]. This distinction parallels our own, except that what Michon calls analytic strategy would instead be the mixed product of estimations based on mnemonic and temporal information. But Michon is right to say that strategy based on mnemonic information, which he calls *impressionist,* dominates in the young child and in certain mental illnesses.

It is necessary to add that this analytic strategy or strategy of parametric evaluation is not found in young children, because it always implies in one way or another, the comparison of two approximately simultaneous durations. This comparison is sometimes explicit as when the subject compares the duration of a race between two horses. At other times the comparison is implicit, as for instance when the subject compares the duration of a present activity to an internal implicit norm that is most often interpreted by absolute judgments (too long–too short).

Piaget (1946) showed that children were unable to make these comparisons in a coherent manner before they reached concrete operations (around 7–8 years old) at which time they become capable of correctly classifying information on the succession and durations of events. Piaget also showed that it is only at the age of what he terms *formal operations* (in adolescence) that man builds an abstract representation of time that separates concrete information of different types.

The problem of the estimation of duration attains all its psychological interest only when we have no direct temporal information available.

It is necessary to distinguish the different situations in which these estimations intervene in order to find the directing principles that allow interpretation of the often contradictory experimental results. We distinguish first of all immediate estimations that are made at the end of an activity from estimations of the past, when we are estimating a previous period of our activity or even our life.

Immediate Estimations. The majority of research belongs to this category. It is limited to fairly brief periods, from several tenths of seconds to several hours. Beyond that, chronometric references changing the nature of the estimation would intervene. In these estimations, prospective estimations must be carefully distinguished from retrospective estimations as stated in Hicks, Miller, and Kinsbourne (1976): "The operational distinction is whether the subject knows before (prospective paradigm) or only after (retrospective paradigm) the interval that a judgment is required [p. 720]."

The general law is that duration seems longer in prospective estimations than in retrospective estimations.

The explanation generally proposed is that in prospective estimations we are not only paying attention to our activity but also to the duration according to the well-known principle formulated by Katz (1906): Each time we bring our attention to the passing of time, it seems to take longer. But more explanation of the role and effects of attention is needed. Estimated durations might be understood in terms of the mode proposed by Thomas and Weaver (1975) for very brief durations, namely a double process, one part of which takes into account the actual duration whereas the other part treats the information or more generally, the nature and level of the activity.

Instead, we think that a more general principle applies to this effect of attention. To know that one has to estimate the duration at the end of an activity leads one to divide the activity into the briefest possible sequences; that is, to multiply the "events." In other words there is more control over the duration of the activity, even if it is automatised.

We could say that in prospective estimations events are actively memorized in order to enable the subject to respond to the request for a posterior estimation of time, whereas when the estimation is retrospective we are in a situation of incidental memory; the latter is always more limited.

This role of attention to duration in prospective estimation is particularly obvious when the situation itself has a dominant temporal component, as in waiting. To wait for a train, to wait at the dentist's, or to wait for a boring task to be finished so as to be able to go on to a more agreeable one always provokes a subjective lengthening of the duration.

However, this attention to duration does not prevent the nature of the activity itself from being a component in our prospective and retrospective estimations. Hicks et al. (1976) rightly showed the connection between the activity and prospective and retrospective estimations. Subjects classified playing cards for 42 sec in a single stack, in two stacks (red and black), or in four stacks (by suits). The judged time in seconds was longer in prospective estimates than in retrospective estimates, especially when the quantity of information treated (response uncertainty) was smaller. When the classification was done automatically (in a single stack) the prospective estimate was 52.9 sec and the retrospective estimate was 28.3 sec. The spread between these two estimates diminishes (42.8 to 38.3) when the cards must be resplit into two stacks.

The available information is largely dependent on the task but can sometimes give contradictory cues. Thus, to estimate the duration of a displacement we are observing or effecting, we can take into account the distance covered as well as the speed at which it was crossed. The adult knows how to reason and compensate for these two parameters, but the young child may make gross errors of estimation by taking only one sort of information into account.

A developmental approach permits a better comprehension of the complexity involved in the treatment of information present in complex situations. In one of our experiments, children between 6.6 and 12.6 years and adults estimated, by using sticks of different lengths, the relative duration of presentation of two series of slides. One had 8 slides and each was presented for 4 sec, and the other had 16 slides each presented for 2 sec. In such a situation, nothing permitted even the adult to judge accurately that the durations were equal, because it would have been necessary to count the number of slides and measure the duration of each. The most interesting result of this test is the criterion taken into account by the subjects, according to their responses to an open questionnaire handed out after the trial. Table 10.1 and Table 10.2 describe all aspects of these responses.

The majority of the children take only one criterion into consideration: the number of slides, ignoring the duration of each slide (or what they sometimes call the speed of the slides). Few children under 10 years consider both criteria. The use of both increases greatly with age but only clearly becomes the strategy of the majority with adults. Overall, the number of slides is the criterion most often cited (Fraisse, 1966a).

In the course of development, the child learns to take many kinds of information into consideration, correcting the effects of each by those of the others. These corrections and the use of the two systems of estimation that we have distinguished explain the noticeable improvement effects of practice on duration estimations in the 6-year-olds (Fraisse, 1963) as well as in the adults (Hicks, 1976).

The differential use of these two systems may explain the large individual differences that researchers find in studies on duration estimation, differences

TABLE 10.1
Percentage of Subjects Having Used One or Several Criteria

	6.6	8.6	10.6	12.6	Adults
One	57	60	65	48	29
Two or three	9	19	35	48	71
Total	66	79	100	96	100

TABLE 10.2
Nature of the Criteria Used When Subjects Cited Only One Criterion (Percentage)

	6.6	8.6	10.6	12.6	Adults
Number of slides	81	60	52	50	39
Duration of slides	11 ⎫	16 ⎫	18 ⎫	22 ⎫	22 ⎫
	⎬ 19	⎬ 40	⎬ 48	⎬ 50	⎬ 61
Speed of presentation	8 ⎭	24 ⎭	30 ⎭	28 ⎭	39 ⎭

that are also present in people's daily behavior. We hypothesize that these differences are due, on the one hand, to the importance that subjects spontaneously attribute to the task or to the accompanying temporal information. We see a confirmation of this in Eysenck's (1959) observation that extraverts judged time to be shorter than introverts: They would attach more importance to the nature of the activity than to its duration.

Estimations of Past Durations. As a general rule, the further a duration lies in the past, the briefer it will appear. Several of Ornstein's experiments (1969) confirm this intuitive observation. The shortening of the duration corresponds to a diminution of the memorized events resulting from reorganizations of information (process of interference) and the degradation of "traces" (Wickelgren, 1974). This diminution is proportional to the square root of elapsed time ($\sqrt{t}$), according to the data collected by Michon (1979). This law is not all specific in nature. The effect of increasing distance in the past appears only when the individual is keeping track of the number of events memorized at the moment when they are being lived. Thus, we conserve many childhood memories because probably everything was new for us then. Inversely, the old person has few memories of his last years, because habit dulls the importance of lived changes. Correlatively, periods of our childhood seem long to us compared to the shortness of our more recent past, which does not correspond to an effect of the $\sqrt{t}$ law. Perhaps to clarify its domain of validity it would be necessary to add "all things being equal at the moment of memorization."

Beyond this, and even more markedly for estimations of past durations than for immediate estimations of duration, there is simultaneous usage of our two evaluation systems. The number of memorized events is compared to temporal references of pragmatic origins (my mother died after the birth of my daughter) or social origins such as those furnished by the dates of events. Thus, dating is often very consolidated (1781, Independence of the United States) but when it remains uncertain it may be remarked that, within certain limits (dating from public events of the last 20 years for example), it also follows a law close to $\sqrt{t}$. The most past events appear relativley less distant in time. Their date is moved forward (Lieury, 1979).

Temporal Perspectives.

At a given instant, though trying to separate myself from the stimulations actually impinging on me at that moment, I have a representation of a time that is in front of me much as is my space. In the circumstances, for time as for space, we employ the term *perspective*. This temporal perspective is made of all the events I have in memory and all the constructions built up from these memories. I distinguish here an *actual present* that is not a *perceived present* but instead that portion of my life that I make present and that serves me as a reference: This afternoon, this week, this year. In relation to this present, I have a representation of the past constituted by memories and knowledge; I have also a representation of the future. Here, apparently, are not memories but mental constructions, products of my imagination that furnish this future.

The Past. This has already been much discussed because all temporal estimations refer to the past. However, it is still necessary to recall that the past is not a simple accumulation of images and memories. It is the fruit of incessant constructions and reconstructions. Piaget (1946), better than anyone, has analyzed the stages of these constructions in the course of the child's development. The child, like the animal, first memorizes objective series of events. A young baby who has dropped a toy may cry but does not search for it. The infant of 7 months looks for the object: A present memory refers him to a disappeared object. When he can move, he goes to search for an object in another room. The past has been released from immediate activity.

An important change occurs when the child, through language, becomes capable of evoking past experience. At the beginning, the child contents himself with transposing onto the map of language what he already knows how to do. But the development of language enables him slowly to organize his memories. It is sufficient to listen to children from 3 to 6 years old giving an account of a previous experience to understand the difficulties involved in the construction of the past. There is often inappropriate juxtaposition of scenes and images. It is only at about 5 years old that everything belonging to the past is not classified without distinction under the adverb "yesterday." The syntactic forms that allow us to indicate simultaneity or succession are not fully mastered until adolescence (Ferreiro, 1971). The more completely we master language, the better we can organize our past. Bachelard (1936) has said what remains in memory most often is "that which has been dramatized by language." In this way we can unfold, with experience and education, increasingly broader perspectives on the past.

The child is helpful with these constructions through familial education, school, and social rites. The recurrence of civil and religious ceremonies helps us to organize our past and to construct chronologies. That these particular recollections in our memory are the result of cognitive-type constructions is proved *a contrario* in the mentally retarded person whose perspectives on the past do not go beyond a span of a few days. This phenomenon is also found in senile dementia, sometimes with islets of old memories.

The Future. At first glance, the future seems to escape from all that we have said because our representations of time have been based on memory. In fact, the future is sketched out from the perception of time because our present perceptions are signals of what will be happening. The newborn who is hungry cries. It stops crying when the bottle touches its lips—a reflex. Very quickly, the stimulus is transformed into a signal through a classic conditioning process. The sight of the bottle and later the preparation for the bottle is sufficient to calm the infant. The present offers information permitting the child to anticipate the future. The child who goes to look for a toy in another room is referring to the past but has a goal directed toward the future. The animal does the same within more narrow temporal limits, except in highly automatized behaviors.

As in the case of the past, anticipatory behaviors are first transposed and then developed by the use of language. Thus it seems clear that the future is first represented only as the repetition of the past. It is notable that it is at the same age that the child begins to use the adverbs *yesterday* and *tomorrow* with relevance.

The representation of the future, as also dependent of the past, is verified in large measure in the adult. At the same time, the richer the past of an individual, the more the future is unfolded in front of him or her. On concrete representations of the past and future, our perspectives depend on many psycho-sociological factors (Nuttin, 1979). Age, culture, and successes (or failures) have also a decisive importance.

CONCLUSION: A MODEL OF DURATION ESTIMATION

Having discussed the principal processes occurring in perception and duration estimation, we can now try to propose a model (Fig. 10.1). We have chosen to draw inspiration from both Sperling's (1967) and Shiffrin and Atkinson's (1969) models. We retain the principal buffers from their models but Fig. 10.1 does not represent the functional relations between these different buffers. To simplify the figure, we have only represented the fundamental relations occurring between the processes of perception and the estimation of duration.

One specific aspect of our model is its orientation to a present instant that we call *now*. On the left, represented by the dotted line, is the progression of

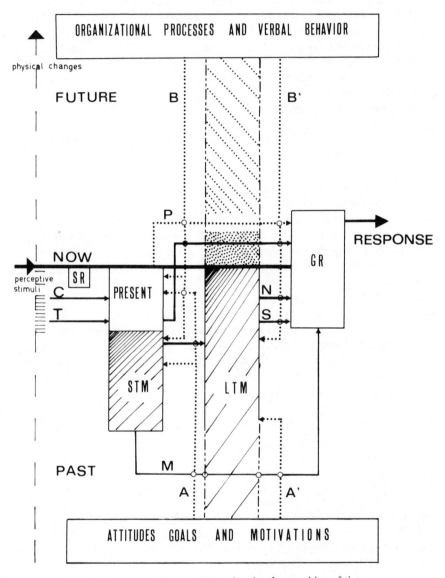

FIG. 10.1. A model of duration estimation for cognition of time.

physical changes that are the source of stimulations. Of these, we have represented only those that can be apprehended in the perceived present. As they appear, stimulations are treated by the sensory register (*SR*). Within *STM,* we have represented with a block the perceived present. It receives the information connected to the duration of the stimulus or stimuli (*T*) and to its (their) content (*C*).

Acting on the perceived present and on the *STM* and *LTM* as well, are control processes that we have divided into two buffers: attitudes, motivations, and goals on the one hand, and organizational processes on the other, because they play a different role as we have seen; their effects are represented under *A* and *A'* and *B* and *B'*. Obviously, the place of these two buffers is not dependent on a temporal order. In a model represented in three dimensions they would be placed on top of the other buffers. The perceived present can directly produce a perceptual response (*P*). It may also register in the *STM* and little by little in the *LTM* and give a memory response (*M*). The immediate estimation of the duration is done starting from memorized events but changes according to whether the subject knows before acting that he has to estimate the duration (prospective order of the response) or whether this estimation is required of him as an afterthought (retrospective order of response *R*). The treatment of data in *STM* or *LTM* changes from one case to the other.

Arriving at the response generator (*GR*) from the *LTM* is specific information related to *N* number of stored events, and temporal information of a cognitive type often socialized (*S*). The response generator is represented astride the *now* because the information furnished at a given instant must still be treated in the near future before being communicated in the response form.

Knowing the effects of the nature of the stimuli, the motivational processes *A* and *A'*, and the organizational possibilities *B* and *B'*, and knowing also that it is a question of perceived present *P*, or of prospective or retrospective estimations (*M*), it is possible, in large measure, to predict the relative results of estimations of the duration.

Different adaptive acts correspond to each of the two modes of apprehending time: perception and representation. The perceived time permits one constantly to gather information about successive events (a sentence, a melody, and scenes from a trip or a theater production). Therefore one can easily take into account various aspects of an activity: duration of phonemes in the comprehension of speech; duration of notes in music; duration of visual or auditory signals in sensori-motor tasks (e.g., when driving a car or operating a machine).

Representations of time reverberate in life sometimes consciously but very often in a hidden manner. One must have on occasion an estimation of the immediate past (e.g., the duration of a conversation) or of an event several years ago. At each moment the duration of past experiences that shaped one and give indispensable reference points are taken into consideration. The individual is also constantly oriented by some project (to go to work, to plan a trip, etc).

These representations of the successive events and of their duration allows for the construction of a general concept of time that is the necessary basis for reasoning about individual time and about the time of the world.

REFERENCES

Anderson, A. C. Time discrimination in the white rat. *Journal of Comparative Psychology*, 1932, *13*, 27–55.

Aschoff, J. *Circadian clocks*. Amsterdam: North-Holland, 1965.

Avant, L. L., Lyman, P. J., & Antes, J. R. Effects of stimulus familiarity on judged visual duration. *Perception and Psychophysics*, 1975, *17*, 253–262.

Axel, R. Estimation of time. *Archives of Psychology*, 1924, *12*, n° 74.

Bachelard, G. *La dialectique de la durée*. Paris: Boivin, 1936.

Benussi, V. *Psychologie der Zeitauffassung*. Heidelberg: Winter, 1913.

Békésy, G. (von). Über die Hörsamkeit der Ein- und Ausschwungvorgänge mit Berücksichtigung der Raumakustig. *Annalen der Physik*, 1933, *16*, 844.

Binet, A. Nouvelles recherches sur la mesure du niveau intellectuel chez les enfants des écoles. *L'Année Psychologique*, 1911, *17*, 145–201.

Block, R. A. Memory and the experience of duration in retrospect. *Memory and Cognition*, 1974, *2*, 153–160.

Bolton, T. L. Rhythm. *American Journal of Psychology*, 1894, *6*, 145–238.

Bunning, E. *The psychological clock*. New York: Springer, 1964.

Craik, F. I. M. The fate of primary memory items in free recall. *Journal of Verbal Learning and Verbal Behavior*, 1970, *9*, 143–148.

Creelman, C. D. Human discrimination of auditory duration. *The Journal of the Acoustical Society of America*, 1962, *34*, 582–593.

Decroly, O., & Degand, J. Observations relatives au développement de la notion de temps chez une petite fille. *Archives de Psychologie*, 1913, *13*, 113–161.

Demany, L., McKenzie, B., & Vurpillot, E. Rhythm perception in early infancy. *Nature*, 1977, *266*, 718–719.

Dietze, G. Untersuchungen über den Umfang des Bewusstseins bei regelmässig aufeinander folgende Schalleindrücken. *Philosophische Studien*, 1885, *2*, 362–393.

Doob, L. W. *Patterning of time*. New Haven, Conn.: Yale University Press, 1971.

Eriksen, C. W., & Collins, J. F. Some temporal characteristics of visual pattern perception. *Journal of Experimental Psychology*, 1967, *74*, 476–486.

Exner, S. Experimentelle Untersuchung der einfachsten psychischen Processe. III. *Pflügers Archiv für die gesamte Physiologie des Menschen und der Tiere*, 1875, *11*, 403–432.

Eysenck, H. J. Personality and the estimation of time. *Perceptual and Motor Skills*, 1959, *9*, 405–406.

Feokritova, I. P. *Vremia kak uslounyi vozliuditel sliunnoi zhelezy*. Doctoral Dissertation, St. Petersburg, 1912.

Ferreiro, E. *Les relations temporelles dans le langage de l'enfant*. Genève: Droz, 1971.

Fraisse, P. Etude comparée de la perception et de l'estimation de la durée chez les enfants et les adultes. *Enfance*, 1948, *1*, 199–211.

Fraisse, P. *Les structures rythmiques*. Paris: Erasme, 1956.

Fraisse, P., *Psychologie du temps*. Paris: P. U. F., 1957.

Fraisse, P. L'estimation de la durée. In *Psychologie et épistémologie génétiques*. Paris: Dunod, 1966(a).

Fraisse, P. Le temps de réaction verbale: Dénomination et lecture. *L'Année Psychologique*, 1964, *64*, 21–46.

Fraisse, P. Visual-perceptive simultaneity and masking of letters successively presented. *Perception and Psychophysics*, 1966, *1*, 285–287.(b)

Fraisse, P. Why is naming longer than reading? *Acta Psychologica*, 1969, *30*, 96–103.

Fraisse, P. *Psychologie du rythme*. Paris: P.U.F., 1974.

Fraisse, P. Latence des réponses en mémoire immédiate: Noms et figures géométriques. *LAnnée Psychologique*, 1977, *77*, 325–342.

Fraisse, P., & Fraisse, R. Etudes sur la mémoire immédiate: I. L'appréhension des sons. *L'Année Psychologique*, 1937, *38*, 48–85.

Fraisse, P., Siffre, M., Oléron, G., & Zuili, N. Le rythme veille-sommeil et l'estimation du temps. In J. Ajuriaguerra (Ed.), *Cycles biologiques et Psychiatrie*. Paris: Masson, 1968.

Fraisse, P., & Smirnov, S. Response latency and the content of immediate memory. *Bulletin of the Psychonomic Society*, 1976, *8*, 345–348.

François, M. Contribution à l'étude du sens du temps. La température interne comme facteur de variation de l'appréciation subjective des durées. *L'Année Psychologique*, 1927, *28*, 186–204.

Frankenhaeuser, M. *Estimation of time*. Stockholm: Almqvist, 1959.

Fraser, J. T. *Time as conflict*. Basel: Birlhauser, 1978.

Gibson, J. J. The problem of temporal order in stimulation and perception. *Journal of Psychology*, 1966, *62*, 141–149.

Gjerdingen, B. B., & Tomsic, R. Recovery functions of human cortical potentials evoked by tones, shocks, vibration and flashes. *Psychonomic Science*, 1970, *19*, 228–229.

Guyau, J. M. *La genèse de l'idée de temps*. Paris: Alcan, 1890.

Harton, J. J. An investigation of the influence of success and failure on the estimation of time. *Journal of General Psychology*, 1939, *21*, 51–62.

Hicks, R. E. Effect of information feedback upon intertrial consistency of time judgment. *Acta Psychologica*, 1976, *40*, 265–270.

Hicks, R. E., Miller, G. W., & Kinsbourne, M. Prospective and retrospective judgments of time as a function of amount of information processed. *American Journal of Psychology*, 1976, *89*, 719–730.

Hillyard, S. A., & Picton, T. W. On and off components in the auditory evoked potential. *Perception and Psychophysics*, 1978, *24*, 391–398.

Hoagland, H. The physiological control of judgments of duration; evidence for a chemical clock. *Journal of General Psychology*, 1933, *9*, 267–287.

Hollingworth, H. L. The central tendency of judgment. *Journal of Philosophical Psychology and Scientific Methodology*, 1910, *7*, 461–469.

Höring, A. *Versuche über das Unterscheidungsvermögen des Hörsinnes für Zeitgrössen*. Tübingen: Laupp, 1864.

Hunter, W. S. Delayed reactions in animal and children. *Behavior Monography*, 1913, *2*, n° 1.

Hylan, J. P. The distribution of attention. *Psychological Review*, 1903, *10*, 373–403.

Israeli, N. The psychopathology of time. *Psychological Review*, 1932, *39*, 486–491.

Janet, P. *L'évolution de la mémoire et de la notion de temps*. Paris: Chahine, 1928.

James, W. *The principles of psychology*. New York: Holt, 1890.

Jaspers, K. *Allgemeine Psychopathologie*. Berlin: Springer, 1913.

Katz, D. Experimentelle Beiträge zur Psychologie des Vergleichs im Gebiete des Zeitsinns. *Zeitschrift für Psychologie und Physiologie des Sinnesorgane*, 1906, *42*, 302–340.

Kleist, K. *Gehirnpathologie*. Leipzig: Barth, 1934.

Koffka, K. *Principles of Gestalt psychology*. New York: Harcourt, 1935.

Kristofferson, A. B., & Allan, L. G. Successiveness and duration discrimination. In S. Kornblum (Ed.), *Attention and Performance* (Vol. IV). New York: Academic Press, 1973.

Laloy, L. *Aristoxène de Tarente et la musique de l'Antiquité*. Paris: Société française de l'imprimerie et de librairie, 1904.

Lieury, A. La contraction du temps dans la datation des souvenirs anciens. *LAnnée Psychologique*, 1979, *79*, 7–22.

Lichenstein, M. Phenomenal simultaneity with irregular timing of components of the visual stimulus. *Perceptual and Motor Skills*, 1961, *12*, 47–60.

Loehlin, J. C. The influence of different activities on the apparent length of time. *Psychological Monographs*, 1959, *73*, n° 474.

Mach, E. Untersuchungen über den Zeitsinn des Ohres. *Sitzungeberichte der Wiener Akademie der Wissenschaften*, 1865, K1, *51*.

MacDougall, R. The structure of simple forms. *Psychological Review, Monographs Supplements*, 1903, *4*, 309–416.

Meade, R. D. Time estimates as affected by need tension and rate of progress. *Journal of Psychology*, 1960, *50*, 173–177.

Michon, J. A. Time experience and memory processes. In J. T. Fraser & N. Lawrence (Eds.), *The study of time. II.* Berlin: Springer, 1975.

Michon, J. A. Le traitement de l'information temporelle. In P. Fraisse et al. (Eds.), *Du temps biologique au temps psychologique*. Paris: P.U.F., 1979.

Minkowski, E. *Le temps vécu. Etudes phénoménologiques et psychopathologiques*. Paris: Collection de l'évolution psychiatrique, 1933.

Mo, S. S. Judgment of temporal duration as a function of numerosity. *Psychonomic Science*, 1971, *24*, 71–72.

Mo, S. S. Comparative judgment of temporal duration as a function of numerosity. *Bulletin of the Psychonomic Society*, 1974, *3*, 377–379.

Nuttin, J. La perspective temporelle dans le comportement humain. In P. Fraisse et al. (Eds.), *Du temps biologique au temps psychologique*. Paris: P.U.F., 1979.

Oostenbrug, M. W. M., Horst, J. W., & Kniper, J. W. Discrimination of visually perceived intervals of time. *Perception and Psychophysics*, 1978, *24*, 21–34.

Ornstein, R. E. *On the experience of time*. Harmondsworth: Penguin Books, 1969.

Peterson, L. R., & Peterson, M. Short term retention of individual verbal items. *Journal of Experimental Psychology*, 1959, *58*, 193–198.

Piaget, J. *Le dévelopment de la notion de temps chez l'enfant*. Paris: P.U.F., 1946.

Picton, T. W., Hillyard, S. A., Krausz, H. J., & Galambos, R. Human auditory evoked potentials. I. Evaluation of components. *Electroencephalography and Clinical Neurophysiology*, 1974, *36*, 179–190.

Picton, T. W., & Hillyard, S. A. Human auditory-evoked potentials. II. Effects of attention. *Electroencephalography and Clinical Neurophysiology*, 1974, *36*, 191–199.

Piéron, H. Les problèmes psychophysiologiques de la perception du temps. *LAnnée Psychologique*, 1923, *24*, 1–25.

Servière, J. De l'instantané au durable: Données perspectives, corrélats électrophysiologiques. In P. Fraisse et al. (Eds.), *Du temps biologique au temps psychologique*. Paris: P.U.F., 1979.

Shiffrin, R. M., & Atkinson, R. C. Storage and retrieval processes in long-term memory. *Psychological Review*, 1969, *69*, 179–204.

Siffre, M. *Hors du temps*. Paris: Julliard, 1963.

Sperling, G. Successive approximations to a model for short-term memory. *Acta Psychologica*, 1967, *27*, 285–292.

Stern, L. W. Psychische Präsenzzeit. *Zeitschrift für Psychologie und Physiologie des Sinnesorgane*, 1897, *13*, 325–349.

Stern, L. W., & Stern, C. *Die Sprache des Kindes*. Leipzig: Barth, 1907.

Stroud, J. M. The fine structure of psychological time. In H. Quastler (Ed.), *Information theory in psychology*. Glencoe, Ill.: Free Press, 1956.

Thomas, E. A. C., & Weaver, W. B. Cognitive processing and time perception. *Perception and Psychophysics*, 1975, *17*, 363–367.

Vernon, J. A., & McGill, T. E. Time estimations during sensory deprivation. *Journal of General Psychology*, 1963, *69*, 11–18.

Vierordt, K. *Der Zeitsinn nach Versuchen.* Tübingen: Laupp, 1868.

Vos, P. *Identification of metre in music.* Report 760N06, Department of Psychology, Nijmegen, 1976.

Wallace, M., & Rabin, A. I. Temporal experience. *Psychological Bulletin,* 1960, *57,* 213–236.

Wallin, J. E. W. Researches on the rhythm of speech. *Studies from the Yale Psychological Laboratory,* 1901, *9,* 1–142.

Wickelgren, A. Single trace fragility theories of memory dynamics. *Memory and Cognition,* 1974, *2,* 775–780.

Woodrow, H. The temporal-indifference interval determined by the method of mean error. *Journal of Experimental Psychology,* 1934, *17,* 167–188.

Wundt, W. *Grundzüge des physiologischen Psychologie.* Leipzig: Engelmann, 1874.

11

Future Time Perspective and the Problem of Cognition/ Motivation Interaction

Hans Thomae
University of Bonn

According to Lewin (1938), change in future time perspective is one of the most fundamental facts of development. Differences in the behavior of children, adolescents, and adults are dependent variables of differences in extension and differentiation of future time perspective. From this point of view, Lewin (1939) emphasized a cognitive theory of behavior according to which the cognitive representation of the situation is the decisive variable in eliciting and directing responses (Baldwin, 1969; Nuttin, 1974). Lewin as well as Nuttin discriminated clearly between the cognitive structure of time perspective and its behavioral correlates on the one hand and on the other hand, the need structure or motivational system that may instigate thought or ideational processes or may become modified by the cognitive structure. The relationships between motivation and future time perspective are defined by these authors in terms of an interactive interpretation. An opposite trend is to be observed in approaches like that of Bergius (1957), Kelly (1955), and others pointing to the fact that the most valid criterion for the "motivational" character of a process is defined by its directedness toward the future. Hence it sounds reasonable to replace the label *motivation* by the name for its fundamental structure, that is, the anticipation of the future or directedness toward the future. The substitutional interpretations of the relationships between motivation and future time perspective may attract new followers according to the increasing trend toward "pure" cognitive theories of behavior. Bolles (1974) summarized this trend by stating that the problem of motivation is no longer of relevance for psychology as any variable that has been "motivational" before has its cognitive aspects. Therefore the behavioral formula for the late twentieth century would be: 'cognitive processes → behavior'. No stimulus, no drive, no need are necessary, as "thought directs action" (Birch, Atkinson, & Bongort, 1974). From this point of view the contemporary trend in theorizing on the "internal" or "external" conditions of behavior asks for a reevaluation of the future time perspective construct in terms of its motivational or purely cognitive status. We try to contribute to this reevaluation by comparing the two opposite interpretations and by examining research findings, mainly coming from developmental psychology. We believe, however, that these findings have some relevance for the issue of motivational versus pure cognitive theories of behavior.

FUTURE TIME ORIENTATION AND PHENOMENOLOGICAL THEORIES OF MOTIVATION

According to the Swiss philosopher–biologist Sganzini (1940), the construct of "anticipation" points to a fundamental structure of processes and being. In a phenomenological analysis of needs the anticipating structure of the state following food deprivation or stimulation of exploratory tendencies was emphasized by our subjects. As translated by the author (Thomae, 1944): " ... Summarizing these reports we have to state that the experiencing subject faced with need situations will reach forward into the time ... The kind of this reaching forward ... can be characterized mainly by subordering need or drive state under the category of "anticipation" [p. 49].

For Lersch (1938) the anticipatory nature of need states was an important aspect of motivational processes. In the first instance, however, he mentioned the perception of deprivation or of unrest. The future relatedness of the reported psychological reactions to deprivation or unrest was seen as a characteristic of motivational processes. There was no intention to replace the motivation variable by the anticipation construct. The same holds for Nuttin's (1974) "relational theory of motivation," which is "trying to do justice to both viewpoints, the cognitive and the affective-dynamic, in an integrated model [p. 12]."

FUTURE TIME PERSPECTIVE AND THE THE STRUCTURATION OF PERSONALITY

One of the theories following Lewin's future time perspective approach in Germany tried to assess different aspects of near or more distant segments of future time in a series of experiments (Bergius, 1957). In agreement with Lewin, degree of differentiation of future time perspective was regarded as a major factor in problem-solving behavior and in the structuration of general beliefs (e.g., about the chances of man reaching the moon). Level of performance in problem-solving tasks was optimal when the differentiation of future time perspective was moderate. Various ways or forms of behavior (like "random behavior," "controlled behavior") were interpreted as consequences of variations in the differentiation and structuration of future time perspective. From this point of view, Bergius (1957) concludes that the construct of future time perspective as conceived by Lewin asks for a revision of motivational concepts. Concepts like need, instinct, drive, and will are not necessary to explain behavior. Even psychoanalytical constructs like sublimation may be interpreted as resulting from specific forms of future time perspectives with varying degrees of differentiation (Bergius, 1957, p. 230). Rather than explaining behavior by the elicitation and modification of one or several drives psychology should try to focus on the structures of time perspectives that are identical with the "personal continuum" (or personality).

In his later publications, Bergius did not pursue these ideas implying a revision of psychological theorizing. As far as he emphasized the replacement of motivational concepts by structural aspects of future time perspective he could have referred to Kelly's theory of "personal constructs" that was published before Bergius' (1957) book on future time perspective. Whereas Sganzini (1940) defined anticipation as a general structural quality of biological processes, Kelly (1955) stated that anticipation is a behavioral form unique for man. The role of anticipation in human behavior is defined in his fundamental postulate: "A person's processes are psychologically channelized by the ways in which he anticipates events (Vol. 1, p. 46)." The results of these anticipations are "constructs" determining behavior. Motivation becomes a redundant construct needed only by those who overlook the fundamental active nature of man. Any aspect of behavior can be predicted by studying the different ways in which man constructs his more or less distant future.

The applications of Kelly's theory in clinical practice gave some validation for his rejection of motivation. However, when trying to test the theory experimentally, Kelly himself developed an instrument in which future time orientation was not a decisive aspect. For historians of motivation like Bolles (1974), Kelly's approach could have served as good evidence for the growing tendency to replace motivational variables by cognitive ones.

FUTURE TIME PERSPECTIVE—A COGNITIVE DETERMINANT OF BEHAVIOR

Most studies on future time perspective and its impact on behavior are ambiguous regarding their interpretation of cause–effect relationships as they are mostly correlational. We evaluate most of these studies as evidence for possible determinants of future time perspective as this is the more plausible interpretation. On the other hand, there are correlational studies that point more to the impact of future time perspective on behavior. In a study on the conditions of success or failure in the training of medical students, Hirsch (1979) showed that the successful ones had more specific and more realistic plans for their future careers than those with low or no success. With the use of theta-based automatic detection program (Morgan & Messenger, 1973), Mudrich (1979) showed that future time perspective was the most powerful predictor of the way adult women experienced the "empty nest situation" (after the youngest child leaves home). Those with a negative attitude toward the future experienced this situation in a more negative way, whereas those with a more favorable future time perspective perceived their lives as determined more by themselves than by others.

Other findings that point to influences of the future time perspective on behavior are coming from the Bonn Longitudinal Study of Aging (BLSA) in which approximately 90 men and women (of originally 220) were followed from 1965 (measurement point I = $m.p.$I) to 1977 ($m.p.$ VI; Thomae, 1976). According to Pfötsch (1979), who used path analysis with various aspects of the future time perspective as the independent variables, we can state that extension of the future time perspective and positive attitude toward the future are "determinants of satisfaction with life situation." The study of Pfötsch is a continuation of the work by Schreiner (1969) who analyzed the data from the first measurement point of the Bonn Longitudinal Study of Aging (Thomae, 1976). In this analysis he compared two cohorts (born, 1890–95 and 1900–05, respectively), both of which consisted of 50 men and 50 women. The following aspects of future time perspective were measured by rating scales: extension of plans, number of plans for the next years, attitude (positive–negative) toward the future, content of plans, perception of own life situation as definitive (unchangeable), and awareness of finitude. As expected, persons with a higher degree of future time perspective and more positive attitude to the future had a higher life satisfaction score. Schreiner (1969) found many other significant differences in the behavior of aged persons with an extended and a restricted future time perspective. The content of future time perspective from most of the BLSA subjects was defined by plans for traveling, plans regarding visits to relatives or changes in one's own family, plans to make changes in one's own house or garden. However, there were also plans regarding continued education, cultivation of one's own interests, and hopes and worries about one's own health. The most consistent differences in the behavior of the subjects with extended or restricted future time perspective were related to activity as shown during a 1-week testing and observation period and regarding feeling competent in this situation (Grombach, 1975).

Another approach toward a longitudinal analysis of our BLSA data on future time perspective was tested by Fisseni (1976). He used the method of

TABLE 11.1
Patterns of Change in Future Time Perspective

Pattern	Scores at m.p. I	Degree and Direction of Change
A	High in all aspects	Decline and consistency
B	High in future orientation, low in other directedness	Decline and tendency to increase
C	Low in future orientation, high in other directedness	Increase and consistency
D	Low in extension and other directedness, high in number of plans	Increase (tendency to decline)

configurational frequency analysis (Lienert & Krauth, 1975) for differentiating patterns of change regarding future time perspective. The number and the extension of plans and the attitude toward others were used as criteria for an "extended life space" directed mainly into the future. Table 11.1 shows the four patterns that could be delineated.

The studies of Schreiner (1969), Grombach (1975), and Fisseni (1976) demonstrated that cohort differences were not related to future-time-perspective variables. This may be explained by the age of the respondents. However, the longitudinal data of Fisseni stressed that also in old age increase as well as decrease of future time perspective can be found. Health was consistently better in persons with more extended future time perspective at m.p.I. However, there were two groups in which future time perspective decreased with consistent good health scores. Therefore it is a very complex pattern of variables that is related to consistency and change in future time perspective. However, even an elaborate system of these impacts would not be sufficient. As change in future time perspective was more observed in the first four measurement points of the BLSA, Fisseni (1976) has stated there was no indication "that in life space of the aged people of this study characteristics of 'fluid' cognitive components predominate over those of 'crystallized' quality [p. 110]." From this point of view, it is hypothesized that future time perspective is an indicator of specific cognitive structures that are related to Cattell's constructs of "fluid" and "crystallized" intelligence. Change as well as consistency of future time perspective point to the operation of these structures. These structures would determine future time perspective as behavioral or attitudinal variables. Therefore the thesis that the construct "future time perspective" can replace that of "motivation" does not receive real support from this study. It would cause many difficulties to reduce all motivational variables to the dimension of "fluid–crystallized" cognitive compounds.

EXPECTED DEFINITIVENESS OF UNFAVORABLE
LIFE CONDITIONS AS AN INTERVENING VARIABLE

The aspect of perceived definitiveness of the present situation (especially of its unfavorable conditions) was selected as one indicator of future time perspective (Pfötsch, 1979). According to Grombach (1975), the scores of rated interview data related to perceived definitiveness of one's own life situation correlated in a highly significant way with bad mood (or low morale) from $m.p.$I (1965) to $m.p.$IV (1970) and with negative attitude toward the future (as measured by the Riegel scales). There was a significant correlation between perceived definitiveness of one's own situation and extension of future time perspective only at one measurement point. On the other hand, significant correlations were found between perceived definitiveness and perception of poor health, low degree of life satisfaction, and prevalence of loss and frustration in the reported life history of all measurement points.

It is evident that perceived definitiveness of the present (unfavorable) situation is related to content or quality rather than to quantity of future time perspective. Continuity of stress, harm or frustration, and lack of differentiation between present and future time are the main qualitities of this cognitive structure. For a cross-sectional study on reactions of aged persons living in high versus low stress situations, we developed a scale for measuring "perceived definitiveness of unfavorable life situations (PEDE)." The scale contains 16 items like: At my age I should not look forward to a better change; all my plans become increasingly restricted due to poor health. The reactions to stress were evaluated from a 3-hour semistructured interview in which all present life stress areas (e.g., regarding occupational, economic, housing, familial, and health situations) were inquired. In subjects with health problems we found mainly the following reactions: achievement related behavior; adjustment to institutionalized aspects of the situation; adjustment to situation in family; revision of expectancies; delaying gratification of needs; hope for change; asking others for help; relying on others; depressive reaction; and active resistance. The great variety of reactions elicited by perceived health problems questions the validity of any classification of these reactions along an "active–passive" or a "coping–defense" (Haan, 1977) dimension. We cannot go into the details of the classification problems (Lazarus & Cohen, 1976). Our main point is related to the intervening role of perceived definitiveness of health problems as measured by PEDE. The significant correlations between perceived definitiveness of own situation and preferred reactions to health problems were related to "delay of gratification," "revision of expectancies," and "depressive reaction." A significant relationship was also found between PEDE scores and preference for active resistance. This reaction includes all kinds of behavior by which recommendations of the doctor regarding eating, smoking, drinking, or physical activity are rejected. Very often the active resistance is directed toward spouse or other relatives who try to remind the elderly patient of these medical recommendations.

The very dangerous influence of high expectancy of definitiveness of unfavorable life conditions is shown especially in a comparison of low, medium, and high scores in the PEDE scale regarding preference for active resistance, depressive reaction, and revision of expectancies (Fig. 11.1). The negative influence of active resistance against medical recommendations and of depressive reactions on health is self-evident and given evidence by many studies.

Revision of expectancies may be defined in this context as a revision of the self-concept, especially in its physical and future-time-perspective aspects. This reaction may be evaluated as well adjusted to the situation of the elderly considering the increasing degree of multimorbidity and polypathy in the elderly organism (Schubert, 1969). In the individual case, however, it may result in behaviors favoring active resistance to medical recommendations, resignation, or similar unfavorable reactions.

From this point of view the interference of the cognitive variable "perceived definitiveness of unfavorable life conditions in old age" with the selection of responses to health problems can result in maladjustment. Any kind of intervention with these reaction patterns would have to change this cognitive variable. Preventive measures would have to change the information input (e.g., on behalf of doctors who are very often decisive in forming cognitive structures of this kind). In any case, the impact of "perceived definitiveness" as measured by PEDE gives evidence that cognitive structures or systems can determine behavior.

One cannot conclude from this finding, however, that cognitive systems can replace motivational variables in the explanation and prediction of behavior. "Perceived definitiveness of a situation" is identical with the anticipation of unchangeability whereas motivation always is an anticipation of change (of outcomes of behavior, homeostasis, increased or decreased stimulation, of "peak experiences", etc.).

As the prestige of some opinion leaders (like doctors fostering a negative stereotype of old age) and the impact of many frustrations belong to the sources of perceived definitiveness, this cognitive variable itself is the result of a complex interaction between motivation and cognitive processes. The construct of motivation is necessary in order to explain the origin of perceived definitiveness.

DETERMINANTS OF FUTURE TIME PERSPECTIVE

Theories of behavior try to explain and predict behavior by the isolation of some antecedent–outcome variables that are supposed to be representative for all sequences of events in the interaction of organism and environment.

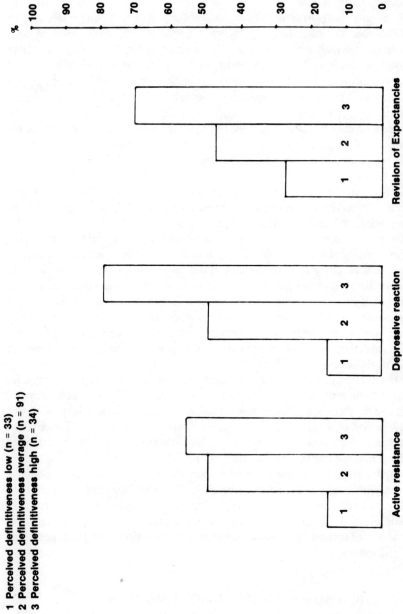

1 Perceived definitiveness low (n = 33)
2 Perceived definitiveness average (n = 91)
3 Perceived definitiveness high (n = 34)

%
100
90
80
70
60
50
40
30
20
10
0

Active resistance   Depressive reaction   Revision of Expectancies

FIG. 11.1. Differences in reactions to health problems between persons scoring low, medium, and high in "Perceived definitiveness of the situation."

The formula cognitive processes → behavior (Bolles, 1974) or the statement "thought directs action" (Birch, Atkinson, & Bongort, 1974) are misleading if they neglect the motivational and other origins of cognitive processes. According to findings of Lehr (1967), Schreiner (1969), Fisseni (1976), and Pfötsch (1979), future time perspective is closely related to health. At *m.p.* I of BLSA, Schreiner (1969) found a significant difference between the amount of plans mentioned by healthy and less healthy aged persons. However, according to the longitudinal analysis of Fisseni (1976), this relationship was not consistent. At *m.p.* I, three patterns of future time perspective and health interactions turned up: A small group characterized by better health but by reduced future time perspective; a larger group with significantly better health and increased future time perspective; and a third group in poor health and with reduced future time perspective. At *m.p.* III, only one pattern proves to be characteristic: poor health in connection with reduced future time perspective. At *m.p.* IV, no pattern turned up. The relationship between health and future time perspective becomes evident in the data. Other variables intervene, however. This is especially true for perceived health status that shows closer relationships to coping with health problems than the health status as assessed by the medical staff (Olbrich & Lehr, 1978).

According to Schreiner (1969), the socioeconomic status correlated significantly with extension as well as quality of future time perspective at *m.p.* I. Fisseni (1976) showed that this relationship is true for the majority of the subjects. However, from *m.p.* I to *m.p.* III persons high in socioeconomic status show some tendency to decreasing future time perspective whereas future time perspective doesn't change from *m.p.* III to *m.p.* IV. There were no persons scoring low in socioeconomic status and high in future time perspective.

Using the technique of hierarchical variance analysis (Sonquist & Morgan, 1964), Kranzhoff (1979) found a close relationship between exposure to economic and/or health problems (stress), activities related to these problems, and perceived definitiveness as measured by PEDE. The highest score for PEDE was found in a group with economic problems, low degree of coping with economic problems and high degree of family interaction, and finally a low score on the Life Satisfaction Scale (Havighurst, 1961; Wiendick, 1970). A larger group with a high score in PEDE is characterized by the same variables except for "high family interaction." On the other hand, we find the lowest scores for PEDE in a group exposed to economic/health problems, low degree of coping with situation, high score of life satisfaction, and a rather low score for PEDE, too. In a group exposed to economic/health problems, high degree of coping and high score of life satisfaction were found. Although there are some indications of a relationship between stress exposure and higher PEDE scores, the decisive variable is life satisfaction. Life satisfation is an index of "successful aging" (i.e., the ability of the individual to restore disturbances in his/her affective–emotional state). From this point of view, life-satisfaction scores result from internal and external adjustments. In terms of the psychological model of stress reaction (Lazarus & Launier, 1978), life-satisfaction scores can be regarded also as indicators of the primary appraisal of the stress that very often is influenced, too, by feedback slopes coming from results of successful coping with a stress situation. From this point of view, the decisive role of life-satisfaction scores in the determination of PEDE scores might be interpreted just as an example of the interaction of several cognitive subsystems within a larger cognitive system that might be labeled as the "image of the elderly of his own situation." Whereas life satisfaction points to past and present life situation, PEDE scores inform about aspects of future time perspective.

As life-satisfaction scores reduce the error variance by 31.6% (Kranzhoff, 1979) whereas objective indicators for stress do so only to a much smaller degree (2.08% for economic problems; 6.1% for health problems), this finding supports cognitive theories of personality according to which the cognitive representation rather than the objective quality of a situation determines behavior (Baldwin, 1969; Nuttin, 1974; Thomae, 1970). However, any cognitive representation is an outcome of motivational processes and life satisfaction is the outcome of processes of restoring emotional-affective balance.

As perceived definitiveness of one's own situation is a component of future time perspective, we have to state that no research evidence allows the dismissal of motivational constructs in favor of the construct of future time perspective. We should rather conclude that future time perspective is a good example of motivation–cognition interactions directing human behavior. This can especially be shown in the discussion of the relationships between age and future time perspective. Whether there is a general restriction of future time perspective in old age may be doubted from more recent research (Munnichs, 1977). Some studies could not find a correlation between chronological age and extension of future time perspective (Eson & Greenfeld, 1962; Kühlen & Monge, 1968; Roos & Albers, 1965; Thomae, 1971). Others point to the increasing relevance of the near future (Kastenbaum, 1963). Nuttin and Grommen (1975) found a general restriction of the depth of future time perspective after 65. They found social-class differences, too, with lower-class people showing an increase of orientation towards the near future, whereas middle-class and high-class persons show a greater interest for the open present. Lens and Gailly (1980) confirmed the hypothesis of Nuttin and Grommen (1975) about a curvilinear relationship between age and future time perspective. They found a restriction of future time perspective from the age of 65 on.

In a study of future time perspective of teachers, Göbbels (1979) found a significant difference between the scores for "far distant personal future" of the age group 25–34 years and all other age groups. The oldest (55–64 years) did not differ from the middle-age groups (35–54 years). On the other hand there was a sharp rise in the scores of the "near personal future" from the age group 45–54 years to 55–64 years. Future time perspective scores related to educational concerns (e.g., "as an educator I hope that I can help my students to cope with life") did not differentiate between the age groups. Apparently future time perspective related to the occupational role of the teacher is perceived in the same way by younger and older teachers whereas there are differences in the personal future time perspective that may appear in early stages or turn up in the oldest age group. In any case we receive some evidence for a concentration of future time perspective on near future or even to the open present in a majority of persons beyond 60 years. From an evaluation of the "themes" that were mentioned in the three annual interviews with our BLSA subjects (duration of all three interviews, 11–13 hours), Tismer (1969) found that "enjoyment of the chances of the present situation" received the highest rank. This "theme" refers to activities and states that offer enjoyment by the friendly aspects of everyday life. Therefore, this theme is connected with a more creative way of experiencing the present and of cultivating the existing moment.

The theme holding the second rank in the older men and women group is "satisfaction in the routine way of living." The third rank is occupied by the "tendency to maintain the social contacts," followed by the tendency to maintain the range of interests. These four themes have one common trend that might be defined by the tendency to concentrate the life space to the present. This cluster of themes centering around present time is surrounded by another one that includes themes like "to be determined by the feeling of definitiveness of one's own situation, to be determined by the feeling of the coming end of life, to be determined by physical complaints, restrictions, and worries, to be determined by disappointment, to be determined by restriction of chances or possibilities." Subjects scoring high on these scales do not show a tendency to concentrate on religious orientations. For most of them present time is defined by disappointment and restriction. Hence the look toward the future can not be avoided. This future then is anticipated even more in terms of restriction, definitiveness, disturbance, and fear.

The structure of these leading themes in the life situation of the aged person, which so far can be outlined in a very vague manner, suggests some hypotheses. Man as an anticipating being is bound to anticipate his own future. With increasing age anticipation is becoming more and more difficult and threatening. Therefore, the tendency to concentrate on the present time is growing. By concentration on the present, the boundaries to the past and the future become subjectively infinite. Therefore, an increasing restructuration of the time perspective takes place, which stresses the present situation. This restructuration offers the illusion of an unlimited range of future and past time perspective, laying the dark around the bright center of the present and some spots in the nearest future. Therefore anticipations seem possible everywhere, even if they are not made unless to the nearest future.

Unfortunately, this is a very rationalized formulation of the critical process. Actually, subconscious regulations are at least as important in these phenomena as in the Freudian ego-id dynamics. These regulations may have some relationships to homeostatic principles. Maintaining the balance of the extensions of time perspectives is the fundamental motivation process in the aging personality, in which the balance is continuously disturbed. This process of maintaining the balance between the different time perspectives has many variations. Individuality, religious orientation, and social as well as physical influences determine it. In this connection we are able only to sketch the contribution of a genuine developmental approach to a theory of motivation. This approach supports those theories of motivation that keep in mind that man as a creature who exists in time, reacts to time, and willingly and unwillingly rides on the back of time. It supports those theories that see meaning and meaningful behavior closely connected with a tolerable balance of future, present, and past in the subjective time perspectives. From this point of view the fundamental motivational structures are only preliminarily formed in infancy. Actually, aging becomes the peak of development with regard to motivational processes—at least of a being who is bound to anticipate and who does not just function in a biological way.

CONCLUDING REMARKS

The evaluation of the functions of future time perspective in directing behavior and the relationships of future time perspective to social, psychological, and biological variables (e.g., age) stresses the relevance of an interaction theory of cognition–motivational processes. As a substructure of the cognitive systems that regulate human behavior, future time perspective may instigate motivational processes (e.g., some discomfort in the situation of the aged). This motivational state can influence content (or extension) of future time perspective as also shown in the special future time perspective of aged people. Any substitution of the construct *motivation* by future-time perspective-related constructs would prevent the study of cognition–motivation interactions, one of the most promising approaches to the interpretation of human behavior. It would be a simplification to reduce the variables that direct human behavior to the construct *anticipation*. On the other hand, only the anticipatory structure of motivational processes explains the specific ways in which human beings live into, within, or away from their future.

REFERENCES

Baldwin, A. L. A cognitive theory of socialisation. In D. Goslin (Ed.), *Handbook of socialisation: Theory and research.* Chicago: Rand McNally, 1969.

Bergius, R. *Formen des Zukunftserlebens.* München: Barth, 1957.

Birch, D., Atkinson, J. W., & Bongort, K. Cognitive control of action. In B. Weiner (Ed.), *Cognitive views of human motivation.* New York: Academic Press, 1974.

Bolles, R. C. Cognition and motivation: Some historical trends. In B. Weiner (Ed.), *Cognitive views of human motivation.* New York: Academic Press, 1974.

Eson, M. E., & Greenfeld, N. Life space: Its content and temporal dimensions. *Journal of Genetic Psychology,* 1962, *100,* 113–238.

Fisseni, H. J. Perceived life space: Patterns of consistency and change. In H. Thomae (Ed.), *Patterns of aging.* Basel: Karger, 1976.

Göbbels, H. *Persönliche und berufsbezogene Perspektive bei Lehrern verschiedener Schularten und Altersgruppen.* Doctoral Dissertation, University of Bonn, 1979.

Grombach, H. M. *Konstanz und Variabilität von Persönlichkeitsmerkmalen.* Doctoral Dissertation, University of Bonn, 1975.

Haan, N. *Coping and defending.* New York: Wiley, 1977.

Havighurst, R. J. Successful aging. *The Gerontologist,* 1961, *1,* 4–7.

Hirsch, M. A. *Die Auseinandersetzung mit Schul-und Studienanforderungen.* Doctoral Dissertation, University of Bonn, 1979.

Kastenbaum, R. Cognitive and personal futurity in later life. *Journal of Individual Psychology,* 1963, *19,* 216–222.

Kelly, G. A. *The psychology of personal constructs* (Vol. I/II). New York: Norton, 1955.

Kranzhoff, E. U. *Reaktionen auf gesundheitliche und ökonomische Belastung im höheren Alter.* Doctoral Dissertation, University of Bonn, 1979.

Kühlen, R. G., & Monge, R. H. Correlates of estimated rate of time passage in the adult years. *Journal of Gerontology,* 1968, *23,* 427–433.

Lazarus, R. S., & Cohen, J. B. Theory and method in the study of stress and coping in aging individuals. *Fifth WHO conference on society, stress, and disease: Aging and old age.* Stockholm: Jena, 1976.

Lazarus, R. S., & Launier, R. Stress-related transactions between person and environment. In L. A. Pervin & M. Lewis (Eds.), *Internal and external determinants of behavior.* New York: Plenum, 1978.

Lehr, U. Attitudes toward the future in old age. *Human Development,* 1967, *10,* 230–238.

Lens, W., & Gailly, A. Extension of future time perspective in motivational goals of different age groups. *International Journal of Behavioral Development,* 1980 *3,* 1–17.

Lersch, P. *Aufbau der Person.* München: Barth, 1938.

Lewin, K. Field theory and experiment in social psychology: Concepts and methods. *American Journal of Sociology,* 1939, *44,* 868–897.

Lienert, G. A., & Krauth, J. Configural-frequency analysis as a statistical tool for defining types. *Educational and Psychological Measurement,* 1975, *35,* 231–238.

Morgan, J. N., & Messenger, R. C. *Thaid: A sequential analysis program for the analysis of nominal scale dependent variables.* Ann Arbor: University of Michigan, Institute for Social Research, 1973.

Mudrich, B. *Der Wegzug des letzten Kindes aus dem Elternhaus im Erleben der Mutter.* Doctoral Dissertation, University of Bonn, 1979.

Munnichs, J. M. A. *Chronological, social, and psychological time.* Paper presented at the World Conference on "Old Age: A challenge for science and policy." Vichy (France), Institut de la vie, 1977.

Nuttin, J. (R.) *A relational theory of motivation and the dynamic function of cognitive contents.* Leuven: Leuven/Louvain Psychological Reports, N° 4, 1974.

Nuttin, J. (R.), & Grommen, R. Zukunftsperspektive bei Erwachsenen und älteren Menschen aus drei sozioökonomischen Gruppen. In U. M. Lehr & F. E. Weinert (Eds.), *Entwicklung und Persönlichkeit.* Stuttgart: Kohlhammer, 1975.

Olbrich, E., & Lehr, U. The influence of ecology on older peoples' behavior. *Gerontology (The Gerontological Society),* 1978, 29–32.

Pfötsch, C. *Längsschnittuntersuchungen zur Zukunftsperspektive im höheren Alter.* Doctoral Dissertation, University of Bonn, 1979.

Roos, P., & Albers, R. Performance of alcoholics and normals on a measure of temporal orientation. *Journal of Clinical Psychology,* 1965, *21,* 34–36.

Schreiner, M. *Zur zukunftsbezogenen Zeitperspektive älterer Menschen.* Doctoral Dissertation, University of Bonn, 1969.

Schubert. R. Verschiedene Formen des Alterns. In R. Schubert (Ed.), *Flexibilität der Altersgrenze.* Darmstadt: Steinkopff, 1969.

Sganzini, C. Vom grundsätzlichen Gebrauch des Gesichtspunktes "Vorwegnahme" (Antizipation). In *Festschrift für R. Herberz.* Bern: Franke, 1940.

Sonquist, J. A., & Morgan, J. N. *The detection of interaction effects.* Ann Arbor: University of Michigan, Institute for Social Research, 1964.

Thomae, H. *Das Wesen der menschlichen Antriebsstruktur.* Leipzig: Bart, 1944.

Thomae, H. Theory of aging and cognitive theory of personality. *Human Development,* 1970, *13,* 1–16.

Thomae, H. Developmental approaches to a theory of motivation. In F. J. Mönks (Ed.), *Persoonlijkheid en ontwikkeling (Festschrift voor Professor Calon).* Nijmegen, 1971.

Thomae, H. (Ed.), *Patterns of aging.* Basel: Karger, 1976.

Tismer, H. G. *Untersuchungen zur Lebensthematik älterer Menschen.* Doctoral Dissertation, University of Bonn, 1969.

Wiendick, G. Entwicklung einer Skala zur Messung der Lebenszufriedenheit im höheren Lebensalter. *Zeitschrift für Gerontologie,* 1970, *3,* 215–224.

Author Index

A

Abelson, R. P., 100, 115, *121,* 153, *157*
Acuna, C., 150, *155*
Adams, F., 104, *119*
Adams, P.A., 74, *84*
Albers, R., 270, *274*
Allan, L. G., 242, *257*
Allen, G. A., 129, 131, *138*
Alpert R., 170, 187, 189, *197*
Anderson, A. C., 235, *256*
Anderson, R. C., 114, *117*
Anderson, R. M., 153, *156*
Anscombe, G. E. M., 11, *13*
Antes, J. R., 241, *256*
Antinucci, F., 10, *13*
Arenson, S. J., 90, *121*
Aschoff, J., 235, *256*
Ashby, W. R., 147, *155*
Atkinson, J. W., 159, 160, 161, 162, 163,
    164, 166, 167, 168, 169, 170, 171, 172,
    175, 176, 177, 178, 179, 180, 181, 182,
    184, 186, 187, 188, 189, 190, 191, 192,
    193, 194, *196, 197, 198,* 200, 201, 202,
    205, 206, 207, 210, 214, 215, 218, 220,
    221, 223, *228, 229, 230, 231,* 262, 269,
    273
Atkinson, R. A., 136, 138, *138*
Atkinson, R. C., 125, 126, *140,* 253, *258*

Avant, L. L., 241, *256*
Axel, R., 246, *256*

B

Bachelard, G., 252, *256*
Bachman, J. B., 205, *228*
Bagshaw, M. H., 153, *156*
Baker, N., 46, 48, 53, *57*
Baldwin, A. L., 261, 270, *273*
Bandura, A., 90, *117,* 127, *138*
Baratta, P., 125, *140*
Barker, R. G., 176, *196*
Baron, R., 144, *156*
Barron, F., 145, *155*
Bartlett, F. C., 69, *83*
Békésy, G. (von), 242, *256*
Bellezza, F. S., 115, *118*
Benussi, V., 241, *256*
Bergius, R., 261, 262, 263, *273*
Berlyne, D. E., 44, *56*
Bernstein, B., 112, *120*
Bernstein, L., 152, *155*
Bernstein, N. A., 5, *13,* 143, *155*
Bernstein, P., 19, *32*
Binet, A., 239, *256*
Birch, D., 160, 175, 176, 177, 178, 179, 180,
    181, 182, 190, 191, 194, *196,* 201, *228,*
    262, 269, *273*

Birney, R. C., 189, *196*
Bjork, R. A., 109, *118, 122*
Blankenship, V., 160, 182, *196, 197*
Block, R. A., 244, *256*
Bolles, R. C., 261, 263, 269, *273*
Bolton, T. L., 234, *256*
Bongort, K., 159, 160, 170, 175, 178, 181, 182, 184, 186, 187, 188, 189, 191, *196, 197,* 262, 269, *273*
Borke, H., 18, *31*
Bottenberg, R. A., 93, *118*
Bower, G. H., 135, 137, *139, 140*
Branch, M. H., 113, *120*
Bransford, J. D., 110, 114, *120*
Brecher, P. J., 208, *228*
Brentano, F., 154, *155*
Brillouin, L., 149, *155*
Brimer, R. W., 110, *118*
Broadbent, D. E., 66, 74, *83*
Broadbent, M. H. P., 66, 74, *83*
Brown, M., 205, 215, *230*
Brown, R., 6, *13*
Bruner, J. S., 4, 5, 7, 8, 9, *13*
Buchwald, A. M., 82, *83, 84,* 88, 89, 100, 105, *118,* 123, 126, 127, 136, *138, 139*
Bühler, K., 15, *31*
Bunch, M. E., 107, 112, *118, 120*
Bunning, E., 235, *256*
Burke, C. J., 128, 131, *139*
Byrne, D., 211, *228*

C

Cannon, W. B., 147, *155*
Carter-Sobell, L., 114, *119*
Cartwright, D., 160, 175, *196, 197*
Ceraso, J., 114, *121*
Cheesman, F. L. II, 115, *118*
Chomsky, N., 3, *13,* 150, *155*
Clark, R. A., 159, 161, 162, 163, 166, 167, 168, 169, 170, 187, *198,* 202, *229*
Claxton, G., 98, *118*
Cochin, J., 97, *118*
Cohen, J. B., 266, *273*
Cohen, R. L., 108, *118*
Cole, M., 128, 131, *139*
Collins, J. F., 238, *256*
Coltheart, V., 110, *118*
Conover, J. N., 92, 95, *120*
Cottrell, N., 192, *197*

Cowan, R. E., 103, 104, *118*
Craik, F. I. M., 63, 64, *83,* 94, 103, 107, 110, 111, 112, 114, *118, 119, 120,* 237, *256*
Creelman, C. D., 242, *256*
Cronbach, L. J., 170, 186, *197*
Cubbage, A., 114, *118*

D

DaPolito, F., 74, *84*
Davidson, T. N., 205, *228*
Davies, G., 114, *118*
Day, J., 115, *119*
Deci, E. L., 220, *228*
Decroly, O., 237, *256*
Degand, J., *237, 256*
Demany, L., 237, *256*
Dembo, T., 23, *31,* 200, *229*
de Montpellier, G., 74, *84*
Descartes, R., 176, *197*
DeVilliers, P. A., 192, *197*
Dietze, G., 239, *256*
Docherty, E. M., 18, *32*
Doob, L. W., 234, 242, 248, *256*
Dowling, J. E., 147, *155*
Duchnowski, A. J., 95, *120,* 127, *140*
Dulany, D. E., Jr., 41, *56*
Duncan, S., Jr., 97, *118*
d'Ydewalle, G., 82, *84,* 89, *118,* 126, 127, *139*

E

Ebbesen, E. B., 35, 36, 38, 39, 42, 43, 44, 45, 51, *57*
Ebbinghaus, H., 72, *84*
Eckhardt, D., 24, *31*
Edwards, W., 175, *197*
Eelen, P., 82, *84,* 89, *118*
Ehrenreich, S. L., 110, *119*
English, L. D., 215, 216, 217, *230*
Entin, E. E.. 202, 203, 204, 206, 208, 210, 211, 212, 213, 214, 215, 218, *228, 229 230*
Entwisle, D. R., 159, 170, 182, 187, 190, *197*
Ericsson, K. A., 99, *118*
Eriksen, C. W., 238, *256*
Erikson, E. H., 226, *229*

Ertel, S., 24, *31*
Eson, M. E., 270, *273*
Estes, K. W., 129, 136, *139*
Estes, W. K., 44, *56,* 74, *84,* 88, 89, 95, 100, 105, *118, 119,* 123, 125, 128, 129, 130, 131, 134, 135, 136, 137, *138, 139,* 142, *155*
Exner, S., 234, *256*
Eysenck, H. J., 251, *256*

F

Falmagne, R. J., 135, *139*
Farbry, J., 91, *120, 122*
Farley, J. A., 127, *139*
Feather, N. T., 160, 162, 166, 175, 178, 192, *196, 197,* 200, 201, 204, 210, 218, 220, 221, *228, 229*
Feld, S., 162, *197, 198,* 214, 215, *231*
Feokritova, I. P., 235, *256*
Ferreiro, E., 252, *256*
Festinger, L., 23, *31, 175, 197,* 200, *229*
Fillmore, C. J., 10, *13*
Fisher, R. P., 107, 110, *119*
Fiske, D. W., 97, *118*
Fisseni, H. J., 264, 265, 269, *273*
Fouraker, L. E., 125, *140*
Fraisse, P., 234, 235, 238, 239, 240, 241, 244, 247, 250, *256, 257,*
Fraisse, R., 239, *256*
François, M., 235, *257*
Frankenhaeuser, M., 235, 244, *257*
Frank, M. D., 97, *121*
Franks, J. J., 110, 114, *120*
Fraser, J. T., 242, *257*
French, E. G., 170, *197*
Freud, S., 33, 43, 46, 52, *56*

G

Gabor, D., 144, *155*
Gagné, R. M., 65, *84*
Gailly, A., 270, *273*
Galambos, R., 242, *258*
Galanter, E., 5, 12, *13,* 123, *140,* 143, 146, 148, *155*
Gardner, B. T., 151, *155*
Gardner, R. A., 151, *155*
Garner, W. R., 153, *155*

Gazzo, B., 216, *229*
Geiselman, R. E., 109, *118*
Gel'fand, I. M., 143, *155*
Gelman, R., 3, *13,* 53, *56*
Georgopoulos, A., 150, *155*
Gibson, J. J., 237, *257*
Gill, M. M., 149, *156*
Gjerdingen, B. B., 243, *257*
Gjesme, T., 208, 210, *229*
Glanzer, M., 110, 111, *119*
Glenberg, A., 104, *119*
Göbbels, H., 270, *273*
Goetz, E. T., 114, *117*
Goldman, S. R., 110, 111, *119*
Granit, R., 143, *155*
Green, C., 104, *119*
Greenfeld, N., 270, *273*
Greenwald, A. G., 59, *84,* 95, 96, 99, 100, 105, 108, *121,* 126, 137, *140*
Gribble, C. M., 42, *58*
Grice, H. P., 5, *13*
Grim, P. F., 40, *56*
Grombach, H. M., 264, 265, 266, *273*
Grommen, R., 270, *274*
Gruendel, J., 11, *13*
Gurack, E., 25, 26, *31*
Gurfinkel, V. S., 143, *155*
Gurin, G., 214, 215, *231*
Guthrie, E. R., 100, *119*
Guyau J. M., 234, 244, *257*

H

Haan, N., 266, *273*
Haber, R. N., 170, 187, 189, *197*
Halisch, C., 24, 28, 29, *31*
Halisch, F., 24, *31*
Hall, G. F., 95, *121,* 127, *140*
Halwes, T., 76, *84*
Hamilton, J. O., 193, *197*
Harter, S., 15, *31*
Harton, J. J., 245, *257*
Hartshorne, H., 40, *56*
Hasher, L., 83, *83*
Havighurst, R. J., 269, *273*
Hebb, D. O., 176, *197*
Heckhausen, H., 16, 21, 22, 23, 24, 26, 27, 28, *31,* 191, *197*
Henle, M., 61, *85*
Herrnstein, R. J., 192, *197*

Hetzer, H., 21, *31*
Hicks, R. E., 249, 250, *257*
Hilgard, E. R., 137, *139*
Hillix, W. A., 90, 92, 94, 95, *119*, 127, *139*
Hillyard, S. A., 242, 243, *257, 258*
Hinson, R. E., 97, *121*
Hintikka, J., 11, *13*
Hirsch, M. A., 264, *273*
Hoagland, H., 235, 242, *257*
Hokanson, J. E., 127, *139*
Hollingworth, H. L., 240, *257*
Honzik, C. H., 105, *122*
Hood, S. Q., 51, 54, *57*
Höring, A., 234, *257*
Horst, J. W., 238, *258*
Hull, C. L., 61, *84*, 123, 127, *139*, 175, *197*
Hunt, E. B., 123, *139*
Hunt, J. McV., 16, *31*
Hunter, W. S., 235, *257*
Hyde, T. S., 63, 64, *84*
Hylan, J. P., 238, *257*

I

Isaacson, R. L., 204, 205, *229*
Israeli, N., 235, *257*

J

Jacobs, B., 187, *197*
James, W., 40, *56*, 146, *155*, 236, 242, *257*
Janet, P., 234, *257*
Jaspers, K., 235, *257*
Jenkins, J. G., 72, *84*
Jenkins, J. J., 63, 64, 76, *84*
Johnson, L. D., 205, *228*
Johnson-Laird, P., 153, *155*

K

Kahn, R. L., 205, *228*
Kahneman, D., 146, *155*
Kanfer, F. H., 123, *139*
Karniol, R., 42, 51, 52, *57*
Kastenbaum, R., 270, *273*
Katz, D., 249, *257*
Kawamura-Reynolds, M., 192, *197*
Keenan, J., 115, *119*

Keller, L., 128, 131, *139*
Kelly, G. A., 261, 263, *273*
Kiekheben-Roelofsen, I., 24, *31*
Kingsley, H. L., 65, *84*
Kinsbourne, M., 249, *257*
Kirker, W. S., 115, *121*
Klamma, M., 23, *31*
Klein, K., 114, *119*
Kleist, K., 235, *257*
Kniper, J. W., 238, *258*
Koffka, K., 236, *257*
Kohlberg, L., 40, *56*
Kolers, P. A., 145, *155*
Koppenaal, L., 111, *119*
Kranzhoff, E. U., 269, 270, *273*
Krausz, H. J., 242, *258*
Krauth, J., 265, *273*
Kristofferson, A. B., 242, *257*
Krug, S., 25, 26, *31*
Krüger, H., 25, 26, *31*
Kuhl, J., 160, 182, *197*
Kuhl, U., 25, *31*
Kühlen, R. G., 270, *273*
Kuhn, T. S., 176, *197*
Kuiper, N. A., 115, *121*

L

Laloy, L., 239, *257*
Lamberth, J., 211, *228*
Lashley, K. S., 76, *84*
Launier, R., 270, *273*
Lazarus, R. S., 266, 270, *273*
Lehman, H. C., 214, 215, *229*
Lehr, U., 269, *273, 274*
Lens, W., 205, *228*, 270, *273*
Leong, D., 153, *156*
Lersch, P., 262, *273*
Levine, D. G., 97, *119*
Levine, M., 135, *139*
Lewin, K., 23, 24, *31*, 60, 72, *84*, 175, *197*, 200, 221, 227, *229*, 261, *273*
Lewis, B. C., 42, *58*
Lichenstein, M., 238, *258*
Lienert, G.A., 265, *273*
Lieury, A., 251, *258*
Light, L. L., 114, *119*
Lim, H., 153, *156*
Lipsitt, L. P., 18, 19, *32*

Lockhart, R. S., 63, 64, *83,* 94, 103, 114, *118*
Loehlin, J. C., 246, *258*
Loftus, G. R., 138, *139*
Longobardi, E. T., 28, *32*
Longstreth, L. E., 108, *119*
Lowell, E. L., 159, 162, 163, 166, 168, 169, 170, 187, *198, 202, 229*
Luce, R. D. 125, *139*
Lyman, P. J., 241, *256*
Lynch, J. C., 150, *155*
Lyons, J., 4, *13*

M

Mach, E., 234, *258*
MacDougall, R., 239, *258*
MacKay, D. M., 148, *155*
MacLeod, C. M., 109, *119*
MacWhinney, B., 115, *119*
Mahrer, A. R., 34, *56*
Mandler, G., 42, *56,* 74, *84,* 202, 209, *229*
Mandler, J. M., 115, *119*
Marcel, A. J., 100, 113, *119*
Marlatt, G. A., 94, *119*
Marx, K., 91, 93, 95, 113, *120*
Marx, M. H., 90, 91, 92, 93, 94, 95, 96, 104, 107, 112, 113, *118, 119, 120, 122,* 127, *139*
Maslow, A. H., 193, *197,* 220, 222, *229*
Massari, D. J., 42, 53, *57*
Masters, J. C., 113, *120*
Matlin, M., 112, *120*
May, M. A., 40, *56*
Mayhew, D., 115, *119*
McClelland, D. C., 159, 161, 162, 163, 166, 167, 168, 169, 170, 187, 191, 193, *196, 197, 198,* 200, 202, *229*
McEvoy, C. L., 64, *84*
McFarland, D. J., 148, *155*
McGill, T. E., 246, *258*
McGuinness, D., 146, 147, 148, 153, *156*
McKenzie, B., 237, *256*
McLaughlin, B., 79, *84*
Meade, R. D., 245, *258*
Mednick, M. T., 205, *228*
Mehrabian, A., 209, 217, *229*
Messenger, R. C., 264, *273*
Metzner, R., 34, *57*

Meumann, E., 69, 73, *84*
Michon, J. A., 235, 248, 251, *258*
Miller, D. T., 42, 51, 52, *57*
Miller, F. D., 99, *121*
Miller, G. A., 5, 12, *13,* 123, *140,* 143, 146, 148, 151, 153, *155*
Miller, G. W., 249, *257*
Miller, N. E., 123, *140,* 175, *198*
Miller, S. A., 18, *32*
Miller, S. M., 41, *57*
Minkowski, E., 235, *258*
Mischel, H. N., 51, 54, 55, *57*
Mischel, W., 34, 35, 36, 38, 39, 42, 43, 44, 45, 46, 47, 48, 49, 50, 51, 52, 53, 54, 55, *57, 58,*
Mitchell, J. S., 206, 229
Mittelstaedt, H., 5, 12, *13,* 148, *155*
Mo, S. S., 241, *258*
Monge, R. H., 270, *273*
Montague, W. E., 63, *84,* 89, *120*
Moore, B., 43, 44, 45, 47, 49, 50, 53, *57*
Morgan, J. N., 264, 269, *273*
Morgenstern, O., 125, *140*
Morris, C. D., 110, 114, *120*
Moscovitch, M., 110, *120*
Mountcastle, V. B., 150, *155*
Mudrich, B., 264, *273*
Mueller, J. H., 91, 110, *118, 120, 122*
Mulhall, E. F., 74, *84*
Müller, A., 23, 27, *32*
Munnichs, J. M. A., 270, *273*
Murdock, B. B., Jr., 129, *140*
Murray, H. A., 161, 193, *198*
Myers, J. L., 126, *140*

N

Neisser, U., 115, *120,* 129, *140*
Nelson, D. L., 64, *84*
Nelson, K., 11, *13,* 115, *120*
Nelson, T. O., 103, *120*
Nilsson, L. G., 108, *118, 120*
Ninio, A., 5, *13*
Nisbett, R. E., 99, 113, *120, 122,* 190, *198*
Nunnally, J. C., 95, *120, 121,* 127, *140*
Nuttin, J. R., 15, 16, *32,* 59, 82, *84,* 88, 89, 95, 96, 98, 99, 100, 105, 108, *121,* 124, 126, 136, 137, *140,* 253, *258,* 261, 262, 270, *274*
Nuwer, M., 144, *156*

O P

Olbrich, E., 269, *274*
Oléron, G., 247, *257*
O'Malley, P. M., 205, *228*
Oostenbrug, M. W. M., 238, *258*
Ornstein, R. E., 146, *155*, 235, 237, 244,
    246, 251, *258*
Osgood, C. E., 112, *121*
Oxendine, J. B., 65, *84*

Paivio, A., 151, *155*
Papoušek, H., 19, 20, *32*
Papoušek, M., 20, *32*
Parisi, D., 10, *13*
Parker, R. K., 95, *120, 127, 140*
Parsons, J. E., 25, *32*
Pattee, H. H., 150, *156*
Patterson, K. E., 74, *84*
Pavur, E. J., Jr., 93, 96, *118, 120*
Peak, H., 227, *229*
Pearlson, H. B., 208, *229*
Peirce, C. S., 151, *156*
Pellegrino, J. W., 110, 111, *119*
Peterson, L. R., 237, *258*
Peterson, M., 237, *258*
Pfötsch, C., 264, 266, 269, *274*
Phillips, J. S., 123, *139*
Phillips, L. W., 74, *84*
Phillips, R. E., 113, *121*
Piaget, J., 15, 18, 21, 28, *32*, 235, 248, 252,
    258
Pichert, J. W., 114, *117*
Picton, T. W., 242, 243, *257, 258*
Piéron, H., 236, *258*
Plotkin, H. C., 153, *156*
Poppen, R., 153, *156*
Postman, L., 63, 74, 81, *84*, 111, *121, 123,
    126, 140*
Prentice, W. C. H., 93, *121*
Preston, M. G., 125, *140*
Pribram, K. H., 5, 12, *13*, 124, *140*, 142,
    143, 144, 145, 146, 147, 148, 149, 150,
    151, 152, 153, *155, 156*
Price, L. H., 159, 160, 170, 175, 181, 184,
    186, 187, 188, 189, 191, *196,*

R S T

Rabin, A. I., 234, *259*
Rapaport, D., 33, *57*

Ratner, N. K., 8, 9, *13*
Raynor, D., 208, *230*
Raynor, J. O., 160, 162, 175, 178, 192, *196,
    198*, 200, 201, 202, 203, 204, 205, 206,
    208, 210, 211, 212, 213, 214, 215, 216,
    217, 218, 219, 220, 221, 225, *228, 229,
    230, 231*
Reddy, B. G., 115, *118*
Reitman, W. R., 171, 188, 193, *196, 198*
Rendle-Short, J., 18, *32*
Restle, F., 135, *140*
Reynolds, P. C., 152, *156*
Reynolds, R. E., 114, *117*
Robinson, C. A., 115, *119*
Roby, T. B., 159, 161, 162, 167, *198*
Roelofsen, I., 22, 23, 24, 28, *31*
Rogers, C. R., 222, *230*
Rogers, T. B., 115, *121*
Roos, P., 270, *274*
Rosen, A. C., 41, *57*
Rosenbaum, M. E., 90, *121*
Ross, G., 4, 7, *13*
Ross, J., 25, *32*
Roy, C., 8, *13*
Rubin, I. S., 202, 203, 206, 218, *230*
Ruble, D. N., 25, *32*
Rundus, D., 104, *121*
Ryan, T. A., 60, 61, 70, 76, 79, *84, 85*
Sakata, H., 150, *155*
Saltz, E., 114, *119*
Sarason, S. B., 202, 209, *229*
Sawusch, J. R., 160, 191, *198*
Schack, M. L., 42, 53, *57*
Schallert, D. L., 114, *117*
Schank, R. C., 100, 115, *121, 153, 157*
Schneider, K., 193, *198*
Schneider, W., 100, *121*
Schreiner, M., 264, 265, 269, *274*
Schubert, R., 267, *274*
Schulman, A. I., 110, *121*
Searle, J. R., 152, *157*
Sears, P. S., 23, *31*, 200, *229*
Seltzer, R.A., 160, 177, 178, *198*
Servière, J., 238, *258*
Seymour, G. E., 93, 96, *120*
Sganzini, C., 262, 263, *274*
Shapiro, J. P., 190, *198*
Shatz, M., 3, *13*
Shiffrin, R. M., 100, *121, 253, 258*
Shik, M. L., 143, *155*

Short, J. C., 211, *231*
Siegel, S., 97, *121,* 125, 126, *140*
Siffre, M., 246, 247, *257, 258*
Simon, H. A., 99, *118*
Singer, J. L., 33, *57*
Siqueland, E. R., 19, *32*
Skinner, B. F., 123, 127, *140*
Smirnov, S., 241, *257*
Smith, C. P., 162, *197, 198*
Smith, E. R., 99, *121*
Smith, R. A., 42, 53, *58*
Smith, S. S., 104, *119*
Sonquist, J. A., 269, *274*
Sorrentino, R. M., 206, 207, 210, 211, 212, *230, 231*
Spence, K. W., 127, *140, 175, 198*
Sperling, G., 237, 253, *258*
Spyropoulos, T., 114, *121*
Stang, D., 112, *120*
Staub, E., 34, *57*
Stern, C., 258
Stern, L. W., 236, *258*
Stern, W., 69, 73, *85*
Stevens, D. A., 95, *121,* 127, *140*
Stroud, J. M., 242, *258*
Suppes, P., 125, *139, 140*
Tart, C. T., 146, *157*
Teuber, H. L., 148, *157*
Teyler, T., 150, *157*
Thomae, H., 262, 264, 270, *274*
Thomas, E. A. C., 240, 243, 249, *258*
Thorndike, E. L., 88, *121,* 126, 127, *140*
Tismer, H. G., 271, *274*
Tolman, E. C., 62, 65, *85,* 101, 105, *122, 175, 198*
Tomsic, R., 243, *257*
Toner, I. J., 42, 53, *58*
Trabasso, T., 135, *140*
Tsetlin, H. L., 143, *155*
Tubbs, W. E., 153, *156*
Tulving, E., 66, 70, 74, *85,* 94, 110, 111, 112, 115, *118, 122*
Turvey, M. T., 143, 152, *157*

U V

Urberg, K. A., 18, *32*
Verhave, T., 123, *140*
Vernon, J. A., 246, *258*
Veroff, J., 214, 215, *231*

Vierordt, K., 234, 240, *259*
Von Holst, E., 5, 12, *13*
Von Neumann, J., 125, *140*
Vos, P., 239, *259*
Vurpillot, E., 237, *256*

W

Wagner, I., 21, 22, 26, *31, 32*
Wallace, M., 234, *259*
Wallace, W. P., 103, *122*
Wallach, H., 61, *85*
Wallin, J. E. W., 239, *259*
Walling, J. R., 64, *84*
Wasna, M., 24, 26, 27, *31, 32*
Watkins, M. J., 74, *85*
Watson, J. S., 18, 19, 20, *32*
Weaver, W. B., 240, 243, 249, *258*
Weinberg, W. T., 216, 217, 218, *231*
Weiner, B., 138, *140,* 191, *197,* 215, 216, *231*
Wendt, H. W., 202, *231*
Whalen, R. E., 178, *198*
White, R. W., 15, 23, *32*
White, S. H., 40, *56*
Wickelgren, W. A., 62, 72, *85,* 107, *122,* 251, *259*
Wickens, C., 18, *32*
Wickens, D. D., 18, *32,* 65, *85*
Wickens, T. D., 136, 138, *138, 139*
Wiendick, G., 269, *274*
Wikler, A., 97, *122*
Wilson, T. D., 99, 113, *120, 122,* 190, *198*
Winograd, T., 153, *157*
Witter, D. W., 91, 92, 95, *120, 122*
Wolff, P., 28, *32*
Wood, D., 4, 7, *13*
Woodrow, H., 240, *259*
Woodward, A. E., 109, *122*
Woodworth, R. S., 70, *85*
Wundt, W., 234, 236, 241, *259*

X Y Z

Yates, B. T., 51, 52, 53, 55, *58*
Zacks, R. T., 83, *83*
Zajonc, R. B., 192, *198*
Zeigarnik, B., 93, *122*
Zeiss, A. R., 38, 39, 42, 43, 44, 45, 49, 50, 51, 53, *57*
Zuili, N., 247, *257*

Subject Index

A

Achievement indifferent subjects, 203–204
Achievement motivation theory (*see also*
    Dynamics of action):
  initial, 159–160, 166, 175, 182, 192,
    200–201
  more general, 160, 175, 199–219 (*see also*
    Theory of personality functioning
    and change)
    contingent and non-contingent paths,
      201–207, 213–215
    length of paths, 201, 202, 207–210
    meaning of success and failure, 199,
      201, 216
    motivation for competence testing,
      215–219
    subjective probabilities of successes in
      contingent paths, 210–215
Achievement motive (*see* Resultant
    achievement motivation, Thematic
    apperceptive measurement of
    motivation)
Ach problem, 60
Acquisition
  action routines, 1
  child's language, 10
  language, 1, 3–5, 7 (*see also* Language
    learning)
  observer, 90–92, 95
  performer, 90–92, 95

Action, 143, 144 (*see also* Dynamics of
    action)
  arguments of, 10
  automatic, 245
  behavioral, 142–154
  cognitive, 98
  communicative, 2
  intentional, 2–3, 5, 12
  mental, 127
  monitored, 245
  motor, 2
  rule-governed, 2
  supportive, 10
  symbolic, 2
  the organization of, 1–13, 145
Activity (*see* Action)
Activation, 3 (*see also* Habit activation)
Acts (*see* Action)
Addiction, 97
Adulto-centrism, 11
Affective transfer, 113
Affiliative motive (n affiliation), 192–193,
    206–207, 215
Aftereffects
  direct versus indirect action of, 126–128
  rewarding or nonrewarding, 116, 136
  satisfying, 136
Agnosias, 151
Alertness, 98
American sign language, 151
Amnesia, 72

Anticipation, 13, 19, 68, 262–263, 271–272
     (*see also* Future orientation)
Association, 147
Associationism, 60, 62, 72, 76, 82, 88
Attention, 141, 145, 241, 249 (*see also* Delay
     of gratification)
  selective, 181
  theory, 146
Attentional control, 145–146
Attitudes, 234, 241, 254–255
Attribution, 215–216 (*see also* Success/failure
     experiences)
Audience effects, 192–193
Automatic strengthening, 89
  of reward, 102
Awareness, 2, 100, 145–146, 244 (*see also*
     Success/failure experiences)
  role of, 123

B

Baby talk, 3
  of adults, 6
Behavior, 142–143
  anticipatory, 253
  goal-directed, 96
  intentional, 2
  modification, 123, 145
  overt, 105
Behavioral contrast, 137
Behavioral system, 221, 224–225
Behavioristic psychology, 59–60, 63
Biological clock, 242, 246

C

Capacity limitation (*see* Memory capacity)
Cells, 143
Centralizing tendency of judgment, 240
Cerebral motor cortex, 143
Choice, 123, 131–136
  model for, 134
  theories, 125
Circadian
  clock, 246
  rhythms, 235
Classification, 136–137
Closed loops, 147, 149
Cognitive factors, 59, 87

Cognitive processes (*see* Cognitive factors,
     processes)
Cognitive psychology, 59, 60, 62, 72, 88–89,
     97, 99, 114, 124, 136, 175, 261, 269
Cognitive reorganization, 227
Cognitive structure, 199, 200
Cognitive theories (*see* Cognitive psychology)
Communication, 152
  gestural, 153
Comparison, 136–137
Competence (evaluation of), 215–219 (*see
     also* Achievement motivation theory,
     Success/failure experiences)
Computer simulations (*see* Dynamics of
     action, thematic apperceptive
     measurement of motivation)
Conditioning, 66, 127, 247
  classical, 97
  operant, 18–20, 76, 88, 123
  Pavlovian, 76
  processes, 253
Congruency principle, 110
Consciousness (*see* Awareness)
Consensual cultural value, 223
Construct validity, 186, 187, 189–190
Consummatory (goal-) activities, 181
Context, 7
  effects, 114
  interactional, 115
  understanding for words, 8
Contingency, 128
  awareness (*see* Pleasure, causality,
     Success/failure experiences)
Contiguity, 61, 100, 115, 147
  association by, 147
  theory, 60
Contingent future orientation, 205, 207 (*see
     also* Contingent paths)
Contingent (non-contingent) paths (*see*
     Achievement motivation theory,
     Theory of personality functioning
     and change)
Cumulative record, 142

D

Decision, 148
  theory, 141, 175
Delay of gratification, 33–56
  aversiveness (frustrativeness) of, 37–38,
     41–42, 46, 49, 53

Delay of Gratification *(cont.)*
  delay rules (knowledge of), 51–56
  effects of
    attention to rewards, 35, 37–38, 40, 42, 44, 46–50
    consummatory (hot) and non-consummatory (cold) ideation, 44–46, 48, 50, 51, 54
    covert self-reinforcement, 34, 42, 50
    trust, 34
    psychoanalytic theorizing, 33–34, 43, 46, 52–53
  waiting or working for rewards, 41
Depressives, 235
Depth of processing view *(see* Levels of processing framework)
Developmental psychology, 11
Discriminative stimuli, 181
Dream, 145
Duration, 233–236, 239, 243, 249
  estimated, 244, 247–248, 250
  memorized, 236
  perceived, 236–237, 239, 240, 242–243
Dynamics of action, 160, 175–195 *(see also* Force, Tendency, Time allocation)
  a theory of operant behavior, 180–182, 191–195
  and stimulus bound cognitive or mechanistic theories of behavior, 175–176, 181
  and the theory of achievement motivation, 178, 182, 192
  applied to thematic apperception, 160, 175, 177–179, 181–195
  changes in activity, 176–177, 179–181, 186, 190 *(see also* Time allocation)
  computer program for, 160, 178
  computer simulation of, 177, 181–187 *(see also* Thematic Apperceptive Measurement of Motivation)
  continuity of behavior, 176, 177, 180–187
  stimulus situation, 176, 181

E

Ecological validity, 115
Econiche, 12
Egocentrism, 11
Ego involvement, 161
Ego-strength, 40
Emotion, 141, 147–148

Encoding, 62, 69, 72, 108, 114, 138, 241
Engrams *(see* Memory traces)
Equilibrium *(see* Homeostasis)
Esteem-income (self-esteem), 200, 206, 220, 222, 224–225, 227
Estimation
  duration, 253–256
  immediate, 249
  past duration, 251
  prospective, 249
  retrospective, 249
  temporal, 252
Ethologists, 142
Event production *(see* Pleasure, causality)
Evoked potentials, 243
Expectancy x value theory, 182, 200–201, 227
Expectation, 68, 75, 81–83, 115, 131
Expression, 148
  intended, 148
Extinction, 107
Eye movement, 148

F

Failure threatened subjects, 203–209, 211–212, 217–218
Familiarity, 104
Feature analysis, 147
Feedback, 2, 131
  control of physiological (internal) stimuli, 147–148
  control of sensory input, 146
  operations, 148
  positive, 135
  rewarding, 116
  servo-loops, 143
Feedforward controls, 148
  open-loop helical, 149
Feelings, 148
Force
  consummatory, 177, 180–181, 192
  exposure to, 180
  inhibitory, 176–179, 181–182
  instigating, 176–178, 180–183, 186, 188, 192–193
  of resistance, 177, 181
  psychological, 179
Forgetting, 65
  directed, 108–109, 116
Formal operations, 248

Fourier
  procedures, 144
  theorem, 143
Free association
  procedure, 154
  test, 113
Free recall, 64
  experiment, 79, 80-81
  technique, 60
  test, 62, 64, 78, 83
Frequency, 103-104, 130
  analyzer, 143-144
Frontal cortex, 141, 153
Frustration tolerance, 37, 42
Future
  importance, 206, 215-220
  orientation, 193, 199-228
  representation of, 253-254
Future time perspective, 261-272
  and age, 265, 267, 270-272
  and definitiveness of life situation, 266,
      267, 270-271
  and health, 265-267, 269
  and motivation, 261-263, 265, 267, 270,
      272 (see also Future orientation)
  and socio-economic status, 269
  behavioral effects of, 264
  content of, 264
  determinants of, 267-272
  differentiation (structuration) of, 261-263,
      271

          G, H

Gambling, 125
Goal, 7, 254-255
Habit(s), 100-117
  activation, 87, 98, 100-117
  coding of, 107
  formation, 76
  motor, 76
Habituation, 147, 153
Holograms
  neural, 143
Homeostasis, 147-149
Hypnogogic period, 145
Hypothesis testing, 135

          I, K

Ideation (see Delay of gratification)
Identity-crisis, 226-227
Image processors, 144
Imaginative behavior (see Dynamics of
      action, Thematic apperceptive
      measurement of motivation)
Imitation, 7
Incidental memory (see Incidental learning)
Indifference interval, 240
Information, 90, 92, 95, 149, 244-246
  acquisition of, 135
  channel capacity for, 5, 240
  episodic, 115
  factors, 117
  mnemonic, 248
  pragmatic, 115
  processing, 62-63, 66, 96, 98, 103,
      105-106, 110, 117, 123-124, 127, 149,
      151, 235, 243
  storage of, 135
  temporal, 234-236, 246-248
  trials, 131
  versus effect, 127
Instrumental
  activities, 181
  value, 223
Intelligence (fluid and crystallized), 265
Intention(s), 1-3, 5, 7, 11, 63, 72-78,
      148-150
  conscious, 105, 116
  deliberate, 116
  to learn, 59-61, 63, 73, 76, 79-80, 83 (see
      also Intentional learning)
Interacting processes (see Interaction)
Interaction, 138
  adult-infant, 1
  mother-infant, 1, 3, 4
  parent-infant, 1
  response systems, 112-114, 116
Internal consistency (see Thematic
      apperception measurement of
      motivation)
Intonation, 7, 8
Introspection, 99
Instantaneity (see Threshold of the lasting)
Instruction, 5
Kappa effect, 240
Knowledge, 68

L

Label
  for an object, 6, 7, 8
  idiosyncratic, 8
Language, 2, 145
  development of, 252
  learning, 68, 75
  pictorial, 145
  sign, 145
  studies of, 150
Language Acquisition Device, 3
Language Assistance Service, 3
Latin Square design, 167, 187–189
Law of effect, 61, 81–82, 88–89, 123, 126,
    129–130
Laws of thermodynamics, 149
Learning, 60, 127, 145, 181
  attitude, 66, 77
  automatic, 83
  by information, 94
  cognitive, 75, 89, 141
  concept, 66
  discrimination, 66, 136
  drive, 66
  effortful, 83
  expectancy, 66
  human, 61, 65, 87
  human selective, 87–89, 94, 96, 98–99,
      105, 116, 129
  incidental, 63–65, 72, 74, 79, 80, 82, 93,
      96, 103–104, 249
  insight, 105
  instrumental, 87, 101
  intentional, 61, 63–65, 74, 78–83, 94, 103
  interest, 77
  motor pattern, 66
  multiple-choice, 90
  observational, 94, 127 (see also
      Acquisition by observation)
  operant, 19 (see also Operant
      conditioning)
  perceptual, 65, 74
  perceptual skills, 68, 75
  serial, 66, 70, 90
  single-trial, 62
  social, 90
  speed of, 128
  symbolic, 98
  theories, 77, 83, 117

Learning (cont.)
  to understand, 68
  transfer, 19
  trial and error, 66, 125, 129
  types of, 65–66, 68–72, 83
  verbal, 98
  without awareness, 61, 76
  with reward, 94
Level of aspiration, 159
Levels of processing framework, 63, 103,
    105, 116
Life satisfaction (-scale), 264, 266, 269–270
Life space, 227, 265, 271
Limbic formations, 153
Linguistic theory, 5
Lobotomy procedures, 141
Locomotion, 227

M

Mastery, 3
Matching law, 192
Meaning, 152
Means-end-routine, 4
Memorization, 69, 72
  meaningful, 68
  of serial lists, 60, 62, 64, 72–73, 78, 80, 83
  rote, 68
Memory, 60, 141
  automatic, 83
  availability in, 131
  capacity, 130, 136
  episodic, 66, 70–72
  for alternative, 131
  for form, 70
  immediate, 244
  internalized scale, 130
  long-term, 89, 115, 131, 136, 254–266
  semantic, 66, 70, 111
  short term, 78, 89, 130, 136, 138, 237,
      254–255
  storage, 146, 150
  store, 154
  theories of, 137
  the role of, 124
  time span, 20
  trace, 107–109, 144
  types of, 67, 68–72, 78, 83
  working, 131

Mental retardates, 235
Mnemonic control, 150
Modeling, 4
Morpheme, 2
Morphine tolerance, 97
Motivation, 59, 77, 87, 98–99, 101, 116,
    141–142, 147–148, 234, 254–255 (*see
    also* Achievement motivation theory,
    Pleasure, causality, Dynamics of
    action, Future time perspective,
    Thematic apperceptive measurement
    of motivation, Theory of personality
    functioning and change)
  consummatory, 101
  effectance, 15–16, 30
  extrinsic, 201, 205–206, 214–215
  intrinsic, 16, 30
  overmotivation, 206–207, 212–213
  satisfaction, 93
  uncertainty related, 211
Motive and motivation, 172–174, 182,
    199–200 (*see also* Achievement
    motivation theory)
Motor skill, 76
Movement (*see* Behavior)
Muscle, 143
  contractions, 142–143
Multimorbidity, 267

O

Operant responses, 5 (*see also* Dynamics of
    action)
Organization, 115
  categorical, 115–116
  helical, 148
  open-loop, 148
  schematic, 115–116
Orienting task, 73, 80, 114
Outcomes, 108, 126–127 (*see also* Pleasure,
    causality, Delay of gratification,
    Success/failure experiences)
  memory for values of, 129
  punishing, 125
  rewarding, 125
  satisfying, 126
  symbolic, 108
  values, 126

P

Paired-associate experiments, 80
  learning, 113
PEDE-scale (perceived definitiveness of life
    situation), 266–267, 269–270
Perceived instrumentality, 204–205, 219
Perception, 141, 144, 146–147
Perceptual grouping, 239
Perceptual skill, 69
Personal constructs, 263
Personal continuum (personality), 263
Personal equation, 241
Personality (stability of), 184
Phenomenal goal/threat, 219
Phonemes, 2
Physiological psychologists, 142
Pleasure
  causality, 15–18, 30
    earliest signs of, 18–21
  ego, 16
  function, 15, 30
  stimulation, 15
Pollyanna principle, 112
Polypathy, 267
Pragmatics, 152–153
Present
  actual, 252
  perceived, 236–239, 243, 252, 254
Primacy, 102–103
Probability
  subject, 125
  theory, 125
Processes
  cognitive, 107 (*see also* Delay of
    gratification)
  control, 255
  mental, 100
  organizational, 254–255
  primary and secondary, 149–150
  sensory, 146
  unconscious, 100
Processing (*see also* Information processing):
  depth of, 94
  elaboration of, 94, 110
  iconic, 151
  image, 151
  indical, 151
  intentional and intensional aspects of
    cognitive, 154

Processing *(cont.)*
  positive vs negative responses, 110–112, 116
  semantic, 63–64, 79, 80, 100, 103, 115
  spread of, 94, 110
  structural, 103
Project, 256
Psychoanalytic metapsychology, 149
Psychogenic needs, 161
Psychological age, 224–226
Psychological career, 200, 220, 222–228
Psychological distance, 208–210
Psychological field, 24
Psychological morale, 200
Punishment, 59, 123, 130, 136
  motivating effects of, 128

R

Random error, 182, 185
Reaction
  affective, 130
  orienting, 153
  self evaluative *(see* Success/failure experiences)
  stress, 270
  time, 106, 112, 241
Recall, 62–63, 66, 68, 74, 102–104, 109
  verbatim, 66
Recency, 102–104
Recognition, 60, 62, 66, 68, 74, 104
  tests, 109, 114
Recollection, 61, 68–70, 72, 74, 78, 83
Reductionism, 12
Reference, 152
Rehearsal, 89, 103, 109, 138
  theories, 60
  unintentional, 60
Reinforcement, 4–5, 12, 59, 76, 103, 107, 112, 123, 128, 130 *(see also* Delay of gratification)
  direct, 113
  effects, 106
  experiments, 82
  principle of, 88
  social, 113
  theory, 60–62, 75, 77, 81–82, 101, 123–125, 127, 138, 141
  vicarious, 113

Reinforcing events *(see* Reinforcement)
Remembering, 69–70
Remembrance *(see* Remembering)
Representation, 3
  brain, 151
  environmental, 151
  episodic, 110
  hierarchical ordered, 152
  iconic gestural, 152
Representational hypothesis, 127
Resistance, 177–181
Responses, 108
  differential, 63
  generator, 254–255
  latencies of *(see* Reaction time)
  memory, 254–255
  perceptual, 254–255
  representational, 63
  "Right", 82
  strengthening of, 101, 107, 123, 136
  weakening of, 136
  "Wrong", 82
Resultant achievement motivation, 202–209, 213, 217 *(see also* Success oriented subjects, failure threatened subjects)
Resultant valence theory, 200
Retention, 93–94
Retrieval, 62, 106, 108, 114, 137–138
Reward, 59, 82, 90, 92, 94, 104, 106, 112, 117, 123, 130, 136 *(see also* Delay of gratification)
  differential, 133
  extrinsic, 104
  informational role of, 105, 116
  memory of, 127
  monetary, 108
  motivating effects of, 128
  stimuli, 44–46, 48, 50, 54
  symbolic, 104
  value, 128–138
Rewarding, 9 *(see also* Aftereffect, Feedback)
Rote memorizing, 60

S

Satisfactions
  consummatory, 104–105
  instrumental, 104–105

Sawtooth-effect, 188–189 (*see also* Thematic Apperceptive measurement of motivation: Effect of ordinal position of stories)
Scaffolding, 4
Schema, 115–116
Schizophrenics, 235
Secondary circular reactions, 15, 18, 20, 30
Self-concept, 267
Self-control, 40–42, 46, 51, 55–56
Self descriptive test, 190
Self-identity, 200, 220–224, 226
Self importance, 206, 215–219, 220
Self-possession, 216–217, 220
Self-system, 221–225
Semantics, 152–153
Semantic elaboration, 115
Sensation
  tactile, 143
Sensory deprivation, 246
Sensory register, 254–255
Serial memorization (*see Memorization of serial lists*)
Simultaneity (see Threshold of succession)
Skinner Box, 5
Socialization process, 12
Social psychology, 11, 190
Social skill learning, 3
S-O-R paradigm (episodic view of behavior), 175–176
Speech, 145
  act theory, 5
Spread functions, 144
Standard of excellence, 27
Stimulus specificity, 107
Storage
  size, 235, 246
  space, 244
Stream of behavior (*see* Dynamics of action: continuity of behavior)
Sublimation, 263
Success/failure experiences, 15–30
  and causality pleasure, 16
  cognitive prerequisites, 16–30
  action-outcome contingency awareness (causality pleasure), 18–21, 30
  attribution of outcome to the self and self evaluation, 22–23, 26–28, 30
  centering on the action-outcome, 21–22, 27–28
  perceiving a standard of excellence, 27–30

Success-oriented subjects, 202–209, 211–212, 217–218
Succession, 233, 235, 239, 247, 252
  perception of, 234, 237
Syntax, 152–153
S-R connections, 76, 82, 88–90, 95, 100, 103, 107, 108, 113, 116–117, 123, 135

T

Tagging hypothesis, 109
Task
  closed, 61, 81–82, 96, 137
  hierarchy, 208–210
  open, 59, 61, 75, 81–83, 96, 137
  solved, 93
  unsolved, 93
Temporal perspective, 252
Tendencies
  action tendency, 176–177, 179, 181, 192, 201
  arousability of, 178, 180–182, 184
  competing, 175, 177, 192
  expression of, 177, 181, 183
  negaction tendency, 177–179, 181
  persistence of, 176, 179, 181, 183
  random oscillation of, 179
  resultant action tendency, 177
  strength of, 177–180, 183
  subordinate, 180–181
Tension, 227
Tertiary circular reactions, 21
Test anxiety (*see* Resultant achievement motivation)
Test Anxiety Questionnaire, 202, 204
Test theory (traditional), 159, 161, 170–172, 182, 184–186, 189–191, 195
Thematic apperceptive measurement of motivation, 159–195
  achievement related imagery, 162–167
  a crude index of motivation, 170, 190
  and theory of motivation, 172–175 (*see also* Dynamics of action, Time allocation)
  computer simulation of, 159–160, 177, 181–195 (*see also* Dynamics of action)
  effect of ordinal position of stories, 167, 169–171, 188–189
  effect of picture content, 167–170, 172–174, 187, 189–190

Thematic apperceptive *(cont.)*
illustrating stories, 164–167
in experimental conditions, 161–162, 167
internal consistency, 160, 170, 182, 186–190
reliability, 160, 170–171, 190 *(see also Internal consistency)*
reliability (objectivity) of content analysis, 162, 190–191
scoring categories, 163
test of creative imagination, 161
validity, 160, 162, 166, 170–171, 182, 186–187, 189–191
Theory of personality functioning and change, 199–200, 219–228 *(see also Achievement motivation theory: more general theory, Behavioral system, Self system, Self possession, Self-importance, Value (sources of)*
and the more general theory of achievement motivation, 219–221
contingent paths, 221, 224–227
psychological careers, 222–228
time linked self images, 220–228
Thorndikean experiments, 81
theory, 89
Thought sampling, 191 *(see also Thematic apperceptive measurement of motivation)*
Threshold
of succession, 238, 242
of the lasting, 238, 242
recognition, 241
Time, 233 *(see also Future, Future time perspective)*
adaptation to, 235
allocation (time spent), 160, 179–187, 191–195
binding, 34, 38

Time *(cont.)*
biological, 236
cognition of, 233–256
conditioning of, 235
estimation of, 234–235, 245, 247, 253
hierarchy, 208–210
historical, 236
knowledge, 236–238
of our own existence, 236
perception of, 236, 238–244, 253, 255
physical, 236
Transaction *(see Interaction)*
trial-error, 3, 12

U, V, W, Z

Unconscious processes, 190
Utility, 125
Utterance, 2, 11
Valence, 221
Value
consummatory, 177, 180–182, 192
difficulty, 222–223
extrinsic, 222
incentive, 180, 193, 200–202, 210
individual cultural, 200, 223
instrumental, 223
intrinsic, 222
sources of, 200, 220–227 *(see also Esteem income)*
Verbal communication, *(see Verbal report)*
Verbal reports, 99–100, 145
Vigilance, 98
tasks, 107
von Restorff effect, 103
Will power, 40
Zeigarnik-effect, 93–94